THE REMINISCENCES OF
Captain
Paul Richard Schratz
U.S. Navy (Retired)

INTERVIEWED BY
Paul Stillwell

U.S. Naval Institute • Annapolis, Maryland

Copyright © 1996

Preface

This oral history is a special one for me, because it was Captain Paul Schratz who recommended me for employment by the Naval Institute in 1974. We had met two years earlier when I was a student at the University of Missouri and he was on the university's faculty. By 1974 he had moved to Annapolis and was most helpful in enabling me to relocate that year. In 1982, after I had been with the Proceedings for several years, I took over the oral history program and have been conducting it ever since. Captain Schratz's memoir is a valuable addition to the collection because of its combination of his splendid operational career with the one he achieved in the educational field.

As a junior officer he served in the heavy cruiser Wichita and a number of submarines during World War II. All told he made nine submarine war patrols against the Japanese. He had his own submarine commands, the Burrfish and Pickerel, in the late 1940s and early 1950s. In the latter he proved to be both aggressive and innovative. Included in the Pickerel's achievements were the longest-ever submerged transit by a guppy diesel submarine and the first submarine patrol of the Korean War.

Following duty at the Naval War College in the late 1950s and early 1960s his horizons broadened, and he achieved a wide reputation for his ability to write about and teach strategic thinking. His students achieved high positions throughout the U.S. military service. He was associated with curriculum reforms at several of the war colleges, including the National War College in Washington, D.C. He was a prolific writer for many years and thereby stimulated a great deal of thought on the part of his readers.

With all of his professional achievements, Paul Schratz was a devoted family man. At all times possessed of a substantial amount of pride, Schratz was probably proudest of his wife Henrietta and their seven children. They, along with his large body of professional work, are a worthy legacy of a lifetime of achievement.

In preparing this transcript for release, Captain Schratz made numerous additions and corrections by hand, befitting his experience as a writer. Thus the smooth version presented here is probably farther from the original verbatim version than are most of the Naval Institute's oral histories. I have done slight additional editing in the interests of accuracy. I regret that the press of other duties prevented me from completing the editing and annotating of this volume during the lifetime of Captain Schratz, whom I was privileged to know as a friend.

In the completion of this volume, Ms. Ann Hassinger of the Naval Institute's history division has made a significant contribution through her diligence in the overall process of printing, proofreading, and overseeing the binding.

Paul Stillwell
Director, History Division
U.S. Naval Institute
June 1996

CAPTAIN PAUL RICHARD SCHRATZ
UNITED STATES NAVY (RETIRED)

Paul Richard Schratz was born in Pittsburgh, Pennsylvania, on 1 October 1915, son of Frank W. and Marie Schlegel Schratz. He attended D. B. Oliver High School and Carnegie Institute of Technology in Pittsburgh. He entered the U.S. Naval Academy, Annapolis, Maryland, on appointment from his native state, on 18 June 1935. As a midshipman he played football, was a member of the crew, and was assistant director and concertmaster of the orchestra. Graduated with a degree of bachelor of science, he was commissioned ensign on 1 June 1939 and subsequently advanced to the rank of captain, to date from 1 March 1958.

Assigned first to the USS Wichita (CA-45), he had gunnery duties as a junior officer on board that cruiser from July 1939 until January 1942, after the outbreak of World War II. During that period he was commended by the President of Brazil at the National Independence Celebration in 1940 and took part in arctic patrol and North Atlantic convoy escort in 1940-41. He was a member of the first U.S. naval forces in Iceland in 1941.

During the first months of 1942 he had instruction at the Submarine School, New London, Connecticut and from April to August 1942 served as torpedo and gunnery officer of the USS Mackerel (SS-204). For 14 months thereafter, he was aboard the USS Scorpion (SS-278) as torpedo officer and first lieutenant. He later was executive officer and navigator and participated in three war patrols in the Pacific area. He was awarded the Silver Star Medal "For conspicuous gallantry and intrepidity in action as Torpedo Data Computer Operator of the USS SCORPION during the First War Patrol of that vessel off the Eastern Coast of Honshu from April 5 to May 8, 1943 . . . " The citation continues:

"Exercising a keen understanding of fire-control equipment and proficiency in operating the torpedo data computer, Lieutenant Schratz rendered invaluable assistance to his commanding officer in conducting successful attacks which resulted in the skillful sinking of eight enemy ships totalling over 13,000 tons and damaging one enemy ship of 7,500 tons. In addition he aided in the successful completion of an important special mission and in evading severe enemy countermeasures . . . "

He also received a Letter of Commendation, with authorization to wear the Commendation Ribbon and Combat "V," from the Commander in Chief U.S. Pacific Fleet, "For meritorious conduct in action in the performance of his duties as Torpedo Data Computer Operator of the USS SCORPION during the Second War Patrol of that vessel in the Yellow Sea from May 29 to July 15, 1943 . . . "

From October 1943 until November 1944 he served as executive officer and navigator of the USS Sterlet (SS-392), which during that period took part in the fourth Bonins raid on 4-5 August 1944. He was awarded the Bronze Star Medal with Combat "V" and cited as follows: "For meritorious achievement as Assistant Approach Officer of the USS STERLET in action against enemy Japanese forces in the vicinity of the Bonin Islands during her First War Patrol from July 4 to August 26, 1944. . . . Lieutenant Commander Schratz contributed materially to the success of his submarine in delivering gun and torpedo attacks which resulted in the sinking of three hostile ships and a small freighter, totaling 14,200 tons, and in evading enemy countermeasures . . . "

In December 1944 he joined the USS Atule (SS-403) as executive officer and navigator and was so serving when she made her first war patrol in the Pacific, for which she was awarded the Navy Unit Commendation, in the Luzon Straits, October 9 to December 11, 1944. He continued service in that submarine during her participation in the Leyte operation, October-December 1944; the assault and occupation of Iwo Jima, February-March 1945; and the assault and occupation of Okinawa Gunto, March-June 1945.

During the latter months of the war and until March 1946 he was attached to Submarine Divisions 361, 212, and 151, being commanding officer of prize crews at Tokyo Bay on 2 September 1945, and during the occupation of Japan the next six months; he was also officer in charge of the ex-Japanese I-203. In April 1946 he began his first tour of shore duty, assigned to the Officer Performance Division of the Bureau of Naval Personnel, Navy Department, Washington, D.C. He remained on duty there until November 1948, when he assumed command of the USS Burrfish (SSR-312). Detached in March 1949, he took command of the USS Pickerel (SS-524) the next month.

The Pickerel, under his command, was the first U.S. submarine in combat in Korea under the United Nations flag. He was awarded a letter of commendation (with star for his commendation ribbon) by Commander Naval Forces Far East: "For exceptionally meritorious service while serving as Commanding Officer of the USS PICKEREL during the period August 1, to October 17, 1950 . . . " when she made her first war patrol. She set a world's speed and distance record submerged during her passage from Hong Kong, British Crown Colony, to Pearl Harbor, Territory of Hawaii, during the period 15 March to 6 April 1950 (5,200 miles in 21 days submerged).

Detached from the Pickerel in August 1951, he returned to the Navy Department, Washington, D.C., where he had a three-year tour of duty in the Office of the Chief of Naval Operations, as special assistant to the Director, International Affairs, and head of the Western Hemisphere Branch. From August 1954 to August 1955 he served as executive officer of the USS Nereus (AS-17), being transferred from that submarine tender to duty as Commander Submarine Division 52, his pennant in the USS Catfish (SS-339). He remained in that command for a year, and in September 1956 he joined the staff of Commander Anti-Submarine Defense Force Atlantic for duty as readiness officer.

He reported in September 1958 as a student at the Naval War College, Newport, Rhode Island, and in June 1959 joined the staff at that college. He remained there until June 1961 and the next month assumed command of the USS Fulton (AS-11). Detached from that submarine tender in August 1962, he next served in the Office of the Joint Chiefs of Staff for Arms Control, Washington, D.C. While in that assignment, he was sent to Geneva, Switzerland, in June 1963 as the Joint Chiefs of Staff representative to the Eighteen Nation Disarmament Conference. He returned from Geneva in September 1964 for duty in connection with plans and policy on the Policy Planning Staff, Office of the Assistant Secretary of Defense (International Security Affairs). In September 1965 he was ordered to the Ohio State University, Columbus, Ohio, for instruction. Upon completion of his studies for a Ph.D. degree, he joined the staff of the National War College, Washington, D.C., in April 1966 and served there to the end of 1968. He officially retired from active duty on 1 January 1969.

Following retirement, Captain Schratz became director of international studies for the four-campus University of Missouri, a position he held until 1973, when he moved to Arnold, Maryland. He then worked as a member of the Commission on the Organization of the Government for the Conduct of Foreign Policy, a bipartisan White House-legislative task force. Subsequently he served on the faculties of Georgetown University, Washington, D.C., and the Air War College, Montgomery, Alabama. He was widely known as a lecturer and writer on civil-military affairs and national security problems.

From 1946 to 1985 he contributed to the Naval Academy Alumni Association's monthly Shipmate magazine, including writing the popular "Sea Breezes" column from 1957 to 1985. He wrote many articles and book reviews for the U.S. Naval Institute Proceedings magazine and three times submitted winning essays in the Institute's annual General Prize Essay Contest. He took the top prize in 1968 with his essay titled "The Caesars, the Sieges, and the ABM." His book of memoirs, Submarine Commander, was published by the University Press of Kentucky in 1988. Captain Schratz died in Arnold, Maryland, on 14 December 1993.

In addition to the Silver Star Medal, the Bronze Star Medal with combat "V," the Commendation Ribbon with star and "V" and the Navy United Commendation Ribbon, Captain Schratz was awarded the American Defense Service Medal with bronze "A"; the American Campaign Medal; European-African, Middle Eastern Campaign Medal; Asiatic-Pacific Campaign Medal with one silver and four bronze stars (nine engagements); the World War II Victory Medal; Navy Occupation Service Medal, Asia Clasp; China Service Medal (extended); the National Defense Service Medal; Korean Service Medal with two stars; United Nations Service Medal; and Philippine Liberation Ribbon. He also received the Korean Presidential Unit Citation Badge and the Submarine Combat Insignia with one silver and four gold stars for nine successful war patrols.

Paul Schratz was married to Henrietta E. Frank of Pittsburgh, Pennsylvania, on 21 June 1941. Their children were born as follows: Regina M., 21 May 1943; Henrietta K., 3 September 1944; Marjorie A., 8 February 1947; Nancy E., 26 July 1948; Paul R., Jr., 27 September 1952; Dorothy J., 30 September 1954; and Mary E., 14 August 1959.

Captain Schratz's hobbies were creative writing, music, real estate, and modern home architecture. He was the first violinist for the Honolulu Symphony Orchestra, 1949-51; The Arlington Symphony Orchestra, 1946-48 and 1951-54; La Jolla Symphony Orchestra, 1954-56; and the Norfolk Symphony Orchestra, 1956-57. He was president of the Arlington Symphony Association in 1954.

Authorization

The U.S. Naval Institute is hereby authorized to make available to individuals, libraries, and other repositories of its choosing the transcripts of three oral history interviews concerning the life and career of the late Captain Paul R. Schratz. The interviews were recorded on 30 November 1984, 4 December 1984, and 11 December 1984 in collaboration with Paul Stillwell for the U.S. Naval Institute.

The undersigned does hereby release and assign to the U.S. Naval Institute all right, title, restrictions, and interest in the interviews. The copyright in both the oral and transcribed versions shall be the sole property of the U.S. Naval Institute. The tape recordings of the interviews are and will remain the property of the U.S. Naval Institute.

Signed and sealed this _eighteenth_ day of _January_ 1996.

Mrs. Paul R. Schratz
Mrs. Paul R. Schratz, for the estate of
Captain Paul R. Schratz, USN (Ret.)

Interview Number 1 with Captain Paul R. Schratz, U.S. Navy (Retired)

Place: U.S. Naval Institute, Annapolis, Maryland

Date: Friday, 30 November 1984

Interviewer: Paul Stillwell

Q: Captain, to start at the beginning, you came from Pittsburgh, so why don't you talk some about your parents and your memories of early boyhood, please.

Captain Schratz: I had the typical Pittsburgh boyhood: public schools, mildly active in sports, lots of tennis and swimming, and active in music and theater. I wrote a play and played the lead role. I was the concertmaster in the symphony, sang lead roles in several operettas, and played first fiddle in the All-City High Symphony, a very good one in Pittsburgh at that time. Many went on to careers in music; at least one, Earl Wild, became internationally famous.

My high school days were extremely happy, despite a reputation as a hell-raiser. I was trying to get into either the Naval Academy or West Point and couldn't get an appointment in those Depression days.[*] They were tough to come by. I went to Carnegie Tech for a year--now Carnegie Mellon--and worked my butt off.[†] I dropped all the freshman shops and phys. ed. and doubled sophomore math and physics. I also bet my dad I could earn all my expenses, and it almost killed me--three outside jobs, a double academic

---

[*] Following the crash of the New York Stock Exchange in late October 1929, the United States was plunged into the Great Depression, from which it did not recover until the nation geared up for World War II at the beginning of the 1940s. The Depression was marked by high unemployment and many business failures.
[†] Carnegie Mellon University is in Pittsburgh, Pennsylvania.

load, playing in the symphony and the string symphony, and a little romancing now and then. I weighed about 180 when I left high school, and at the end of a year at Tech, I weighed 140. I was working 20 hours a day and skipped lunch to study.

When I got to the Naval Academy, 10:00 o'clock taps was impossible. I was up for hours later or sitting in the head reading.

Q: How did you get into music to begin with?

Captain Schratz: Most of our crowd was musically involved. A cousin taught violin, and I soon found it an entrée to a very interesting life. In my last year in high school, I was so determined to become the concertmaster, I spent the whole summer practicing at least six hours a day, sometimes ten. I earned the concertmaster's chair, qualified for the all-city and won runner-up honors in a national contest as a member of a string trio. I graduated from Wickersham School of Music in Pittsburgh, and Carnegie Tech made an exception to allow me, an engineer, to participate in their fine music school symphony. Incidentally, I was in the ROTC at Tech also.[*]

Q: What was the play you wrote? How did that come about?

Captain Schratz: That happened during the George Washington Bicentennial year, and my high school decided to put on a play.[†] The activities director asked if I would write one to keep me out of trouble, and then it was only natural for me to play the lead. I think the play is in the Library of Congress with the Bicentennial materials.

Q: What sort of occupation did your father have?

Captain Schratz: My father was a special insurance adjuster.

---

[*] ROTC--reserve officers' training corps.
[†] George Washington was born 22 February 1732.

Q: Did your parents place an emphasis on education and learning?

Captain Schratz: They were always supportive, although many people told me later that they didn't supervise me as closely in high school as they might have, or I probably wouldn't have been in as much trouble. With three inseparable friends, we decided we could learn as much in four days a week as the others learned in five, so the four of us made every Friday a holiday. I did this for about two and a half years until finally my very understanding guidance counselor, in a heart-to-heart talk, suggested the foolishness had gone on long enough, and it was time to grow up. I was suspended about eight times either for AWOL or academics, but I still stood pretty high in my class--top quarter.* I usually had a musical activity of some sort that required my services, and they were willing to cancel my suspension for the good of old alma mater.

Q: How did you spend your Fridays?

Captain Schratz: There was usually a big athletic event on Friday, so we'd usually go downtown to the natatorium and swim all morning, then go to an away game in the afternoon. Sometimes rehearsals of the All-City Symphony came that afternoon, too, and it eased the trolley ride. And one of my friends had a camp on a stream in the middle of Cook Forest. It was nice to take a three-day weekend and plan further mischief.

Q: How much participation did you do in sports?

Captain Schratz: I played some football and baseball, a good-hit, no-field baseball player, and a lot of tennis. We had a court behind the house. I found a main interest in tennis because girls play that too. The regimen of sports interfered too much with my social life.

Q: Well, how much of that was there?

---

* AWOL--absent without leave.

Captain Schratz: Quite a lot of that.

Q: How intense was the competition for appointments to the Naval Academy?

Captain Schratz: Extremely. I didn't have much chance until a congressman came in with a new broom, giving all applicants a Civil Service exam in math and English. I ranked two in 135 on that and got an appointment as a first alternate. When the principal made it, the congressman felt obligated to give me the principal the next year.* That's why I took the year at Carnegie Tech as a prep school.

Q: Did you win the bet with your dad?

Captain Schratz: Just about. I paid a high price for it. I had had so little sleep, my memory was about gone at the end of the year at Tech. I vividly recall trying to take an oral exam on something. Before I could answer a question, with the answer on the tip of my tongue, I had forgotten the question. Just a total blank. I couldn't have kept that up much longer.

Q: What had led to your interest in going to the Naval Academy?

Captain Schratz: Parents and superb high school advisers. The family had always thought highly of a service academy education. I set my goal that way early in high school. The life sounded far more exciting than what Pittsburgh had to offer.

Q: Had you read the fiction of the time that inspired young boys of that generation to go?

---

* The "principal" referred to here was the individual who had won the congressman's principal appointment for that particular opening at the Naval Academy. Someone with an alternate appointment would get in only if the person with the principal appointment was found to be unqualified or if he decided not to accept the appointment.

Captain Schratz: I read all kinds of stuff. I was always an avid reader. More likely a normal high school urge for change.

Q: When you got to Annapolis, did you find it an advantage that you did have a year of college under your belt?

Captain Schratz: Very much. Probably 60-75% of my class had some college; two were graduates, Archie Fields of Harvard, and Jim Dunford from the University of Washington.[*] We had some really rough competition.

Q: What do you remember about induction of plebe summer and events that followed?

Captain Schratz: As a free spirit, I didn't take the hazing too seriously. The class of 1936, administering our plebe year, was a small class, hence with too much competition for midshipmen stripers. They took it too seriously and had more than their share of sadists. I was less concerned for myself than for a roommate who wasn't gifted with as rugged a frame.

Q: Are there any incidents or people that you particularly remember in that context?

Captain Schratz: Well, I guess the incident my classmates still mention is a bet with somebody that I could wear my p.j. trousers to noon formation and get away with it. That was in the days, before uniforms were issued, when we wore white works.[†] It wouldn't have been tough except that it was a windy day; the p.j.s had shrunk so much that I had to drop them halfway to my knees to get them down over my shoe tops. From a mile away you could see them flapping in the breeze, whereas the white works were stiff. No

---
[*] Midshipman Arthur Mortimer Fields, Jr., USN, stood number five of the 581 graduates in the Naval Academy class of 1939; Midshipman James M. Dunford, USN, stood number three.
[†] White works was the name given to the white uniform, comprised of bell-bottom trousers and jumper, worn by enlisted men.

upperclassmen noticed. I'm afraid I did a lot of foolishness like that and was high on the demerit list by the end of plebe summer.

Q: Are there other examples of foolishness?

Captain Schratz: One I vividly recall as a first classman, I was invited to play bridge one night in the room next door. We needed an extra chair, but rather than upset the mate-of-the-deck in the corridor, I decided to go by the window, carrying my chair with me. I completely overlooked the fact that the main office was in full view below me. As I got out on the fourth deck windowsill dragging a mahogany chair, I was eye-to-eye with the DO, standing with hands on his hips, looking on with horror.[*] He was on his way up in a split-second, so I passed the chair back to my own room. When Lieutenant Burford banged on the door, everything was serene.[†] He was going to put us all down for playing bridge during study hour, but two of my bridge partners were midshipmen three-stripers who weren't supposed to get demerits. So he put me down for "hazarding government property," i.e., the chair, and let it go at that.

As you may gather, discipline didn't come easily, then or throughout my career. The only discipline I ever learned was as a violinist. For instance, once when I was playing with the Norfolk Symphony, we had a special rehearsal one Saturday afternoon before a concert. Unfortunately, it conflicted with a Dizzy Dean baseball telecast, and I thought, "Can't I be the guy who didn't get the word just this once so I can watch another inning before going to the rehearsal?"[‡] I arrived at the rehearsal half an hour late, slid into my chair, and later apologized to the conductor. He was quite a martinet.

That night, as we were about to walk on stage for the second half of the concert, he put his hand on my arm and mentioned that during my half-hour absence at rehearsal, they

---

[*] DO--duty officer.
[†] Lieutenant William P. Burford, USN.
[‡] Jay H. "Dizzy" Dean was a flamboyant pitcher for the St. Louis Cardinals in the 1930s. In the 1950s he was one of the announcers during the CBS network's game of the week each Saturday.

had worked very hard on the Haydn second movement and didn't feel quite confident about me in the concert.

I said, "But I know the music by heart. We played the same symphony in a concert just a few nights ago."

He said, "I just don't feel quite safe. I think you better not play the second movement."

I said, "You can't be serious." He was.

Out on the stage, I sawed my way through the first movement, then sat there with my fiddle in my lap while the orchestra went on about me, then I went to work again for the third and fourth. Before a packed house, I felt totally naked. My wife, in the audience, couldn't wait to get backstage and find out what was going on. She found me as the conductor walked up. To her inquiry on what had happened, he answered simply, "We have discipline in this outfit too." Perhaps a major reason for favoring submarine duty is the informal, small ship atmosphere.

Q: Did you wind up spending any time on the Reina Mercedes?[*]

Captain Schratz: I got lots of demerits but never came close to a "black N."[†]

Q: That was a somewhat perverse badge of honor, wasn't it?

Captain Schratz: Yes, very much so. But I think some of the finest naval officers I've known spent time on the ship.

Q: Who were some of your classmates that you particularly remember?

---

[*] USS Reina Mercedes (IX-25), captured during the Spanish-American War, served as a station ship at the Naval Academy from 1912 to 1957. Until 1940, midshipmen being punished for various disciplinary infractions slept and took meals on board the ship but continued to go to classes ashore.

[†] Midshipmen confined to the ship for punishment were denoted by a black N beside their names in the class yearbook.

Captain Schratz: Ned Beach was prominent.* Lou Roddis, my summer roommates Jim Dunford and Bill Sawyer, my regular roommates Larry Geis, Bing Gillette, and Layton Goodman.† Bing, Layton, and I all went to submarines; Layton was lost in <u>Barbel</u> in 1944. Vic Boatwright was also a good friend, perhaps the most brilliant man in the class.‡

Q: Are there any specific memories of these individuals that you have, incidents, personality characteristics, what have you?

Captain Schratz: We had about five people who later became prominent in the nuclear program: Laney, Roddis, Dunford, Sawyer, Reich, who are just plain brilliant.§

My prepping at Carnegie Tech was excellent, especially in math and sciences, and I felt I was way ahead of much of the class at the academy. I always hated to carry books or equipment while marching, so I never took anything to class if it could be avoided. The slide rule, an essential tool, I took out of the case and slipped into my breast pocket. Everybody thought that I was the only guy in the class who would go through the exams without even using his slide rule, so I let the myth perpetuate itself. The myth sometimes propelled me to the elite of the super brights, a place I never deserved.

Q: Your entry in the <u>Lucky Bag</u> said that you were very capable intellectually but perhaps by choice did not become a star man.** Why was that?

---

* Midshipman Edward Latimer Beach stood number two in the class of 1939 and subsequently retired as a captain. He has written a number of books, most notably the submarine novel <u>Run Silent, Run Deep</u>.
† Midshipman Louis H. Roddis, USN, stood number one in the class. Midshipman James M. Dunford, USN; Midshipman William T. Sawyer, USN; Midshipman Lawrence R. Geis, USN, who retired as a rear admiral; Midshipman Robert C. Gillette, USN; Midshipman Claude Layton Goodman, Jr., USN.
‡ Midshipman Victor T. Boatwright, USN, stood fourth in the class, behind Roddis, Beach, and Dunford.
§ Midshipman Robert V. Laney, USN, stood 46th in the class.
** Star men are those at the top of the class academically.

Captain Schratz: Several reasons. Partly, I think, I was somewhat burned out as a student. It was a real grind for years before entering. I was also bored with rote courses and courses that didn't catch my interest. Perhaps I just hadn't matured enough. I know if I had been interviewed by Admiral Rickover for the nuclear program, he would have been very upset with my attitude, but I was interested in too many things to waste time with trivia.[*]

Q: What did you do instead of applying yourself on your studies? Was it similar to the high school pattern?

Captain Schratz: Not quite. I never had any interest in going over the wall at night or anything like that, although many did. I was active in a lot of things, doing some writing and reading. Classes themselves, I thought, were incidental. I rarely took time studying. Two of my roommates had academic problems. When they asked for help, I learned enough for my own preparation and didn't have to study on my own.

Q: Was it emphasized at that time that your class standing would have an effect from then on throughout much of your career?

Captain Schratz: No, unfortunately. The Navy juniors like Bing Gillette generally learned that, but I doubt it would have made that much difference anyhow. Academic grades didn't seem all that important and "grease" ratings even less so.[†]

Q: You say you were writing. What sorts of things were you writing?

Captain Schratz: I wrote a couple of essays in competitions, and I did more than my share of themes in English classes. I stood very high in English, I think, and wrote a pretty good

---

[*] Rear Admiral Hyman G. Rickover, USN, was considered the father of the nuclear Navy. He ran the Navy's nuclear-power program for many years. In interviewing candidates for the program he had the reputation of being tough and demanding.
[†] "Grease mark" is Naval Academy slang for an individual's grade in the area of aptitude for the service.

translation from the German of Stefan Zweig's dramatic book on Scott's voyage to the Antarctic.*

Q: You have gone on to get advanced degrees and so forth. What comments do you have to evaluate the quality of the Naval Academy education during the time you were here?

Captain Schratz: Well, having just come from a top engineering school, it never occurred to me to evaluate the Naval Academy as an engineering school. I looked upon it primarily as a professional school for a career in the Navy. I don't think I was nearly as critical in evaluating the educational quality then as I was many years later when I took a much more direct interest in it. I think when I came here, the academy had been recognized as a degree-granting institution only a year or two before.† But the civilian instructors who had been here a long time were extremely good; the military instructors, some very good, or they at least knew where to find answers in the book and tried to stay one assignment ahead. I had no complaints. I felt, in comparison with my civilian peers, that I was quite well educated.

Q: I had been under the impression that this system sort of forced you to keep up with the work because of the requirements to man the boards and write out things for the homework. With your penchant for avoiding that, how did you manage to prevail?

Captain Schratz: The first section in math and a few other subjects--the top-ranking mids were put into a special section to compete against each other, and they weren't nearly as rigid in their approach to manning the boards. I was in and out of the first section a fair amount of time. But with the same academic courses for everybody, only a language as an option, it really wasn't all that tough for people who had a superior background. Again, I was doing a lot of reading in other subjects, and the fiddle was taking so much time, and

---

* Robert F. Scott led a British party to the South Pole in early 1912, but his men perished.
† Congress enacted a law on 25 May 1933 so that the degree of bachelor of science would be conferred on graduates of the Naval Academy.

other activities I just found more challenging. I translated a couple of German texts into English.

Q: What was your background in the German language?

Captain Schratz: I had taken German in high school for about two or three years, and at the Naval Academy I naturally opted for German. It was also a common belief then that to be a scientist, German would be important, certainly more than Spanish or French. As my career worked out, French would have been far more important, so I used French for my doctorate.

Q: What extracurricular activities were you involved in at the academy?

Captain Schratz: I rowed in the 150-pound crew until I regained my 180-pound high school figure, and I played a fair amount of tennis. I had played scads of tennis before the academy, but my plebe summer roommate, Andy Lyman, was a very hot tennis player and he beat me so bad, I never tried for the varsity.* I also played some battalion football. Varsity sports here demanded too much time. I'm sorry only that I never took up golf here.

Q: What recollections do you have of people in the commandant's organization?

Captain Schratz: Almost none. They were fairly remote from the mids. We knew them by name. The name I heard most was Captain Thaddeus A. Thomson, a true martinet, who had been the head of the executive department the year or two before we arrived.

Q: He wound up being your skipper in the Wichita.

---

* Midshipman Andrew I. Lyman, USN, dropped out of the Naval Academy and subsequently became a colonel in the Marine Corps.

Captain Schratz: That's how I first met him. I didn't realize, when they told me the skipper was Thad Thomson, that it was "TBT--That Bastard Thomson," about whom we were often quizzed as plebes.

Q: Are there any specific memories you have of Roddis, the man who stood tops in the class?

Captain Schratz: Just as extremely bright and a very nice person, always willing to take time to help other people out. He was never a slash, a cutthroat at academics. We had more than our share, I think, of very brilliant, very nice top scholars.

Q: Any others that you would mention specifically?

Captain Schratz: Boatwright comes immediately to mind. Vic Boatwright has been a close friend since plebe summer. He had one of the best fitness report records as a naval officer I have ever seen. Unfortunately, he was retired for glaucoma after World War II, almost losing his eyesight.

Q: What memories do you have of the social life?

Captain Schratz: Not too much. I still have a certain revulsion for the dancing lessons, ballroom dancing. I seemed to get as my partner Ben Jarvis, who was about 6 feet, 5 inches and 250 pounds, and we shared over 100 inches of chest between us.[*] I didn't think we made a very good couple for ballroom dancing.

Q: There must have been some girls at some point in this endeavor.

---

[*] Midshipman Benjamin C. Jarvis, USN.

Captain Schratz: As a plebe, I was going with my high school OAO--or maybe TAO.[*] Then when younger sister grew up, I had a tough time shifting down one notch around the family table. Both families were near neighbors in Pittsburgh, both with six children, who frequently paired off, usually boy-boy. I fouled up the pattern by taking two girls from the middle. Things were tense for about a year until big sister married.

Then there was a redhead I had dated casually in Pittsburgh. She came down for a few weekends, seemingly bent on seduction, but I couldn't do that in uniform. In time, Henrietta and I married and lived happily ever after.[†] But I didn't date much as a mid, rarely attending the hops. I played with the NA Ten for one or two dances, where they needed fiddles, but I was pretty much a "red mike."[‡]

Q: What's a "red mike?"

Captain Schratz: That's a guy who doesn't date.

Q: Are there any of the professors or instructors that you particularly remember?

Captain Schratz: One in particular was Harry Hawkins, an English teacher, and very active in athletic programs.[§] I wasn't in his English section until first-class year.[**] He invited the new class each month to his home for a Coke and social hour with several local gals. I thoroughly enjoyed it, and wrote him a wholly sincere bread-and-butter note after, expressing my delight. It happened that bread-and-butter notes were part of the material covered in English class that month, but I made no special association, even when I stood one in the class in English that month.

---

[*] OAO--one and only; TAO--two and only.
[†] The future Mrs. Schratz was Henrietta Frank of Pittsburgh.
[‡] The NA Ten was a musical group comprised of midshipmen.
[§] Lieutenant (junior grade) David D. Hawkins, USN.
[**] First-class year is the fourth for a midshipman, the equivalent of a senior at a civilian university.

Two or three years later I was in Wichita in Norfolk, and Harry, a lieutenant, was in New York, and we were both coaching the basketball teams. At his home for a social one night, he mentioned that at the academy, they had entertained something like 2,200 midshipmen at their home and only one ever sent a bread-and-butter note. It suddenly became clear how I reached the top of the class in English that month.

Q: Whatever works.

Captain Schratz: Another favorite professor taught German. He was very good, not only with the language but German culture and our own obligations as future officers. I was very disappointed when he was later interned as a Nazi sympathizer. He influenced us as a philosopher as well as a teacher.

Q: What was his name?

Captain Schratz: Herr Thomas--I don't recall his first name.[*]

Q: How much awareness did you have of the country at large? Were you insulated from economic problems in the nation?

Captain Schratz: In post-Depression years one could hardly be uninvolved. Things were grim in Pittsburgh during the Depression. My family was fairly fortunate, but you couldn't live in the city without knowing an awful lot about economic problems.

Q: How about of the world at large, the encroachments of Hitler and the Japanese and so forth?[†]

---

[*] Dr. C. R. Walther Thomas, an assistant professor in the department of modern languages, was on the faculty of the Naval Academy from 1935 to 1940.
[†] Adolf Hitler was Chancellor of Germany from 1933 until his death in 1945.

Paul R. Schratz #1 - 15

Captain Schratz: The world political problems were too much a part of our careers for us to stay aloof. I was deeply interested. I recall vividly some of the wardroom discussions in Wichita. There was a surprising amount of anti-British feeling among the officers, who couldn't see that we had any role whatever in opposing Hitler, that it was someone else's problem. We had agitated discussions then and a few at the Naval Academy prior.

Q: What was the basis for their anti-British feeling?

Captain Schratz: In some form it has been in the Navy for about 150 years. After all, we had war plans against the British at least until the 1920s, and when President Wilson forbade the Army to plan a war against Germany, they used the plan for war against Britain when the emergency came in 1918.[*] When Admiral Sims went to London to handle U.S. Navy-Royal Navy cooperation, the CNO, Admiral Benson, briefed him that "we would just as soon be fighting the British as the Germans."[†]

Q: That late?

Captain Schratz: Yes. Part of the Anglophobia came from parents bitter about the British failure to repay their war debts from World War I. My mother reflected some of this, an attitude I could never change.

Q: What do you recall of your various midshipman cruises?

---

[*] Woodrow Wilson was President of the United States from 1913 to 1921.
[†] Vice Admiral William S. Sims, USN, became Commander U.S. Naval Forces Operating in European Waters in May 1917. He served in that billet until March 1919, being promoted to full admiral in December 1918. Admiral William S. Benson, USN, served as Chief of Naval Operations from 11 May 1915 to 25 September 1919.

Captain Schratz: They were great. The training squadron went to Europe, and many of us got to Berlin on youngster cruise.* I think I spent about 20 hours sleeping in a baggage rack getting from either Denmark or Sweden to Berlin, but it was worth it, especially when I was back there 30 or so years later to see the same Adlon Hotel, now in the Eastern sector and a real fleabag. Later on that cruise, we were diverted to Spain, during the Spanish Civil War, to evacuate Americans. They were great experiences.

Q: What ships were you embarked in?

Captain Schratz: I was in Wyoming for youngster cruise and for first-class cruise.† These old battleships made excellent training ships. I thoroughly enjoyed them.

Q: What do you recall about that operation during the Spanish Civil War?

Captain Schratz: We were diverted from Cherbourg or Le Havre, I believe, to Bilbao, Spain. We anchored off Bilbao and brought some people off by boat, getting under way about dark to head back out to sea. I understand that the rebel Navy came in and took over Bilbao just after we left, passing us in the night. The mids, of course, were not directly involved.‡

Q: Do you have any specific recollections of the training during your cruises?

Captain Schratz: One of my favorite subjects was celestial navigation. It still fascinates me today. I looked forward to "communion with the stars." Another favorite Naval Academy

---

* At the Naval Academy, the "youngster" year is the second one. This cruise was in the summer of 1936.

† The USS Wyoming (BB-32) was commissioned as a battleship in 1912 and served in that role until being demilitarized as a result of the 1930 London Treaty on the limitation of naval armaments. She was redesignated AG-17 in 1931 and thereafter served into the mid-1940s as a training ship for gunnery and for midshipman cruises.

‡ This event was in July 1936.

professor was Roy Benson, a navigation instructor.* He has a favorite sea story about rambling on in his classroom, but always keeping his eye on Lou Roddis. As long as Roddis nodded in agreement, it was smooth sailing. But if Lou Roddis stopped, Benson knew he'd better get careful.

On the cruise, we did the routine of celestial navigation: noon sun sights, plotting, and piloting. One day, by chance, the other battleship was obstructing our line of sight to the southern horizon at the time of our noon sun sight. I simply turned around and took the big angle of the sun from the northern horizon, and worked out the sight in the usual manner but reversing some of the corrections. Since I was the only mid who got a noon latitude that day, Roy was very interested in how I had done it. The big angle told the tale.

Then I started thinking that maybe the same thing would happen again the following day, plus clouds, and I planned on this assumption. As anticipated, the horizon was blocked again and the sun itself at LAN. So I took a series of sun sights ten minutes each side of LAN--local apparent noon--and faired a line through my plot to determine what the altitude should have been at precisely noon, and again got a fix when nobody else did. I thought celestial navigation was one of the most fascinating arts a naval officer ever learns. I regret very much young officers know so little about it now.

Later, as navigator of a submarine on a war patrol, one gorgeous southern seas night I decided to shoot every navigable star in the sky, and actually got about 59 of the total 110 in the book. My fix was a great big blob of 15 to 20 through one point, a score of lesser clusters close by. The heavens were all on station that night and I moved into a separate world in the center of the universe.

Q: In his oral history, Admiral Benson talked about his time both as an instructor in the classroom and on the midshipman cruises. A name he mentioned was Commander Denebrink.† He was very much impressed by him. Do you remember him?

---

* Lieutenant Roy S. Benson, USN. The oral history of Benson, who retired as a rear admiral, is in the Naval Institute collection.
† Commander Francis C. Denebrink, USN, who subsequently became a vice admiral.

Captain Schratz: Yes, I remember him well, although I never was in his classroom nor later in his command. I met him years later in Pearl Harbor, when he made flag rank, the first time I'd seen him since midshipman days. He was a popular midshipman instructor--if you knew your stuff--and was ruthless otherwise. He claimed to be an avid reader of my Shipmate column, proving he was a superior being.*

Q: Did the cruises serve the useful purpose for you of demonstrating how the enlisted men lived?

Captain Schratz: Not to any great extent. You couldn't help but learn a lot, especially if you had no previous shipboard experience. The midshipmen were well isolated. As third class, they did enlisted chores, but nobody considered them enlisted. And we were pretty ignorant. I think the authorities went out of their way to make sure we were isolated.

Q: Why would you think that was?

Captain Schratz: Primarily because we were officers, or at least officers to be. We started at the bottom to learn their way of life. We did the chores as enlisted men but never with the men, always separate. When we stood engineering watches, the chiefs were quite helpful, especially on the ships which made the cruises every year. But there was no real connection. The isolation was fairly complete, I thought.

Q: What was the mood of the people when you were in Berlin? Did they seem to be supporting Hitler fairly strongly?

Captain Schratz: My German was far from conversational, and I can't recall talking politics. I think we were more interested in a glass of ale and the Sans Souci and a few things like that. My political thoughts, if I had any, or impressions of those days, have long faded.

---

* For many years Schratz wrote a monthly column for Shipmate, the magazine of the Naval Academy Alumni Association.

Q: You said you went to Europe twice. What was the third cruise?

Captain Schratz: The second-class cruise was a destroyer cruise on the Atlantic seaboard for about a month. It gave a fine opportunity to see small-ship operations, particularly the wardroom camaraderie. Virtually all the officers and men were long-term careerists. My skipper in J. Fred Talbott was a non-Academy type with a superb sense of humor.* His officers and the mids fit in well at West Point, Newport, and Norfolk--a good career experience.

Q: At the present time, midshipmen are shown during the course of these summers the options for Marine Corps, aviation, submarines, and so forth. Was there anything comparable during your time?

Captain Schratz: No. The Marine Corps probably didn't feel they needed it. So many in my class wanted to go to the Marines, me included, that it took almost being a star man to make the cut. I stood in the top third, and missed the Marine Corps by, I think, one or two numbers. With so many people opting for the Marines, the rules were changed by limiting the Marine Corps selections to one-fourth from each quarter of the graduating class.

I later decided I was fortunate that I stuck with the Navy, especially as the war turned out. Many classmates volunteered for the Marine Corps at least partly because they wanted to get married. The Navy had a two-year prohibition against marriage at graduation. Unfortunately, many who went to Basic School and got married were sent to the Philippines or Peking a year later, leaving their young brides behind. When the war broke, they died at Bataan and Corregidor or served out the war in prison camps in China, the Philippines, or Japan. We lost a heavy percentage of fine officers.

---

* Lieutenant Commander Clarence H. Pike, USN, was the commanding officer of the J. Fred Talbott (DD-156) in the summer of 1937.

Q: What had been your motivation for wanting to go to the Marine Corps? To get married?

Captain Schratz: That may have been on the list of priorities, but I don't think so. I liked the attitude, knew some great people, and liked the small service. Perhaps this is why I was so happy later in submarines.

Q: Any other memories of the Naval Academy, various aspects that you want to cover while we're still on the topic?

Captain Schratz: I don't think so. I was ready to move by the time the four years were up, anxious to go somewhere. I had been going to school just too long.

Q: Any recollections of the final weeks, the graduation and so forth?

Captain Schratz: No, except my mother often stated that the peak of her ambition was to see her son commissioned in the Navy, and it didn't quite come off right. The Secretary of the Navy mispronounced the name. I became a Schwartz, and she almost fainted.

Q: How then did you get ordered to the Wichita?

Captain Schratz: In those days, we drew numbers for assignment preference, and I happened to draw a very low number, so I could write my own ticket. As it happened, Henrietta, my wife-to-be, graduated the same week and had a fine offer of a job as a home economist at the H. J. Heinz pier in Atlantic City, New Jersey. I asked for Wichita, which was fitting out in Philadelphia.* I spent my first six weeks of sea duty with about 2,600

---

* The USS Wichita (CA-45) was commissioned 16 February 1939. She had a standard displacement of 10,000 tons, was 608 feet long and 62 feet in the beam. Her top speed was 32.5 knots. She was armed with nine 8-inch guns, and eight 5-inch guns. The ship served throughout World War II before being decommissioned 3 February 1947.

miles by Greyhound bus between Philadelphia and Atlantic City and about 800 feet by sea, moving out of dry dock.

Q: What are your recollections about reporting aboard the ship, your early duties?

Captain Schratz: Well, Thaddeus Thomson's shadow fell over almost everything.[*] We had a fine wardroom, so united against the skipper's iron hand that it unified us into one of the closest knit groups ever. There was always a new horror story about one incident or another involving the skipper.

Thad was a disciplinarian, but to his credit, he set very high standards of performance and was willing to give junior officers all the responsibility they could handle. He didn't know squat about engineering or ship handling or most of the running of the Navy, but he was a person you could look up to. He had served several tours of attaché duty, had a very gracious wife (incidentally, a fine ship handler), and they did entertaining in the grand scale. On the cup and saucer side of the Navy, they enforced protocol with a checkoff list--excellent training in that respect. He also had a super exec, who did most of the ship handling.

Q: Was this Commander Moyer?[†]

Captain Schratz: Yes, classmate Johnny Moyer's dad.[‡]

Wichita duty, in spite of the pain and heartache, was a good experience for me. Not so for my classmates aboard. Of the six ensigns in my class who went to the "Witch," I was probably the only one who didn't get fired--i.e., recommendation to have a commission revoked for some minor problem as an ensign. The only reason I missed was because I was in the engineering department in my rotation of duties during the tough period. I think I

---

[*] Thomson was the first commanding officer when the ship went into commission. He held the command from 16 February 1939 to 27 December 1940.
[†] Commander John G. Moyer, USN.
[‡] Ensign John S. Moyer, USN, who reported to the heavy cruiser Louisville (CA-28) after graduating from the Naval Academy in 1939.

was also the only one of my Wichita classmates who made all of his promotions on time after that experience.

Thad simply took the fact of our probationary status as an administrative tool to enforce an impossible level of compliance. He assigned us responsibilities as top watch in port about three or four weeks from reporting aboard--a tough job for a fresh-caught ensign fitting out that big ship. Fires were breaking out every watch. There were problems with everything. It was tough when we got to sea. We stood JO watches for not very long until we were given top watch, and if you succeeded, life was great.[*] If you didn't, God help you. There was no in-between.

Q: Did your classmates actually wind up losing commissions?

Captain Schratz: No. The bureau killed it, but the letter is on the record.[†] I think they all eventually made captain but several years late.

Q: You say engineering helped you. Was that less under his scrutiny?

Captain Schratz: Yes. Engineering was a big mystery to him. For example, we were going down the Delaware River one day and a temperamental steam whistle, on a routine blast, didn't turn off. On the bridge 20 feet away, the sound was deafening. Orders couldn't be heard; confusion reigned. The other ship in the passing situation had no idea what was happening. There aren't rules for a three-minute blast. It was an awkward situation. Thad screamed to the engine room officer to cut the steam to the whistle. Well, that's like calling up the power company to turn off your TV set. I was the JO and ran aft to the signal bridge, jumped the rail to the forward stack, climbed up about three steps, and shut off the steam supply to the whistle. The immediate silence was deafening.

---

[*] JO--junior officer.
[†] The Bureau of Navigation was responsible for officer assignments and record-keeping in those days.

Q: How did he manage to get command of this ship if he didn't really seem to have all of the qualifications?

Captain Schratz: Without question, he had a great record over 32 years of service, not including much sea duty. And ship handling is not a test for command. Even his wife was a better ship handler.

Q: How did you find that out?

Captain Schratz: When he entertained on board, which he did frequently, she generally came out in the gig to do the flower arranging, seating, the menu, and everything else, usually running the stewards like Cleopatra and the slaves. I usually had the chore of being the boat officer and would take the gig in to where they were staying in Newport or Bar Harbor to pick her up. We had many adventures on some of those foggy afternoons at Newport, trying to get that gig into places where he would like it to pick her up.

Q: Are there any other horror stories you remember?

Captain Schratz: Yes. I was standing a JO watch, and Thad's seamanship, his rather primitive knowledge of relative movement made him intolerant of human error in station-keeping. If SOP called for 600 yards interval, he allowed about ten yards tolerance, which is impossible, given different engineering plants and performance data. As a JO, I operated the stadimeter, which is a miniature range finder. Counting on Thad's poor eyesight and lack of a seaman's eye, rather than moving the range knob, I kept it on 600 yards and twisted the masthead height to keep the range from changing. Screwing the knob this way and that, I reported, "Steady on 600."

Everybody on the bridge could see that the ship was all over the place--far beyond the allowable limits for station-keeping. Even Captain Thad finally got suspicious one day, walked across the bridge and grabbed that stadimeter from my hand, put it to his eye. Everybody on the bridge froze. They all knew what was going on. The captain screwed the stadimeter into his eye, twirled the same knob (mast height), and looked at the range, which obviously had not changed. He shoved it back to me without a word. I never tried that trick again.

Q: So he caught on.

Captain Schratz: Hardly. He made the same "mistake."

Q: There was a great emphasis on station-keeping in that era, wasn't there?

Captain Schratz: Yes, and without radar.

Q: How was it in fog situations?

Captain Schratz: It was tough. Our temperamental whistle failed again one day. We then had on board an ensign out of the class of '34, already six years in grade and not likely to get much beyond it. He'd been on a ship in China getting unsat fitness reports. To give him a break, the bureau gave him a new start--with Thad. The superannuated ensign was still standing JO watches.

The whistle broke down in a heavy fog off New England during a four-hour full power run. So Alan Ingling was sent forward to the eyes of the ship, with a tiny fog horn from a motor boat, blowing his guts out.* He was also prematurely bald and had shaved off what little hair remained. While he was blowing that puny foghorn, his transparent skull turning purple with the effort, the skipper yelled to blow louder. Even on the bridge he could barely be heard. Well, the big whistle was finally repaired and commenced its stentorian warning. Unfortunately, as often happens, nobody remembered Alan down in the eyes of the ship. About five minutes later, one of the lookouts reported, "Fog signal dead ahead."

---

* Ensign Alan L. Ingling, USN, who resigned from the service in October 1940.

The skipper screamed, "All back emergency!" We backed and backed, changed course 90 degrees and stopped to listen. Dead ahead was this little "peep" again. Another back emergency, our endurance test now gone to hell. By the time we backed halfway to Atlantic City, it finally occurred to somebody on the bridge that Alan was still up there with his toy. He wasn't alert enough to realize his meager services were no longer needed. The skipper put him in hack. This is typical of some of the not very high standards of seamanship we occasionally achieved on behalf of the skipper. Sea operations were clearly not his dish. But he did many other things extremely well.

Q: What things did the skipper do well?

Captain Schratz: Primarily, he had a very solid understanding of the professional naval officer: training, bearing, standards of performance. He routinely invited two of the ensigns to his cabin for dinner every night at sea. He would talk about our role in preparing a new ship for war. "We took this inanimate mass of steel and breathed life into it, placed our stamp upon it to form a reputation it would bear years after we have gone, for good or ill." Here I admired him greatly. I used that line myself over the years. As I say, if you could pay the price, if you could stay out of trouble, he was not a bad guy to get along with.

Q: She was a one-ship class, essentially.

Captain Schratz: Yes.

Q: Did you go through extra trials and tests and so forth because she was a new design?

Captain Schratz: Not to my knowledge. The Navy hadn't built a new capital ship for years. We were more or less the prototype for the new North Carolina-class battleships just then coming along.

Q: What sorts of things were involved there?

Captain Schratz: Perhaps not too much. Those long eight-hour full-power runs, backing and crash backing at full power, I thought, were excessive. The crash backing, from ahead full to back emergency, I thought, aged the ship 25 years for no purpose. The gunnery tests were important to test new 5-inch/38 and 1.1-inch battery designs. In <u>Wichita</u> the stops on the 5-inch/38s allowed firing too far into the superstructure, and wiped out half the sheet metal on the ship at first firing. On the main battery we had problems in getting the range keepers to integrate the whole system. Here a very bright officer, Tom Davies, '37, solved in a few minutes a problem which had stymied the Ford Instrument folks for weeks.[*]

Q: Were there innovations in the gunnery system other than the 5-inch/38s?

Captain Schratz: I think we started off with the 1.1 AA battery, which failed miserably. They disappeared very early in favor of the 20-millimeter and 40-millimeter guns, both foreign-made.

Q: How much contact did you have with the exec?

Captain Schratz: Oh, quite a lot, even though he was a generation older than we were. We did a lot of operating in the Caribbean--out of Guantanamo, Cuba, where he was always the super athlete: shortstop on the softball team, a number-one athlete in everything, and by far the biggest party pusher of all of us for a trip to Caimanera, especially the Red Barn. We invariably took the exec's motor boat for our sprees in the worst of old Caimanera. Usually a boat full of JOs would spend that night partying, the other half trying to drag the XO back to the ship in time for morning quarters.[†] But he was on deck after a change of clothes. If

---

[*] Ensign Thomas D. Davies, USN. Davies later became an aviator and achieved public notice for the long-distance flight of the P2V patrol plane "Truculent Turtle" from Australia to Ohio in 1946. He retired as a rear admiral.

[†] XO--executive officer.

the JOs weren't with their divisions at 0700, he personally would drag us out of the sack. A solid guy; we loved him.

Q: Did the JOs go on liberty as much as possible to escape their onerous routine in the ship?

Captain Schratz: I don't think so. I went on liberty because that's why the ship took us to all these glamorous places. The ship was always under way, and the JOs, primarily unmarried, rarely stayed aboard. The captain, even during the fitting-out period, was living down on Cape May, and the informal call on the skipper was mandatory. We made our formal call in his cabin within 48 hours of reporting aboard, in full dress. The call at his home within six or seven days, I recall, was required even if we had to rent a car to drive across New Jersey to get there.

Q: That was expected?

Captain Schratz: More than that. Mrs. Thad--Lillian--kept a checkoff roster behind the front door. I think she checked us off, "In, 1620; out, 1644." But once there, it was very pleasant, very gracious, both inspiring and educational. Sometimes, late in the evening, he allowed their son to stop calling him "sir" and use "Dad." In my later career, I always encouraged the routine of calls by my officers. I tried to make them be just as valuable for a young officer as they were for me in my early days.

Q: What value did you see in seeing the CO in that situation, as opposed to the meetings in his mess?

Captain Schratz: Social rather than professional. In the mess, he was a very charming conversationalist. They were stag, naturally, and he had spent a lot of time around the world and was a superb raconteur. An experienced attaché, he was well-read and an interesting talker. He also owned half of Texas and was hardly unknown in the business world. Always a charming host, these evenings were quite inspirational for a young lad.

Q: How was it different than the calls at his home? What was the benefit of having this additional call?

Captain Schratz: Well, there were usually more people. It allowed us to meet his wife and family, to match wits in the teacup set. An occasional cocktail or two often loosened a tongue. You talked. He was interested in your personal life, your ambitions, your sweethearts, your goals in the Navy.

Q: This ship had an extensive cruise down to South America, and one might presume that was one reason he was sent there, because of the diplomatic background.

Captain Schratz: That could be, but I rather doubt it. We went because of a political crisis in Rio. It was necessary to redouble the size of the Marine brigade, so we carried an augmented group with us. We spent about three months, eventually visiting almost every port in South America we could get that ship into. It was a great cruise. We were all social butterflies in Rio. I think we brought the samba and gin and tonic to the U.S. at that time. Every American or native stage show or ballet or symphony soon found most of the gals attracted to young Wichita bachelors, and we had most of them in the wardroom quite frequently.

The Philadelphia Youth Orchestra under Leopold Stokowski was playing in Rio when we were there, and later in Buenos Aires. I knew a few young musicians in the group, and it was nice meeting them again. It was the real Navy life of song and legend, a way of life gone for all time. The ship was always on the move. As a bachelor, I loved it-- the Caribbean in the winter, Norfolk, Newport, or Bar Harbor in the summertime. We operated as far north as above the Arctic Circle and south below Uruguay. I loved the duty and the life.

Q: Did you get involved in the receptions with the local dignitaries?

Captain Schratz: Wherever possible, yes.

Q: Any specific recollections along that line?

Captain Schratz: In Buenos Aires, yes. On one occasion, four young studs were needed to escort the four daughters of the Secretary of State, and I was one of those picked. Argentine gals were not allowed out after sunset without a chaperone, and there were only two nightclubs they could go to in town. We usually went to their home for cocktails, during which the gals would disappear, emerging later to put on a show, a dramatic play or something, always quite clever. They could never be present while liquor was being served. Then we'd go to one of the nightclubs, the chaperones sitting together at distant tables. Invariably we enjoyed a thick steak near midnight, after a pleasant evening of dancing. There was never any hanky-panky. I recall, on saying good night to this charming young lady who was my companion, shaking hands with her at the door of the club one night, and slipping my finger up her wrist for a mild caress. She gave me a sly wink, but, my God, I felt I had raped her. It was just good, plain fun and companionship.

We were always met at the ship with special government cars with white license plates, and we always expected an open parking space in front of the restaurant or club. Then one day they invited us to their summer camp up in the mountains, where we spent the day. Here there were no chaperones once we left the city. Still, the standards of conduct were no different. Chaperones were necessary in the city only for appearance sake. Truly, I hated to leave Buenos Aires when the time came.

Q: Had the Graf Spee incident occurred by the time you got to Montevideo?

Paul R. Schratz #1 - 30

Captain Schratz: Yes, <u>Graf Spee</u> was sunk in the middle of Montevideo. Her action with the British cruisers <u>Ajax</u>, <u>Achilles</u>, and <u>Exeter</u> had occurred in December '39, about six months prior.

Q: Did it make any difference in the shipboard routine after the war had started in Europe?

Captain Schratz: Not to us. The Atlantic Fleet went to war in the summer of 1941. I went to Iceland in <u>Wichita</u> in July 1941. We '39-ers were first allowed to marry in June of '41.[*] I left a few weeks later for Iceland with the first U.S. occupation forces.[†] When the ship left for Iceland, Captain Thad was long gone, but another of his social mores emerged. The junior officers were criticized for the "maudlin display of farewells" on the dock. One officer was holding his wife's hand almost until the crane hooked onto the brow. We learned that an officer should say goodbye to his wife four hours before sailing, then tend to his shipboard duties.

We were on essentially a war footing at that time. We made routine patrols north of Iceland, along the coast of Greenland to the Arctic Circle. We also left Iceland to go to Argentia for the meeting of FDR and Churchill in August '41, when the Atlantic Charter was announced.[‡] President Roosevelt at that time was bringing along American opinion very carefully to support the inevitable war--brilliantly, I thought.

Hitler had proclaimed a danger zone, including Iceland and reaching to the coast of Greenland, in March 1941. It overlapped the Roosevelt "security zone." FDR countered two weeks later by extending the Western Hemisphere security zone, ostensibly to help the Royal Navy, then in late May 1941, proclaimed an "unlimited national emergency." A week before <u>Wichita</u> sailed for Iceland, he broadened the security zone to include Iceland.

---

[*] The Schratzes were married on 21 June 1941.
[†] The <u>Wichita</u> sortied from Newport, Rhode Island, on 27 July 1941 as part of Task Force 16.
[‡] President Franklin D. Roosevelt of the United States and Prime Minister Winston Churchill of Great Britain had their first face-to-face meeting during the Atlantic Charter talks, held 9-12 August 1941 at Argentia, Newfoundland.

In August '41, FDR indicated to Churchill that American escort of convoys to Iceland would soon produce an incident leading to U.S. entry into the war. When USS Greer was attacked-- unsuccessfully--by a submarine in early September, FDR countered on the 11th with his "rattlesnake" fireside chat, deliberately misrepresenting Greer as the victim of an unprovoked attack when, in fact, she was clearly the aggressor and had made the first attack.

The President sent orders to Rear Admiral R. C. Giffen, ComCruDiv 7 in Wichita, to "eliminate" the U-boat and publicly ordered the Navy to attack German vessels on sight.* Since the U-boat had long since cleared the area, Giffen could do nothing not already done. He may also have had doubts about the validity of the sub contact. To the great displeasure of Admiral King, then CinCLant, he did nothing.† That he couldn't do anything not already in progress was less important than the image created in Norfolk and Washington.

Affairs continued to heat up in October. The FDR "shoot on sight" order brought another retaliation from Hitler that any American ship doing so would become the mark for German torpedoes. The day before, 17 October, Kearny had been hit amidships by a German torpedo, killing 11 men, and made a dramatic entry into Hvalfjordur. Steaming between the new British battleship King George V and the USS Mississippi at anchor, each heavy reversed tradition by rendering honors to Kearny. We all gave her a rousing three cheers. Then on Navy Day, 27 October, Roosevelt revealed the existence of a captured German map showing German ambitions to set up five vassal states in Central and South America. He never produced the map for public inspection, but Hitler's Mein Kampf gave all the information necessary.

---

* Rear Admiral Robert C. Giffen, USN, Commander Cruiser Division Seven.
† Admiral Ernest J. King, USN, served as Commander in Chief Atlantic Fleet from 1 February 1941 until he was transferred in late December 1941 to Washington, D.C., to serve as Commander in Chief U.S. Fleet (CominCh).

Paul R. Schratz #1 - 32

Q: After the Kearny was damaged and Reuben James sunk, did these incidents combine to produce any change in mood aboard the ship that you might be next?*

Captain Schratz: I don't think so. I think we were pretty well up to speed on that. Again, a total contrast with the Pacific. We had the feeling we were at war, very poorly prepared in lots of ways, wretched in some ways, but we did the best with what we had.

Q: Was there any feeling of resentment that you were not better prepared for essentially wartime duty?

Captain Schratz: I don't think so. I think we understood. At least I don't recall wardroom discussions along that line.

Then, less than two weeks later, a strange incident occurred. Wichita and Tuscaloosa were sent from Hvalfjordur, Iceland, to a point about 100 miles off the coast of Londonderry, Ireland. We went out with no escorts, no darkened ship, no particular antisubmarine alert, no zigzagging, nothing; just cruise ships wandering across the ocean. Many of us were quite sure that FDR was deliberately trying to provoke an episode with Hitler to involve the U.S. formally in the war. I personally had long before seen that war was inevitable. I sympathized wholly with the President in his attempt to get the American people moving. His attempts were not limited to the Atlantic. Admiral Kemp Tolley published something in Proceedings years ago about FDR sending three or four escort types to sea from Indochina at that time in almost the same type of operation, and, he thought, for the same purpose.†

---

* On 31 October 1941, the U-552 torpedoed and sank the four-stack destroyer Reuben James (DD-245) with the loss of 115 lives while she was escorting a convoy from Halifax, Nova Scotia.
† Rear Admiral Kemp Tolley, USN (Ret.), "The Strange Assignment of USS Lanikai," U.S. Naval Institute Proceedings, September 1962, pages 70-83. The oral history of Admiral Tolley is in the Naval Institute collection.

Q: Was it fairly common knowledge in the ship that there had been specific orders from above to operate in this fashion?

Captain Schratz: It was common knowledge in the wardroom, yes. We had absolutely no defense against submarines, except turn tail and run. We had no sound gear, we had nothing but a surface or AA battery. We debated about what to do in a crisis with a submarine. Our instructions were, on sighting a periscope, to open fire on it. We questioned what possible use a 5-inch shell could do against a submerged submarine. We didn't even know enough about a submarine to know the answer. After the cruise to Londonderry, ship's force built some depth charge racks on the stern for the big 600-pounders, but the ship had no detection gear. All we could do is make a lot of noise, at the risk of blowing off the fantail.

Q: Had you routinely been escorted by destroyers prior to that?

Captain Schratz: Generally, yes, but it depended on the operation. On a November patrol north of Iceland we were looking for the German surface raiders Admiral Scheer and Prinz Eugen. There were three patrol areas. The destroyers searched from the coast of Iceland to the Arctic Circle; the cruisers from the Arctic Circle to the ice pack, the battleships Mississippi and Idaho to the south. Augmenting our force were British Home Fleet units, the battleship King George V, three cruisers, and six destroyers. A Coast Guard ship, North Star, had the far north area, to get himself frozen in the ice pack in the fall and come down the next spring. She was successful in destroying a German radio transmitter on the coast of Greenland. As winter set in, these operations, invariably in terrible weather, became intolerable.

Q: Did you have a feeling at all that you were sort of sacrificial bait?

Captain Schratz: In a way, yes. That idea came to many of us over time. We were in the war and may as well get the benefit along with the hazard. It is strange that no comparable feeling pervaded the Pacific. During all these months, we were corresponding with academy roommates and friends in the Pacific Fleet, and couldn't believe their totally different attitude toward the approach of war. They were training, training, training like mad, but it was just ordinary old peacetime training with a wartime urgency, not really realistic. We didn't think it bore much relation to our task.

It was grim duty. There was no logistic tail; supplies were rare and unreliable; mail was chancy and usually came in drenched. Several times we were forced to drape letters over the lamps in the wardroom to dry, then try to locate a familiar handwriting. If mail was doubtful, fresh food was worse. A commercial stores ship would arrive, generally while we were at sea. Ships in port and the battleship division grabbed off everything they could, and the merchantmen wouldn't unload outside union hours. We adapted to that. You've heard the old stories about the German black rye bread in World War I? We used those big general mess coffee urns to keep our yeast culture going with potato peelings and all that, from which we made bread. An ordinary loaf weighed about five pounds and it was very, very damp and sort of rancid. It was delicious.

You can't imagine, for example, that for a crew of 660 people on a cruiser in wartime operations in the North Atlantic, our allowance was six suits of foul weather equipment. We were standing AA director watches continuously. My watch was in sky forward. When gale winds or snow or green water broke over the foretop, it was no picnic. We borrowed every piece of warmth we could find. The enlisted men rotated every 20 minutes; we officers every four hours: four on, 12 off. On being relieved, we would crawl into our bunks, spend the next eight hours shivering, trying to get warm before the next watch. Peacetime ops? Great. Iceland at best is hardly a great place to live. There were sound strategic reasons why the Americans and British were there; I could never find out why the Icelanders were there.

Q: How much antiaircraft practice did the ship get?

Captain Schratz: Quite little realistic training. We worked hard at it, though, with occasional gunnery exercises on home-made targets. I recall those fantastic visibility conditions, fantastically good many times and bad many others. Anyhow, my director watch picked up a German Focke-Wulf flying boat once, visually, perhaps 40 miles away. We tracked him visually before we could even get that great big 28-foot stereo range finder on him. We were reporting all this to the bridge, and they were going wild because they couldn't find him. In the post-mortem we figured this initial sighting had been in excess of 40 miles.

Q: Did you have any radar at all in the ship while you were on board?

Captain Schratz: We added a big mattress type, probably air search, just before departure for Iceland, as I recall, but of performance or real use, I draw a blank.

Q: And yet this was the first line against Hitler.

Captain Schratz: It ruins your sex life, didn't you know? That's what they said about it then.

Q: Oh, really?

Captain Schratz: Yes.

Q: Admiral Pickens spent some time on board the ship.* What do you remember about him?

Captain Schratz: Great guy.

---

* Rear Admiral Andrew C. Pickens, USN, Commander Cruiser Division Seven before Admiral Giffen took that billet.

Q: In what sense?

Captain Schratz: One of the boys, very pleasant and congenial. Just a nice guy to have around.

Q: How much contact did he have with the junior officers?

Captain Schratz: Everything he could. He was a good party man with the JOs. One night in Rio he invited me to join him on a yacht cruise around the harbor, hosted by the U.S. consul general. I don't recall why I in particular was chosen, other than the obvious need for a raconteur and a wit adept at the social graces.

Q: Did you spend time on the bridge when he was there?

Captain Schratz: No. Howard Orem, I guess, was part of the first CruDiv 7 staff as flag secretary.* I knew him before and subsequently.

Q: Where did you cross paths with him?

Captain Schratz: At the Naval Academy, later in OpNav.

Q: What do you remember about your new skipper, Captain Alexander.†

Captain Schratz: He was okay. I would say average. I left a matter of several months after he relieved. I got my orders to sub school on 7 December '41 in Iceland. At that time I would have sold my soul for orders to anywhere. We'd been married then less than six

---

* Lieutenant Commander Howard E. Orem, USN.
† Captain James T. Alexander, USN, commanded the USS Wichita (CA-45) from 27 December 1940 to 20 February 1942.

months. I had a pregnant wife at home and hadn't seen her since three weeks after we married.

Q: Where was the ship when you got married?

Captain Schratz: New York City.

Q: How much stateside liberty did you manage to get?

Captain Schratz: Well, in trying to rush through wedding plans, she had a delicate situation, because her older sister had set the date for her marriage for three weeks later, and it wasn't "fittin'" for the younger sister to slip in ahead after the other date had been set. It didn't make much difference that the ship wasn't going to be available later. We might never get married if we didn't do it then. So I traded off so many of my duties, going to Pittsburgh to work out details, that when we got back from our honeymoon, I had the duty almost every night. Our three weeks were wonderful.

Four of us JOs were married that month, three Naval Academy '39-ers and one reserve officer. We all lived in the same apartment building in Kew Gardens in Forest Hills. Our wives shopped together and prepared the same menus, often saving a big penny by buying two loaves of bread and sharing. Since Henrietta had run the cooking school on the Heinz pier, she was sharp and usually did the menu planning and use of leftovers. All too soon our three happy weeks were memories. The wardroom gave us a fantastic party, customary in those days, complete with wedding cakes to match each gal's wedding dress, and four beautiful gifts, sterling coffee service or sterling trays--impressive and absolutely unforgettable.

Q: Was the ship home-ported in New York afterwards?

Captain Schratz: No. Philadelphia.

Q: You said Forest Hills. What was the connection with Forest Hills?

Captain Schratz: We were in the Brooklyn Navy Yard. My gosh, did we go back there for a piece of radar gear? I think we might have, one of these big old bedspring air search types.

Q: CXAM.

Captain Schratz: Yes, but I have no recollection of its use at sea.

Q: The second exec was Commander Cooley, who later became flag rank.*

Captain Schratz: Ross Cooley, yes.

Q: Remember him at all?

Captain Schratz: Yes. Another great guy, but he had left before we went to Iceland, and Harry Need relieved him.†

Q: What are the characteristics of Cooley that stand out?

Captain Schratz: Another one of the boys, always a nice party guy. I remember a big wardroom party in Norfolk at the skipper's home, and Ross Cooley was there. The Thomsons' son, about ten years old, was a very meek little thing, and the Cooleys had a daughter about the same age. Of course, Ross Cooley was a horse and their daughter was well-built too. During the party, the girl and boy began fighting out on the lawn. The

---
* Commander Thomas Ross Cooley, Jr., USN.
† Commander Harry W. Need, USN.

young Thomson was losing badly, and it was terribly embarrassing, with everybody trying to prevent the skipper finding out about it.

Q: The usual combination is a good guy-bad guy with the skipper and exec. Did that prevail in both combinations?

Captain Schratz: No, I don't think so. Johnny Moyer had a tough time with Thaddeus--who didn't?--but Moyer was a superb ship handler and greatly admired by all. He didn't seem at all intimidated by the skipper. By and large, they made about as good a combination as they could under the circumstances. I just don't recall enough about Alexander professionally. Ross Cooley was a super exec.

Q: It's sort of curious that you got two captains in the same pattern there in a row.

Captain Schratz: No, there was only one Thad Thomson.

Q: But you were saying both were not too adept professionally in some of the seagoing things.

Captain Schratz: Yes, but in many ways the ship was not ready for war. I spent a lot of my time in Iceland and later trying to learn the ship. I started off in AA battery central and later with the main battery on the big range keeper, and time in engineering. Coincidentally, I thought the damage control system of that ship was unsat. Then I found in the magazines and handling rooms the air-conditioning had been overlooked. Well, when the Brits built the King George V, they overlooked an air-conditioning/ventilation contract until well along in construction. Then it was necessary to cut the ship apart to put a very poor jury-rigged ventilation system into it.

Later, in her action with the Bismarck, she was at general quarters for a little over an hour and had something like 100 heat casualties in the lower handling rooms. We would have had the same thing. Even though we had good ventilation and air-conditioning, we used it improperly in battle conditions. So I became more and more curious about the "Witch's" damage control bill, even though I was in the gunnery department at the time. I got more and more deeply into damage control and eventually rewrote the bill for the whole ship. But that ship would have had a tough time had she ever had a serious battle damage problem to take care of.

Q: In what sense?

Captain Schratz: Systems designed to be kept open for clearing away fumes were shut down; emergency ventilation was all screwed up. Thaddeus had insisted that the emergency bills be completed before we got the master plans from the shipyard. It may have been the best that could have been done under the circumstances.

I was scheduled to brief the wardroom officers on my new plan on 8 December 1941; dispatch orders for submarine school came through on the seventh, for immediate departure. What with other things happening on that date, I never gave my lecture. I still recall the first lieutenant walking down the gangway with me to this decrepit launch taking me off the ship, trying to explain to him what I'd really done, give him the whole meat of it. But I still don't know how I got involved. It just had to be done and I did it.

Q: Damage control was really a new thing at that time, wasn't it?

Captain Schratz: I was just going to say that. Although our ships were built extremely well, damage control wasn't a prestige assignment, and sometimes we didn't do our best. What was often needed was good practical plumbers, carpenters, and electricians, to show what can and can't be done.

Q: It's remarkable it developed as quickly as it did.

Captain Schratz: Yes. We got help from the British experience, and the Pearl Harbor disaster probably had a major effect.

Q: What do you recall about the various gunnery stations in which you served--both the main battery and the antiaircraft?

Captain Schratz: I was the range keeper operator in the main battery, and I always liked that very much. Then I went to the AA battery. I learned much from a brilliant officer, Tom Davies, class of '37. Aircraft tracking by rate control fascinated me; I spent hours at it. Our system was far inadequate for war needs, however. Thanks to this training, when I went to submarines, I aimed to become the world's best torpedo data computer operator. We'll get to that soon.

Q: Tom Davies later became an aviator.

Captain Schratz: Yes. He and I were catapult officers in Wichita. Tom was controversial in lots of things, but he had a damn good head on his shoulders and had the courage of his convictions. He thought the catapult doctrine was wrong. Instead of firing on the rise in the catapult--on the uproll--one should fire just after reaching the peak. On the rise, the catapult is pushing into the sled, friction is near maximum, and aircraft launching speed is reduced. On the downroll, the catapult is falling away from the sled and produces less friction and higher launching speed. I was on the port catapult doing it the conventional way, so the Wichita became known as the ship with catapults, one high and slow, one fast and low.

Q: Did you determine which produced better results?

Captain Schratz: I think Tom was right. But the reason I mention it is his equal shrewdness in another area. One of the bugs I mentioned earlier in the main battery was the failure to get a ship's speed input into the range keeper, a very important element of the fire control system. We had the Ford rep out there time and time again, almost enough to earn him an officer's commission. He couldn't figure out what was wrong. Tom at that time was in the AA battery and overheard a wardroom conversation about the problem. He asked to take a look at it. After studying it for a few minutes, he said the problem was a misdesign. The speed input was a linear function; the rest of the system was non-linear. What was needed was a converter, which he rapidly sketched on the proverbial envelope.

The Ford expert looked at him in amazement and said, "My God, you've got it." He disappeared, and in due time delivered the alteration, for about 50,000 bucks, which was Tom's idea. That was typical of Tom's approach. He was very sharp.

Q: Did you have any plotting room time in addition to your range keeper duty?

Captain Schratz: What do you call it?

Q: There was a stereoscopic range finder up top, plus the director, then there was the range keeper down in the plotting room.

Captain Schratz: What do you call that damn main battery computer thing?

Q: That's the range keeper.

Captain Schratz: Yes. I ran that. Then Tom and I later shifted. I went to the AA battery, so I was up there in sky forward.

Q: How accurate was the ship's gunnery?

Captain Schratz: Generally pretty good. We were very good and very lucky with several drone experiences off Norfolk.

Q: That was strictly visual, or did you have a fire control on it?

Captain Schratz: Visual, plus rate control in automatic.

Q: Another one of your shipmates was Ensign Miles Libbey, who later went with Rickover.* Do you recall him?

Captain Schratz: Yes, he was in the class of '40. Mike got in trouble with Thad, but I don't recall the circumstances. It didn't help his career much.

Q: Sounds like everybody had that problem.

Captain Schratz: Oh, yes.

Q: There was also a period when the ship trained naval reservists for a while in 1940. What do you remember from that?

Captain Schratz: Well, those were, I think, the V-7 reserves, and we'd had groups on board for a month at a time.† I remember it mostly because in one group of about 20 or 30 I found a remarkable pool of basketball talent. Since I was coaching the ship's basketball team at the time, I set up two basketball squads. One of these reservists, whom you probably never heard of, was a teammate of Hank Luisetti, the Stanford all-American.

Q: He's the guy who perfected the one-hand set shot.

Captain Schratz: Yes--you surprise me. Several in the group showed real basketball talent, so we had some great basketball games with that group. We took on anybody and everybody.

---

* Ensign Miles A. Libbey, USN.
† V-7 was a Naval Reserve officer training program in which individuals with enough college education (normally a bachelor's degree) were trained as deck officers for surface ships.

Q: Was there any feeling of contention between regulars and reservists at that point?

Captain Schratz: Very little, really. The reserves of that era were bright, carefully selected, and, with rare exceptions, did extremely well.

Q: I just wondered if there would be any resentment that you had to spend four years getting your commission and they did it in much less time.

Captain Schratz: It wasn't quite that simple. When the war came, there was a job to do. If they could perform, that's all I cared about. I wasn't really evaluating them for their potential for flag rank. With a war on, all that came later.

Q: They were a source of needed manpower.

Captain Schratz: Vital. They were damn good.

Q: Are there any other incidents you recall involving the ship's planes, other than the catapulting?

Captain Schratz: Well, anybody who's seen one of those--what do they call them, "Cast" recoveries--is looking for adventure, especially up north in heavy seas when it became pretty hairy to see an airplane chugging its way through oceans and oceans of salt water.* Our <u>Wichita</u> senior aviator was a little bit cautious, prone to land way at the back of the slick and chug his way to the mattress. He avoided casualties by a whisker several times. Two others tried to land on the mat and almost ended up in the fantail on occasion.

---

* "Cast," which was a letter in the phonetic alphabet of the time, designated a recovery method whereby the airplane landed on the water, rode up on a sea sled, and was lifted aboard by a crane on the ship's fantail.

Q: How helpful were the planes in spotting the main battery gunfire?

Captain Schratz: I don't recall ever using them except on rare occasions while operating out of Iceland.

Q: Why not?

Captain Schratz: I don't know. If we were in Norfolk and went out for a gunnery exercise, the aviators went ashore to the naval air station and were in a different world. I don't think it often occurred to us that we should have them up there as spotters. I just don't recall.

Q: If not for that role, why were they there?

Captain Schratz: Well, if you wanted to take a ride now and then, they were fine. While in Iceland dying from boredom, we had a special thrill--zooming down Mount Hekla at treetop level if they had trees, maybe 30 or 40 feet off the ground. And we used them for a lot of antiaircraft training at that time.

Q: Were they the ones that towed the sleeves?

Captain Schratz: No. A support service did that. They needed a special rig.

Q: Did you get ashore at Iceland at all?

Captain Schratz: Oh, yes. It was about a 30-mile trip into Reykjavik. We all rushed there first chance we got, but it took a destroyer used as a liberty boat, taking a mob in and a mob back. After being there once and looking right, left, up and down, there wasn't much else to do. At that time Iceland was prohibitionist. The only way you could get a beer was with a ration ticket and with a full meal at one of two hotels in town. The beer was guaranteed less than 1% alcohol and tasted like dog-flavored tree bark. Of course, there were few trees in Iceland. So the thrill of liberty in Reykjavik was limited. For souvenirs, the smallest pair of ladies' gloves was for a hand about a foot long. Nor were the Icelanders all that friendly to Americans. I much preferred going ashore in Hvalfjordur for some superb fishing or to hike up to a mountain top. And the natives were often unfriendly. That was the only place I was ever spat on, while walking down a main street in mid-day.

Q: Any more memories of the Wichita that you'd like to include before we move along?

Captain Schratz: No, I don't think so. Great duty.

Q: What had motivated you--beyond the undesirability of duty in Iceland--to volunteer for submarine school? Why submarine school as opposed to something else?

Captain Schratz: My wife's sister knew Jane Porter, wife of George Porter in '32, a-red hot submariner, and I heard lots about submarines indirectly from George.[*] I always had a hankering, I think, for small-unit duty, gradually focusing on the submarine life.

Q: Then how long a period of time did it take for the system to work to get you into the submarine school?

Captain Schratz: We weren't eligible for submarines or aviation until we had two years in the fleet. My two years were up in June of '41. By that time the war emergency was on and one didn't ask; he was sent for. CruDiv 7 was asked to nominate one individual, apparently because they didn't have enough volunteers for the class entering sub school in January '42. I had just written a letter requesting submarine school about three days before, and so I was the automatic. But I had to be detached immediately, a sacrifice I was only too happy to make.

---

[*] Lieutenant George E. Porter, Jr., USN.

Q: Especially because things got worse for the Wichita after that. She got stuck in some wretched weather.

Captain Schratz: Yes, the terrible storm of January 1942. She had three collisions--merchantmen drifting down on her--and one grounding in one day.

Q: I guess that brought a period of reunion with your wife back in the States.

Captain Schratz: Very pleasant.

Q: Did you then move to New London for a while?

Captain Schratz: Yes, we moved to New London. Starting with my class, sub school was cut to three months from the old six months' course. Unfortunately, during that time we lost our first child just before graduation. It was quite a shock to both of us. Karl Hensel, head of the sub school, knew of a billet which just came open in the Mackerel, one of two small new subs used largely for running the PCO school.* He nominated me for it.

I qualified in submarines after three months in Mackerel.† It used to take a year to 18 months. Nobody ever qualified as soon as I, but I really worked my butt off for that. Those PCO operations, with a half dozen or so skippers of new fleet boats, involved very intense operations. It was superb training for me, too, as torpedo officer, showing them how to run the torpedo data computer--as I learned myself. These hotshots were going off to their submarine commands, and with a war fresh upon us, the motivation was extremely high.

---

* Commander Karl G. Hensel, USN, was officer in charge of the submarine school and submarine base at New London. PCO--prospective commanding officer.
† The USS Mackerel (SS-204) was commissioned 31 March 1941. She had a displacement of 825 tons on the surface and 1,179 tons submerged. She was 239 feet long, 22 feet in the beam, and had a draft of 12 feet. Her speed was 16 knots surfaced and 9 knots submerged. She was armed with six 21-inch torpedo tubes and a 3-inch gun.

Q: Are there some of the PCOs you remember as students from that period?

Captain Schratz: One I remember most prominently was Bill Wylie, '30, because as soon as he got to the Scorpion in Portsmouth, he pulled my chain to join him in taking Scorpion to sea.* Bill had been my engineering boss in Wichita, and we hit it off extremely well. By a strange coincidence, when Bill left the Wichita to go back to submarines, his relief was Max Schmidt.† Two years later, when Bill was detached from Scorpion, Max was again his successor and I the JO both times.

Q: What do you remember about your course as a student in submarine school?

Captain Schratz: It was a good, basic course. I and most of my classmates were very much interested in the attack trainer: running problems against zigzagging, escorted targets, trying to get into attack position and out again. We often went back at night, accompanied by wives. The duty personnel would set the thing up for us and run some problems, some weird and some ridiculous. It was not unknown that we'd have a couple of martinis beforehand, just to keep us loose. It was excellent training, and I think we all became very good approach officers by the end of the course. And one or two of the wives may have been better than one or two of us on occasion.

Q: How much classroom instruction went along with the practical work?

Captain Schratz: It was usually mornings in the classroom and practical work in the afternoons: submarine trainer, attack trainer, or ship handling on the old O-boats at the piers. I felt that after three months, I could dive a submarine by myself if I had to. I could start the engines or shut down the plant, dive, run an approach, surface, and make the landing.

---

* Lieutenant Commander William N. Wylie, USN.
† Lieutenant Commander Maximilian G. Schmidt, USN.

Q: That was an advantage that submariners had over, say, sailors, who couldn't run a destroyer by themselves.

Captain Schratz: True.

Q: Is that a common thing, that submariners take that kind of a hands-on approach, to be able to do the kind of things as well as telling others to do?

Captain Schratz: That's really common, normal practice, at least before the nukes came along.

Q: Who were some of your fellow students in the course?

Captain Schratz: I guess Ben Jarvis was the number-one student in the course, "Big Ben," my football-playing classmate and plebe summer dancing partner. He was so hot to get at the Japs, he was determined to stand number one in the class just to get the choice of assignments on graduation. Not noted as a scholar, Ben made it by hard work and determination. A Little Rock, Arkansas, farmboy, he made a fine officer and an excellent shipmate. Many other students did extremely well, but we were just becoming eligible for command when the war ended. The few who got war commands had too few Japanese ships left to earn a reputation.

Q: How competitive was that atmosphere compared with the Naval Academy?

Captain Schratz: Not nearly as much. We knew early in the course that there would be more billets than graduates. With the war just starting, we did our best simply to be better submarine officers. But those who stood high obviously were favored for the better assignments.

Q: Favored in what sense?

Captain Schratz: To get a new boat. Some went to old S-boats in Australia, which was hardly a choice assignment. I regretted the personal need for which I was sent to the Mackerel, but she was newly commissioned, and the duty couldn't have been better while I was working to qualify. We also made a war patrol while I was aboard en route to and from Norfolk. We were sent down primarily to test a new defensive minefield off Dahlgren. We met a German submarine off Hampton Roads and fired some torpedoes at it and missed, fired a few others at one of our own Coast Guard ships and missed, but it was good combat experience, a tester-outer. Johnny Davidson was my skipper.[*]

Q: What do you remember about him?

Captain Schratz: A good skipper and a very nice guy. He was having personal problems over a divorce and custody of a daughter.

Q: I would think you had a considerable advantage over your contemporaries because of that experience.

Captain Schratz: I was halfway home on qualification before my sub school classmates arrived on their boats. I also had the super experience of eavesdropping on all the PCO school attacks. A major factor was the contribution of Commanders Karl Hensel and "Silent Pat" Patterson, who ran the sub school and PCO school.[†] Hensel was a tough nut to crack, and he was ruthless on the unzealous student of any rank. They set the pace for a very punishing schedule, particularly with the PCOs. Hensel was much more admired than loved. When he finally got his own command and learned that on a perfectly good submarine approach, one can fire his torpedoes and still miss, it gave him a little humility.

---

[*] Lieutenant Commander John F. Davidson, USN. The oral history of Davidson, who retired as a rear admiral, is in the Naval Institute collection.
[†] Lieutenant Commander George W. Patterson, Jr., USN.

But I was always solidly in his corner. Pat Patterson had physical problems, unfortunately, and wasn't qualified for even limited shore duty.

My career also benefited when Bill Wylie grabbed me off--I guess Bill grabbed me; it looked like more than coincidence when I went to Scorpion. Of course, the fitting-out period in the Portsmouth, New Hampshire, shipyard, further delayed me in getting to the Pacific until December of '42 or early January '43.

Q: You had been in a new cruiser and now a new submarine. What comparisons can you draw between the two?

Captain Schratz: Wichita was a fine ship but with some design defects--fireroom arrangement, for one, which would have made her vulnerable in combat. For our new fleet submarines, thank God somebody was smart enough back in 1938 or so to actually try depth charges on a hull section, exploded close aboard to check durability of structure and systems. The experience generated lots and lots of changes to design and construction techniques. The new fleet submarine, which started coming out just prior to the war, was a superb submarine. Perhaps the biggest factor in our morale throughout the war was absolute faith in our boats. We operated far beyond their limits, including half again the maximum test depth. We put enormous demands on the ships, and they always delivered.

I thought many times about the German submarine force losing 900 subs and 28,000 dead out of a total force of 35,000 and still keeping morale high at the end of the war. I admired that because their subs did not get better; construction suffered as losses increased. Why waste scarce facilities in making a superb ship if it could last only one patrol? We had the great morale advantage of faith in our submarines.

Q: I wonder if sometimes that faith wasn't too strong if people tended to ignore the limits.

Captain Schratz: Yes, but you're between a rock and a hard place.

Q: And those are the ones that never came back to tell what they tried.

Captain Schratz: A choice between the devil on the surface and the deep blue sea below. Yet some of our subs had serious defects. The Scorpion, for example, wasn't the best that Portsmouth was building, mainly because they were the last of the old thin-skinners.* The shipyard probably cut a few corners when materials ran short while tooling up for the deeper-diving thick-skinned Balao class. Scorpion was in the Runner class of about six submarines. All but two were lost in the war, a record much worse than the classes both preceding and following.

Q: Were there experienced skippers who had already come back with some war patrols to inject into the PCO course?

Captain Schratz: Not in New London while I was there. The war was too young. Mike Fenno was in Portsmouth then, already a big hero and a god to most of us.† Lew Parks was another.‡ I saw a lot of Lew during the war. We learned much from their wartime patrol experiences. Additionally, all SubPac war patrol reports were circulated throughout the force and they were a gold mine.

Q: Lew Parks was a very innovative guy, from what I understand. Slade Cutter served with him in Pompano and said he was always trying new things.§ He said he was one of the few of his generation as well suited in wartime as in peacetime.

Captain Schratz: I concur.

---

* The USS Scorpion (SS-278) was commissioned 1 October 1942. She had a displacement of 1,526 tons on the surface and 2,410 tons submerged. She was 312 feet long, 27 feet in the beam, and had a draft of 15 feet. Her top speed was 20 knots surfaced and 9 knots submerged. She was armed with ten 21-inch torpedo tubes and a 3-inch gun.
† Lieutenant Commander Frank W. Fenno, Jr., USN.
‡ Lieutenant Commander Lewis S. Parks, USN.
§ The Naval Institute oral history of Captain Slade D. Cutter, USN (Ret.), contains detailed recollections of his service in the Pompano (SS-181) under Parks's command.

Q: Do you have any specific memories of Parks?

Captain Schratz: Only one of that era, and it had little to do with his innovativeness. He arrived in Portsmouth to take over the squadron. That was when I was fitting out Sterlet, my second tour in Portsmouth. Anyhow, on our first tour we had become friendly with shipyard deputy commander, Captain H. F. D. Davis, who owned a very nice retirement home in town.* Because of a very strong recommendation for us as tenants from our previous landlady, the Davises offered us their home for our Sterlet tour when Mike Fenno moved out. She sent us a lease, then she called down to Mike Fenno's office and asked if they could send a working party out to clean up the house for one Lieutenant Schratz. Fenno's number two screamed a mighty oath and snarled, "When a hero like Mike Fenno arrives here, I wouldn't mind cleaning up the house for him, but I'll be goddamned if I'll clean it up when he leaves for somebody I never heard of before." So he sent the working party down, but I heard nothing about this until much later.

When Lew Parks arrived to relieve Mike, he assumed he would take his house. Mike didn't know it had been leased to us. It was a bit tense for us. I was sent off for a routine trip to the Torpedo Station, Newport, for two weeks, and suggested that Lew move into our place temporarily while house-hunting.

When I returned, Lew not only hadn't found a house, but came down with pneumonia. He was carried out on a stretcher, and we moved in. It was not the best way to start off duty with a new squadron commander.

Q: No, it isn't. Had the word come back by that time of the torpedo failures in the Pacific?

Captain Schratz: Yes. That became my special problem as torpedo officer. So I went down to Newport for briefings at the Naval Torpedo Station. I was particularly curious about the instructions on the magnetic exploder. When I was torpedo officer in Mackerel, the exploder was so secret that nobody could work on it. To install or remove one, only the

---

* Captain Henry F. D. Davis, USN, manager of the Portsmouth Navy Yard.

torpedo officer and one torpedoman's mate were allowed in the torpedo room, and we weren't allowed to touch the exploder insides.

When I got to Newport for classified briefings, the exploder didn't look at all mysterious. The major point of weakness, it seemed obvious, was a propeller which armed the torpedo after making 400 revolutions. Instructions called for exactly 15 ounces of tension on the blades to make sure they wouldn't bind when the torpedo was fired. But the danger of leakage if fired from deep seemed much greater. And so I asked, "What would happen if I tightened those glands up to maybe 20 or 30 or 40 ounces tension on the blades just to make sure they'll stay watertight? Will the impeller still rotate when the torpedo is fired?"

They confessed to having a warehouse full of tests with tension up to almost 90 ounces, beyond which they failed very quickly. But tension increased to 50, even 75 ounces, caused no problem.

Since we were having so many prematures when the warhead exploded as soon as it armed, this would indicate the exploders were shorting out. So I asked why they didn't put a change to the fleet. Some justification was offered; my impression was an attitude which was to let sleeping dogs lie.

When I completed the instruction period, I returned to my room and sketched from memory the whole circuitry on the exploder, then got my chief petty officer to do the same. Then we compared our drawings, returned to the exploder lab once more to recheck a few details and to make sure we had a good working diagram of the circuitry. This was totally illegal, of course, but all's fair in love and war. For the rest of the war, all my submarine patrols were successful. Despite all the agonies of torpedo failure, all ours were "hot, straight, normal," and we had one of the highest hit percentages in the force. When we stopped using magnetic exploders, it was still the same mechanism with one side negated.

I am sure that a very high element of the problem of torpedo failure was nothing more than that damn simple little propeller. It was criminal not to change the procedures. We still weren't able to touch them at sea. This, I thought, was more bureaucratic stupidity. Checking the after bodies--engines--of torpedoes was a time-consuming chore at sea which I thought largely unnecessary. That torpedo had been in service forever and was totally reliable. There seemed no more need to check the power plant than to check my Chevrolet at 2:00 A.M. to make sure it would run when needed at 8:00. The exploders were new and were causing problems, and we weren't allowed to touch them. My people checked exploders carefully after every unusual submergence, but Newport never changed the rules. I thought it was a waste of New Mexico scenery to use Alamogordo for the nuclear test; they should have used the Newport Naval Torpedo Station.

Q: So that's what you did to make our torpedoes work?

Captain Schratz: Yes. the torpedomen thought I was mad, but the results were conclusive. I insisted we had the evidence, and I had the responsibility. The other problems of running too deep and warheads crushing before the exploder could activate were solved by Admiral Lockwood, ComSubPac, in Pearl.* Again, Newport denied any responsibility.

Q: Did you spread the word informally?

Captain Schratz: I did what I could, but, you know, if the torpedo station itself actively opposes a change, what can you do?

Q: Well, what you can do is tell other people, "This works for me, and here's how I found out."

Captain Schratz: Yes, I told everybody I could. I had one other advantage. Just before we arrived in Portsmouth for Scorpion, Tony Gallaher had run an informal torpedo attack seminar based on some brilliant tactics for a deep submerged sonar attack he had developed in Key West with an R-boat.† When Tony left Portsmouth as CO of Bang, I was nominated to take over the seminar, thanks to Bill Wylie, Wally Ebert, and others who had worked

---

* Vice Admiral Charles A. Lockwood, Jr., USN, served as Commander Submarines Pacific Fleet from February 1943 to December 1945.
† Lieutenant Commander Antone R. Gallaher, USN.

with me as PCOs in Mackerel.* As a tyro in the sub force, instructing wartime skippers, it was easy to be modest, yet I thought the seminar was very useful, not only to me. Many of those ideas deserved a wider audience. I used this audience to publicize the word on exploders.

Other things we developed in Scorpion merited wider attention. One had to do with night lighting. When the war started, all Navy ships used dim blue lights at night. These were later found to be the worst possible for night adaptation. A certain frequency of red was far better. Prewar subs had no idea about how to illuminate the inside of a submarine for night operations, a severe defect. Most lighting worked great by day, useless by night. The "bubble" in curved tubes at the diving stations indicated the up or down angle. The shipyard built a big old sheet-metal screen to shine direct light on the bubble. I thought it a stupid way to go at it.

Remembering a high school physics experiment where light was bent through a plastic tube, I suggested using a tiny light at the end of the tube which would illuminate the bubble at the top of the arc. The shielded light would pass right through the tube, illuminating the bubble clearly by day or night. The yard agreed and very shortly "invented" the same idea themselves. Months later when we checked into ComSubLant for operational training, we proudly showed off the latest in submarines. The only thing the admiral really wanted to see was that insignificant bubble lighting. It became standard for all submarines. I wondered why it hadn't happened years before.

As a bug on night lighting, I believed that the best lighting is the least. Instrument lighting must be minimal to avoid destroying night vision. Modern car makers don't yet know this. Many needless accidents are caused through blinding by improper instrument illumination. Gradually we got very good at daylight lighting in subs where one didn't destroy the other.

Q: Were there any other modifications that built into the Scorpion as she was coming along?

---

* Lieutenant Commander Walter G. Ebert, USN.

Captain Schratz: Submarine radar by then was excellent, particularly the periscope radar, new then to almost all of us. The SJ surface search was excellent but hard to keep at peak efficiency. Somehow the submarine always seemed to find a brilliant technician to keep it operating. And we didn't yet have a PPI scope.[*] The newest sonar gear then was the deck-mounted JT, very good, but that also came later.

Q: How far along was the submarine when you reported?

Captain Schratz: It hadn't been launched yet.[†] I guess it was launched maybe within a month, which meant all the major (large) equipment was installed but not much else.

Q: How much work still had to be done?

Captain Schratz: Quite a lot. And here I would like to add a special kudo for the constructor at the Portsmouth Navy Yard, Captain Andrew I. McKee.[‡] There's a new submarine tender named after him now, and nobody deserved it more.[§] Andy was one of the true heroes of the submarine war. He knew every part of every submarine by its first name. If we recommended that the potato masher be moved six inches to the right or left, he'd go down and talk with the cook about it. Everything, every detail, if it was a good idea, he wanted to do for every ship in the force and save money for the yard. If it was a bad idea, he wanted to know about that, too.

When we produced weep lists at the shipyard commander's conference, McKee would say, "Well, when I talked with your torpedoman's mate about that, he said . . ." He

---

[*] PPI--plan position indicator, a type of radar that presents essentially a geographical picture with one's own ship in the center of the scope and surrounding ships, planes, and land areas shown in their respective positions in terms of range and bearing.
[†] The Scorpion was launched 20 July 1942.
[‡] For more on this remarkable submarine designer, see John Alden, "Andrew Irin McKee, Naval Constructor," U.S. Naval Institute Proceedings, June 1979, pages 49-57.
[§] The USS McKee (AS-41) was commissioned 15 August 1981.

made us much more careful about sending requests in until we really checked them out from every angle. He was an absolutely super gentleman, a genius, yet extremely modest.

Q: Design was his real forte.

Captain Schratz: Yes, that and salvage. Squalus had sunk off Portsmouth, and at that time he gave an example of leadership, one of the best I've ever learned.* When a submarine is lost or unheard from, the Navy goes to general quarters to minimize loss of life. Time is vital, and every command seemed to have--or must have insisted on--a role: BuShips, the fleet commander, the naval district commander, BuMed, SubLant, the yard, everybody.† People swarmed in from all over. Everybody had an idea on how to get Squalus off the bottom. Andy had worked out a detailed salvage plan which he laid out just as soon as all the experts gathered around the table. But every person there had objections of every description.

Andy said, "I think you're all correct. Maybe I did that a little too hastily. Let's put it aside and look at another plan."

When the new plan had been studied, again a series of objections emerged around the table. Finally somebody said, "You know, Andy, I don't think this is as good a plan as your first one." The others quickly agreed and rolled out the first one again, on which they soon found full agreement, arguing for what they previously argued against. What Andy had done, of course, was to allow each person to show that he, too, was an expert. Once they'd made the point, they could look at the plan objectively. So he let the others argue to save the plan he really wanted in the first place. His plan was adopted and worked

---

* The USS Squalus (SS-192), commanded by Lieutenant Oliver F. Naquin, USN, sank in 243 feet of water while conducting exercise dives on 23 May 1939 off Portsmouth, New Hampshire. Twenty-six men died, but 33, including Naquin, were recovered through the use of the McCann rescue chamber. The submarine later was salvaged, refurbished, and renamed the Sailfish. For details, see Carl La VO, Back from the Deep (Annapolis; Naval Institute Press, 1994).

† BuShips--Bureau of Ships, which actually came into existence a year later, in 1940; BuMed--Bureau of Medicine and Surgery; SubLant--Submarines Atlantic Fleet, a command established later.

successfully, saving the lives of 33 men in the forward section of the sub. I never forgot the story and I've used it many times. It's typical Andy McKee.

Q: Sounds like he was a good psychologist.

Captain Schratz: He really was.

Q: Do you have any other recollections about him?

Captain Schratz: Yes, he later became a big hero in Okinawa when we lost so many ships to kamikazes. He was responsible for salvage--another chance to work a few miracles. A very brilliant officer, modest, unassuming, easy to talk with, no matter who you were, ship's cook to CO. Many submariners believe he deserved a Medal of Honor for his work at Portsmouth.

Q: So he spent a fair amount of time in your boat as it was coming along?

Captain Schratz: Yes, he was wholly on top of the job, ensuring we got the best product the shipyard could produce.

Q: What were the tasks of the ship's officers when construction was being completed?

Captain Schratz: Well, I can tell you a story when I returned to commission Sterlet, which answers the question. Do you want to wait until then?

Q: Let's wait. Anything else about the building period in the Scorpion?

Captain Schratz: Yes, the most important point of all. The exec was Lieutenant Commander Reggie Raymond, '33.[*] The first time I met him at a party in Portsmouth on the evening of our arrival in town, I walked into the room, looked casually around and fastened my eyes on Reggie. Almost from first meeting, I believed him to be the greatest naval officer I'd ever met, and absolutely brilliant. He and I became very close. For my part it was hero worship from first meeting. Frequently in hot water at Naval Academy, he was on the Reina Mercedes earning his black N on graduation day. He stood 15 in his class, only because demerits dropped him from the top. An inspirational leader, the crew worshipped his footprints. He and I were totally simpatico and frequently got Bill Wylie, a fine skipper, into all kinds of trouble. From the earliest Portsmouth days, Reggie and I became a very effective team. He was exec and navigator, I, fourth officer, was torpedoes, gunnery, and first lieutenant.

Q: Do you think there is any correlation between the time in the Reina Mercedes and being a superb naval officer?

Captain Schratz: I don't know. Why?

Q: I'm just wondering if there was a stream of insubordination that helped.

Captain Schratz: Oh, sure. That was George Marshall's credo, wasn't it?[†] If you can't disobey an order, you'll never become a leader. Clay Blair, in his Silent Victory, talks about over-eager, over-aggressive execs serving with timid skippers.[‡] Slade Cutter was a good example. Blair put me in that category for both the Scorpion and the Sterlet. We can discuss Sterlet later, but it was not at all true for Scorpion. Reggie and I talked the CO into

---

[*] Lieutenant Commander Reginald M. Raymond, USN.
[†] General of the Army George C. Marshall, USA, was Chief of Staff of the Army throughout World War II, later Secretary of State and Secretary of Defense.
[‡] Clay Blair, Jr., Silent Victory (Philadelphia: J. B. Lippincott Company, 1975) provides a candid, detailed account of U.S. submarine operations in World War II. Pages 458-460 deal with Wylie's command of the Scorpion during this patrol.

doing things he might not have done otherwise, but he had great faith in us and it was a very harmonious wardroom.* As a long-time friend of Bill Wylie, the skipper, we understood each other and worked extremely well together. Clay's book really upset me. He had about six hours of interviews with me on tape and was merely trying to sell some books in this deliberate misinterpretation. I defend Bill's actions completely, and I had known him for five years by then.

Q: Here's a good chance to correct the record. Why don't you have your say about Commander Wylie and what you feel about him?

Captain Schratz: For the first patrol, March of '43, we had a good patrol area off the Japanese home islands, but the force was short of torpedoes, so Scorpion went out with a half load of mines. Operating south of Honshu on the approaches to Tokyo Bay, we were ordered to lay a mine field. We laid two fields of 10 Mark 10s in one, 12 Mark 12s in the other. We later got credit for sinking three ships, sank three others by torpedo, and had an all-around good patrol. But more was to come. On the way to the area from Pearl a few weeks prior, we met a Japanese patrol vessel off Marcus Island. Facing the first real enemy with a green untested crew leaves a tense lump in the pit of the stomach. The pucker factor makes the palms sweat and creates a nervous urge to urinate. We had to avoid detection until completing the mining mission, but there was a lot of talk--false bravado perhaps--"Wait till we come back. We'll catch you, you bastard."

Reggie had made earlier patrols with the British in the Mediterranean with Tony "Crap" Miers, who earned the VC for his patrols, many of his sinkings by gunfire.† Reggie's sea stories about life with Tony Miers were enough to turn anybody's hair.

On return with torpedoes and mines expended, we were looking for trouble--a gun target. One remaining torpedo in the tube had been taken down to 200-300 feet, exposed

---

* CO--commanding officer.
† Commander Anthony Miers, Royal Navy, received the Victoria Cross, Britain's highest decoration for valor, for following an enemy convoy into a harbor on the island of Corfu on 4-5 March 1942. Miers was then commanding officer of His Majesty's Submarine Torbay.

to sea pressure. Despite careful routing and our special treatment on the exploder impeller, there was strong doubt it would work. We met the patrol vessel again and decided to take him on with our 3-inch popgun and our two 20 millimeters, .30-caliber machine guns, and automatic rifles. We put the enemy's five-pounder out of commission, but he returned heavy small arms fire.

A few minutes later, Reggie, firing a Browning automatic from the bridge, was instantly killed by a machine gun bullet.[*] I was on deck alongside the gun and about the same time, I got hit with a ricochet, bouncing off the conning tower and catching me in the center of my jacket, tearing the zipper loose and fusing into it. I got only a small scratch in the center of my chest. Two of our 20-millimeter crewmen were also hit and slightly wounded.   Well, the shock of Reggie being killed--it's just impossible to describe. The skipper ordered the last torpedo made ready, we backed off to 500 yards and fired. The torpedo ran perfectly and in a spectacular explosion, sent the patrol vessel to the bottom in a matter of moments.[†] Our troubles were not over. Simultaneously, a lookout reported an aircraft coming in out of the sun to attack.

We dived as soon as we could get people below, but we were forced to leave Reggie's body behind. The crew was in a state of shock, me above all. We were both expecting orders after the patrol to be CO and XO of Runner, which Mike Fenno was giving up. We surfaced after dark, and, while lying to, Bill Wylie and I conducted a burial service. Many of the crew broke into uncontrollable sobs, the only time I've ever known of it happening.

Our first daughter, Regina, born a month later, commemorates his memory for me. I've often wondered, had he and I taken over Runner, what sort of record we would have made. Surmises are free, but this is history. Of one thing I'm sure: he was the greatest loss the submarine service suffered throughout the war. And because of him and Bill Wylie, Scorpion became the sentimental favorite of all the ships I served on. The crew was also

---

[*] Raymond was killed 30 April 1943.
[†] The target was the converted gunboat Maiji Maru Number 1, sunk on 30 April 1943.

superb; a real tragedy that only one or two men got off before she was lost.* Reggie was the type we needed to get the nuclear Navy out of technological domination and into solid strategic thought and operational use of this enormously powerful weapon.

Q: In view of what happened, it would have been just as well to go on with the torpedo first.

Captain Schratz: Possibly but probably not. The mood of the men was for a gun action. With only one doubtful torpedo against a shallow-draft vessel, it was important that my torpedo exploder didn't flood, even at 300 feet.

But to get back to the question of the skipper being a reluctant dragon--when we got back to Pearl, the division commander, Captain Leo L. Pace, said he would dedicate one torpedo nest by each ship in his division to Reggie's memory.

For our second patrol, we again had a good hunting area in the Yellow Sea between China and Korea. The new exec was a classmate of Reggie's, Harry Maynard, six years my senior.† He had been ashore for several years, working on a design for a new torpedo--the Mark 18 electric, I believe. Surprisingly, Harry was not qualified for command, having left the force as a JO for shore duty in his ordnance specialty. It was probably an impossible assignment despite his academic brilliance. For one reason or another, he still hadn't formally relieved me as exec and navigator during the entire second patrol. And I still had torpedoes, gunnery, and first lieutenant, and was acting informally as assistant engineer.

The mood of the patrol was that the one attack dedicated to Reggie was going to be our absolute best. The chance finally came off the north Korean coast near today's DMZ line.‡ Wylie made a superb attack, the one time when everything fit together perfectly. The target was a merchant convoy of five ships with two escorts. With three ships overlapping, we fired three torpedoes forward, three aft, and got five hits, the three ships' screws

---

* In early 1944 the Scorpion failed to return from a patrol into the East China Sea, presumably the victim of a Japanese mine.
† Lieutenant Commander Harry C. Maynard, USN.
‡ DMZ--demilitarized zone.

disappearing amid breaking-up noises. A long time later postwar analysis gave us credit for sinking two and damaging one, but at the time we were jumped on immediately by the escorts and had other problems.*

Going deep to evade, we passed 140 or 150 feet and hit bottom, wiping off the sound heads, leaking air and oil, and deaf with no sonar, it was tense until finally getting clear late that day. Lacking good charts of the area and leaving an oil slick, we couldn't stay in that area. Under the circumstances, in water too shallow for good submarine operations and lacking sonar gear, the CO decided to terminate the patrol. I suggested that we move a couple hundred miles to the southern part of the area where the water is 300 feet or so, and patrol the Nagasaki-Shanghai sea lanes for the last week in the area. Bill decided against it and set course for Midway. The submarine tender Sperry at Midway did a superb job in replacing those sound heads while we were tied up alongside, keeping the forward torpedo room pressurized the whole time--never before attempted.

Meanwhile, my orders were waiting to return to Portsmouth and put Sterlet in commission as exec. Harry still hadn't relieved me, even on the last day of the training period before the next patrol. At 0800 that morning, I said, "Harry, I leave the ship as soon as we get back in today. You must relieve me as navigator and exec as of this moment."

At 1100 we grounded on Midway and wiped off those new sound heads again. Well, Bill was really in deep kimshee then. He was in the doghouse with SubPac. After all, it's almost impossible to go aground on Midway. You're either in no water or you have 1,000 fathoms. If you cut across a corner of the island, you're going to hit ground. Since the water is so deep, nobody was navigating. The real responsibility was with the OCE, the officer conducting the exercise, who should have laid a course in a safe direction. He could see we were heading for trouble and should have turned the target seaward to take us out of danger. A letter to this effect was sent to Bill by the CO of one of the escort vessels, but Bill didn't introduce it into evidence at the investigation. Then we had a tough time getting back into Midway because of a storm, and were then sent to Pearl for hull repairs and a board of investigation.

---

* This attack was on 3 July 1943. The victims were the Abzan Maru and the Kokuryu Maru.

Q: What was your capacity after you'd been relieved?

Captain Schratz: During that last sea phase, I was simply the training officer. The CO had sent several telegrams to the bureau to cancel my orders. Then they delayed my detachment and return to the mainland so I could testify on the grounding. The board recommended that both the CO and XO be relieved. Bill took it very hard. He was grieving over Reggie's loss. A lot of people criticized him for the gun action. We were really very close by then and shared many thoughts. But they wouldn't give him credit for any sinkings on that perfect attack, which really fried me off. This came later, on intelligence info.

Harry Maynard, the real culprit, though not qualified for command, was given command of the Litchfield, the destroyer target ship in Pearl Harbor. So Harry came out smelling like a rose. But it broke Bill's spirit. He died not many years later.[*] A broken heart is the best analysis I can give. Max Schmidt relieved Bill.[†] The announcement that Scorpion went down with all hands was made just after my arrival in Portsmouth for Sterlet. Bill wrote me almost immediately and stated that he thought my detachment was the primary cause of Scorpion's loss. The point of all this is that Clay Blair's inclusion of Scorpion as an example of wardroom friction is an affront against the reputation of a fine naval officer.

Q: Can you give me more about Captain Wylie? You said he had been misrepresented in Blair's book. How might you defend him?

Captain Schratz: As for any lack of aggression by the CO, the surface attack on an armed patrol vessel is a pretty good indication. He may not have done it had Reggie and I not egged him on, but the decision was certainly his, and he carried it out aggressively. A vital element of our team, he was a good, solid submarine skipper. What we did, we did damn well. I didn't agree with his decision to withdraw from the area on the second patrol, but

---

[*] Wylie, who retired as a rear admiral, died 10 May 1960.
[†] By this time Schmidt held the rank of commander.

the average submarine CO then would have done the same. Going in against an alerted, armed escort with no sound gear--we had no surface-mounted sound units then--and leaking air and oil made the decision one of judgment, not courage.

Q: Were you being depth-charged during that time you were on board?

Captain Schratz: Frequently. That's part of the price of admission.

Q: Describe what that's like.

Captain Schratz: Well, it's unpleasant. You're very happy when they quit.

Q: There must be more to it than unpleasant.

Captain Schratz: Above all, submarine war is almost wholly unique. Battlefield or surface combat brings to mind noise, confusion, stress, activity, violent action, chaos. In a submarine attack and evasion thereafter, none of that. Nothing pumps adrenaline. The handful who are active try to work in dead silence. Few can divert the punishment of one's own thoughts. The urge to urinate comes quickly after sounding general quarters. Then the only thing active is the imagination. The silence reverses the whole psychological idea of warfare.

One is prey to his own secret fears; every sound takes on a special, eerie significance. Sounds through the hull--dropping a depth charge, the click of the exploder if they're close enough--tend to put a knot in the stomach. The time between the click and the boom gives a split second to think about your past and possible future. It can be emotionally shattering. The sound is magnified many times in seawater, especially in shallow water. Before the war, it was commonly believed that a depth charge anywhere within half a mile may be fatal.

We found that even as close as 15, 20, 30 feet, we were surviving. But you can imagine the racket when they go off that close--light bulbs burst, loose gear flies into space, the pressure hull may dish inward. It doesn't seem possible that the ship can survive such treatment; many survived some God-awful punishment. In that heavy depth-charging Sterlet received, one was so close that a piece of the casing on the charge gouged out the teak decking a half inch deep and a foot and a half long. That really was close to have 300 or 500 pounds of explosive detonate.

If one were inclined to offer a silent prayer to Andy McKee and those superb yard craftsman, it was generally deferred until later. If the evasion tactics didn't succeed, it might be time to try something else. Meanwhile, the tension builds for the next attack. As the minutes or hours drag on, the air gets stale, the battery gets low. If a decision is made to bleed oxygen into the boat to help breathing, there's no way it can be replaced, and the next crisis may be worse. It takes a certain psychological attitude to be a good submariner.

One submarine CO, very capable, asked to be relieved after two patrols. He showed every indication of lack of courage in attack situations. On return to port, he said, "It's not for me," and asked to be relieved. The Navy was wise enough to put him later into another combat environment. In time he got command of a cruiser and did a superb job. Submarine warfare is just a bit different; it isn't for everybody.

Q: Was there any kind of screening process that sought to pick out this type of individual in the submarine service?

Captain Schratz: That started for the first time, I believe, while I was in sub school. The bird doing the screening should himself have gone to a psychiatrist. He earned nothing but ridicule. To a very large extent, suitability for submarine duty is largely a self-selection process. One who is not up to that type of warfare is hardly likely to be a volunteer. From the earliest days of the war, most of the new officers were reserves. Normally, at the end of every patrol, we'd transfer one-fifth of the officers and men to keep a planned rotation. For officer replacements, we invariably picked the reserve officer. Anybody who volunteers for active service, for combat duty, and for submarine duty is likely to be a thoroughbred.

Some individuals must have used the Naval Academy as a delaying device to keep them out of combat. The odds were that with comparable records, the reserve was a safer bet. The record bore it out. Those I served with were really super. In fact, in <u>Scorpion</u>, they used to chide me on my USN and challenged me to earn my "R." For each heroic deed, I advanced one letter; USNA, USNB, USNC, etc. I think on departure I had reached only a USNC-minus. The point is that the reserve officers were very good. Many came from solid engineering schools like Georgia Tech and had lots of experience. But a depth charge attack is something for which there is hardly a training ground.

I don't recall but one man who ever broke down at sea in a submarine; it was a very rare phenomenon. For one thing, the submarine force never expanded to the degree of aviation, for instance. Most of our people got into combat, a very small percentage of aviators. The men I saw at the end of the war were the same I knew at the beginning, less those who didn't make it. In my peer group, there were many who made a dozen or more war patrols, and we were a haggard and beaten-down group at the end, physically and mentally exhausted.

Q: What kind of a communications network, either official or unofficial, was there for spreading throughout the submarine force such things as tactical improvements, changes in doctrine, and so forth?

Captain Schratz: The submarine patrol reports followed a standard format designed specifically to capitalize on every phase of submarining, and they went to all of us. The sub school and the PCO school also did a great job in keeping the course up to the minute, analyzing patrol reports, operational testing, and the like. The seminar I ran in Portsmouth on tactics, thanks to Tony Gallaher's pioneering, was an eye-opener for many, me included, and I was happy to keep that sort of thing going. We always knew instinctively about use of small gyro angles, straight shots, and all that for maximum effectiveness. But there were nuances, operational tricks, which acted to cancel out normal errors and greatly improve accuracy.

The "Tenth Fleet," an operational research organization, made a major contribution. For instance, the bathythermograph, or BT, was designed to help diving officers during large changes of sea water temperature when changing depth. We'd come in off patrol, and such a piece of gear would be on the dock until they got permission to drill some holes through the hull for one thing or another, which we normally resisted. The BT was like that.

When we got to sea, what we noticed immediately was that we could now tell major breaks in the sea temperature, layers, under which we could hide and escape or minimize detection by sonar. Very quickly the BT became the most vital antisubmarine weapon we had, whatever its value to the diving officer in ballast changes. Soon we would go to sea with a questionable torpedo, but never with a BT on the fritz. It was a vital tool of evasion technique. In some areas of the world, such as in the Japan Sea during certain seasons, the thermal just below the surface was so great that it must have been almost impossible to detect a submarine just below that tremendous thermocline.

The Tenth Fleet also analyzed operational success and failure from a dozen perspectives. Manuals, doctrines, operational suggestions emerged. We also read most patrol reports and drew our own conclusions. If the Japs tried a new technique--dropping a grapnel or some kind of hook for out-of-season fishing, an experience which three or four of us shared, it's terribly disconcerting the first time it happens. The tremendous clank of iron on iron, tearing away the superstructure, the normal plunge to the depths as he tries to haul you up for the gaff, or perhaps to slide a depth charge down the line--this gives one the idea to get out of there ASAP. The sound of tearing away of metal is ghastly inside the ship. Nevertheless, it was apparently never a very successful tactic. Any information on enemy innovations naturally, as Ben Franklin suggested, helps to concentrate the attention.

Q: Who told you what the priority of targets was?

Captain Schratz: ComSubPac in the op ord.[*]

---

[*] Op ord--operation order.

Q: Would that be put out at the beginning of each patrol?

Captain Schratz: Yes, if appropriate. In addition, the skipper and exec were briefed on information developed from codebreaking. We were generally briefed on the planned course of the war during our two-month patrols, the progress of the strike carrier offensive across the Central Pacific. It was important to us, far more than to an aviator, for example, to know what was coming up during our time at sea. So we generally had a fair picture of how the war was expected to develop.

Q: When was your first awareness of Ultra?*

Captain Schratz: I think in Sterlet. Even before then, we would get mysterious reports that a Japanese ship was expected to be at a given position, proceeding from point A to B. If Scorpion knew this, I didn't, because I was never formally the XO, and hence didn't merit the briefing. Harry may have received the information, but I doubt it. Most of us had no idea just where the information came from. The CO and XO were under strict instructions to control it. They disclosed the information needed, and the rest didn't care where it came from. We soon became expert at laying out a retiring search curve to develop the information over maybe a six- or eight-hour period.

Q: What was your role during an attack while you were in the Scorpion?

Captain Schratz: I ran the torpedo data computer and more or less controlled the tempo of the attack, suggesting courses and speeds to close, predicting enemy zigs, when to get

---

* Ultra--short for ultra secret--was a special security classification given by the British to information gained from breaking the code of the German radio enciphering machine. It has come to be used more broadly to encompass other information obtained from interception and decryption of German and Japanese radio communications.

torpedoes ready, cutting in the gyros and actually firing. The graphic plotters worked independently on the data--very helpful over long periods of tracking.

Q: Wasn't that normally the exec's job?

Captain Schratz: No. The CO and XO roles varied. Most COs were on the periscope; some put the exec on the scope or on the bridge in night attacks, and the CO concentrated on the overall attack. This depended on personal style, visual acuity, and a number of factors. Most often, the exec acted as the overall attack coordinator.

Q: Describe the usefulness of the torpedo data computer as a tool in making an attack.

Captain Schratz: It was, in essence, an automatic plotter giving a visual picture of our own and enemy ships. The TDC takes inputs of range and bearing from periscope--or bearing transmitter on the bridge, or radar, or sonar--and solves the fire control problem. It was a very, very effective piece of gear. I insisted that all my officers work out canned problems on the TDC every day to improve their skills, to better understand relative movement, to anticipate all sorts of zigzagging, including specialized "continuous clock" maneuvering. It was amazing how good one can get with practice. Sometimes I used to practice while catching a breath of fresh air on the bridge; I'd solve relative-movement problems mentally on data passed to me from the conning tower. They'd set up a problem, pass me periodic ranges and bearings of the "enemy," and I'd try to solve enemy course and speed on three observations. After hours and hours of daily drill, techniques get very sharp.

Q: That's another way of describing what the term "seaman's eye" used to describe too.

Captain Schratz: Sure.

Q: A sense of judgment that you develop with constant practice. How much did you rely on that internal mechanism of your own as compared with the mechanical device?

Captain Schratz: The question is whether you're mastering the machine or it's mastering you. Tracking on sonar, for instance, bearings aren't accurate--or weren't then. It's tougher to know if you're still on one target or if your operator accidentally shifted targets. With radar, your bearings can be out a bit and the range is exact. Sonar ranges are usually terrible; operators tend to pick out the range you want to hear. One has to learn how to choose an attack position which minimizes or cancels the unknowns. Anything which minimizes errors improves chances of success. A wealth of practical knowledge developed in wartime experience is lost today, even though entirely relevant to current attack techniques.

Q: You described the "pucker factor" as you went into the first attack. How soon did you get over that feeling and sort of take things in stride?

Captain Schratz: It depends on the individual. There's always an element of fear, if only of the unknown. In the attack in which Reggie was killed, that bullet with my initials on it convinced me that the Japs had their chance and blew it. Even in the most tense situations thereafter, I could feel no apparent effect. It was probably no more than psyching myself up, but it worked. I quickly developed the reputation as unflappable.

Q: Describe the rest periods during patrols.

Captain Schratz: Except for the first day, I forget. No, that's not true; they weren't drunken brawls. In truth, they were a major element of continuing readiness. Depending on where and when, it was a great device to take the mind off the war, engage in athletics, swimming, a bit of body building, maybe a few beer busts, poker, and the indoor sports. The officers and men got together for sports, depending on where we were.

Pearl, which I didn't see too often, was different from Midway, where there was nothing but volleyball, basketball, swimming, or horsing around with the gooney birds. The overall routine was always the same: ten days at the rest facility with only duty days on the ship, or necessary supervision of refit work. Back on board for fitting out, an intensive three-day training period at sea, final loading, and departure.

Q: You got sort of short shrift compared with the submariners operating out of Pearl Harbor.

Captain Schratz: Oh, I don't know. I liked Midway or Majuro or Guam. Even Saipan had a grim fascination, a little better than being poked in the eye with a sharp stick.

Q: How much contact did the people in the boats have with the division commanders and squadron commanders?

Captain Schratz: The submarine force organization was unique in command relations. Our parent squadron and division staffs might be in Pearl or Fremantle, or in one of the tenders, wherever they were--Midway, Majuro, Saipan, Guam. We refitted and went under the training and admin of whatever squadron happened to be in the refit port. Sub COs rarely saw their own divcom or squad dog. They, in turn, never had the whole division together. The system worked superbly well for simplicity and effectiveness of training, but I hardly recall who my divcom was most of the war. With those who happened to be in ports where I refitted, relations were always very friendly, but we didn't see much of them.

Q: Are there any names that you remember in particular among the commanders?

Captain Schratz: Division commanders? Well, in a place like Midway, all the senior officers hang out in the skippers' hut, so you see them there and on the tender.

Q: Apparently for your own well-being, you got off the Scorpion just in time. Did you ever give any thoughts to that afterwards?

Captain Schratz: Many times. Bill sent about four messages to the bureau or force commander to cancel my orders. They didn't even answer but one of them. I wanted to stay aboard. It really was a great ship. Max Schmidt, who relieved him, was a fine officer, very sharp, but he had almost a new wardroom. I think we had a very high percentage of submarine losses with new wardrooms in the first or second patrol. Bill Wylie's letter, mentioned above, that he thought my detachment was a primary factor in the loss of the Scorpion, I've thought of a thousand times. I just wish he had never written it. I really felt sad when I saw that. I never considered anyone an indispensable sailor. Remember, I was only the fourth officer in Scorpion.

Q: In what sense did he mean that?

Captain Schratz: Obviously we had some deadwood, or I wouldn't have done what I did as fourth in seniority. Also, the morale in the wardroom had fallen apart, especially during-- no, I shouldn't mention this. Things were different. They changed the day Reggie was lost. You can't have an episode like that not affect you for quite a long time, both ashore and in the wardroom, particularly when Harry's shortcomings directly caused Wylie's relief as well. These were some of the reasons I wanted to stay aboard. Even though my wife was pregnant, with a strong possibility that her life might be endangered, I still thought my duty was to the ship, and I supported Bill all the way in trying to cancel my orders.

Q: Of course, that's one of those imponderables that could never be resolved.

Captain Schratz: Yes.

Q: I've read George Grider talking about the Wahoo.[*] He said maybe if he'd still been there, the ship would have survived because he and the exec, I guess, had the tendency to

---

[*] George Grider, with Lydel Sims, War Fish (Boston: Little, Brown, 1959).

curb some of Mush Morton's more daring things, and without that dampening influence, he probably went beyond what was reasonable.[*]

Captain Schratz: But Mush also lost a superb fire control party when O'Kane and others left.[†] Scorpion had a superb group of enlisted men too.[‡] I think of them many times and the tragedy of their loss. I lost some really good friends on that ship. I've often thought that the men back aft had no vote in what kind of a ship they were on or how capable the officers were to lead them. If a ship shouldn't have gone to sea for some reason, only the officers could do something about it. They gave unquestioned loyalty, even to the death. But enough of that.

Q: You went from there to the Sterlet.[§] Describe the process of putting her in commission. You said you had a good sea story to go with this one.

Captain Schratz: Oh, yes. Of course, I was the experienced hand, one of the very few in the wardroom with combat experience.[**] The CO was Orme Campbell "Butch" Robbins, out of '34. He had been a submarine JO at the time of the Pearl Harbor attack and had been relieved for physical reasons on his first patrol. He went back to sea as exec of one of the

---

[*] Commander Dudley W. Morton, USN, was the commanding officer of the submarine Wahoo (SS-238) when she was lost on a patrol in the area of the Kurile Islands in October 1943. For more on this submarine see Richard H. O'Kane, Wahoo: The Patrols of America's Most Famous World War II Submarine (Novato, California: Presidio Press, 1987) and Sterling J. Forest, Wake of the Wahoo (Philadelphia: Chilton, 1960).
[†] Lieutenant Commander Richard H. O'Kane, USN, had served as executive officer of the Wahoo before getting command of his own boat, the Tang (SS-306).
[‡] For a list of the crew members at the time of the Scorpion's loss, see United States Submarine Losses: World War II (Washington, D.C.: Government Printing Office, 1963), page 79.
[§] The USS Sterlet (SS-392) was commissioned 4 March 1944. She had a displacement of 1,525 tons on the surface and 2,415 tons submerged. She was 312 feet long, 27 feet in the beam, and had a draft of 15 feet. Her top speed was 20 knots surfaced and 9 knots submerged. She was armed with ten 21-inch torpedo tubes, a 5-inch gun, and a 40-millimeter gun. The Sterlet was built at the Portsmouth Navy Yard.
[**] Commander Orme C. Robbins, USN.

Squadron 50 boats, which saw little combat while operating out of the U.K.* He had a good reputation for smarts, particularly as an engineer, and started off well in putting our organization together.

When in the shipyard getting the ship ready for war, the average JO looks to his allowance list of spare parts and equipment. He'll do a very conscientious job of getting a full suit of spares for anything that can come up. What I suggested was that if we were in Formosa Straits and the radar broke down and he didn't have a spare part because it didn't happen to be on the allowance list--that was really not my concern; it was his concern. He was supposed to look at that gear and everything he had in the ship, to check the allowance list and scrounge everything he could possibly think of in case he did need it. Whether or not it's on the allowance list, the Navy yard is the big PX. To emphasize, I added, "There is no such thing as a Seventh Commandment in a Navy yard." Well, I didn't learn until a long time later that there are different Seventh Commandments in different bibles.

At one of our first meetings with all the officers, I put the above ideas into a memorandum literally on the back of an envelope. The CO asked me to write it up formally for him to promulgate and give each officer a copy. He took the letter to the divcom: "Here's a memorandum I wrote for my officers. I thought you might be interested." The divcom prepared a copy for the squad dog: "Here's a memorandum I prepared for my officers," which he sent to ComSubLant, who sent it to CinCLant, who sent it to CNO.† It was then made part of the commissioning packet for every new construction skipper for the rest of the war. But in all the reissues, nobody ever changed the Seventh Commandment to the more common King James version, where stealing violates the Eighth.

By coincidence, a very bright <u>Sterlet</u> junior officer got himself involved in a scandalous relationship with the wife of an officer on the submarine following ours. A few months later, when <u>Sterlet</u> left the shipyard, her husband's submarine was about a month behind. She decided to leave with the <u>Sterlet</u> wives. She arrived in Newport for the torpedo trials. I think she was almost the only "wife" waiting when we arrived in New London one rainy midnight for our final shakedown training.

---

* U.K.--United Kingdom.
† CinCLant--Commander in Chief Atlantic Fleet; CNO--Chief of Naval Operations.

There was a big party just before we left New London, and by this time Bob was in really deep trouble. The skipper told him he could not bring "that woman" to the ball; she appeared draped on his arm. The next morning, he compounded his troubles by failing to show up when we got under way to shift into the dry dock. That afternoon I got hold of Bob and really told him off. I said, "I've done everything I possibly can for you, and you've just gone too damn far."

And he said, "Sir, you gave me permission."

I said, "What in the name of God are you talking about?" And out came this tattered old memorandum, where, as far as his Bible was concerned, we forgave him--not for the consequences of stealing but of adultery. Well, I learned a lesson too.

Even during the fitting-out period with a fine group of officers, minor problems began to emerge. The CO was often reluctant to stand up for his officers against anybody who happened to be senior.

Q: What kind of circumstance would bring that about?

Captain Schratz: Well, one of our training officers thought that the fire control organization, mechanical plot, firing procedures, etc., should be exactly the same as he had on his ship. Since the system on any ship must, within limits, be responsive to the CO's personal style--in this case markedly different from our procedures--there should have been enough flexibility to allow individual variations. I had worked very hard on that fire control team and they were shaping up extremely well. To suddenly get a suggestion to change it around, even though our equipment was not compatible, generated considerable heartburn when the CO concurred. The officers had become pretty disenchanted by the time we left New London on our way to Honolulu. When we got to Pearl and for our final training before going off on patrol, that same officer again was our training officer. He'd been transferred from New London to Pearl in the meantime.

Q: Is this a person whose name we can mention?

Captain Schratz: Yes. Donc Donaho.* I admired Donc greatly. We later served together in OP-61 and became good friends. Donc was wrong in this case, and in Sterlet things were pretty tense in the wardroom when we went off on patrol. We made an excellent first patrol, but we suddenly found out that the skipper was lacking in aggression. The fire control party simply took control during general quarters and ran the approach, and the captain might disappear to the wardroom and have some breakfast or wander through the ship. I ran the fire control team, with or without help from the CO. The attack ran very much without his help.

It was a good patrol. We sank enough shipping for a Navy Cross for the CO. But the CO seemed to change for the worse after a heavy depth charging during the patrol. We got a good going-over in shallow water, four miles off the beach, bad enough to cause considerable damage to bow planes, teak decking, piping, and electrical systems forward. The Japanese credited this depth charging with a positive kill--as they had the one in the Yellow Sea on Scorpion--but we survived.

We went to Midway for refit, where several officers got a little beered up and told the skipper off, including remarks that if I ever left the ship, they'd never remain on board. Looking back on it now, I might have seen the handwriting and gotten off myself then, but that wasn't my way of doing things. As long as he let us run the attacks, I thought I could control things. But the second patrol was grim. He was under great stress. I don't know how to classify it. He frequently called me into his cabin to talk, lying in his bunk, and I'd sit on the heater or somewhere.

A submarine cabin is damn small. I'd sit there and listen to him for maybe an hour, to unintelligible mumbling. I'd ask for a repeat a half dozen times, but you can do that only so long, then you simply let him mumble. There was no conversation; he was just talking. On two other occasions, he asked me to read deeply personal letters to his wife. He told her how terrific his officers were, what a really great job they were doing, each of us,

---

* Commander Glynn R. Donaho, USN, who had previously commanded the Flying Fish (SS-229). In the summer of 1944 he took command of Submarine Division 222 in Hawaii and the Picuda (SS-382).

individually, right down the line. And, of course, the officers themselves never heard such praise. They were being chewed out for everything and were demoralized, the exec included.

Things went from bad to terrible, and more and more I had to think about the very difficult choice of relieving him and assuming command myself. Aggravating the problem was the fact that this was early in the patrol; we still had a long time at sea. If I did--for what cause--and sent a report to ComSubPac on it, what would he do? I couldn't imagine him leaving Butch on board to complete the patrol. It seemed likely we'd be ordered to rendezvous somewhere to get him off the ship, lest something worse might happen. But there were no surface units nearby, and we couldn't send him to another submarine. The ship was needed on the firing line at that time.

It was the middle of the Philippines campaign and the tide of war was reaching a crescendo. The Battle of Leyte Gulf and the last challenge by the Japanese fleet put us in traffic between the Philippines and Okinawa and Japan. I had no cause for concern about the integrity of command. I had been careful not to let rumors of a problem with the CO get out of the wardroom. The officers talked symptoms but not a solution, at least to my knowledge. I contributed little, lest I add fuel to the fire unnecessarily.

The decision before me to relieve the CO, I, of course, could discuss with no one. I felt some loyalty to the CO, some sympathy, some obligation merely to retain the structure of command. I confided in nobody about the late night mumbling sessions in his cabin and other irrationalities of behavior. There was no concern for our ability to carry on in his absence; we were already doing so. The system used for surface or submerged attacks put the exec in charge, the CO as an overall observer concerned with the general safety of the ship. If I relieved him, no change would be required. I finally decided to sweat it out as long as I could. I believed then that we were successful in keeping any information on wardroom problems from the men back aft.* But for every deterioration my problem became more difficult. I was neither able nor inclined to consult him and took virtually full independence in running the ship, prepared to assume command formally on short notice.

When things looked darkest, fate took a hand. We were able to pick up some naval aviators shot down over Okinawa, and that added three more officers to the wardroom, a half dozen enlisted back aft. It helped just to get more people. We started a bridge game and kept it going for two weeks. The CO was pretty much frozen out of it by all of us. There was no plan; it just happened. All contact with him by the officers was avoided. He'd come into the wardroom for something and everybody else would get up and leave. He ordered a couple of junior officers to sit with him at breakfast. Well, it's intolerable for a submarine wardroom. I continued to do my damnedest to keep the crew in ignorance, and I thought they knew little of what was going on. The aviators' adventure stories kept us occupied. One of these aviators had been picked up in a mined area, very close under the cliffs in Okinawa. I suggested to the skipper that I'd navigate in the conning tower and he could stay on the bridge, doing what comes naturally.

He said, "I don't want to go inside 100 fathoms."

Well, 100 fathoms would have left this guy about five miles to row, and the pilot was being set on the beach with a pretty good current. So I kept reporting fathometer readings divided by five or ten or something; it didn't matter. We got in to ten fathoms or less. Finally we were so damn close, I was really concerned myself. What I didn't know was that the deeper areas were freshly mined. Swordfish was lost in that minefield about six weeks later. Where we were was probably safer than in deeper water.

---

* Captain Schratz's note: By an unusual coincidence, I had just edited the above when a second class petty officer, who had served in Sterlet from commissioning to the end of the war, phoned me to report he was in the area and would like to pay a visit. Not having seen him in over 40 years, I was delighted. We chatted for several hours. I pumped him as subtly as I could on CO-XO relations. He claimed to have full knowledge of the CO's problem, citing strange orders the CO had given in the general mess while wandering around during general quarters. He expressed the view that the men were thoroughly confident of the professional ability of the CO and exec and had no concern whatever as long as I was there in an emergency. He also stated confidently that the crew had full knowledge of everything going on in the wardroom, "sometimes before the officers did."

So we finally pulled this bird aboard, one very fine officer. He had given up any hope of rescue and had written his thoughts in a memo notebook during the three or four hours in this tiny lifeboat, later showing it to several of us. Well, our visitors helped break the tension considerably. We were then looking for Japanese warships, stragglers from the Battle of Leyte Gulf returning to Empire waters. A whole line of subs was looking for them. That's when you check the rosters to see who the TDC operator is on each boat to make your own professional guess as to how good their contact dope is likely to be.

Well, the two boats to the southwest were both hotshots, so I knew I could bank on their information. Exhausted, I turned in late one night but first gave instructions to the OOD that if they made radar contact, to immediately come to a northeast course, the known track of the enemy heading back toward the Inland Sea, at flank speed, and start tracking. The idea was to parallel them at maximum speed. I didn't want to let them draw ahead while we were trying to get into attack position. Given the enemy speed advantage, getting into attack position depended on how far off the track we were.

Events worked out just as anticipated, except that the CO had gotten up for a cup of coffee or something and happened to be in the control room when the report came of a radar contact. He ordered the OD and put our tail to the guy at flank speed.[*] By the time I got to the conning tower and reversed the order, we had lost position so that there was no hope of making an attack and just watched a battleship-cruiser force pass by. We got off a contact report, but it was not worth much to anybody. I really, really wanted those guys. It was a big opportunity thrown away.

Q: How could you go about countermanding the skipper's orders?

Captain Schratz: Well, the tracking team took over to get the ship into attack position.

Q: Well, how does the crew know whom to obey?

---

[*] OD--officer of the deck.

Captain Schratz: There was no problem with that. I controlled the attack team and did what was natural when I got to the conning tower. Probably only a few minutes were involved, but he couldn't really disagree; he knew I was right. There was no real loss of control, and I don't think it bothered anybody. But we lost that gorgeous attack opportunity.

About that time Salmon got badly damaged to the south of us, and the three subs in the wolf pack were ordered to her assistance with orders either to take off the crew and take them back to Saipan or to escort her back, and if she gets sunk by somebody en route we would surface later and pick up any survivors.[*] Well, Sterlet was first to make contact. I think Jack Coye in Silversides and Fritz Harlfinger in Trigger were also en route.[†] Dick Laning, XO of Salmon, came over by boat to see what we could do to help.[‡] We couldn't talk by radio; they had no communications intact beyond a weak SOS frequency transmission every 15 minutes on the emergency radio circuit.

As Dick Laning came alongside, bobbing in his tiny rubber boat, he greeted me on deck with a cheery, "Great to see you, Paul. What can I do for you?" Having survived so far on pure luck and pluck, they weren't about to give up the ship. We may have taken off a few men and escorted the ship back to Saipan. The campaign for Saipan was still continuing hot and heavy in the hills, but Tanapag Harbor was okay, with two submarine tenders already there, Holland and Fulton. Incidentally, I was to command the latter 15 years later.

---

[*] The Salmon (SS-182) was badly damaged by a Japanese depth-charge attack while she was operating in the Ryukyus Islands on 30 October 1944, a few days after the Battle of Leyte Gulf.
[†] Commander John S. Coye, Jr., USN; the oral history of Coye, who retired as a rear admiral, is in the Naval Institute collection. Commander Frederick J. Harlfinger II, USN.
[‡] Lieutenant Commander Richard B. Laning, USN. The Naval Institute oral history of Laning, who retired as a captain, contains a vivid description of the Salmon's problems.

The day before arriving in Saipan, the CO figured this was his opportunity. He told me he was going to ask for my detachment when we got into Saipan. Sterlet was due to refit in Pearl; he could control the rest of the wardroom in Pearl, when the stories started to come out about the ship. So he went to the commodore in Fulton, reporting that his exec was hot for combat, didn't want a rest period, and wanted to go back out again at the first chance. I didn't know about that for a long time. But it happened that Atule came through shortly and detached as exec for his command.

So I joined Atule with Jack Maurer as the skipper, and went back out to sea again as XO.[*] My final word to the skipper on leaving Sterlet was, "You know you'll never take this ship to sea again after I've left. I wish you luck somewhere in the world, but not in the submarine force."

And that's about it on the fighting Sterlet. He took the ship to Pearl Harbor, received a Navy Cross for another great patrol, then turned in his suit in favor of a staff job in Australia for the rest of the war.

Q: I bet you emerged with a real wonderful fitness report with that scene, though.

Captain Schratz: He had mentioned that I would get a satisfactory fitness report only if I promised not to discuss Sterlet with anybody. I kept my word for a long time, although I did talk it over in general terms with Dick Laning and Kenny Nauman, his skipper in Salmon.[†] They were very helpful. I think Dick had gone through the same thing in one of his boats.

Q: That almost sounds like extortion on the part of the CO.

Captain Schratz: Well, you've got to put yourself in his position. I pity him a lot, you know. Certainly 40 years after, I can't carry a grudge. I couldn't carry a grudge even two days after. I pitied him during the patrol. I pity the other officers there, too, who had to

---

[*] Commander John H. Maurer, USN.
[†] Commander Harley Kent Nauman, USN.

serve under him, but you win some, you lose some, and I survived. It was an intolerable ordeal. I was physically and mentally exhausted from a situation building up for almost a year. I lost more than the usual 15 pounds on patrol. If the break had to come, it was just as well it happened in the boonies.

Q: What kind of help did you get from the Salmon officers, what suggestions, whatever?

Captain Schratz: Well, Kenny said he'd intercede with anybody if I wished, which I did not. I was quite disappointed that the squadron commander, division commanders, or CO of Fulton, all senior submariners, didn't quiz me on what really had happened. Maybe I should have broken the ice, but I had given my word not to.

There was a war going on in Saipan. Jap formations were flying over every night as the campaign reached its final stages, treating us to a wild display of tracer fire from the ships in the harbor. A day or two later, we had an air raid at noon. The Japs had built a fighter strip secretly on nearby Pagan Island and caught us by surprise. Fulton couldn't hit anything with her AA battery--they were ship repair specialists, not warships. I offered to assist as director officer. These were the same old 5-inch/38s I had encountered in my Wichita days, and the CO was happy to get some help. And it helped me too.

Of course, when Atule signed me up, the problem was solved.* Jack Maurer was a great skipper. He had put Atule in commission, made four war patrols, made a trip under the arctic ice from New London after the war, and put it out of commission. He and I were both a couple of square-headed Dutchmen, and we got along like brothers. Jack was having some personal problems at that time. We soon became very close in everything, did everything together, and had great support from another superb crew.

Q: How was he as a professional submariner?

---

* The USS Atule (SS-403) was commissioned 21 June 1944. She had a displacement of 1,525 tons on the surface and 2,415 tons submerged. She was 312 feet long, 27 feet in the beam, and had a draft of 15 feet. Her top speed was 20 knots surfaced and 9 knots submerged. She was armed with ten 21-inch torpedo tubes, a 5-inch gun, and a 40-millimeter gun.

Captain Schratz: Great. He later became my divcom after the war when I had command of Pickerel, and he's always been top-notch. He was eventually ComSubPac.*

Q: Did you have a situation to observe his aggressiveness?

Captain Schratz: Oh, yes. His patrols were superb. We made one patrol up in the Yellow Sea up off the Shantung promontory, and we apparently caught an antisubmarine decoy sent out to lure us into a trap. We were just about to make a surface attack on it when an airplane came screeching out of the sky in a steep dive, heading right for us. We barely got down before some nasty old bombs straddled us. It was a close call but didn't shake him. The Japs credited this, too, as a submarine kill, the fourth time I was "lost." We had several good patrols, sinking whatever tonnage was left. Atule got a Navy Unit Commendation.

Q: You must have thought you went to heaven compared with the previous situation.

Captain Schratz: Well, I liked action. I spent hours developing prospects for each patrol so that we could find the activity. There's nothing more deadly boring than sitting around waiting for him to come to you. And I made Jack a bargain: "Let me write the patrol report, and I'll guarantee you a successful patrol, no matter what we do."

Well, for the third patrol, I had the chance. We didn't do a lot, but we were aggressive in all directions. We didn't sink any ships. I think we blew up 57 mines floating on the surface. They were all over the East China Sea and southern empire waters then, so we all had our mine episodes. Even that we did aggressively. In fact, we hit one flush on the bow while making flank speed. Ever hear the sound of a 1,000-pound sledge hitting a steel hull at 18 knots? It was a very noisy dud. When you read through that patrol report, it's a masterpiece of nothing.

---

* As a rear admiral, Maurer served as Commander Submarine Force Pacific Fleet from 1966 to 1968.

The last paragraph of the ComSubPac endorsement, however, tells the story: "This patrol is considered successful." We picked up an aviator. We were lifeguarding for a B-29 raid in shallow waters of Bungo Suido, the sea exit to the big Jap submarine base at Kure, close to a Japanese lighthouse. The Japs sent two antisubmarine floatplanes out looking for us. Our B-29 air cover had just headed for the barn. We saw a Jake and a Rufe coming in, and recalled the B-29, then dived to periscope depth to watch the show.[*] The Jake fled; the B-29 let go one burst from all guns and the Rufe just disappeared. Surfacing immediately, we pulled a survivor out of the water, an antisubmarine officer.

This bird was an amazing intelligence catch. He had the tracings from his MAD recorder, almost identical with the U.S. gear.[†] From his tracings made on an antisubmarine patrol, we could tell that their gear was very weak on detection when the submarine was on an east-west magnetic heading, a potentially valuable assist in evasion tactics. This man was wearing three suits of clothing, carrying everything he owned: a wad of money, several condoms, perfume. He was ready for anything. He had his log books from ASW school, almost as though he was about to defect. It took us about two days to dry him out, but he was a useful intelligence find, and I guess this earned us the successful patrol.[‡] He, incidentally, later became a rear admiral in the Japanese Self-Defense Forces and is still in communication with his saviors.

Q: Do you have any more general observations on patrol reports, their value, what goes into them, and so forth?

Captain Schratz: Again, it depended a lot on the patrol report writer. Some COs masked fine patrols behind poor writing. Someone like Gene Fluckey had everybody reading his

---

[*] "Jake" and "Rufe" were Allied names given to Japanese aircraft to eliminate the need for pronouncing the Japanese names during combat.
[†] MAD--magnetic anomaly detector, a device used on aircraft to detect the magnetic signatures of submarines below.
[‡] ASW--antisubmarine warfare.

reports.* They were brilliantly written--and executed. He was a supreme activist in developing some marvelous and very aggressive patrols, highly successful patrols. He always had new ideas that made his patrols very valuable. Some COs were overcome by false modesty and didn't really try to make contributions on tactics. Even mistakes are valuable if somebody else can benefit. And some were short, simple checkoffs of the items in the standard format without interpretation, analysis, or a real contribution. By and large, the patrol reports were well worth reading, always sought after, and with a lot of previous patrols in one assigned area, added much to the briefings.

Q: You mentioned you hadn't had too much contact with Ultra before. How was it when you were an exec?

Captain Schratz: At sea we were getting Ultra information, not identified as such. We didn't know where it came from. SubPac made every effort to cover up the fact that it came from codebreaking. We assumed it was a report of contact, a reported enemy convoy disposition and destination, number of escorts, and so forth. The information was sometimes extremely good, sometimes useless because of poor navigation or operational changes. Late in the war, it got really good.

Q: How was the health of the crew living under conditions in submarines?

Captain Schratz: Great. Late in the war, when we were able to spend most of our time on the surface, we'd pass the word below that sunshine and fresh air were available on the bridge for two men at a time. Few came up. You'd ask them, "Why not? My God, you've been below for a month."

They'd reply, "Well, I got my bunk lamp, I got a good book I want to read, there's some good music on the radio, and I got a steak frying in the galley." So we got pale, some

---

* Commander Eugene B. Fluckey, USN, received the Medal of Honor for his exploits in command of the USS Barb (SS-220).

more gaunt than others, but health was excellent. The pharmacist's mates sent on submarines--I don't know where they found them, but they were magnificent.

Q: These are the guys that performed the appendectomies and so forth?

Captain Schratz: Yes. They were told not to after that <u>Grenadier</u> experience.

Q: When I talked to Captain Cutter, he said it was very difficult for him to sleep in a submarine. I wonder what your experience was in that regard.

Captain Schratz: I always survived with minimal sleep anyhow, so I saw no problem in a submarine. I was an avid reader, and I played a lot of solitaire simply to keep the mind off current problems. The reading had to be selective, requiring little concentration. A shoot-'em-up with action on every page was fine. Otherwise, I'd find I had read five pages and didn't know what I'd read. So my guess is the general state of tension probably operates against sound sleep, especially on the surface. We could go deep in the daytime, perhaps to avoid a big typhoon on the surface. There's not much point in fighting the sea, so we could go down to 400 feet, take a cold shower, tell the cook to call you maybe in 16 hours with the biggest steak he can find. Then you really slept like a rock. When you got back on the surface to fight Japs, they'd been beating themselves out fighting on the sea for two days, and the submarine had a big advantage.

Q: How frequently did you get those experiences and opportunities for that kind of sleep?

Captain Schratz: I think we talked about that more than anything. Only once I recall for sure. But every day, when submerged all day, there was a good opportunity to sleep. It was quiet, still, and comfortable. Sleep--I was never bothered by either too much of it or too little. I just didn't consider it other than to resent the amount of time wasted.

Q: Did you have a constant concern, though, that you were more vulnerable than, say, a surface ship or whatever?

Captain Schratz: No way. I felt sorry for those people who could take a big dive only once.

Q: Really?

Captain Schratz: Definitely. With some of those storms, to sit up there and slug it out brought back too many of my Wichita days in those God-awful storms north of the Arctic Circle. You fight through one of those with seas breaking clear over sky forward 100 feet up; you can't eat, you can't serve plates. You live on soup and sour rye bread. No, a submarine is the life. I really felt sorry for the others.

Q: Are there any specific memories you recall of being in the Atule as the war wound down, the closing campaigns?

Captain Schratz: I was anxious for a command. I had been qualified for command since Scorpion days. My Naval Academy class had become senior enough for command, I guess, about the time I joined Atule. At that time there was apparently a decision at the fleet level that they had better give some of our hotshot reserve officers a chance. I mentioned before some of these Georgia Tech engineer types, with lots of active duty and well-qualified. Clay Blair has a good discussion about my class being delayed for command for this purpose, as well as I've seen it done. So we were getting pretty feisty about getting command before we burned out.

One or two of my classmates were very fortunate when the skipper stepped down and asked that his exec be given the job. I learned later that I was considered for command of Sterlet in Pearl when my CO threw in the towel, again when his relief was ordered ashore. Others happened to be in the right spot at the right time. Another factor was that my class had borne the brunt of the war, first entering subs six months before Pearl Harbor.

Many were veterans of a dozen or more patrols, walking skeletons. We could have taken school boat commands--submarines then being taken off the firing line--but the force commander didn't want to lose the experience from the war zone. I personally wanted a command badly but not a non-combat one.

So when I left Jack Maurer after our third patrol, I went to Guam on the command list, and I was overdue. That's when I started suffering from "non-combat fatigue." I conned General LeMay into allowing me to fly on a B-29 mission.* ComSubPac gave the authorization to fly in the lifeguard plane cover over the submarine. I wanted to see what it was like in an airplane as a liaison officer. With few Japanese ships left, we were doing lots of lifeguarding, and Admiral Lockwood authorized a Super Dumbo B-29 flight.

When I met LeMay, I folded the message in half. He glanced at only the first line, that I was authorized to fly a mission, muttered, "Great!" and put me in the Pathfinder--the lead plane over the target, which started the fires for the others to dump on. I went through the briefings and pre-flight with the crew, made the mission, and it was really a superb operation. Our target was near Nagasaki, where I had recently made a patrol in Atule. Having spent 30 days as exec-navigator analyzing the harbor, shipping, traffic patterns, resources, economy, etc., I had a better idea of the area than the briefers.

Q: What period of time was it when you made this flight?

Captain Schratz: Late in the war, probably in July or August of '45. So I made a night raid. Carrying an extra person, they listed me as a machine gunner, which means that I had to carry my flak suit, coveralls, rations, and the rest. Weighing about 200 then, not quite my gaunt patrol weight, it was a big addition to the "cargo." And unfortunately, the trade wind off Guam reversed that night, so instead of the 15-knot head wind, we had a 15-knot tail wind, and we almost didn't get off the ground. The runway was marked off in ten-mile-an-hour ground speed increments. If a plane fell short of one of those, SOP called for pulling

---

* Major General Curtis E. LeMay, USA, was commanding general of the 21st Bomber Command, which was running B-29 strikes against the Japanese Empire from bases in the Marianas.

off to the side and a standby plane takes your place back a mile or so at the end of the line.[*] We were below minimum at every marker, passed the end of the paved area and crossed about half a mile of coral, blowing dust all over the western Pacific, still bearing down hard.

There was a shack at the end of the runway and beyond, the steep northeast cliff at Guam about 100-125 feet above the water. At the last moment the pilot humped the plane into the air, over the shack, then tried to regain airspeed as we fell toward the water. Was it 10,000 pounds of incendiaries they carried? Oh, it was a thrill, but I thought it was like this all the time. Not a sound came over the intercom until we finally started to climb. Then, tail gunner to pilot in a very weak voice: "Jack, do you want me to fly all the way to Japan and back with this load of shit in my pants?"

I just burst out laughing. What you don't know doesn't hurt you. It was a great show, and I wanted to try it again. I volunteered for a day raid on Tokyo and was on the field after going through the briefing, ready to man my plane, when I was ordered to come back and see ComSubPac. LeMay apparently thought my bravery rated an Air Medal. But when ComSubPac received it, he blew his stack, because I had an Ultra clearance, carrying a ban on any flying over enemy territory. So in place of the Air Medal, SubPac recommended me for a general court-martial. Well, it was an interesting day.

Q: Tell me about it.

Captain Schratz: The day the recommendation came through was the day the Japs made the first surrender offer, about two days after Hiroshima.[†] I think we had four submarines either going on patrol or coming back from patrol, and special briefings were necessary. The Russians also entered the war against Japan that day, and it looked like there were many more things of concern than my episode. The verdict: "We'll pit one against the

---

[*] SOP--standard operating procedure.
[†] B-29 bombers of the U.S. Army Air Forces dropped atomic bombs on Hiroshima, Japan, on 6 August 1945 and on Nagasaki, Japan, on 9 August 1945. The Japanese surrendered shortly afterward.

other and tear them both up." I probably played that wrong. I've always thought I should have--I'd like to have--that Air Medal. But I never got it.

Q: Were you in kind of a limbo status then?

Captain Schratz: No, I was actually on the command list, serving as a CO of relief crews of submarines in refit when the regular COs go off to the rest camp.

Q: Why don't you describe some of that process.

Captain Schratz: Each submarine has a great big work book, covering every system on the ship--a checkoff list of all routines. They filled this out before they came in for a refit and turned it over to the relief crew. The relief crew skipper shifted berths, and whatever else was required. It was a superb system and worked like a charm.

    The regularly assigned officers and men had qualified reliefs to run the refit and let them enjoy the ten-day rest between patrols. Then there was an intensive three to four days to check the work, test new gear and do intensive training. The relief crews were attached to a flag allowance. These were mainly people coming off the subs for a rest after five patrols or waiting for new construction needs. And all with almost no paperwork. The PCOs gave the necessary level of experience in the refit to make the whole thing work.

Q: If a ship or submarine came in with a list of things to be fixed, would all the items on the list get done?

Captain Schratz: At the first meeting of ship's crew with the repair personnel, they went through the whole book. Some things they couldn't do for time or spares, some things they had to defer to a shipyard, but by and large, if they could do it, they did. It was simply a matter of possibility, and a lot of those which weren't possible got done, too--for instance, replacing the sound heads and mounting on <u>Scorpion</u> alongside the tender at Midway. But the tenders did one unbelievable job. The Japs rightly called them our secret weapon. At one time we were transferring so much scarce gear from one sub to another--pulling it off a fresh arrival and sending it out on a departure--that it was claimed we kept 129 submarines in action with only 128 hulls.

During the early part of the war, when equipment was short, a gun, a radar, and air-search radar, maybe a piece of sound gear, never got a rest period. It was a remarkable job, no accountability, just do it, and it worked beautifully.

An indication of how sharp some of the people were is illustrated by a story on Atule. We had an electronics officer named Fred Oyhus, a jaygee, who was unqualified for sea duty because of a birth defect involving one eye.* He talked himself into submarine duty and was an electronics genius. On Atule's first patrol, we had a severe problem with the air-search radar, the old SD. Apparently the Japs homed in on that thing like a beacon. It apparently just happened to coincide with their radar search gear frequency and became dangerous to use. Well, I asked Fred what he could do. "Why can't you send out one single pulse?"

He said, "Sure, I think I can do that. I can soup up the screen voltage so that it will retain the image from the single pulse, then modify the transmitter from continuous to a single electronic pulse of about one-tenth second. But it's a violation of BuShips' directions to alter it, you know."† He had already disappeared into the pump room and emerged about four days later, with my brand-new air-search radar. We were the only submarine in the force able to use our air-search radar.

When we came in off patrol, the force materiel officer couldn't approve an unauthorized shipalt, but said, "Okay, we'll submit it, recommending approval, and you use yours in the meantime."‡

The next patrol, the one off Nagasaki, I again went to Fred and said, "Look, here we are as close as we can get, but we're ten miles off the harbor. If I use the 8,000-yard sweep on the search radar, it won't reach the harbor. If I use the long-range sweep, the

---

* Lieutenant (junior grade) Frederick A. Oyhus, USNR.
† BuShips--Bureau of Ships.
‡ Shipalt--ship alteration.

harbor is so tiny I can't discriminate. Why can't I use my 8,000-yard sweep right over the harbor?"

"I can do that. That's easy. I'll just put a delay in the outgoing signal." Well, these are common now. But that was the first time it was actually done, and he did it while at sea on patrol. He did that in a day or so.

The third patrol, I had a new problem. By then we knew the precise location of all the Japanese air defense radar stations along the Japanese coast. I wanted a radar receiver so that I could use these signals for navigation. We had no radar receivers in the Navy then. The Japs and Germans had to get good at it, because our radars were so good. I wanted to mount it on the target bearing transmitter on the bridge and use it to sweep around and get bearings on enemy transmissions. Again, his answer was yes, with only the small disadvantage that we had to run a cable through the hatch to the bridge. In a quick dive, it could be a hazard. I soon had excellent navigation using a passive receiver of enemy air-search radar signals, just as good as lighthouses. We could also identify when antisubmarine search frequencies were used, to warn us of an unfriendly. So we now had the first air-search radar receiver aboard a U.S. submarine.

Fred couldn't stand watches and spent his days decrypting, encoding, keeping his electronics in top condition, or inventing, with the prospect of an unsat fitness report because he wasn't physically qualified for sea duty. Just don't ever take him off my ship. He came from somewhere in Nebraska. I'm trying to find him again. A true genius.

Q: How much contact did you have with your family back home during the time you were on patrol?

Captain Schratz: We had a daughter born while I was in Sterlet, our second daughter. In cases like this, if the wives sent personal news like that to ComSubPac, we soon got the word. As you know, to keep radio traffic at a constant level all the time without peaks and valleys during major operations, space was often available for personal messages. To ease the load of decoding, especially if using a strip cipher, noninvolved subs were told they need decode no further, although we usually did because we were interested too. So we were kept fairly well informed of major personal events. Except I had told two people to make sure that I got the birth announcement, and both followed through a day apart. I wasn't sure whether I had twins or just one. Before I finally got back, that child was almost two years old, and I hadn't met her yet. Our first daughter was three years old then, and I'd known her for only three months. Except for one refit, I hadn't been back as far as the International Dateline for two years. Admiral Nelson was at sea for over two years in Victory, but even he got ashore often enough to run a flagrant romance with Lady Hamilton.[*]

Q: You said mail service was poor when you were in the Wichita. How was it in the sub?

Captain Schratz: Excellent. Extraordinary efforts were made always to have mail waiting, even in case of reroutings to different ports. My wife and I serialized our letters back and forth, and she kept all of mine. During that long absence, we were both in the 300s, and the mail lost only a couple because of my sudden departure from Sterlet and two other changes to Atule. I have a contract now to write a book on my submarine experiences in World War II and Korea, and I went through those letters just recently.[†] There were 350 letters during that period, and even without anything of any vital military value, they will be very useful on the human side of submarine life.

Q: Did you impose a system of self-censorship then?

Captain Schratz: We censored all the enlisted and each other's mail. The CO and exec were franked without reading, as a privilege. It was never much of a problem. What men

---

[*] Lord Horatio Nelson was a British naval hero, killed in the Battle of Trafalgar in 1805. Emma Hamilton, whom he met while she was the wife of the British ambassador to Naples, was Nelson's mistress.
[†] The book, Submarine Commander, was published by the University of Kentucky Press in 1988. It duplicates and expands on some of the material in the oral history, but it does not cover Captain Schratz's entire career.

did know about operations, they were good about keeping to themselves. It was a rare occasion that we had to use the razor blade.

Q: How did you get from that duty into taking over the captured Japanese submarine?

Captain Schratz: When the first surrender offer came through, CinCPac ordered a submarine tender, Proteus, with Lew Parks, ComSubRon 14, embarked, to Tokyo Bay a few days before the surrender.* We got the call to take over the submarine base tucked away in the big Yokosuka Naval Base. There were three of us, the first people ashore-- Bernie McMahon, recently CO of Drum, Rob Roy McGregor, and I, with a couple of squads of enlisted.†

Each of us wanted to be the first to put his foot on the next step up from the landing, but wanted the others to test it for booby-traps first. A dark, rainy night, we were frozen from the long ride in an open motor launch, and there wasn't a soul around. We finally located a room full of submarine officers sitting around, waiting to get receipts signed for their subs, etc., so they could go home.

We spent, I don't know, a day or two ashore in Yokosuka, taking over the submarine base. It was ghastly. No food, some cold coffee soaked with sea water on the way in, and the gnats, lice, mosquitoes, and flies welcomed fresh meat. Yuck. A horrible, horrible period. I was scratching for two months after.

Q: Where did you stay?

Captain Schratz: Sleeping on a desk, sleeping on the floor, sleeping anywhere. It was one massive hunt for souvenirs--technically for intelligence material--and we were also looking for information on POW camps, for submarine POWs primarily, who were then brought in to a repatriation center.‡ I found two of my classmates, one in particular, a very good

---

* Captain Lewis S. Parks, USN.
† Commander Bernard F. McMahon, USN; Commander Rob Roy McGregor, USN.
‡ POW--prisoner of war.

friend. I flew back to Guam with several of them and sent them on the way home. Everybody else made tracks for the U.S. But the other tender in Guam, the Euryale, was sent to western Japan to dispose of suicide submarines and to assemble the surviving submarines in Sasebo awaiting action by the Allied Control Commission. Because of my Tokyo experience, I was transferred to this group as a PCO. We spent several days in Okinawa, then went to Sasebo and Kure.

Q: Who was the classmate?

Captain Schratz: Al Toulon.[*] He had been in the Grenadier and in prison camp for three or four years.[†]

Q: What kind of shape was he in?

Captain Schratz: Horrible. Almost total loss of memory, didn't recognize me, asked the same questions 50 times, starved, ate everything in sight at meals. He carried a can of dry ice cream mix and a tablespoon, and every 15 minutes he'd spoon some down. He had a prominent wound on his forehead. One of their greatest shortages was soap, and when the B-29s started dropping supplies to them in the last days of the war, he was hit in the head with a full case of soap. Oh, it was sad.

One of my good friends, also in prison, was the chief engineer in Wichita, Don Giles.[‡] He had left Wichita to go to Guam as the deputy governor just before the war broke and was captured on 10 December when Guam fell. He received much better treatment in a camp for senior officers, but was down to about 125 pounds. I have his manuscript on his

---

[*] Lieutenant Alfred J. Toulon, Jr., USN.
[†] The Grenadier (SS-210) was scuttled on 22 April 1943. A Japanese merchantman rescued eight officers and 68 enlisted men, who became prisoners of war.
[‡] Commander Donald T. Giles, USN.

experiences in prison, which he wanted me to edit and publish for him.* He died about a year ago, a real nice person, our favorite "Dutch uncle" to all the JOs.

With the Euryale flag allowance, we went to Sasebo, where I took command of His Imperial Majesty's Ship I-203, a high-speed attack submarine, just then completing sea trials. Then later I added to my command a division of ex-Japanese submarines, including the I-58, in which Captain Hashimoto had sunk the Indianapolis.† Hashimoto, shortly after, got his orders to go to Washington to testify against Captain McVay, CO of Indianapolis.‡ He was scared half to death. "What they do to me now? Put me in public square and shoot me?" He didn't want to go.

Q: Can you blame him?

Captain Schratz: I said, "Don't worry," but he gave me his A chronometer as a guarantee of safe conduct. He knew the chronometer would be somebody's souvenir, and figured he better get some mileage out of it.

Q: Did he speak English at all?

---

* Giles, who retired as a rear admiral, died 28 February 1983. Subsequently Schratz turned the manuscript over to Donald T. Giles, Jr., who had not seen it previously. The younger Giles then edited his father's work and wrote additional material to produce a book, Captive of the Rising Sun (Annapolis: Naval Institute Press, 1994).
† See Mochitsura Hashmoto, Sunk: The Story of the Japanese Submarine Fleet, 1941-1945 (New York: Avon Publishers, 1954).
‡ The Japanese submarine I-58 torpedoed the heavy cruiser Indianapolis (CA-35) on 30 July 1945 while en route from Guam to the Philippines. Because of delays in discovering the loss, rescue forces were able to save only 316 of the 1,199 men in the ship's crew. The cruiser's commanding officer, Captain Charles B. McVay III, USN, was subsequently court-martialed after his return to the United States.

Captain Schratz: Oh, yes, they all spoke some English. All the surviving Japanese submarines, about 15 to 20 of them, were then in Sasebo for disposition by the Allied Commission. Since the COs in my division all spoke some English, I got Hashimoto and six, seven others around the table to talk submarine tactics to see how Japanese doctrine compared with ours, just informal, just for my own curiosity. Naturally, I quickly learned how to run their torpedo data computer, which I found was very interesting. It had some good features in it. It worked fine.

Q: Do you recall what they had to say about tactics?

Captain Schratz: Yes. In fact, I wrote a paper on it back in those days for somebody. In general, not too much different from ours. They preferred the straight bow shot as we do, and, with far better torpedoes, much faster and much bigger warheads, they didn't have to use as many, normally. They could risk getting one hit anywhere to get a sinking. But their radar was junk, and night surface attacks, which we favored, were rare. Their sonar was superb, and I mean superb, far better than I'd ever seen. So this encouraged them toward submerged attacks also. They could make a sound attack, perhaps with no visual observation, that was simplicity itself.

At first, they couldn't recall ever having attacked a U.S. warship, never heard of that happening by a Japanese submarine. When we'd been there maybe a week, we found the charts of I-58 with the track of the Indianapolis attack. When they realized we knew and they weren't going to get shot just for having made the attack, they became much more open about warship attacks. You'll recall, they followed our prewar doctrine of using submarines as the eyes of the fleet and never did use them extensively as commerce raiders. Overall, of course, they were unsuccessful.

The most vivid memory of that era was the extreme interservice rivalry between the Japanese Army and Navy. For instance, to resupply outlying Army garrisons cut off by our carrier march across the Central Pacific, the Japanese Army asked for Navy support by submarine, some food, and maybe some ammunition. The Navy did so initially but gradually became so uncooperative that the Army decided to build its own submarines. The

Army contracted for a boiler factory in Korea to manufacture cargo submarines. They had a cargo hatch about six feet in diameter, extremely vulnerable. They looked like boilers, sailed like boilers and sank like boilers. They were death traps.

Another example of rivalry--one of the casualties of the Hiroshima A-bomb was a Japanese Army aircraft carrier fitting out at the docks at the Army base. The Navy refused to give tactical air support to the Army when the war approached the inner perimeter. So the Army built its own aircraft carrier, just fitting out when partially destroyed by the A-bomb.

One more example--I was in Kure demilitarizing midget submarines and suicide craft in those early days and met a relative of ex-premier Koiso, the head of the peace party which had gone out of office just before the war.[*] He spoke beautiful English; many of his personal staff were educated at U. Cal. Berkeley and returned to Japan in 1938. I was interested in talking with him about the future, about the war, about anything. We spent many afternoons in discussion.

One subject I recall quite vividly was the question of dropping the A-bomb on Hiroshima. He echoed the same feeling I had received in discussions with Japanese submarine officers. The Jap Army could probably not have faced surrendering under the threat of conventional weapons alone. They realized fully by then their technological shortcomings. The A-bomb allowed them to save some of their dignity in defeat by claiming they didn't lose the war; only this scientific stuff beat them.

One day while we were chatting, two of the maids came in all excited, chattering to him, apologized for the interruption and when they left, said, "I really must extend to you my very sincere apologies. My maids have been doing laundry down below for the U.S. Army enlisted men. Two of your Army men came by to pick up their laundry, and my maids didn't realize there were Navy men in the house. And so I apologize for allowing U.S. Army people under my roof while you are here." That's what I call harmful interservice rivalry.

---

[*] Retired General Kuniaki Koiso.

Q: Yes. Do you have any specific memories about Hashimoto himself?

Captain Schratz: Yes, a very nice person, highly respected by his peers. Quite senior then, he was one of the few surviving veterans.

Q: Did he seem very competent as a submariner to achieve what he did?

Captain Schratz: Yes. In the Indianapolis attack, contrary to Ned Beach's flyleaf endorsement of the book by Hashimoto, he did not use suicide torpedoes.* He had them on board, but said the attack was so simple, it was a waste of human life to use a suicide weapon. Close to midnight, he made visual sighting at 10,000 meters, Indianapolis not zigzagging and making only 15 or 16 knots. He simply took the normal approach course, closed to 1,500 meters and fired a salvo. But from the discussions with the Japanese COs, he was known as a skilled tactician.

Q: Did you get any feeling from these various submarine skippers on their views toward the use of the kaitens?

Captain Schratz: Yes, but not quite the published version.

Q: Was it something they were reluctant to do?

Captain Schratz: Late in the war, the Japanese submarines were increasingly jealous of the airmen because of all the publicity they got through the kamikaze attacks. The Japanese did not call them "suicide" attacks. They were operationally successful tactics that allowed men to die honorably for their country. They said, "We're losing as many submarines and as

---

* Captain Edward L. Beach, USN, a Naval Academy classmate of Schratz, wrote the foreword to Hashimoto's memoir. In the 1990s, through additional investigation, Captain Beach has come to the conclusion that, in fact, the I-58 did not use kaiten suicide torpedoes against the Indianapolis.

many people as the aviators, and getting no glory out of it." So they formally adopted the kamikaze insignia and set up departure rituals prior to going on patrols, dressing in white coveralls with special white headbands with a rising sun "meatball" in the center of the forehead. They invited their relatives and friends for a commemoration ceremony and big saki party in a very dramatic farewell. They were proud of the kaiten insignia on the conning tower, looking like a surrealistic chrysanthemum, and carefully painted them out at the time of the surrender. They, too, wanted to die gloriously and not simply disappear to an unknown fate.

When I took over the I-203, we called it the Sasori, Japanese for "scorpion." It was also a "so sorry" submarine. I wanted to repaint the kamikaze insignia on the periscope shears. "Oh, we can't do that. We forget how to do it." There was probably a ritual significance which made them reluctant. So it took a long time to get that insignia back up there.

Another good friend from Wichita days, Phil Berkeley, was then a Marine colonel with General "Howling Mad" Smith's Fifth Amphibious Corps in Sasebo, in charge of demilitarizing Japan.[*] Through Phil, I got all the passes, keys to the warehouses, and so forth, to look for "submarine intelligence material," translated "souvenirs." At a big New Year's Eve party at the corps headquarters to welcome in 1946, there was a midnight presentation of awards.

The general presented me the Japanese Order of the Sacred Treasure. It's a beautiful, eight-pointed, solid silver medal with a triangular ribbon, somewhat like a Medal of Honor. It fit right over a row of U.S. medals, and for several years, when large medals were called for, I wore it. When a senior pair of eyeballs would pop out and questions were about to follow, I usually turned, slipped it off quickly and dropped it into my pocket. But the citation mentioned something about "Schratz's Raiders," who left so little behind that his task of demilitarization of Japan was very simple. A really clever citation. But we were all Asiatics by then. To add a cover of legitimacy, I did need his help officially.

---

[*] Colonel James P. Berkeley, USMC; Lieutenant General Holland M. Smith, USMC.

We had had one tough time finding spares to make the submarine work to get it back to Pearl Harbor. Few people realize that these attack Guppies, designed to make 25 knots submerged, had a perfectly streamlined hull, which I thought would make a good antisubmarine target.[*] But we could never get both engines on the line at the same time from the takeover until around January of '46. The battery had 4,192 cells in it. We'd go to sea daily for training, operate for a whole week, and never have an engine in commission. We could do the whole exercise on the battery. At low speed it had unlimited battery power. Twenty-five knots, even at the one-hour rate, takes a lot of juice. However interesting the operating, we were all anxious to get home, now over two years since I'd left.

Japan was really flat, physically, economically, emotionally. When we first went ashore, no one was in the streets, no living human anywhere. I guess it was about the third day that we finally found a couple of children out, the old G.I. candy bar routine, and maybe in four days the old men would appear, maybe an old lady, and finally you'd see young women appear. They were totally convinced that it was going to be the rape of Nanking all over again.[†] "To the victor go the spoils," and they expected the worst. They couldn't believe that the American G.I. wanted little more than to take a picture and hand out a candy bar, do some sightseeing. The surrender stunned them. MacArthur's great skill in running the occupation, plus his imperial presence, were major elements in the ease with which the surrender was accomplished.[‡] The Japanese referred to him as "the blue-eyed Emperor."

Q: How devastating might those Japanese Guppy boats have been had they gotten into action?

---

[*] The term "Guppy" grew out of the initials for the postwar modification fitted to World War II fleet boats to give them greater underwater propulsion power (GUPP).
[†] Japanese troops had brutalized civilians in Nanking, China, during the Sino-Japanese War of the late 1930s.
[‡] General of the Army Douglas MacArthur, USA, commanded Allied occupation forces in Japan from 1945 to 1951.

Captain Schratz: Great if they could work out all the bugs. The engines were junk. They had a lot of other defects. In a crisis, say, against elements of the invasion fleet, they could have been a powerful force. The sonar gear was so super, on the surface with engines running, I could find ships all over the whole place. Their standards of construction seemed okay, but only a shipyard could tell. They were suffering all sorts of shortages. Vital pieces of equipment were missing, sections of voice tubes and other piping would be missing. There were no gaskets in the main engines; some head blocks were unmachined castings.

They had no fossil fuel left and were using a soybean base for the diesels. It worked just as well. We used it in our submarines with no problem. But the soybean is a vegetable, and when it collects on bulkheads or bilges, it ferments with a very rancid odor. With no gaskets, the cylinders were crunching oil all over the place with every combustion stroke. The engine room looked like a yard of a goat and smelled worse. When our people first took over those big I-400-class plane-carrying submarines, there was a standing offer of five bucks for anybody who could walk down the forward torpedo room hatch, all the way through the boat and up the after torpedo room hatch. There were no takers.

Q: Just the odor?

Captain Schratz: Everything. Rats, great big rats and little rats, rancid cooking stench, primitive head facilities, worse for showers if you couldn't get topside. No first aid. I asked what they'd do to care for routine cuts and wounds. They said, "We urinate on them."

I couldn't wait to report this gem to the squadron medical officer that night. He said, "Well, young man, if you will take a look some time at the average antiseptic, you will find that about 90% have crystals of urea in them somewhere. It's an ancient technique." But hardly socially redeemable under the circumstances.

Q: Was there liberty in Japan for Americans?

Captain Schratz: Oh, yes. We had few limitations, except a curfew. Ed Spruance, commanding one of the big submarines, and I made a couple of liberties together, using his barge to get us ashore from the tender to check out the geisha houses for some music and entertainment.*

Q: What do you recall of him?

Captain Schratz: Ed was a wild man. I think he spent his life trying to shock his father by being everything which his father was not, unfortunately. He had lots of ability and, I suspect, was a fine submariner.

Q: He was overshadowed by having that famous a father.

Captain Schratz: Unfortunately, yes. And I think something of the same happened to Chester Nimitz, Jr.†

Spruance had commandeered the admiral's barge for his submarine gig, and so we were using that as a gig to get around the harbor without depending on the tenders. We went ashore one night near the air station at Sasebo, to go to a geisha house up in the boonies about ten miles or so. He had a very Italian Jeep driver to take us there in style. We were sitting around that place, sipping our saki and enjoying the entertainment late one night when Ed had to make an urgent call of nature. He stepped out the rear door of this place and accidentally stepped right into one of those big honey pots full of "night soil," and he sank up to his chest. When he came back in, he stank so bad even the Japs couldn't stand him. It was offal.

Q: Offal?

Captain Schratz: Right. That spoiled the party; nobody wanted to dance with him. We went out to the Jeep and got back to the landing about 7:00 o'clock in the morning.

---

* Commander Edward D. Spruance, USN, was the son of Admiral Raymond A. Spruance, USN, Commander Fifth Fleet.
† Commander Chester W. Nimitz, Jr., USN, was a submarine skipper during World War II.

Meanwhile, the tide had gone out, leaving the barge high and dry. We commandeered a rowboat and rowed our way back out. Ed had dropped all his clothes off except his 'Lil Abners and skivvies. We arrived at the tender and walked up the gangway just at the stroke of morning quarters, and you could smell Ed halfway to Chefoo. He went in his cabin. He was living with Joe McDowell, and he took off his 'Lil Abners as he climbed into the shower.* When Joe woke up about an hour later, why, the stench was all over the room. Joe couldn't stand it.

Q: This was the tender Euryale?

Captain Schratz: Yes.

Q: So she just stayed out there to support you and the Japanese boats?

Captain Schratz: Yes. We had serious materiel problems getting those subs ready for sea. I sent my engineer officer all over Japan to try to get spare engine parts and battery cells. We needed lots and lots of battery cells.

I sent my engineer, a solid mustang, to Maizuru on the Inland Sea.† He commandeered one of these little old four-wheeled passenger coaches and two four-wheeled flat cars and "hitchhiked" his way on local trains, telling the Japanese where to drop off his fleet. It was a question whether they'd starve or freeze to death first. They didn't have enough food and were freezing to death. This was December, and they couldn't scrounge firewood in Japan. In desperation, they cannibalized their passenger car to keep a fire going on the metal strip which ran down the center of the car. He found the batteries, but by the time they got back to Sasebo, he had burned one of the flat cars and the coach,

---

* Commander Joseph M. McDowell, USN, was commanding officer of the prize crew of the former Japanese submarine I-400.
† "Mustang" is Navy slang for a former enlisted man who has risen through the ranks to become an officer.

leaving little but the wheels and the metal strip down the center. Miserable, dirty, starving, racked with insect bites, that's how we got Sasori ready for sea.

Q: Did you disarm any of their submarine ordnance, take possession of it, or what?

Captain Schratz: Yes. This was our primary task initially, while in the Tokyo Bay area at the time of the surrender, and later in Kure and Shimonoseki. Many of the two-man types were human torpedoes, with a large warhead in the bow. They had been hauled out of the water under terms of the surrender, but they could be put back in again, and for our own security, they had to be disarmed. My team in Yokosuka consisted of a demolition expert and an interpreter. But the subs were so small, only one of us could get forward at a time. I had to take the lead to find which were submarine fittings and which were warhead equipment, then make the first attempt at defusing it.

You can let your imagination fill in the blanks. A 200-pound man in a 100-pound space, the sub lying partially on its side, only weak flashlight illumination, the few identifying labels in Japanese, the equipment totally foreign and stinking. Was it booby-trapped? After a few agonizing mistakes, we found that the Japs had removed the detonators, perhaps for their own safety. The submariners inherited that task in many parts of Japan. At least it created the opportunity for some excellent sightseeing.

One such task got me in trouble again in Kure. In the Kure naval base, there's an island in the middle of the harbor used as a base for the six-man kaitens. About 130 of them had been destroyed in the Kure dry dock, but on this little island, there were about 16 in a warehouse. My guidance on demilitarizing them was to use a cutting torch to cut through the pressure hull at a frame. This seemed very inadequate. They could weld them up about as fast as we could cut them and all systems were "go."[*]

We had expert demolition specialists flown out from the States, and two were with me at the time. They thought this was a poor way to use their talents and suggested using a

---

[*] For a differing opinion, see the Naval Institute oral history of Rear Admiral Norvell G. Ward, USN (Ret.), who was also disarming Japanese submarines during this period. His recollections contain a comment on Schratz's methods.

controlled explosion with shaped charges in the control room. They went to an Army depot and "borrowed" a big motor launch full of explosives. We did a test run on one sub, and it was just beautiful. The hull was puffed out but not ruptured and the inside was a shambles. I suggested wiring 14 of them to go off at 30-second intervals and clean up the problem in no time. The remaining hull in the center of the warehouse had been marked to save for analysis by the Pacific Joint Intelligence Center--JICPOA. What I didn't realize was that our demolition experts were disappointed at the first blast--no fire and brimstone. Without telling me, they put two charges in the control room instead of one and added additional charges in the fore and aft compartments.

The first sub went off like a clap of thunder, clearly heard in my commodore's cabin on <u>Euryale</u> four, five miles away. These subs still had all the fuel and equipment aboard. The blast blew burning fuel oil all over that building. When the others went off at half a minute intervals, it was an inferno. An oily black smoke cloud rose, which was so bad the U.S. seaplane on the regular afternoon mail trip had to divert. The commodore took one look and blew his stack--white smoke, probably.

Admiral Halsey had put out an order forbidding any incidents of pillage, looting, etc.[*] Anyone involved in an "incident" would be presumed guilty. The commodore could see his whole career going up in smoke, and he took off in the barge. In the meantime, Japanese officials came out of the woodwork, asking who was going to pay for it. Most of the island was in flames, and I had to get them off my back before the commodore arrived. I wrote out, on a stray piece of cardboard, a receipt for 15 submarines, two warehouses, two barracks buildings, one fire engine house, one pumping station, and signed it Charles A. Lockwood, Vice Admiral, U.S. Navy, Commander Submarine Force. Then we rushed them out of there as fast as we could. They were barely out of sight in one direction when the commodore came storming in from the other. He asked me the same question about who's going to pay for it, only he knew the answer. Shaking a bony finger at me, he said, "You stay here until every ember is out."

---

[*] Admiral William F. Halsey, Jr., USN, Commander Third Fleet.

Q: Who was he?

Captain Schratz: Captain Stanley P. Moseley, another fine submariner but a little tense. I spent several days there. Some of my people sent in some food now and then to keep me alive. That thing burned and burned. With no fire engines, thanks to my experts, these submarine hulls, fed by fuel, the battery jars and other combustibles, turned cherry red, igniting the steel framing in the warehouse. I couldn't believe it. It left little but a pile of slag. And the "Save for JICPOA" sub was right in the center.

Q: Those explosive guys had their jollies.

Captain Schratz: Oh, they loved it. They _loved_ it.

Q: What about the torpedoes? What did you do with those?

Captain Schratz: There were none on these subs. The Japs kept them in nearby caves-- water dripping all over them. What seemed more precious to a Jap is his fishing industry. In the best of their air-conditioned, waterproofed caves they stored glass fishing floats, impervious to the weather; in some leaking like a sieve, they stored torpedoes and electronic gear. Everybody wanted to get a souvenir torpedo to mount outside headquarters buildings.

I was in the doghouse for a couple of weeks and missed the big trip to the Japanese Naval Academy at Eta Jima. We also did some business in Shimonoseki to see what could be done about U.S.-laid mine fields all through the area. The B-29s had mined Inland Sea areas quite heavily in the last stages of the war. Their instructions were to set them to sterilize in six months, but my hotshot young B-29 buddies claimed they weren't going to risk getting their tail feathers shot away for something that's going to fizzle out in six months. So they managed to set them on the maximum, 12 years, and as a result, closed the Inland Sea for almost all navigation until the late 1950s. They were excellent mines, almost impossible to sweep. A lot of mine-damaged shipping had grounded all around the bay.

Q: How long did it take before the Japanese populace at large began to go back to its normal way of doing business?

Captain Schratz: I would guess about 48 hours, maybe 24. The response to the Americans was really quite incredible.

Q: Had you expected there would be some treachery on their part?

Captain Schratz: We were very suspicious at first. Many hot-heads, particularly in the Army, refused to recognize the surrender, and we anticipated trouble. The occupation could have been tough. If we had ever made that landing, the Olympic and Coronet operations, it would have been God-awful.* Half the Japanese seemed to be living underground in caves. Having seen how they had to be rooted out in Saipan, Iwo, and Okinawa, it could have been terrible. The only incident we experienced was in Sasebo on December 7 when a radical group staged some demonstrations, but nobody was hurt.

Q: On the torpedoes, did you have any procedure for destroying them?

Captain Schratz: No, that was somebody else's responsibility. Their torpedoes were so good that everybody wanted them for study and analysis. They had a torpedo they could fire from Kyushu all the way to Okinawa. They tied three, four, five, six fuel compartments together to make a "torpedo" 150 feet long, put a cockpit in the middle to guide it, and it would go anywhere. They were ships but very, very dangerous, potentially.

Q: Are there any memories you have from that journey from Japan to Hawaii in that submarine?

---

* Olympic was the code name for the U.S. invasion of the island of Kyushu, scheduled for 1 November 1945. It was to be followed by Coronet, the invasion of Honshu, in March 1946.

Captain Schratz: Yes. I read the manuscript by Tom Paine on the I-400, which I believe you are considering for publication, and the relative luxury when he came back.* Well, that bore no relation to our story. The Japanese skipper in my ship was about 5 feet, 5 inches, and his bunk was 5 feet, 6 inches. I had to take out his ancient mattress and throw it over the side, which was maybe eight inches thick, then try to fit a U.S. Navy mattress in there. I took the door off a locker at the head of my bunk and slept with my head in the locker. The first time I dozed off, the rats came out of the paneling and started playing in my hair, and I almost lost my teeth when I tried to sit up in bed. One food treasure we preserved to save our lives was candy bars, and the rats loved them, even though they had never tasted chocolates before.

Q: The rats or the Japanese?

Captain Schratz: The rats. Both of them. In our training, we operated from September through January in and out of Sasebo. Allen B. "Buck" Catlin, '42, my exec, was very sharp. I suggested that he specialize in the spoken language, so he could work with the "press gang," and I would concentrate on how to operate the gear, translating nameplates and the like. We worked very well together. We took a half-hour of instruction of Japanese, and a week later, Buck was talking to these guys like a Toyko teenager. We got rid of the last Japanese crews in maybe a couple of weeks, a very short period, and we were operating on our own. We never dived it; that was forbidden, which I think was a fair precaution.

For the trip to Pearl, we had a fleet tug plus Euryale. The deck was rounded, with absolutely no projections to violate the streamlining. The radio antenna folded into the deck; even the gun disappeared from sight. On diving, the bridge personnel fitted fairing pieces into the lookout positions. This was great for underwater speed, but hell if one had

---

* Lieutenant Thomas O. Paine, USNR (Ret.), "I was a Yank on a Japanese Submarine," U.S. Naval Institute Proceedings, September 1986, pages 72-78. From 1976 to 1982 Paine served as president of the Northrop Corporation.

to go on deck at sea. To pass a towline at sea would have been perilous without a special rig, so prior to departure Euryale rigged a towing cable on deck which could be cut free quite easily. The first night out, a good storm came up and that round-bottomed bucket rolled all over the place.

Sasori also had fixed stabilizer fins about three feet below the waterline, extending out 17 feet from the hull. These "wings" made berthing very tough, and in a storm at sea, slamming into the sea, we didn't think they'd last if we couldn't dive. The battery cells, all 4,192, were a particular hazard. The jars weren't laminated, just single plastic pressings, and not well-secured to the hull. Rigged in stacks of eight, as soon as the ship started working in a sea, the stacks started to sway and many of the jars cracked, dumping sulphuric acid electrolyte into the bilge. Soon we had about 100 gallons of acid sloshing around. We could jump the damaged cells but had nowhere near enough caustic to neutralize all the acid spill. The engine rooms offered other problems. No strainers were installed in any of the engine room sumps, so the black gang had to clean them by hand once a watch. The bilges would fill over the deck plates, given half a chance, so the offgoing watch had to pearl dive every watch. And this fuel, remember, was vegetable oil which got exceedingly rancid when it fermented.

That first storm brought other problems. We had used so much caustic to purify the fresh water tanks that the shaking up in the storm made the water taste like lye. It was undrinkable. The only hot water for washing or shaving came from a big old five-gallon coffee urn we had installed. If you wanted to shave, you shaved with coffee and looked like a coffee parfait. If you wanted to bathe, you washed down with ship's water but an ordinary washup was with coffee.

The second day out, the main refrigerator failed beyond ship's force repair. We had squirreled away lots of frozen strawberries and real goodies to last the cruise. The wardroom steward was ordered to load up the wardroom refrigerator with delicacies from aft before they went bad. The following day, the gasket in the wardroom refrigerator failed, with a stinking ooze dripping on the deck. That's how we discovered that the main part of those delicacies he had saved for us was fish. Meanwhile, the troops polished off everything they could.

If you have gathered by now that it was a miserable trip, you're right. Fighting to keep at least one engine on the line, we spent 1,500 miles on a towline and did everything else at maximum speed, averaging about six knots overall. In our tiny cribs, sleep was fitful, standing up not much better. To keep the morale up, I took advantage of a hot shot young communications officer. Jack Ahearn and I, in deepest secrecy, decided to try something to take people's minds off their problems.[*] At that time, Charlie Chaplin was involved in a Hollywood scandal in court over some gal.[†]

Q: A paternity suit.

Captain Schratz: Yes. So we just twisted the story around a bit. We said it was Shirley Temple who was involved, then began putting out a ship's paper.[‡] I couldn't believe the way these guys went absolutely ape over any stigma involving Shirley Temple. Their same age group, she was a lifelong idol and to involve her in a scandal got them boiling, steaming, yelling mad. So after the first issue of this paper, we had a real tiger on our hands. So we made exactly three copies and we checked them very carefully to get them all back again, for protection just in case. Soon we had to put out special editions and bulletins. The idea worked; terrible living conditions were forgotten or overlooked. But then we arrived for the first stop, in Eniwetok. Our men swarmed all over the tender looking for the latest on Shirley Temple. The tender hadn't heard anything, of course, but got just as upset trying to find the whole story, exaggerating the details further in the retelling. Our men came back with fresh new tales.

Jack sought me out, asking plaintively what in the devil could we do now to get out of the mess. Well, we still needed the trickery, so I was forced to wait until one day out of Pearl Harbor, and decided it was time for a confession. I told the troops that they'd been had. "For what I thought were very good reasons, we dreamed up the Shirley Temple story, every bit of it, and it just isn't true. It's total bull. But now I've got to ask you to

---

[*] Lieutenant John A. Ahearn, USNR.
[†] Charlie Chaplin had been a star comedian during the silent film era early in the century.
[‡] Shirley Temple was a child movie star in the 1930s.

cover for me. You may want to kill me later, but put yourself in my position. Something had to be done to get your minds off our serious day-to-day problems. I had no idea she was the goddess of your generation. But think. Now she's just as pure as you always believed." Well, it all came out just fine.

For the great day of arrival in Pearl Harbor, we had planned some real showmanship. Buck Catlin and I decided on an all-Japanese landing. The Japanese Navy used a little bugle decorated with dangling red tassels, and a small two-foot range finder to assist in making a landing. We schooled the line handlers in three or four basic commands so we could do everything in Japanese. Alas! It was such a smooth landing, nobody even noticed. We were terribly disappointed.

It was now February '46. I had left the East Coast just after Christmas 1943. No decision had been made on disposition of the Japanese fleet remnants, nor on what to do with Sasori. Of transcendental importance, one thing I couldn't do was to sit around waiting. I was on the point of writing that famous letter to the bureau: "I request that I be transferred to any ship or station. My reason for making this request is that I think I would like that kind of duty." But in the nick of time, orders came through, and I went to shore duty in the Bureau of Naval Personnel.

Q: That's quite a contrast. Had you put in for that specifically?

Captain Schratz: No, I didn't. One didn't ask for preferences then. He went where sent and when. My only preference was to get home.

Q: So that this was the first extended period you'd had with your wife since you were married, really.

Captain Schratz: Yes. And that's a long separation, with two years of it beyond the International Dateline.

Q: Where did you wind up living then when you served in BuPers?

Captain Schratz: Arlington, Virginia. Also at that time my Naval Academy class started monthly luncheons almost the day I arrived in Washington. They decided I should start writing a column for Shipmate. I just now entered my 40th year, which will be the last. But Wes Hammond still thinks I am not serious about quitting.*

Q: You were in the officer performance section, I believe. What did that entail?

Captain Schratz: I was in the retirement section of officer performance, working with officer retirements and those very basic problems of physical disability. There was a backlog of close to 1,000 officers lying around hospitals or on leave somewhere waiting for retirement, waiting for a survey board, waiting for their attorneys or congressmen to pull strings. They were all on full pay and allowances until their cases were disposed of. My billet called for a law specialist. I relieved two reserve officer lawyers, both of whom then set up shop in Washington, specializing in appealing the cases of people they had turned down while in BuPers. A lot of money was involved in each case. Some--very few--mistakes had been made. The laws were a hodgepodge of Civil War relics. This is part of the price of an all-or-nothing retirement system, with no possibility for a percentage of pay based on degree of disability.

The Reserve Officers' Association, the Fleet Reserve, and a lot of lawyers and members of Congress were trying to influence or change government decisions. A handful of shyster lawyers around town really made things tough. Knowing nothing about law--no training, not even a good briefing--I was lost. I'd take one case home every night and try to make rhyme or reason out of it, find out its merits, the governing statutes, and where justice really entered. The JAG was looking over one shoulder and the Comptroller General over the other.†

---

* Colonel James Wesley Hammond, Jr., USMC (Ret.), was then the editor of the Naval Academy Alumni Association's Shipmate magazine.
† JAG--Judge Advocate General, the Navy's top legal officer.

It took about a month to find out half of the answers, in which I was able to draft a recommendation for SecNav or the President's action.* In another month I produced about 45, 50 standard paragraphs, from which I needed fill in only a few dates or numbers for the secretaries to draft the final recommendation letter for the President's signature. If we wrote the wrong letter or used the wrong law, the presidential signature made it final, and only a special act of Congress could undo the damage. The pressure is terrible when you're so unsure. It probably took six months before I felt comfortable. Then I could put a piece of paper the size of a calling card on top of each one of those thick files, itemizing about eight to ten paragraphs which could be turned over to a battery of secretaries to type out the retirement letters. I could go through 100 in a day. And the more the pressure of outside interests for special treatment, the more a shyster I'd become.

Q: Let's have a few examples of what these cases were and how you had to wade through them.

Captain Schratz: Well, one of the flagrant pieces of stupidity was that tombstone promotion law and its interpretation during the war.† That was put in the books back in 1925, because the Army had a battlefield promotion law from World War I days. For heroism in the field, they were advanced one grade. When the tough years of cutback, no promotions, and forced retirements came in the 1920s, most of the Army officers with battlefield promotions were one rank senior to their Navy peers who were getting forced out for non-selection. It wasn't fair in many ways. The Army still had no promotion by selection, only by longevity. If you lived long enough, you became a general. Navy officers were justly angry because their classmates with identical careers were almost all one rank senior. The law passed in 1925 specified that naval officers retired for non-selection and

---

* SecNav--Secretary of the Navy.
† In the years after World War II, naval officers who had received combat decorations received a one-grade honorary promotion widely referred to as a "tombstone promotion." Although the individual still received the retired pay of his actual rank, he was authorized to assume the title of the higher grade. The practice ended in 1959.

specially commended for performance of duty in combat would be advanced one grade on the retired list. The law was passed simply to equalize the two services.

Well, by the end of World War II, the Army and Air Forces still had battlefield promotions, but the legislators forgot about injustice to the Navy. Then in 1946, just before I arrived in BuPers, Congress granted the additional benefit on retirement of the highest temporary rank under wartime legislation. This created three major problems for BuPers. First, the JAG erred seriously in allowing the tombstone promotion to be added to the temporary wartime grade. The JAG said, in effect, that, "If an officer retires as a temporary rear admiral but a permanent commander, then he can pile a tombstone promotion on top of rear admiral and go out as a vice." That was well-intended but dead wrong from the beginning.

I had two powerful supporters, one a very sharp lady in the Bureau of Supplies and Accounts, a liaison who worked with my section. The other was Charlie Moses, my boss.* The lady was a fearsome personage, a yeomanette in World War I, who had stayed in government. She knew every law by its first name and either loved you or hated you. She saved my ashcan countless times. Where the JAG screwed up, we would choose a fairly airtight test case and submit it to the Comptroller General. If we advance an officer to this rank, will the CompGen approve retirement pay? And the Comptroller General invariably sided with us.

The second major problem had to do with mustang officers. Many fleet reservists, prior to World War II, were serving in federal jobs as prison wardens, government agents, postal clerks, and the like. When ordered to active duty in the war, virtually all earned temporary promotions to officer status. Most were released to inactive duty commencing about 1944, reverted to their enlisted status, returned to their Civil Service jobs and hoped to earn a full retirement eventually from both the military and Civil Service. The two pensions would give them enough to live on.

But to them, the 1946 law granting temporary ranks and pay on the retired list was a cruel hoax. First, it made them retired <u>officers</u> and hence subject to dual compensation

---

* Captain Charles W. Moses, USN.

laws.* Second, it was retroactive to the date of their release from active duty. All their Civil Service employment after release suddenly became "illegal," and all pay for that employment was therefore subject to forfeiture. Since they had these enormous checkages against their accounts, their retired pay was withheld; hence they lost their total income. It is hard to imagine the heartache and panic this caused among many of our most loyal retired people, hard even to believe that "the system" could be so cruel. With a stroke of the pen they lost their jobs, their total income, and their retired pay. I talked with many who came to Washington to protest, promising that the department would do everything it could to get emergency legislation enacted. Yet despite the clearest evidence of major misfortune, I must confess that I did not think our Navy leadership was as energetic as it should have been in pushing amendatory legislation through.

Q: Can you suggest any reasons?

Captain Schratz: Yes. People don't like to go public asking for Congress to correct their mistakes. The two offices primarily involved were the JAG and the Fleet Reserve Affairs Office in BuPers, and hence BuPers himself. Even though it was a case of pure oversight, it should never have happened.

The third major problem arose in trying to give reserve officers the benefit of the tombstone promotion. Again, under procedures directed by JAG, we got into hot water. The law stated that an officer is to be <u>advanced</u> on the retired list to the highest temporary grade, hence he must be at that permanent grade in order to be advanced. Therefore we terminated all temporary assignments the day before retirement, reverting the officer to his permanent grade that day so he could be "advanced" on the retired list.

That worked okay for regulars, but it didn't work for reserves, whose laws were different. It surely seemed to them like a device by the bureau deliberately to screw the

---

* Laws against "double-dipping" were designed to prevent retired regular officers of the armed services from collecting U.S. Civil Service wages on top of their retirement pay. The pension would be reduced by the amount of the civilian pay. The provision did not apply to retired enlisted personnel.

reserve officers out of benefits which they appeared to have earned. So I did some research and finally found my gimmick. Under the Uniform Retirement Date Act of 1 March 1933, all retirements must be effective on the first day of the month, but rank and pay are determined as of the date of approval of the retirement by the President, generally a few days prior. This gave the leverage needed. I drafted a request to the JAG that under the 1933 law we had no authority to change rank and pay status by administrative action in the few days after approval of the retirement and before the first day of the following month. By this device we saved the benefit for the reserve officers, and saved the rank but not always the pay for the regular. The JAG could still approve promotion under both the temporary and permanent legislation, but the CompGen would authorize payment on either one or the other law, whichever was more advantageous.

Then there were always the hot political cases to keep life interesting--Admiral Richard E. Byrd trying to get his retirement pay above lieutenant commander, and I lost that.[*] There was a James K. Vardaman, Truman's naval aide, good old Missouri folk.[†] He created minimal admiration in our office.

Q: In what sense?

Captain Schratz: Well, he wanted to get a combat advancement too. He had been in Sicily, and he conned the skipper of a cruiser in the Med to recommend him for a commendation for an adventure while ashore sightseeing. Then he tried to pyramid his benefits by proving a highly questionable arthritis disability was the result of the combat, so that his entire retired pay would be tax exempt. There were statements in his record that when it happened, he was nowhere near combat, nor could the incident have disabled him in any way.

He simply couldn't support his case. He was then in Bethesda trying to steer a physical retirement, primarily for arthritis, which is particularly tough to incur in combat, or

---

[*] Rear Admiral Richard E. Byrd, USN (Ret.), famous for his exploration of Antarctica.
[†] Commodore James K. Vardaman, Jr., USNR, served as naval aide to the President in 1945-1946.

at least to prove. He stated publicly he would draw no pay while there was any doubt as to his status. Drew Pearson published something about him having drawn no pay for about a year, whereupon, the day following, he conned some poor little lady paymaster to shell out everything he had on the books, 10,000 bucks or so.* It was such a conniving thing, it made everybody look bad, so we went to great lengths to prevent that sort of miscarriage, despite pressure from the White House.

Q: What about the Byrd case?

Captain Schratz: Well, Byrd was retired for physical disability in 1916 in the grade of ensign. He was promoted to lieutenant commander on the retired list by a special act of Congress sometime in the '20s, likewise rear admiral in the '30s. But the special acts of Congress overlooked his pay status. When he re-retired as a rear admiral, he ruefully discovered he was still a lieutenant commander as far as retired pay was concerned. His brother, the senator, introduced a piece of legislation to correct this terrible injustice.† It had to be in general terms, however, and the gimmick they used was that any officer who served for a year on active duty as a rear admiral after retirement shall be entitled to upper-half retired pay.‡ In the normal case, a rear admiral made upper half in about a year, but a retired officer couldn't improve his pay status no matter how long he was active thereupon. The bill, therefore, seemed to be serving a plausible equity.

When it came to us for comment, I ran an IBM list of all persons who would be involved. There were only about half a dozen, and the top name on the list was Richard E. Byrd. It then became clear that he was trying to go from a lieutenant commander's pay to upper half pay, and this didn't look like a very good thing to me. It also made possible that any tombstone rear admirals who had retired as captains and came back on active duty as

---

* Andrew Pearson was a muckraking syndicated newspaper columnist, the predecessor of Jack Anderson.
† Senator Harry F. Byrd (Democrat-Virginia).
‡ For pay purposes, the rank of rear admiral is divided into two grades, lower half (grade O-7) and upper half (O-8).

rear admirals would also qualify for upper-half pay. So we recommended against it but lost that one for lack of political influence.

I asked for a law PG at the end of my tour in BuPers.* I loved that job and knew I had quite a knack for the law. A lot of people made flattering predictions that I would be a sure shot for the JAG in about 15 years. My submarine folks, however, suggested that coming off shore duty tour and asking for another shore duty tour tends to foul up one's image. After much thought, I finally withdrew my request.

Q: Any other cases that were particularly interesting from that period?

Captain Schratz: Yes, many. One of the young officers in Scorpion was Lieutenant Bob Brown, son of Congressman Paul Brown of Georgia, a longtime friend of the Navy in Congress.† He had looked forward all of his life to having Bob take over his seat in Congress. When Bob was lost in Scorpion, I sent him a letter and offered, when I got back to Washington, to help him in any way I could in cases involving the Navy Department.

As it happened, the major case I handled was that of an enlisted man, temporary officer, who was on the point of death in a naval hospital in Georgia on the day of his scheduled release to inactive duty on the retired list. The medical officer in command of the hospital should have canceled his orders and continued him on active duty, under treatment. But the doctor thought he got hospitalization either way and processed him for release to inactive duty. Actually, it made a great difference financially if he died on active duty, then far more than now. He died two days after.

This case happened to be in Congressman Brown's own district, and everybody who handled it screwed it up. The American Legion got into it, the veterans' groups in Georgia, congressmen, and others. Brown wrote me for help, little knowing it was to be my own responsibility. When it got to my desk, it looked like there was nothing we could do about it, having been executed in good faith by his commanding officer. I prepared the case for

---

* PG--postgraduate education.
† Lieutenant (junior grade) Robert T. Brown, USNR, was the son of Paul Brown (Democrat-Georgia), who served in the U.S. House of Representatives from 1933 to 1961.

submission to the Secretary of the Navy's Board for the Correction of Naval Records, just then being set up. Congressman Brown then asked if I would represent the widow when the case was heard. Well, having prepared the Navy's case, it was a clear conflict of interest for me to represent the widow in the appeal.

I thought everybody understood that we were seeking justice, trying to reach the best verdict possible. I prepared the best case I could on the basis that the lieutenant, at the point of death, had never seen orders to release him from active duty; there was no evidence in this record that he accepted the orders, that he might have requested his release be delayed to continue treatment.

The day I went to the Secretary's hearing, I pulled his jacket out to refresh my memory, and I can still see the first piece of paper which opened before me, "To: Lieutenant (j.g.) Cosby Homer Dawson, U.S. Navy; Subject: Release from active duty. I hereby acknowledge my orders releasing me from all active duty in the Navy. Signed, Cosby Homer Dawson." The paper had been misfiled and made its way back to the proper jacket, perhaps a year after the event. I stared at that thing for a long time, then made my decision. I pulled that page out and ate it. (It was only an onion skin flimsy, but it didn't taste like a hamburger.) I ate it right there at my desk, then went over and perjured myself, testifying before the Secretary that there was no evidence of Dawson's release. On the spot the Secretary found in his favor and restored all due allowances to his widow. Well, complicating the case, the widow was young, a very attractive Georgia peach, a honey blonde, and very appreciative.

Q: As well she should have been.

Captain Schratz: I was just then being detached to return to Portsmouth for command of the Pickerel. This was my last official act. When I arrived in New London en route to Pickerel, a shipment was waiting in the railroad station. This was back when we used trains. Unfortunately, it had been there for weeks while I was on leave. She had sent me a bushel of gorgeous Georgia peaches, and lying out there in the August sun, every one was rotten all the way through. I took one look at it and muttered to myself, "You deserve that, you lying, perjuring bastard. You don't deserve any better." Well, I thought justice was served all around. I had no pangs of conscience about it whatsoever.

Q: How much involvement did you have with Congress during that tour of duty?

Captain Schratz: Not too much beyond routine draft of replies to scores of inquiries. One memorable incident involved an investigation of retirements, primarily the case of an Air Force general. Secretary of Defense Forrestal, who had just set up his office, called me directly to prepare his opening statement for the congressional hearing.[*] In my draft, I tried to point out the great difficulty the department had in administering retirement laws.

The existing system had been set up in 1861 for the sole purpose of improving the readiness of the Union forces along the North-South fracture line. President Lincoln wanted to bring in more vigorous officers, and at that time, there was no way to take care of an officer who had "grown old and tired" in the service, other than by discharging him. If his state had a pension plan, he could benefit, but there was no federal plan. So it was the humanitarian thing to do to keep these people on active duty long after they had outlived their usefulness.

There were 12 officers involved, one of whom, I said in my speech draft, was General Winfield Scott, hero of the Mexican War, then in command at Fort Sumter. Congress passed a law to take care of these 12, "incapacitated through long and faithful service," who were to be "retired with retired pay." On the basis of that law, with only one amendment in 1938, to entitle reserves to the same benefits as regulars, the services administered disability retirements for 12 million men in uniform in World War II. Few incapacities came from "long and faithful service." Many disabilities were situational to be relieved merely by changing the situation--sending them home.

Well, when Forrestal gave the presentation to Congress, it was very impressive. I went back to my office feeling quite smug. Unfortunately, putting my feet on the desk, I happened to kick over a file on which I had been working, baring to view a statement that

---

[*] James V. Forrestal served as Secretary of Defense from 17 September 1947 to 27 March 1949.

General Winfield Scott had been nowhere near Sumter; he was actually the commanding general of the Army in Washington. I was horrified. It being long past quitting time, I figured I'd try a martini and think about it at home. I finally decided that the Army, due to testify the following day, would certainly correct the record. Well, the Army did. They picked up the Winfield Scott statement only to elaborate further on the difficulty in administration generated by these ancient laws. Now I was doubly concerned. At home I had two martinis, but I still couldn't see the answer. Finally I relaxed. I muttered, "If the Navy comes through tomorrow and says the same thing, I don't care what the facts are. Three times in the Congressional Record establishes its own veracity." The Navy did, and now it's a fact. Such is the life of a speechwriter.

Q: You mentioned many of these men who were shyster lawyers that would represent people. What sorts of things were they trying to achieve on their clients' behalf?

Captain Schratz: First, retirement pay where it was doubtful or undeserved. Second, keep their wartime temporary officer clients on active duty in a hospital or home on leave for unspecified lengths of time and take half the active duty pay for that period as compensation. One favorite technique took advantage of the backlog in the bureau. An officer discharged from Bethesda would be advised by counsel to check in at Fort Worth or somewhere--south in the winter, north in the summer--and start over again with the same symptoms. By the time the system caught up to him again, he may have had four more months of active duty.

To counter this type, we put the word out through the department that nobody could touch these cases without clearing it with our office in BuPers. If one of our malingerers asked for leave, for travel outside the country, for reimbursement for a move--anything--we soon found out. If he took leave in a certain area, we alerted the nearest hospital to advise us if he requested admission. If he did so, we immediately ordered him brought before a board and if fit for release, he was processed immediately, or possibly held in outpatient status until the last day of leave, and released to inactive duty. It simply took an organization closely coordinated in BuMed, BuSandA, JAG, and BuPers, to catch up with them, and some of the testimony and statements by counsel were pretty sleazy.*

Q: Were there some cases, though, that legitimately deserved consideration?

Captain Schratz: Definitely, but they didn't make the headlines. An officer rarely used a lawyer if he had a good case. "The system" didn't require an attorney. The Navy was quite humane about it, even bending a terribly complex structure of laws to fit. We believed the laws were to take care of the individual.

Q: What was the balance between people discharged for physical symptoms as opposed to mental, emotional, psychological problems?

Captain Schratz: Senior officers were generally circulatory system. Junior officers, more often mental, and frequently situational. Take a man off the farm, put him on a destroyer in combat, it may be too stressful. Return him to the farm, he'll have no problem.

Q: So the situational ones would get a much smaller percentage of disability?

Captain Schratz: In those days there were no percentages. All or nothing.

Q: I see.

Captain Schratz: Retire them or not retire them. Of course, whether or not retired, they could still go to the VA and get a percentage based on disability.† The amendment to the law in 1938 gave reserve officers the same "retirement pay" as regulars. The Navy took that to mean retirement as well--PX, commissaries, hospitals--all coming out of the regular Navy budget. The Army didn't do that. They took the literal interpretation that retirement

---

* BuSandA--Bureau of Supplies and Accounts.
† VA--Veterans Administration.

pay doesn't mean retirement. If the reserves were found to be disabled, they merely certified them to the VA for retirement pay, and it didn't come out of the Army budget. So we were really in a tough spot at the time.

Q: Did you in that office have any concern or input to the new promotion legislation that was going in around that period?

Captain Schratz: Very minor. We prepared some statistical data. For instance, the percentages of officers who'd break down physically or mentally, or retire voluntarily for any reason--all those percentages are fairly fixed over long periods of time. Unless you took those data into account in planning selection mortality, you might end up with gross disparity against certain Naval Academy classes. That happened to my class. The accelerated wartime promotions hadn't taken us quite as far as we were supposed to go, and the classes of '37 and '38 held on to their wartime gains. Hence, they had very low mortality from ensign through captain, somewhere around 10%. If an officer kept his nose clean and didn't retire for some other reason, or die, only 10% would fail to go before a board for selection for flag rank. In our class, we had about a 60% mortality from commander to captain alone, and we did very poorly in selection for flag rank.

Q: Why so much disparity in such a short span?

Captain Schratz: Primarily for the failure of BuPers in orderly career planning. I was elected class president just before my class came up for captain. I had known this inequity from my time in the bureau, yet I couldn't see clearly what my obligation was to my class. Then stationed in Norfolk, I flew to Washington at my own expense to talk with either the Chief of Naval Personnel or the Secretary of the Navy. I had my audience with the Chief of Naval Personnel and he assured me, somewhat patronizingly, I thought, that he had just that day approved a mortality of 15% for my class in going to captain, which I thought was reasonable. When it happened, the 60% figure was shocking. I was more than a little bit upset, but it was too late then.

Q: Who was that Chief of Personnel?

Captain Schratz: It was Admiral Holloway, Lord Jim.[*]

Q: The big event in Washington in the late '40s was the fight between the Air Force and the Navy. Did that have any effect at your level?

Captain Schratz: No, the unification battle didn't involve me until later. If not involved, though, I was interested. I became more involved in '49 and '50 in the "revolt of the admirals." I did a good piece on that, looking back after 35 years, which the Proceedings bought but hasn't yet published.[†]

Q: After a while, I would think the wartime disability retirement business would tend to fall off. Was that the case during the course of your tenure there?

Captain Schratz: Well, I left BuPers in the middle of '48, and it hadn't fallen off much by then. It was still brisk, including a small backlog of people on the active list hanging around the hospitals, mostly under prolonged treatment. That had eased significantly.

Q: Any more interesting cases from that period?

Captain Schratz: Hundreds, but let's not overdo it.

Q: I don't know that you could top the swallow-the-letter routine.

---

[*] Vice Admiral James L. Holloway, Jr., USN, served as Chief of Naval Personnel from 1953 to 1958.
[†] Captain Schratz's article was published as "The Admirals' Revolt," U.S. Naval Institute Proceedings, February 1986, pages 64-71.

Captain Schratz: Anything to serve justice and protect a client. That's what they call accepting responsibility, isn't it? I thought then that I'd make a very good lawyer.

Q: I'm sure you were looking forward to your submarine command. How did it happen to become the Pickerel?*

Captain Schratz: I don't know. I had my morning and afternoon cup of coffee in the submarine detail office in BuPers in those days. The submarine detailer was my old Mackerel skipper, Johnny Davidson, and his assistant was Ebby Bell, a close friend and classmate.† But I saw so many people pinging on those poor guys for one job or another, I swore I would never do it. They had my record on file, and I never brought up my future assignment until they mentioned they had me slated for Pickerel. Since she was the newest, first Guppy submarine after the war, the best we had, and slated for Honolulu duty, all I could say was, "Thank you."

Then the next problem--all your old shipmates write to get aboard also. "We've done it before, let's do it again." These were fine people, and I'd love to go to sea with them. But on a small ship, I always thought it was a mistake. The submarine force never sent the same skipper and exec together for successive tours for a lot of reasons. A CO and exec who repeat tours together know each other's style and won't learn much new. With younger officers in a small wardroom, it tends to set up cliques, talking about the good old days, and creates the appearance of favoritism.

I sent a letter to the submarine detail officer and said, "I have all sorts of requests from fine officers who want to go to sea with me again. I would prefer that none of them be sent." And I added brashly, "If you send me the worst officers you've got, and if I have

---

* The USS Pickerel (SS-524) was commissioned 4 April 1949 with Lieutenant Commander Schratz in command. She had a displacement of 1,570 tons on the surface and 2,428 tons submerged. She was 312 feet long, 27 feet in the beam, and had a draft of 15 feet. Her top speed was 20 knots surfaced and 9 knots submerged. She was armed with ten 21-inch torpedo tubes.
† Captain John F. Davidson, USN; Lieutenant Commander C. Edwin Bell, USN.

anything on the ball as a skipper, I'll make an average crew out of them. If you send me any better than that, I don't have to have much on the ball."

Well, that's egotistic, I realize now, but it's also terribly good psychology, because it put the detailers on record as more than ordinarily responsible for the people they sent. I think they must have looked over the whole Navy list to find the most superb people for Pickerel. I had a wonderful group of officers.

Q: Tell me something about them. Who were they and what made them so good?

Captain Schratz: Well, my exec was Bill "Pappy" Sims, out of '42, a super athlete, captain of the football team, later a nuclear submariner, an all-round top-rate professional officer, skilled in handling the men, a very congenial person to have around, and tough as he had to be.[*] For instance, we both disliked the habit of cussing in the crew and let the men know how we felt. With 220 pounds of exec, they soon thought it was a good idea, too. I had two officers out of the class of '44; Mike Elliott handled navigation and operations, Ralph "Snuffy" Jackson, engineer and diving officer, both very capable.[†] Two young sub school graduates joined us later.

There were several things we did differently in fitting out Pickerel. One of my concerns was the standard ship's organization. An OpNav board had standardized the format for all ships, but even reduced to submarine needs, it produced a loose leaf volume several inches thick.[‡] By fiat throughout the Navy, every new man reporting aboard is required to read and understand the organization within a minimal time, usually 48 hours. The language was obtuse, inspissate, imprecise legalese. Pap and I chose the most oafish man aboard and made him the captain's yeoman. Every two-syllable word was tested on him. If his eyes didn't blink happily over "promulgated," out it went.

---

[*] Lieutenant Commander William E. Sims, USN.
[†] Lieutenant Michael M. Elliott, USN; Lieutenant Ralph F. Jackson, USN.
[‡] OpNav--the extended staff of the Chief of Naval Operations.

We took liberties with many accepted routines, in the interest of safety--backing down on all man-overboard drills, for example. We could find no way a man could be pulled into the screws and found much hydrodynamic information to justify our position. Contrary to all fleet practice, when in danger of collision at sea, the submarine's best and quickest defense is to dive. In 40 seconds no fixed part of the ship is within 20 feet of the surface. On an operational readiness inspection off Pearl a year later, I couldn't seem to make this clear. When the drill came, the OD thoroughly drenched the inspection team on the bridge when he immediately pulled the diving alarm. Our organization was short and sweet, in clear prose, and a third the size of anything else in the fleet. I wonder what shape it was in when the ship was decommissioned several years ago.

Q: One well-known thing from your days in the Pickerel is when you had a picture taken of your boat coming up at a severe up angle out of the water. How did that come about?

Captain Schratz: On the way around from New England to Pearl Harbor, we stopped at various ports down the Atlantic Coast and the Gulf of Mexico, where we volunteered to take the local reserve group to sea at every opportunity. Most submarines, when they take reserves out, tend toward "show and tell" more than putting them on the gear and letting them run the submarine. We were terribly proud of this hot-rod Guppy submarine, and it was really a marvelous piece of gear. After the reserves rotated through all the ship control stations, helped fire a torpedo or two, my hot-rodders took over to put the ship through all these steep turns, up and down angles, and so forth. It's really thrilling, quite different from any other ship. We always ended our show with what we called an Event 500, surfacing at a very steep angle, usually about 50 degrees. [The code name for a lost submarine is Event 1000--two really good 500s and ...] One of the reserves in Houston was a newspaperman, and he claimed if he could ever get a picture, his fortune was made.

We started then to get a picture. It isn't easy to get a photographic ship which has sonar gear for tracking and communication while submerged in quiet seas and all that. Just after reporting in to Pearl, we were sent to the Singapore area for a combined fleet exercise with the British. The day before arriving in Manila on the way out, it looked like everything was hunky-dory for a try for a picture. The submarine Queenfish was operating with us. They had a cameraman on board, and we gave them the plan. We started at 525 feet--I think test depth was 450--making maximum speed of 18 knots. We blew the forward tanks, holding the ship on an even keel as long as possible, then threw the planes to full rise. We hit 72 degrees on that one, a gorgeous day for photography off Manila, bright blue sky and everything, a foamy wake all around us. It was quite spectacular, but the camera was a 16-millimeter movie and we could make only small prints. It wasn't until laser techniques for blow-ups made it possible about three years ago to get a 14 x 16 print. This is the one published on the cover of Shipmate last year.[*] But we had some excellent small prints.

We arrived in Manila the following day, and in my incoming mail was a letter from the force commander, Admiral Babe Brown, commenting on certain of his Guppy submarine skippers using large angles.[†] He didn't want to discourage aggressiveness, but he really did hate to write those 89 letters to next of kin, and didn't see what was to be gained by any angle over, say, ten degrees. Well, having just done the stern hinger, we got hold of the camera film and we put it in deep limbo for a while. Babe Brown was another famous athlete, All-American all the way back in 1913 or 1914. He had been the shipyard commander in Portsmouth when Pickerel was built, and there was no question that we were his favorite submarine. We were delighted when he became the new ComSubPac.

He still had the same aide, a classmate of Pappy Sims, who was trying to get the pictures released and kept us advised of the heat on Capitol Hill. A few months later, Admiral Lockwood in Los Gatos celebrated his 50th year since commissioning.[‡] Admiral Brown sent for me a few days prior, and we chatted for a while. After much hemming and hawing, he mentioned Admiral Lockwood's big celebration and said he would like to give him "one of those pictures." He suggested how it should be autographed, to which I agreed. But something else was clearly on his mind. Finally, placing a great big paw on my

---

[*] A blurred color photo of the surfacing appeared on the cover of the July-August 1983 issue of Shipmate.
[†] Rear Admiral John H. Brown, USN, served as Commander Submarine Force Pacific Fleet from 1949 to 1951.
[‡] Lockwood was commissioned in 1912. The celebration must have been on some other occasion, perhaps his 60th birthday on 6 May 1950.

shoulders, he asked for one for himself, too, "and I don't care how you autograph that one." So I autographed it, "To Admiral Babe Brown, proving that ComSubPac knows all the angles," or something like that.

We took that as permission to release the photo. Because the 72 degree ones were small, we did some others. The one which was so highly publicized, however, was one we were trying to work out with professional photography just as I was detached. My relief gets credit for that one, which was 45 degrees. Movies of that episode were used in "Silent Service," the movie of our submarines in World War II, and in many other places.

Q: Was there indeed a risk in doing something like that?

Captain Schratz: Oh, sure. You shouldn't start below test depth in any case. When you start up at any time, the bow starts to rise but the stern goes down quite a distance. The ship pivots about one-third from the bow, so the latter two-thirds may be a lot deeper than you think. At a 30-degree angle, the stern is 100 feet below the center of buoyancy. There are always things that can go wrong at that enormous pressure and under maximum speed.

I worried lots about torpedoes, a highly machined surface, greased for easier manhandling. If one in the racks should carry away and start thrashing around, the 3,000-pound air flasks could rupture or the engine start a hot run in the room. We had them double and triple chocked down to be sure they couldn't move. Those exercises weren't done haphazardly; it took months of preparation to train people on the planes, to the point we thought they could handle it. They were such great ships, though!

Q: Did it become a fad at all? Did others try to imitate it?

Captain Schratz: Ned Beach had pioneered it in the Amberjack in the Atlantic, frequently using 30-35 degrees. Nobody else in the Pacific was interested. I believe we were the only two.

Q: Was it something you could do only in a Guppy because you had to be deeper to pull it off?

Captain Schratz: Speed and power were more important. You could do 35-40 degrees up in a fleet submarine, but you didn't have the control and other things to pull out in a step down angle. Later, when I had a division, one of my units was nominated for an ASW movie, The Good Shepherd. I was asked for technical advice on surfacing at a steep angle, using a fleet submarine to simulate a German submarine getting depth-charged to the surface before sinking. I thought they could use 35 degrees for that. The skipper was a little tense, so he sent a letter to Mare Island and asked for their ideas on the maximum angle. Because the transverse bulkheads in fleet subs, and in Guppies, were not reinforced, they suggested 15 degrees as a max. The weight of the forward battery on that bulkhead in particular might allow the battery cells to move toward the pump room at angles above 15 degrees. I hadn't thought of that, but we surely disproved it many times.

Q: Tell me about your long submerged run from Hong Kong.

Captain Schratz: When I got to Pearl with the Guppy snorkel submarine, the general attitude in the Pacific was that the snorkel was tested, evaluated, and proven--and therefore need not be used. Quite the contrary. No one had any idea of the strategic and tactical values--and limitations--for snorkel operations. Pap, Snuffy, and I were inquisitive. We were sure there was much to be learned. For one thing, nobody wanted to snorkel for long periods because it was sometimes hard on the ears. Second, at that time there was a problem with the diesels when snorkeling. Operating 60 feet below the surface created heavy back pressures on the diesel exhaust, discharging against sea pressure. Air to the engines pulled down a narrow tube, created a high vacuum in the engine intake blowers.

Operating with a high vacuum on the intake and high pressure on the exhaust sets up stresses in the engine never visualized when the engines were built. The Fairbanks-Morse engines were the best in the world, but they were wiping those heavy aluminum scavenger blower lobes after less than 100 hours of snorkeling. After careful study and operational testing, some bright chiefs back aft, again led by Pap and Snuffy, found that the critical temperatures and oil pressures occurred where there was no instrumentation to warn of approaching danger. Snorkeling puts a doubly heavy load on the engine when starting up. If you begin with a hot engine recently on the line, there is less temperature change between the blower lobes and the housing, but you start near the maximum temperatures with very little tolerance before wiping the lobes. Starting with a cold engine allows a maximum range of expansion but different expansion of different parts again causes a danger of wiping the blower lobes.

Our solution, with the wisdom of Solomon, was to start snorkeling with neither a hot nor a cold but a warm engine, to take the best of both worlds. We also relocated and added thermometers and pressure gauges at critical points not previously protected. I tried to talk this over with some BuShips people. They weren't interested even though they had tried everything else. They put a diesel engine on a test stand here at NSRD in Annapolis and wiped those also in less than 100 hours.[*]

We learned all this just before departure for Hong Kong for the British exercise. I asked permission--at no higher a level than the SubPac assistant operations officer--on coming back from Hong Kong to try a long-range snorkel cruise. We weren't sure how far we could go, so I asked only to reduce our speed of advance to ten knots. I don't think anybody higher in the force staff had any idea what we were attempting. Departing Hong Kong with many warm farewells from British units, we started off snorkeling at 10 knots from the usual 15, requiring 100% load on the engines, the normal four-hour rate. We left that 100% load on for 21 days.

A few problems arose, one potentially serious. <u>Pickerel</u> had a new method of spring-loaded cam locks to secure the plating around the conning tower fairwater. On routine dives some had popped loose. When we couldn't get topside to tighten them, they became progressively worse. Soon heavy pieces of sheet metal were tearing loose and bouncing down the deck. One or two went through the screws, reducing our speed

---

[*] NSRD--Naval Ship Research and Development Center.

somewhat for the last four days. They also tore away all of our antenna, so that we couldn't transmit to ComSubPac. Anticipating the worst, somewhere around near Midway, I reported to ComSubPac that "because of progressive loss of all transmitting antenna, this may be my last transmission." Just in the nick of time. The average force commander, when a submarine is unreported over 24 hours, has a lost-submarine routine to go through.

Admiral Radford was CinCPac at the time, and when we were unreported for 48 hours, he said, "Order her to the surface."[*] Admiral Brown, our great friend, asked for a delay, assuring the big boss of his great faith in the ship. He couldn't be sure we were still able to receive messages, however, and sent out an air search team. They couldn't find us, so the second day he ordered us to broach enough to show running lights and fire flares. Although they knew our track accurately, unfortunately they couldn't find us. The running lights had grounded out. We were four days unreported before they finally found us a day out of Pearl.

Because somebody had claimed that a French or German submarine had been submerged for 500 hours, we asked by VHF to be allowed to stay off Pearl Harbor in the operating area just long enough to pass 500 hours.[†] On surfacing at the entrance to the channel, we had covered 5,187 miles in 21 days--505 hours--continually submerged, with two engines continually on propulsion.[‡]

Lots of small problems greeted us. We lost topside grease lines, fittings, cabling, the entire conning tower fairing, the whip antenna, some deck plating, and the periscope protection. Of major logistic significance, we found that fuel consumption was about 60% higher than for normal cruising, which meant that the range of a snorkeling submarine was reduced very seriously. Granted, we were at 100% load, but nobody realized the difference. Even with the nuclear submarine just over the horizon, the reduced fuel endurance was an important logistic factor.

---

[*] Admiral Arthur W. Radford, USN, served as Commander in Chief Pacific/Commander in Chief U.S. Pacific Fleet from 30 April 1949 to 10 July 1953.
[†] VHF--very high frequency radio.
[‡] This voyage took place from 16 March to 5 April 1950.

The Bureau of Ships was delighted, however, that we had succeeded without wiping an engine blower. By then we had 1,600 snorkeling hours on each of the four engines. They were still trying to get one to run for 100. Curious to learn the secret of our engine endurance, they first asked for a fuel analysis. Their theory was that the fuel we got in Hong Kong made the difference in engine performance. We sent a sample for a routine analysis. The report: excessive sediment, excessive moisture, insufficient flash point, insufficient pour point, does not meet submarine standards, do not use. Clearly this would have only increased our difficulties.

I forwarded this report to BuShips without comment and waited for their next reaction as to the secret of our success. They sent two engineers out to see for themselves. The crew had been alerted beforehand that our secret--adding a few gauges at critical points to monitor performance better, and always starting a warm rather than a hot or cold engine to snorkel--would stay with us unless they were willing to give us full credit for it. If they insisted on snooping around to find out for themselves and then invented the idea when they got back to Washington, no go.

Well, their first shock came when they found we had disconnected the snorkel safety circuits which cut out the engines if the men on the diving planes lost depth control and ducked the air intake under water. These were over-engineered and oversensitive, many times operating when they weren't supposed to. When you duck the head valve under water, three spark plugs trigger a system to shut the valve and keep the ocean out. Those big diesels then pull all the air out of the boat unless shut down quickly. It's quite painful on the eardrums, a questionable add-on for engine shut-down.

Our men dreamed up a better idea. At the maneuvering controls, they had an ordinary milk bottle--this was back in the days when milk came in glass bottles--in front of the controllermen and put a condom over the top of the bottle, with the head painted red. Well, when the sea breaks over the head valve, it slams shut. The vacuum rises, and the condom gets rigid right in front of their noses. Well, these youngsters' minds were on sex as much as engineering, and they immediately responded to pull the engines off the line. That was <u>our</u> snorkel safety circuit; the model designed by old men was bypassed.

This didn't impress the BuShips people very much. With some doubts, I had decided to include our modification in my patrol report. Admiral Brown also deliberated before passing it along to CinCPac, Admiral Radford; he didn't think Radford would appreciate it. We learned later that he broke up laughing over it. He said he wanted to come down to congratulate us--and obviously to get a firsthand look. It's the first time CinCPac personally visited a submarine since the Nimitz days during the war--all because of a contraceptive. But BuShips never learned the secret. Meanwhile, we offered to donate $500.00 to the Damon Runyon cancer fund if any plant could beat our record. To cover my tracks, I told Colonel Fairbanks at Fairbanks-Morse of the bet, knowing full well he'd pick up the tab if ever necessary. But in 34 years now we haven't been challenged. The diesel submarine era in the U.S. is a thing of the past, and I suppose the secret died with it.

Q: Was there any secret beyond this milk bottle?

Captain Schratz: Well, that plus the thermometers on the blowers, you know, and the idea of not overloading the cold or hot engine. It was just high school physics, no more.

Q: Had you monkeyed with the fuel at all? You say it was unfit.

Captain Schratz: No, it was just a lousy batch; the fuel issue was irrelevant. Just a remote possibility. They thought the Hong Kong fuel might have been different. It was different but not in the way they expected. Since it didn't meet standards, it merely increased our problems.

Q: I see.

Captain Schratz: Indonesian fuel has very low sulfur content, for one thing. The crude burns almost like refined. I suspect that was what was on their mind.

Q: Well, do you want to go on some more today?

Captain Schratz: A few additional points on snorkeling should be in the record. The greatly increased electrical power in the Guppy submarine caused some other engineering problems not fully appreciated in the design. The transfer switches used to place the batteries in parallel or series carried very heavy amperage and should have used the commercial, oil-immersed type rather than standard submarine open air. They were also poorly located where salt spray could make them hazardous. Combined with the hydrogen gas routinely given off by the battery, there was a serious potential for a fire when submerged.

Before leaving the Atlantic on our shakedown cruise, we had recommended a shipalt to replace the switches with commercial oil-immersed types. About two to three days later, while our letter was in the mail, <u>Cochino</u> had just such an electrical fire off Norway, eventually causing loss of the boat. But again BuShips went overboard with the antidote. They decided the danger was the hydrogen and set up new directions to "purge" the battery every hour by pulling a big vacuum in the boat to evacuate the hydrogen bubbles off the battery plates. This was a nuisance, also painful on the ears. Bakers couldn't bake cakes--it purged them, too, so they wouldn't rise. Sealed containers either crumpled or burst when opened, throwing their contents in one's face.

We got the BuShips order while in the Philippines. Again, Snuffy Jackson thought he had a better idea. His men found a small wet-cell battery in a glass jar while ashore in Manila. We hooked it up in the wardroom, charged, discharged, and purged it just as we did the big batteries below our feet. We could watch the action as the hydrogen bubbles formed on the plates and learned very quickly that the purging routine was wholly ineffective. We were soon able to recommend a quite different procedure to eliminate any danger involved, which soon became standard throughout the fleet.

The purging routines added one more headache. The leading torpedoman in the after room had an aquarium with an expensive collection of fish. The yard made a mount out of torpedo gyros to prevent spillage on the steep angles, but every time we purged the batteries, it pulled all the oxygen out of his tank. He had to fit a complicated aerator system to counter the purging routines.

Navigation submerged offered another problem. We had Loran but wanted to stimulate new ideas on navigation for the officers.* Bowditch, who wrote the gospel of seamanship, disposed of the problem in a single sentence: "When long-range submerged cruises of the future become possible, the means of navigation will be at hand."† The Naval Institute Proceedings published an article on this subject by one Paul R. Frank in April 1945 with which I was quite familiar. It advocated use of a subsolar fix via a series of timed periscope bearings of the sun for ten or 15 minutes on each side of the noon transit. An excellent device when near the subsolar point, we found the value under other conditions to be somewhat overstated. Coincidentally, I was Paul Frank; the incident reported occurred while navigating Sterlet, with both author and ship masquerading under a wartime nom de plume.‡

During the Pickerel cruise, Pap and I decided to keep the Loran to ourselves, and the watch officers took turns for two days at a time as navigator, using any conceivable means: soundings, celestial transits by periscope for longitude lines, sun sights by measuring the altitude in the periscope crosshairs, and so forth. Despite the limitations, we knew our position accurately throughout. At constant speed of 10.2 knots, before the screw damage from topside plating reduced speed somewhat, and with no steering loss from sea action on the hull, navigation was far more accurate than normal. Our landfall was exactly as predicted.

When the story broke after our arrival in Pearl, the public reaction throughout the U.S. and internationally was unbelievable. We received messages of congratulations from the Secretary of Defense, SecNav, CNO, and numerous public officials. The media went

---

* Loran--long-range aid to navigation, a system based on plotting radio signals transmitted from various locations.
† Nathaniel Bowditch (1773-1838) was an American mathematician and astronomer.
‡ Frank was the maiden name of Schratz's wife. The article, "Submerged Celestial Navigation," appeared on pages 424-425 of the April 1945 Proceedings. A small box at the end of the article contained the following: "Due to security reasons, we are unable to give the usual biographical information on the writer of this article."

ape over it, creating one immediate problem. Nobody had thought to photograph our surfacing and arrival in Pearl. So three days later, we got under way, went to sea, turned around and snorkeled back to the entrance buoys for our "official" welcome, all photos carefully air-brushed to hide the loss of plating and collateral damage to the periscope fairwater plating.

Interview Number 2 with Captain Paul R. Schratz, U.S. Navy (Retired)

Place: U.S. Naval Institute, Annapolis, Maryland

Date: Tuesday, 4 December 1984

Interviewer: Paul Stillwell

Q: It's good to see you again today to start off session two. Maybe the best place to begin would be to catch up on anything that you might want to mention covering the first interview that was omitted.

Captain Schratz: Yes, a couple of points. The most important one was command of Burrfish. While en route to command of Pickerel in--I think it was October of 1948--I was diverted first to PCO school and the PCO-XO sonar school in Key West. While relaxing on the beach at Key West, I received urgent orders as CO for the emergency reactivation of Burrfish from the mothball fleet in New London.*

Somebody in OpNav decided it would be a great idea to test the readiness of the back channel fleet, and so they started a grand experiment at midnight, 1 November 1948. I was chosen as CO to report immediately to New London. The other officers and men came from wherever they could find warm bodies. While simulating a war emergency and reactivation of the whole reserve fleet, they actually reactivated one submarine and one

---

* The USS Burrfish (SS-312) was commissioned 14 September 1943. She had a displacement of 1,525 tons on the surface and 2,415 tons submerged. She was 312 feet long, 27 feet in the beam, and had a draft of 17 feet. Her top speed was 20 knots surfaced and 9 knots submerged. She was armed with ten 21-inch torpedo tubes and a 5-inch gun. After being decommissioned on 10 October 1946, she was recommissioned 2 November 1948 for conversion to duty as a radar picket submarine. The Burrfish was redesignated SSR-312 on 27 January 1949.

rescue vessel. Unfortunately, it coincided with a major Atlantic Fleet exercise, and nobody was available except people in hospitals, a few from the brig, some they could pull off leave. I had a very rag-tag bunch of officers and men. The exec was a super officer, Bill Walsh, out of '41.[*] Unfortunately, Bill came down with a very serious appendicitis attack the day we first moved away from the pier, and I haven't seen him since. All the officers except one were on temporary duty, largely mustangs, very capable but unconventional and quite loose about regulations.

Existing war plans called for having the submarine ready for duty within 30 days. Actually we did far better. We cleaned up tons of preservative, doused liberally even on the wardroom silver, tested all equipment, guns, torpedoes, engines, made full power runs surfaced and submerged, and reported for duty in 20 days.

Q: How long had the boat been out of commission?

Captain Schratz: About two or three years. <u>Burrfish</u> was chosen because she was thought to be exactly average of the mothball fleet. A superior job of deactivating had been done and helped us greatly. Just before our sea trials were scheduled to start, I asked permission to make a shakedown cruise, and, since Christmas was coming, I suggested St. Thomas.

ComSubLant at the time was Admiral James Fife, a teetotaler and a martinet.[†] He had changed a number of careers in a major direction for the mildest sort of infractions, especially involving alcohol. He sent for me for a briefing before we left on shakedown, noting that St. Thomas is a great place to visit just before Christmastime--beautiful port and great for shopping. Then he added, "Liquor is very cheap too." I couldn't fathom why he made the last statement. Was he trying to tell me that the lid's off if I want to bring back a little Schnapps for Christmas? I had carried alcohol before in my ships, but I always followed one cardinal rule: that everybody in the ship shares equally. If the officers bring some back, the men could do so also.

---

[*] Lieutenant Commander William C. Walsh, USN.
[†] Rear Admiral James Fife, USN, served as Commander Submarine Force Atlantic Fleet from 15 April 1947 to 1 June 1950.

Arriving in St. Thomas after a photo reconnaissance of San Juan, we posted a price list and, for cash on the barrelhead, offered to order and have it delivered on board, sealed in the magazine. This worked fine; the magazine was almost full. Only two hours out of St. Thomas, on departure, however, I received a message from ComSubLant that he would meet me at the entrance buoy off New London at 7:00 A.M. on our arrival date for an operational readiness inspection. I almost died. I ordered flank speed, planning to reach the sub base the night before and off-load our special cargo. No sooner was the heavy throb of the engines felt when my engineer came charging up to the bridge to ask what was going on.

I showed him the message and he said, "But captain! Since we're going to go into the yard for conversion to a radar picket immediately upon return, I didn't see any point in filling all the fuel ballast tanks and then pumping it all off again. So we have just enough fuel for a gentlemen's trip back."

I said, "Well, you rascal, since you falsified your fuel reports, you can start thinking about what we do when we run dry. Meanwhile, that flank bell is going to stay on because I've got to get up there the night before." Well, we did run dry, but we had enough to get into Long Island Sound, including everything greasy we could scavenge in the bilges, then shifted to the battery.

I couldn't request a berth in advance, couldn't tip my hand, and it happened to be the day the Christmas leave started at the base. It was snowing heavily and a maximum ebb tide was running. We were lucky to find one berth open so that we could land on the high side of the pier and let the current put us alongside, but I had only enough juice left for a one-bell landing. We had no line handlers, and we had to lay the ship alongside and then put line handlers on the dock to tie us up. Midnight, nobody was around. We had to knock on the conning tower of the ship across the pier and get some people up to give us some fuel. We also scrounged a Jeep, off-loaded the liquor, and put it up in a set of transient quarters on the base being used by one of my junior officers. His wife got up shortly after, saw some great big cockroaches looking out at her, and carried all the cases outside, stacking them alongside the Dempsey dumpster. The snow was falling pretty heavily by then, and by dawn, it just looked like one more dumpster.

But we had other problems, getting enough fuel, getting a battery charge in, and getting back out to the sea buoy by 0700. The men were exhausted, but we went through really an excellent operational readiness inspection. The staff made it as tough as they could. After all, they wouldn't look good if some rag-tag outfit could come out of nowhere and get an excellent on an ORI in a month when the rest of the force trained all year and could do no better. But we did a super job.

When I got back to the sub base, I asked my divcom what the story was. He said, "We were trying to help you out. I knew you were living up in Portsmouth and wanted to get back with the family in time for Christmas. I was going to save you a couple days of operating to give you a break on Christmas leave."

All's well that ends well. We recovered all the booze, knocked the snow off it, dealt it out, and were on our way for holiday break.

Q: What did you do to get a crew trained that quickly to pass an ORI so well?

Captain Schratz: Well, two or three of my officers were mustangs, very good at their trade, and very good at cracking the whip. They weren't tied down by trivia that might have held us back in the normal routine. We ran things fast and loose. It was fun, but there was no fooling around about training. I was always serious about that. I missed being without an exec, normally responsible for training, and I tried to saddle each of the department heads with his responsibilities, which worked extremely well. Part of the purpose of the exercise was to put a crew together, as well as getting the ship ready as part of a highly compressed experience primarily to evaluate the status of the mothball fleet. We concentrated also on the technical, taking a good look at everything, every system on the ship. And we were lucky, too, in the way it did work out. It was just a nice, happy experience all the way through.

Q: What are some examples of doing things in a non-routine, not-bound-by-regulations way?

Captain Schratz: Well, we performed services for the submarine school while operating from the submarine base. Normally the school boats get under way about 0800 and go out and make a dozen or so dives to rotate the students through each operating station and come in about 1500. Since most of my crew was on temporary duty, with other things to do, I told the sub school I was going to get under way at 5:00 o'clock. So we'd go out at 5:00 and run through those exercises like nothing they'd ever seen before, and really put it to the students. The others tried to fill a day. We stressed the training, finishing the day's work, and would be heading home up the river when the rest of the boats were going out. And generally the CO was off to Portsmouth for a long weekend and a quick look at progress with Pickerel. So we had a whole day at the base to do our normal chores. It took a lot of cooperation by the submarine school to rouse their students out a couple of hours early for that sort of thing, but we worked together very well. And I worked my gang long, hard hours on what had to be done.

Another example tells the story even more vividly. One Friday morning the division commander notified me he had a special operation he wanted us to do the following day. Normally, of course, I went to Portsmouth for my "other" career over the weekends. That particular Saturday I had important plans. The divcom was entirely sympathetic, assuring me the commitment was not yet firm. Also, a heavy fog was rolling in which might cancel all operations.

When I returned to the boat, my acting exec came up with a compromise, suggesting I go ahead with my plans, drive north, and call him from Boston. He'd know for sure by then if we were to go out, and I could return if necessary. When I phoned from Boston, he said, "Have a good weekend, Captain." He was quite busy, and I was only too happy not to get into a long discussion. Returning on Monday morning, we agreed we'd played that one right. I asked how bad the fog was. "Clear as a bell, Captain."

"Oh, the operation was canceled?"

"Oh, no, Captain. We went out."

In a state of semi-shock, I asked if he had explained my absence to the divcom. "No, sir, Captain. We just pulled the curtain on your cabin and told him you had a bad night."

All I could do was roar, "Bob, you ruin my reputation as well as my organization. Do you realize how far up the creek we were if anything went wrong?" He did. I don't think it bothered him. I could only wonder at the reaction of Admiral Fife, so ruthless toward human frailty, had he known one of his subs went on daily operations with no CO or XO on board.

Q: I take it, then, that this reactivation test was a success.

Captain Schratz: A very great success.

Q: Did she then stay in commission for a while?

Captain Schratz: Yes, she stayed in commission as a radar picket, but the role of the picket didn't last but a few years in the fleet and they did away with them.

Q: Was there any stimulus to this from the international situation, the Berlin blockade, for example?

Captain Schratz: For the picket idea, no. Merely a new look at the prewar idea of the submarine as the ears and eyes of the fleet. I never learned what prompted the readiness operation. All I learned was the order from CNO to do it as a realistic test of readiness of the mothball fleet. It's something which I think should be done routinely anyhow, if we ever plan to use these ships. I've always regretted the lack of realism in the training exercises that we do routinely. When I had my turn as a division commander--later we can get into some of those ideas.

Q: Was there a work package that had been left behind by the decommissioning crew so you knew what needed to be done to fix her up?

Captain Schratz: Yes. It was all very well organized, extremely well organized. I was so impressed, I dug out the name of the officer who had been in charge of Burrfish and sent him a really sincere letter of appreciation for a very conscientious job.

Q: Do you recall who that individual was?

Captain Schratz: I'm racking my brain. Yes, Fred J. Ruder.[*]

Q: Did you get a good degree of cooperation from the shipyard in reactivating her?

Captain Schratz: Yes. Submarine base; no shipyard.

Q: And that was enough to do it?

Captain Schratz: Essentially it was almost entirely ship's force, relying on the base for very little.

Q: So it was a case of reversing the inactivation. The real overhaul came on the conversion to the picket.

Captain Schratz: The base took off all the cocoons over the guns and exposed equipment. Once they towed the hull out of the back channel and put it alongside the dock, it was our show. I think I arrived late on the second of November. My first concern was submarine pay, not for myself, of course, but for the troops. So I went to ComSubLant, then based in

---

[*] Lieutenant Commander Frederick J. Ruder, USN.

New London, as soon as I reported in. He asked how soon I would be ready for commissioning, suggesting about three weeks. I remonstrated, "I hate to take these men off submarine pay and keep them in a non-sub pay status for three weeks before commissioning while we conduct this grand experiment. I don't like to punish the wives and children that way."

He said, "Well, that's a good point. How soon will you be ready? Could you make it next week?"

I said, "How about tomorrow?"

So they set up the commissioning ceremony, the first in New London since the heyday of World War II. I had no idea it would snowball into such a big event. Everybody on the whole Atlantic seaboard showed up for it--bands, admirals, visitors, a real holiday. After making this pitch for the troops, there were, on my quarterdeck, just four officers and four enlisted men. SubLant had prepared a fine inspirational address. Without the guests, he had only a four-man audience in front of them. As he walked off the ship, he looked around at me and snarled, "All for the holy enlisted man and his submarine pay, are you?" I, of course, was the big beneficiary. I wouldn't rate sub pay at all until the Pickerel commissioning, so this from Burrfish was just a nice Christmas bonus.

Q: What kind of shape were the batteries in after that lay-up?

Captain Schratz: The electrolyte had been drained. No problem. The only temporary difficulty was that the records were incorrect; they thought it was a Gould battery, and it was an Exide. So we had a very excited Gould man around trying to get the proper procedures for the initial charge. Although both batteries are almost identical, the companies had quite different initial charge procedures. I don't think it made a bit of difference.

Q: Was there any reactivation of reservists in connection with this drill?

Captain Schratz: Only simulated, as a test of the mobilization plan. We used all active regulars.

Q: Do you have any specific recollections of Admiral Fife besides those you've mentioned?

Captain Schratz: Yes. I had never really served directly with him before, and somehow we developed quite a warm friendship after that. He was a bachelor and didn't have many friends. When I was in New London later, while commanding the submarine tender Fulton after he'd retired, we were always on his party list for numerous evenings at his home. I thoroughly enjoyed them.

Q: Any aspects of his personality that you particularly recall other than his teetotaling?

Captain Schratz: I'm not even sure he was a teetotaler. He was then because he lived in the BOQ on the base. But he was certainly a sundowner, a renowned sundowner, one of the few who married the U.S. Navy. He is one who prompts the rumor that his wife divorced him and named the Navy as a co-respondent. He was a very sincere, dedicated, no foolishness, outstanding flag officer.

Q: Then that was terminated and you went on to Pickerel. That's credited with being the first submarine to take part in a United Nations action.

Captain Schratz: That's correct. The first submarine in combat since World War II.

Q: What were your activities in connection with the Korean War?

Captain Schratz: We had gotten so much publicity from the snorkel cruise in March and April of 1950 that as soon as the Korean emergency broke, CNO sent an aircraft carrier, Boxer, out for gravely needed tactical air support in Korea. Then, on his own, Admiral

Radford decided, "Send the Pickerel, too." We had no idea what sort of a mission he had in mind, nor did he, probably; he liked the way we operated.

We went out there at full power. You recall the grave emergency in stopping the North Koreans before they pushed the defenders into the sea. When we checked in to Commander Naval Forces Far East after crossing the International Dateline, somebody apparently misconverted the date and changed our arrival to 24 hours earlier than anticipated in our normal ETA.[*] Well, the news was grim enough from the front that I thought it might have been necessary. I didn't question it but laid on 150% overload to get there a day earlier, the maximum four-hour rate, and ran at that speed for four days. We set an all-time speed record for submarines getting from Pearl to Japan, averaging 19 for the last 1,000 miles and 17 knots overall.

When we got into Yokosuka, I tried to make a trim dive before entering port, only to find that we had so many pieces of piston ring from the engines lodged in the outboard exhaust valves, I couldn't get a "green board," couldn't get them closed so we could dive. So we tied up in Yokosuka on time but with four engines about to die. It took the entire Pacific fleet stock of gold seal piston rings to re-ring four engines. In one engine we lost three pistons as well, charred beyond repair. Arriving in Yokosuka late Friday night, we went off on a war patrol Monday morning. Two engines were back on the line by then; the other two by about Thursday of that week, just before arrival in the patrol area.

The immediate crisis then was the threat of General Chiang Kai-shek moving from Formosa back to mainland China, and the equally dangerous threat of Mao Tse-tung and the mainland Chinese making an assault on Formosa.[†] You'll recall that Chiang offered troops to save our skins in Korea and used the threat of going back to the China mainland to pressure the U.N. command into using him in Korea. I had a very strange operation order to patrol Formosa Straits with orders to prevent either one from crossing. I think

---

[*] ETA--estimated time of arrival.
[†] Generalissimo Chiang Kai-shek served as President of Nationalist China on the mainland from 1943 to 1949 and as President of the Republic of China on Taiwan from 1950 until his death in 1975. Mao Tse-tung was head of the Communist Party in the People's Republic of China from the time the Communists seized power in 1949 until his death in 1976.

there was one other submarine and somewhere to the south a pair of surface patrol units. All we could do in case something happened was to get the word out and stay alive.

Q: Were you supposed to wait for a specific order?

Captain Schratz: Yes, and keep the radio ready. We spent a considerable amount of time looking way into Foochow, Amoy, and Swatow, primarily Amoy Harbor as far as we could navigate. I did quite a lot of operations with the lower sound head frequently in the mud, slogging through 60 feet of water with a 58-foot submerged draft.

Q: Who briefed you on your mission?

Captain Schratz: Admiral Tex McLean, who was then . . .[*]

Q: He was the commander of the base at Yokosuka.

Captain Schratz: Yes. When we got back from that mission, I made a second war patrol. It was a special operation off China, following a dry run off Iwo Jima.

Q: Do you have any recollections of Admiral McLean? He has something of a reputation as a submariner also.

Captain Schratz: Yes, but I never knew him in submarines. The little I saw of him left me much impressed. My officers were very specially treated. I was a frequent dinner guest when we were in port and also for the Friday night boxing matches. We had a very warm, friendly relationship, which I thoroughly enjoyed. I hadn't met him before.

Q: Surface officers have not spoken well of him. Perhaps that's the explanation.

---

[*] Rear Admiral Heber H. McLean, USN.

Captain Schratz: Could be. Then our third patrol was again a classified operation up off Vladivostok. I had a problem then. We could see all sorts of traffic at great distances and could hear all sorts of screw noises at very long range on the sonar gear, but we weren't of much use on an intelligence mission unless we could penetrate the closed sea area. By terms of the op ord, we were to remain clear of the closed sea area the Russians maintain around Vladivostok, perhaps 50 miles.* As I saw it, I could either carry out my mission of observing shipping movements, or I could carry out my order to not violate the closed area, but I couldn't do both. I decided that the mission must take precedence.

After a careful initial penetration with no observed reaction, I conducted the whole patrol inside the zone. Then one evening we were fortunate in finding, while submerged, a division of Soviet submarines transiting on the surface. It immediately presented a problem. They could have been bound for Vladivostok. They also happened to be on the same course to take them to the U.S. carrier force which had just moved into the southern part of the Sea of Japan. I was gravely concerned at that latter possibility. We were also aware that that particular part of the world's oceans is unique in probably being the most impossible for antisubmarining, because of tremendous temperature differentials between the surface and deep waters.

My orders were quite specific that any hostile attack on my part must be clearly in retaliation. As a precaution, a full salvo of torpedoes was ready forward, but we were not detected. We were quite close to their track and observed them carefully as they went by. To make sure of our identification, the exec and I took turns taking looks. We were able to observe men on the bridge and such details as who was flying the command pennant. We also noted the hull numbers painted on the conning tower, one of the best means I know of identifying a ship. Two were quite unmistakable; on the third, we had a question of whether one numeral was a three or a nine. After they had gone by, we compared notes and punched the recognition books and found that we had agreed completely on all the details.

---

* Op ord--operation order.

When we got into Yokosuka shortly after, MacArthur's intelligence chief came down to interrogate us. When he received our contact report, it was assessed in the lowest category, as a "doubtful submarine." I really blew my stack. I sent a rather sharp message that as a trained observer under highly favorable circumstances, I believed without question they were submarines. Based on other evidence, he thought the three submarines were in the Atlantic with the Northern Fleet. But we were right. I learned much later that we had seen the summer transfer through the northern ice from Atlantic to Pacific. The flagship was correctly identified, as were the other two, but since it conflicted with his intelligence book, he dismissed our sighting.

Q: Did Admiral Joy's staff go to bat for you in that case?[*]

Captain Schratz: Very strongly. Admiral Joy was another great guy to work for.

Q: What do you remember about him?

Captain Schratz: I hadn't known him previously and saw him very rarely, but he and his staff were very supportive. We were busy out there and usually at sea. We made three patrols and a special mission. Oh, yes, the second patrol, in August 1950, was a photo reconnaissance for the amphibious landing around Wonsan on the east coast of Korea. It was a two-submarine operation, Pickerel and Perch. Pickerel had the mission of going in to reconnoiter and photograph the area to pick out some beach landing areas. Perch, which had been converted to a troop transport, carried the landing force. The mission was to cut the rail traffic and road traffic through a couple of tunnels down the east coast of Korea, to cut off possible reinforcements to Pusan just after the Inchon operation, and later to cut off the North Korean retreat.[†]

---

[*] Vice Admiral C. Turner Joy, USN, was Commander U.S. Naval Forces Far East.
[†] On 15 September 1950, troops under the command of General of the Army Douglas MacArthur made an amphibious landing at Inchon, the port for Seoul, South Korea. The surprise landing, 150 miles behind enemy lines, temporarily turned the tide of war in favor of United Nations forces.

We had no camera for radar scope photography and had to use one of our men's cameras and jury-rig an operation to prepare radar scope photography for commando use. Admiral Joy had asked the Air Force for a bird's-eye perspective of the objective areas, but they did their photography from about 30,000 feet and produced a photograph of most of Asia. You could see the entire Korean peninsula, the Shantung promontory in China, and the Yellow Sea, the Sea of Japan, and the Japanese coast. Interesting, but totally useless for a boat crew. We went in quite close and did a typical formal submarine photo recon operation, which under stereo viewers gives excellent depth perception. Only later did I learn that the whole area of most of our operations had been mined quite heavily. We were operating in about 60 feet of water with the keel frequently sliding through the mud, in a minefield. But we got some really fine photography. This was done under very high priority--19-knot speed of advance for the 1,000 miles into the area and return--and turned out to be an extremely strenuous operation. Pickerel and Perch were awarded the submarine combat insignia for this operation, the only time it was awarded since World War II.

Q: Did that wind up being used in the operation?

Captain Schratz: Oh, yes. The landing force Perch used were Royal Marine commandos flown in from Singapore. They were wild men, but did a super submarine amphibious operation which was quite successful.

Q: Did you have confidence that you were not detected during the time you were shadowing the Russian submarines?

Captain Schratz: I was quite sure. Having finished maybe a dozen war patrols and always worked very hard on my periscope technique, I was as careful as one could be under the circumstances. The odds were much in our favor, too, because of twilight. It was ideal for us.

Q: You'd been involved in several high-recognition things already: the steep dive, the long submerged transit, and the Korean War. I would assume that the morale of your people was pretty high.

Captain Schratz: Oh, it was great. We always went all out to give the troops a chance to at least capture bragging rights, and we usually did things with class. As the fair-haired ones with so much publicity, we were on the harbor cruise itinerary in Pearl Harbor and were always assigned Pier Number 1 nearest the ComSubPac headquarters. We made all the VIP cruises that came by. Shirley Temple visited us, for one. I didn't tell her about ruining her reputation in the Sasori episode. I suspect some of the other skippers in the area were pretty jealous. I might have been under the circumstances. But the troops were superb and very proud of their ship.

Q: You had an anecdote in the Proceedings about leaky periscopes in order to illustrate the informal atmosphere on board. Are there other examples of that?

Captain Schratz: I don't recall that one.

Q: You told the quartermaster either to get the periscope fixed or bring the sou-wester, and he said, "What size, sir?"
   How does one go about conducting religious observances in a vessel as small as a submarine?

Captain Schratz: It depends on the submarine. Normally you use the forward torpedo room.

Q: Did you have some designated lay leader?

Captain Schratz: On Sterlet, one of the stewards was an ordained minister in some church I wasn't familiar with. He was a southerner and a remarkable character. I attended first as a matter of propriety, or felt that I should, simply to give support, but I thought his homilies were outstanding and attracted a very high attendance of the crew.

Q: Was this a black man in that era?

Captain Schratz: Yes.

Q: Did you ever see any correlation between attendance at services and the degree of danger in the mission?

Captain Schratz: Oh, that happens, yes. I had one officer, to go back to Sterlet for a moment, who was a mustang, and he made quite a thing that he was a lifetime church-goer, baptized in the church, married in the church, and he would die in the church. But he figured that those three visits would take care of it, and he would think about it in the meantime with nice thoughts. He didn't want to be coerced into anything more. Yet he became a regular attendee at Sterlet services.

Q: Did the Pickerel, by virtue of her fame, demand any extra goodies in terms of supplies or food and so forth?

Captain Schratz: No. As a matter of fact, quite the contrary. She was the worst feeder in the fleet for quite a long time. For one thing, we were under way almost continuously, and once you start that routine, the married johns tend to get off the ship and single people fight to get on board. The more single people you have, the more people eat on board and the cost of the mess increases. At that time there was also a gang of some sort in Pearl Harbor stealing from the submarines, falsifying inventories and shipments. The other submarines either accepted it or didn't realize they were getting ripped off. But we were in the red and blew the whistle as soon as we found out.

Before we found out, we ran way in the hole in a quarterly mess statement. I cut the rations down to almost nothing, sent a report to the squadron commander that the exec was now the commissary officer, and promised to make up the differential in the next quarter. Well, the next quarter we were in Japan and with everybody on board, we went still further in the hole, so we started stealing from the rest of the ships. Any time we tied up near a carrier or a heavy, we stole them blind. We even stole food from the Japs and Koreans. We probably had the lousiest meal service in the submarine force by then.

I went on tropical duty hours. We would work from 7:00 o'clock straight through until 1:00 o'clock, then grant liberty before serving lunch, maybe after 1:30 or 2:00 o'clock, and served breakfast before they came back aboard in the morning. Well, six months of that, and we were back in the black. The unsavory situation in Pearl Harbor was cleaned up; the bad guys were punished, and we could regain our early reputation as a good feeder. But guests rarely came on board for meals in that period.

Q: How was the maintenance support when you were deployed after the Korean War period?

Captain Schratz: Superb. We had a submarine facility at Yokosuka, a shore-based supply outfit, which was extremely good. For underway training, we were on our own. I took the submarine rescue vessel <u>Greenlet</u> from Yokosuka and picked some sheltered bay or small port in Japan. We used the ASR for target practice, to fire exercise torpedoes, to recover the torpedoes back on board for the next shot. Then we went ashore in the ASR boats for liberty every night. We'd pick a different location each time. Excellent training, lots of ship handling and thoroughly enjoyable.

Q: What was your pattern of operations after you finished up on those war patrols in the Korean area?

Captain Schratz: On finishing the fourth patrol, the North Koreans were about finished too. We left there just after General MacArthur declared the enemy routed and peace at hand--late October 1950, just before the big Chinese offensive. I recall my farewell visit with Admiral Joy. At that time, things were heating up with the French in Indochina, and so I predicted--now that we had Korea wrapped up--we would be back out in about six months for Indochina. He said, "Well, I'll send for you when we get down there." We were just well out of the area when the Chinese made it a new war.*

Q: Did you then go back to Pearl?

Captain Schratz: Yes.

Q: How long did you operate out there?

Captain Schratz: Let's see, I think I had been in command about two and a half years then. I was relieved in August 1951 after only a few more months in Pearl.

Q: One thing you talked about last time after the recorder was shut off was your pattern of operations around the base in Pearl Harbor. So if you could cover that, please. This involved going in and out, making the twists, and so forth.

Captain Schratz: Yes. Again, I always stressed total realism in training operations. Nothing bored me more quickly than the routine of fire drills and the rest of the emergencies carried out in a routine manner. We liked to put drills into a damage control problem, a broad problem. It involved the routine emergencies, of course, but we liked to achieve a higher level of training and really fighting the ship under a wide variety of circumstances and that took far more than routine exercises.

For instance, if we were supplying ASW services, the hottest antisubmarine ships in the Navy were in Pearl Harbor, where superb sound conditions offered great training. One

---

* In late 1950 Chinese Communists entered the war on the side of the North Koreans, leading to two and a half years of stalemate before an armistice was signed in the summer of 1953.

of these ships was a DDE, the Carpenter; the skipper was an old submariner, Jim Grady.[*] Many times we would sit around the club and challenge each other to exercises. I challenged him once to a special test, offering to be lying to on the surface at 10,000 yards from him and his whole division of four DDEs at the start of unrestricted ASW search, and he would never lay a glove on us. That was too good to turn down, so we made a fairly decent bet on it.

He, as a submariner, knew I would head toward him at maximum speed and try to get off the initial diving point as quickly as possible. And I did head directly toward him. A Guppy, at 18 knots, offers a lot more speed than in his experience in submarines when the maximum was about eight. We also were a knot or two faster than the other Guppy subs. I made a steep dive down to about 500 feet, bent on everything the electrical plant could handle, and headed for him until the minimum time he could possibly make passive contact, then slowed down below audible detection range and kept on going at that speed until they thundered by overhead.

Well, four destroyers churning away at maximum search speed of 25 knots make quite a lot of noise, and we could guess pretty accurately how much noise we could risk putting in the water and still be undetected. He missed us on the first pass-by, and once you lay on a search curve with four ships at 25 knots searching against an 18-knot target, the circle is so big the second time around, the wing ship is halfway to Tokyo. At those speeds, the normal destroyer antisubmarine search plans fall apart almost immediately. It was less than 45 minutes from "go" time until we were on the surface with nobody inside the horizon. We tried to tease him by first asking for a time check. It took several minutes before it dawned on him that we were on the surface. They came charging back to datum again and found us enjoying a leisurely swim call. But we all learned a lot from these exercises. It was excellent training, interesting, and kept the people on their toes, just trying to outwit each other.

Q: At that point were the submarines and ASW forces fairly evenly matched?

---

[*] Commander James B. Grady, USN.

Captain Schratz: Oh, I don't think so. Subs were way ahead. For instance, that first operation off Singapore was the first time they ever had a Guppy in the Far East, the first time the Brits had had any contact with them. It was also the first, and a rare occasion, when the submarine was allowed unlimited evasion without any restrictions on speed, on depth, or on cavitating. Except for those unofficial exercises off Pearl, I can't recall in my years of antisubmarine work of ever being allowed to use full evasion tactics.

We were limited in speed or depth or required to cavitate--operate screws at high enough speeds to produce audible sound--or limited in time without showing something on the surface. Such artificialities were necessary. You couldn't get much training time if the sub disappeared after the first contact or never made contact at all. The ASW forces got no training. But I think the surface forces and the antisubmarine air squadrons should keep in mind, lest they get too confident about their ability, that they have limited their opponent very severely.

Q: Could you cover the operations around Portsmouth, please, when you were trying to get back to watch baseball games on TV?

Captain Schratz: I had always believed that the day's duty officer should get the ship under way and bring her in. But the Portsmouth Harbor offers extreme problems for ship handlers--very strong currents, a few sharp bends in the channel, a narrow channel, and a rock bottom. It's no place for the tyro ship handlers. The normal routine in the Portsmouth yard is to get under way or dock only at slack water. During sea trials, however, this required taking two yard shifts out, each of whom worked half the time at sea.

I decided to get under way every morning at 0700, when the shift came on, and return at 1400, before they went off. The yard saved lots of money, but not even the yard pilot thought a submarine could be handled at that strength of current. He refused even to go to sea with us. Many others said we were asking for trouble.

Well, we had checked the tide tables carefully and learned that we would never get a maximum adverse current on both going out and returning. If the current was near maximum on returning to port, the next morning under way would be close to slack. So we used the current to help our landing. If return to port were made on a maximum flood, I let the current help us make a 180-degree turn in the river so as to berth heading downstream as the current pushed us alongside. If landing on or near a maximum ebb, I made an upstream landing and again let the current put us alongside. And, remember, the current runs five to eight knots. If the ship needed ten knots for normal steerageway, we were making perhaps 18 over the ground--or perhaps only two.

We always anticipated the next underway time, so as not to have to get under way on a maximum ebb with the ship heading upriver, or on a maximum flood with the ship heading downstream. Believe me, though, it was always a thrill. I took the conn until I felt comfortable, no matter what, then let Pappy Sims try it until he developed the same feeling of confidence. After that we turned the conn over to the regular duty officer, and they did a beautiful job. Only once did we get into trouble.

Q: What was that?

Captain Schratz: The conning officer, while backing clear of the dock, let his tail get caught in a maximum ebb, and we started down the river sideways. I had to get her headed properly before the sharp 90-degree turn in the channel at the naval prison. Making that turn normally on the ebb at 18-20 knots over the ground was enough of a thrill without trying to do it sideways.

Q: You followed also the pattern of operating hours that you had brought in with the Burrfish?

Captain Schratz: Yes. We accommodated the yard. And it also enabled the CO to get home every afternoon early enough to catch the Boston Red Sox or Braves--their National League team then--on television.

I also managed to fail my promotion exams about that time too.

Q: They had been reinstated then after World War II.

Captain Schratz: Yes. My class took them for promotion to commander.

Q: What happened when you failed your promotion exams?

Captain Schratz: You got a second chance a few months later. It had no effect on the date of promotion. I think there were three of us in the same squadron at Pearl who took a re-exam together. Quite a number busted them. The main question I blew involved internal operations and organization of a carrier, an area foreign to my world, and one I had not reviewed in my studies. It was embarrassing, a nuisance.

Q: How thorough were those exams?

Captain Schratz: They were quite searching, but also a matter of luck.

Q: What topics did they cover?

Captain Schratz: I don't recall the subject areas anymore, nor how many exams there were. I managed to put that out of my mind very nicely.

Q: Do you think the Navy is at somewhat a disadvantage now that it no longer has such exams?

Captain Schratz: I do for a fact. I think every officer should have a periodic examination, not so much on his ability to go to sea in a ship or his knowledge of ships in operations; I think he should have an exam of some sort on his professional knowledge, of how to fight a ship or develop a war plan. I would make that mandatory for every promotion to lieutenant and above and ensure that standings on those professional exams on the art of war be a requirement for selection first to the command and staff level, and second, the senior war college. It think it is absolutely necessary, particularly for the Navy, to raise the level of instruction at the war colleges adequately, so that we can compensate for the fact we in the Navy get a maximum of only two years in graduate education and study of the art of war, in what we're supposed to know thoroughly as professionals.

Q: Is there anything else from your notes or otherwise that you want to mention on the Pickerel before we move on?

Captain Schratz: Yes, there's one episode. Because we were the fair-haired boys around Pearl Harbor, we usually drew the VIP visitors. One of these visitors was a friend of my commodore, a baker who made a lot of dough in Omaha, didn't know an awful lot about much else and nothing about the Navy. We took him out to sea and gave him the usual tour of the ship, but he appeared totally disinterested, either non-comprehending or didn't care. I got a bit irked and decided to put a scare into him. We started dipsy-doodling, high-speed down angles, sharp up angles, turns, and so forth. He thought that was fantastic. But I made a serious mistake. I overlooked the commodore's reaction. I was in the conning tower, and the diving officer asked if I'd come down to the control room immediately.

The commodore was hanging onto the gyro table, and I think still today there is a complete set of his fingerprints in the aluminum cover. I thought he had had a stroke. He was rigid, couldn't talk, and I had to break his hands loose from the gyro table and try to ease him into the wardroom, physically lifting his feet over the coaming. On the verge of panic, I sent a message to the base that I was returning immediately. By the time we got into the harbor, however, he had recovered almost completely and was able to get off the ship without any particular difficulty.

Well, the next morning he sent for me, first to present me with a very expensive bottle of Scotch from the baker, who claimed it was the biggest thrill of his life. Then he added an explanation for his own reaction. When he came into submarines, the normal dive involved a one-degree down angle, normal surfacing a one-degree up angle, maybe two degrees. And it was "documented" over the years a three-degree angle was the safe maximum. Even during the war, that was the maximum for most diving and surfacing. One didn't have enough speed to control steeper angles, and it didn't make an awful lot of difference anyhow. He was correct.

During the war, one skipper, Benny Bass in <u>Plunger</u>, claimed he could control his ship with a ten-degree down angle.* I know at that time there were serious thoughts about relieving Benny for perhaps having gone off the deep end. The commodore realized we had worked up to large angles, thanks to greater speed and more responsive controls, very carefully over a period of a year or more. For him to suddenly experience it, knowing we were doing these things, flew in the face of all the precautions of 20 years of experience in submarines. I understood the point he was making. I also noticed that he never went to sea in my ship again. He was a very pleasant and capable person, had made several patrols in the war, neither the best nor the worst.

Q: Was this the division commander?

Captain Schratz: Squadron commander. He also took my ship off the "E" list. We had the battle efficiency award locked that year. He told me privately that though we had earned it, we had had so much publicity over our other exploits that it was bad for the rest of the boats, and he had to give it to somebody else. I didn't complain. But everybody knew which was the hottest ship in the outfit.

Q: Many of the individuals I interview say the command of one's own ship is among the most satisfying duty in an entire career. Did you find that to be the case?

Captain Schratz: No question about it. I think I was very fortunate, too, in the way my career worked out. Less than a year out of sub school, I was acting exec in <u>Scorpion</u>, and I never again was anything but XO or CO. I had more than my share of command and loved every minute.

---

* Commander Raymond H. Bass, USN.

Q: Did the next tour of duty seem sort of anticlimactic after that?

Captain Schratz: I went from Pickerel to duty in OpNav, OP-35, now OP-61, the political-military policy division. My boss was Charlie Moses again, whom I had worked for in BuPers. At least Charlie was in the same division. I was in a different branch. I went there as special assistant to the director, who was initially Jimmy Thach, then Count Austin, and later Smedberg.*

Q: How did you get into that, since you hadn't had any postgraduate education in that field up to that?

Captain Schratz: Well, nobody else had either, although the other services do much better. When I look back now and see the influence which some lieutenant commander paper-writers have on the policy structure in Washington, I see serious flaws in it. The Navy in particular has never felt the need for international relations specialists to the degree that the other services have.

I came to discover this in full force when I later asked to be allowed to accept a doctoral fellowship. I pointed out to the Chief of Naval Personnel in my interview that the Army and the Air Force had extensive programs of graduate education in international relations and the Navy had essentially none, and really the Navy has major influence around the world in that field, more than the other services. This drew a very patronizing response to the effect that just being in the Navy is an education in international relations: "We take our ships into the harbors; we understand the little people, and they understand us. Wearing that uniform is your education in international affairs."

I didn't quite agree with that, naturally. I violently disagreed. But the prevailing attitude in the Navy is very resistant to change in that respect. We produce technicians, not warriors.

---

* Rear Admiral James H. Thach, Jr., USN; Rear Admiral Bernard L. Austin, USN; Rear Admiral William R. Smedberg III, USN. The oral histories of Austin and Smedberg are in the Naval Institute collection.

Q: You get to meet the little people that way but not the big people.

Captain Schratz: True. Good point.

Q: What do you remember about Jimmy Thach?

Captain Schratz: He left very shortly after I arrived. This was the brother of the aviator.[*] Count Austin was just selected for flag rank and he became the director shortly.

Q: Let's talk about Count Austin then.

Captain Schratz: He was a very nice person to work with, a bit pompous but very easygoing. I thoroughly enjoyed the duties. Special assistant didn't mean an awful lot then except trying to keep him properly briefed. My early concern was the enormous amount of time flag officers spent at their desks and the very little percentage of it dedicated to long-range thinking about something. People were spending enormous amounts of time in the offices, largely wheel-spinning. Nobody went home until the big boss quit. The long hours weren't necessary and were very tough on family life.

    I suggested a plan to Count Austin one day. I thought he should take out at least one hour a day and do nothing but think broad thoughts, the broad future of the Navy, of the nation, whatever. If he would pick one hour of each day most suitable to him personally, I would ensure, up and down the line, that we would respect that, keep all the calls and everything else away from him, to free him for Big Think. He agreed it was a super idea, so we tried it. The first day it went fine. The second day, something urgent, I believe from Jimmy Fife, OP-06, simply couldn't wait.[†] So I grudgingly allowed the

---

[*] Captain John S. Thach, USN, who later became a four-star admiral, was the younger brother of James H. Thach, Jr.
[†] Vice Admiral James Fife, USN.

interruption. And about the fourth day, there were two or three interruptions. A week later we were back to business as usual--a great idea which lasted about a week.

At that time I also inherited a collateral duty on the Antarctic Policy Committee. Admiral Richard Byrd, my old nemesis from BuPers days, had been the antarctic expert for years, but he was a very strange individual. The International Geophysical Year was coming up in '57, and the Navy was planning an antarctic expedition, which Byrd wanted to head, naturally.[*] There were others who also wanted to be the leader, Finn Ronne, for one, the Norwegian who had been Byrd's deputy on a previous trip, once great friends but no longer. So, looking forward to both the IGY and the antarctic expedition, the National Security Council set up an inter-agency council on the Antarctic, with representatives from State, CIA, Interior, Defense, and everybody else with an interest in it. Byrd was appointed head of the committee, and I was named his deputy. Since he was such a prestigious person, the other agencies nominated a deputy chief or assistant secretary. The State Department member was Andy Ronhovde, head of European Affairs.[†]

Then I found to my horror that Admiral Byrd had a personal fear of the Pentagon. He had an office in the old Main Navy building for years but never visited the Pentagon. He had a real phobia against people in general and the senior people in the Navy in particular. Even though he was intensely interested in the U.S. activities for the Antarctic, he never attended a meeting. When he came to town, it was usually for a private meeting with me at his hotel, the Hay-Adams, where Tom Siple or Bernt Balchen or some of the other old sourdoughs from the past would join.[‡]

I suddenly discovered that I would have to chair all those inter-agency meetings. As a fresh-caught commander, I was far junior to anybody else and had no competency in polar affairs that came easily to mind. I made the obvious decision. I suggested to Ronhovde,

---

[*] The International Geophysical Year ran from 1 July 1957 to 31 December 1958 as a cooperative endeavor to study aspects of planet earth.
[†] Andreas G. Ronhovde.
[‡] Paul A. Siple went on Byrd's 1928-30 expedition to Antarctica; Siple had been chosen from among 600,000 Boy Scouts in order to be included. Bernt Balchen was a Norwegian who was chief pilot on Byrd's late-1920s trip. He was credited with piloting the first flight over the South Pole on 29 November 1929. He entered the U.S. Army Air Forces in 1941.

next senior to Byrd, that since Byrd would rarely be present, that it would be far more appropriate if State Department would chair the meetings. This worked out fine.

The task, of course, was to prepare a draft of U.S. policy on the Antarctic for approval by the NSC and the President. State Department was reluctant on this issue. Any policy would cause disagreements with other nations having territorial claims in the Antarctic. Every time the issue came up, State supported a policy "to reserve all our rights, whatever they may be." They favored as the best time for a declaration of a U.S. claim in the Antarctic to be 20-25 years prior. For the Antarctic policy paper, a claim had to be made, and the key to U.S. policy was a formal U.S. claim to territories in the Antarctic based on U.S. explorations which were far more extensive than those of any other nation. Here I thought I could make a contribution. What was necessary, it seemed, was a gimmick approach to sell an idea when possible opponents don't realize it's being sold.

Of all the nations with territorial claims to the Antarctic, only the Russians had the logistic capability for extensive exploration of the interior of the Antarctic at this time, and this area caused the most contention. Other nations' claims were based on the sector principle. If they explored a coastal area, they claimed the pie slice from the coast clear to the Pole.

For a number of reasons, State Department opposed the sector principle out of hand. The Russians had made no territorial exploration and based their claim only on circumnavigation of the Antarctic by Bellinghausen way back in 19th century.* I reasoned that since only the U.S. had both a legal basis and a capability for exploration of the interior, why not simply exclude all those areas in the center from our draft policy, make a U.S. territorial claim for the areas where we do have extensive rights based on exploration, and reserve the interior for scientific exploration by all nations.

I put this into a draft policy paper, working out some of the details with the polar areas desk officer in State. But to introduce it, I had an unusual problem. Byrd was totally uninterested. He gladly signed off on anything, usually if I took it to Boston for the purpose. My boss, Admiral Smedberg, wasn't interested either. Few in OpNav would

---

* In January 1820 Captain Fabian von Bellinghausen of the Russian Navy reached a point only 20 miles from Antarctica.

touch anything Byrd was involved in, and this was for an inter-agency committee anyway. The fact that I was committing the Navy to a position made no difference. The committee accepted it enthusiastically, and it eventually became the U.S. policy for the Antarctic. I then carried that paper through OpNav, through the three services, through the JCS, and through the National Security Council staff for final approval.

During this time the collateral problem of the details of the U.S. claim became quite urgent. There was no central depository of U.S. polar exploration. The historical records of major expeditions could be found, along with rumors of exploration by New England whalers of which there was no record. I suggested to my boss that the best way in the world to track these down was to hire a researcher. My specific suggestion was to find a hotshot young graduate student in geography, for example, and send him off on a three-month boondoggle through these old whaling museums in New England.

BuPers produced one young ensign, recently married and not averse to a three-month honeymoon at government expense, working with his hobby. He had just graduated from the University of Michigan, a geologist or geographer or similar specialty, and recently commissioned. He was more than delighted at the opportunity and returned in due time with, among other things, a pregnant wife and a log. The incident is still etched on my brain. Nicholas Burdick, a whaler in the schooner Huntress, had taken his old logbook and made a scrapbook out of it. Peeling off the old newspaper clippings, most of them falling off, revealed the story of his antarctic whaling voyages. He sailed down the Palmer Peninsula and stated in the record, "I see before me a vast area which I take to be a continent." That was about 1818, far earlier than any other claim identifying the Antarctic as a continent, and a vital bit of evidence in support of the U.S. claim. This was a real gold mine, a key document for our claim. Of course, it was immediately classified, but I believe it is now available to anybody.

Q: Why was it classified?

Captain Schratz: To assist our diplomats. We didn't want to tip the hand of negotiators in the early days of the new policy, pending the reaction of other claimants. Anyhow, my paper became the basis for the Antarctic treaty, the treaty which just came up for renewal, I think, last year.

Q: Did Admiral Byrd make any substantive contribution?

Captain Schratz: Never. I received nothing from him but "Attaboy." He was actively planning a new Antarctic expedition, talking with Tom Siple--remember, the All-American Boy Scout who made the 1925 expedition with Byrd?

Q: I've heard the name.

Captain Schratz: Yes. Tom was chosen of all the Boy Scouts in America for the 1925 expedition to the Antarctic. Not too far from his own age, this was very dramatic for me at the time. Siple made his career with Byrd, and we became quite friendly. He did a dissertation on the Antarctic for his doctorate from Clark University.

It was Siple who tipped me off one day that Admiral Byrd had never seen the South Pole. That was amazing enough that I went to the Naval Photo Lab at Anacostia and examined the records of Operation High Jump photography, with millions of exposures photomapping the entire region. Unfortunately, he overlooked any ground control locations and the mass of photography is largely useless. Nor could I find a single exposure claiming to be of the South Pole itself. On the widely publicized trip when Byrd flew to the South Pole from Little America, there is no photograph of the Pole. There are plenty of photographs inside the plane--dropping the U.S. flag through the bomb bay, for example-- but nothing of the Pole. Tom said Byrd had actually flown toward the Pole from Little America until he was out of sight over the horizon, then flew it back to a remote section of the coast at the end of the ice shelf, and orbited over the area until enough time had elapsed, then reversed his track and flew back to Little America, and that Tom was convinced himself that Byrd had never seen the Pole.

I completed duties on the Antarctic committee just before my detachment from OP-61 for sea duty. Arriving in San Diego for a submarine division command, the first mail included a letter from Admiral Byrd expressing his appreciation for all I had done in getting the expedition approved. But he asked, "What is it that you really did? I want to make sure you get the proper commendation out of this. If you would like to write the commendation, I'll add the flowery details and take care of it from here." I stared at this document for quite some time. I had been criticized by Smedberg because polar affairs had taken too much of my time from my "Navy" duties--little choice I had. After deep thought, the Byrd letter found a place in the wastebasket.

Q: Could you please tell me your memories of Rear Admiral Milton Miles from the time you were in OP-61?[*]

Captain Schratz: Yes. He was the director of Pan American affairs at the time in CNO, OP-02 then, and I had the Latin American desk, so policy items frequently involved both offices. Miles generally did not care to operate within the Pentagon operational structure. He was a free spirit going his own way and doing his own thing. I don't think he agreed with much of U.S. policy toward Latin America, claiming it showed little knowledge or appreciation of internal problems. He was right more than wrong. His own wide experience and his closeness to all the Latin American military was a pretty sound guide.

At that time I was also on the Antarctic policy committee. Argentina and Chile were running a little comic opera naval war over Deception Island in the Antarctic. Deception Island was the center of disputed antarctic claims of both Argentina and Chile. At that very tense moment, Miles was invited by the Argentines to go to sea with them on their cruiser flagship to visit Deception Island. Neither OpNav nor State would ever clear such a visit, so he decided to go without their clearance or knowledge. He wanted somebody up here to know he was going, however, so he told me about it and made me the patsy. I was put in an awkward spot, because it was probably my responsibility to inform my boss of it and let him carry the load. Could I rat on a rear admiral? If I didn't, I was disloyal to another.

---

[*] Rear Admiral Milton E. Miles, USN.

Q: Admiral Austin?

Captain Schratz: Admiral Austin. Since I had a strong empathy with Miles and felt he might ease the Chile-Argentine crisis, even though he was apparently taking sides with the Argentinians, I thought I'd accept responsibility and pray that nothing went wrong. Nothing did, fortunately.

We had much in common. I found him a soulmate in the way we operated, even for ordinary things like watching baseball games on television. I was in his office with a small group. This was the time of the famous Bobby Thomson home run in 1951.[*] As Thomson went to the plate, Leo Durocher called him aside for a few moments before he stepped into the batter's box.[†] In that quiet office with about 15 people watching the screen, I mentioned matter-of-factly that Leo Durocher just told Thomson that if he got a home run, he could spend the weekend with movie actress Laraine Day, then Durocher's wife. When he hit that memorable home run, one of those sports events nobody forgets, every eye turned to me. Everybody in Miles's office remembers the fairy tale about Laraine Day more than the home run. I'll never forget it.

Q: Any other stories about your relationship with him from that period?

Captain Schratz: No. Having known and admired him, I was much interested in digging more deeply into his unbelievable experiences in China. At the Air War College, I did a paper on U.S. policy in the Pacific for the biannual history conference at the Air Force Academy, and I tended to overemphasize Miles's role in China during the war, certainly one

---

[*] Robert B. Thomson was the third baseman for the New York Giants as they played the Brooklyn Dodgers at the Polo Grounds in New York City on 3 October 1951. The two teams had tied during the regular season and were engaged in a playoff to determine which team would represent the National League in the upcoming World Series. Thomson hit a three-run home run to win the final game, 5-4.

[†] Leo Durocher was the manager of the New York Giants.

of the all-time heroic episodes in our history. I read all I could get my hands on about the China expedition. A great character; we lost a lot when he shoved off.*

Q: What other things did you work on during that period? Was the Southeast Asia thing a concern?

Captain Schratz: Not for me. Midway through my tour, I took over the Latin American area as my responsibility. The major concern during that time was Iceland. That was in my area, and we were having a lot of trouble with the Icelandic Government on unreasonable limitations and hostility toward U.S. servicemen in Iceland. I spent a lot of time on that.

Q: Nothing new there. Do you have any other specific recollections about Admiral Austin in addition to his one-week long-range planning course?

Captain Schratz: He was excellent to work for, very unassuming as a flag officer, but rather pompous. I didn't put the story about the boxing gloves on record, did I?

Q: No.

Captain Schratz: Well, typically he had a tough time making up his mind and really laying down the law on points where indecisiveness made it tough on the staff. One of these cases was over a three-service issue of some sort which had been thrashed around every way possible without agreement. A deadline arrived where he had to come up with a decision. Briefing him for that meeting, I put a large briefcase on his desk. In it was a pair of boxing gloves I had borrowed from the Pentagon athletic club, enormous boxing gloves, and a bottle of bourbon. I said, "Admiral, everybody around the table knows everybody's position. There's no point in trying to argue for a new position. You simply must decide today and make it stick."

---

* Miles died in March 1961 at the age of 60.

I suggested he go to the meeting, open the briefcase, pull out the boxing gloves and the bourbon and say, "Okay, we all know where we stand and must reach an agreement. How do you want it, the hard way or the easy way?"

A funny look came over his face. I guess it really appealed to him. So he went off to the war and came back shortly, all smiles. It broke up the meeting; the issue was solved.

But I couldn't often find that solution to some of the problems. One of his deputies also was a very, very cautious person who couldn't get up on his hind feet to get a paper forward. He compounded the problem. Although the duty was rewarding and I accomplished a great deal, it was a very unhappy tour. There were so many things I thought should be done that weren't getting done. Admiral Burke, then OP-60, strategic plans, was a workhorse, but too much of the effort of the planners was wasted in direct competition with the Air Force for roles, missions, prestige, or visibility around the world.[*] I thought the Navy was really dropping the bricks in our own role in international affairs in not taking a dynamic approach rather than simply reacting to crises as they happened. Far more should have been done beyond the routine of ship clearances, visits, training areas, and transitory issues.

Q: What types of things do you think might have been accomplished that weren't?

Captain Schratz: First, I thought the realism, the operational feasibility of our Navy crisis procedures was dreadful. It was more than ten years after the surprise attack on Pearl Harbor, yet crisis procedures in OpNav were primitive, perhaps even unchanged. I first ran across this in standing the Navy Department duty officer watches, the senior awake DO in the Navy. In a crisis alert, the duty officer was responsible for notifying close to 100 seniors, civilian and military, and furnishing them transportation to the Pentagon. He had one car, one telephone, one enlisted assistant. The DO was required to draft and send out a dozen emergency messages to the fleet, notify local radio and TV stations to air emergency notices for all personnel to return to their duty stations. This was in direct contradiction to

---

[*] Rear Admiral Arleigh A. Burke, USN, who became Chief of Naval Operations in 1955.

JCS instructions and to regional disaster plans, but nobody would take the initiative to change.

Two of the people the Navy did not notify in crisis were the JCS and DoD duty officers. The DO was required to open the CNO safe, get out "the briefcase," and meet the CNO when he arrived in the Pentagon. The DO had not even a chart to translate the latitude and longitude of the crisis into an identifiable piece of real estate. And all of this "immediately," by two individuals.

I assure you, there is no exaggeration here. I drafted a letter to the CNO pointing out the need for some sort of a crisis plotting facility, but Count Austin wouldn't sign it. I therefore signed it myself and sent it via him to the chief. The result: I was appointed a member and recorder of a board to come up with recommended changes. The other members, all flag officers, were remarkably undistinguished, probably chosen for that reason. I did my homework and was easily able to prevail, if not overwhelm them. The result was the eventual establishment of the CNO chartroom, a very fine facility for day-by-day and crisis operations, and a revision of the whole concept of department watch-standing.

Second, fleet operational training seemed unrealistic, dull, and unimaginative, a responsibility to some degree of all the CNO operational deputies. I thought we needed the sort of worldwide exercises such as the Soviets were doing in their Okean operations. Our exercises did not well simulate wartime challenges. This was not primarily Admiral Austin's responsibility; it was partly the responsibility of all, and hence nobody did it.

The first of this type of exercise happened some time later. Shortly afterward, my submarine division on the West Coast began antimissile operations, of which CNO was quite doubtful, simulating a defense against incoming submarine-launched missiles. This became a very important operation, long before we had a real missile capability, when we had nothing but the surface-launched Regulus missile.* We did little in those days really

---

* The two Regulus missiles were designed to be fired from surface ships or surfaced submarines. Regulus I was 34 feet long, weighed 12,000 pounds, and had a speed of Mach 0.9 and range of 500 miles; Regulus II was 57 feet long, weighed 22,000 pounds, and had a speed of Mach 2.0 and range of 1,000 miles.

challenging to the entire fleet. Bud Zumwalt as CNO much later tried to break down the three "unions" in the Navy--air, subs, and surface.*

Many of us were pressing along these lines far earlier. The submarine fleet went its own way, the aviators went their own way, the surface ships were dying of starvation and neglect. I didn't think we were really integrating naval operations anywhere to do what we had to do everywhere, to influence political ideas and concepts around the world. A show of force served national goals. When used strategically, it served a political goal. When used only tactically, it fostered military goals. We were not looking at the rest of the world as it is, and using what we had to influence events rather than react to initiatives of others and be influenced by events. How can we do what we must do when lack of ships and the day-to-day routine absorbs all our energies in over-concentration with our own resources rather than a broader look at the world?

Q: Did it make any change in the leadership, in action in that area when Admiral Smedberg came in?

Captain Schratz: I don't think so, no.

Q: What memories do you have of him?

Captain Schratz: I was really disappointed in him as a boss. We didn't seem to see eye-to-eye on much. Where Count Austin was often hesitant, Smedberg was prone to act too quickly on too little information. For one thing, I felt I had far too many duties. The antarctic problem, despite the great importance the policy was to have on the IGY planning, was peculiarly my own; nobody had any interest. As a collateral assignment, it was natural to assume that it was at the expense of what I should have been spending my time on, and I was left in a very awkward position on it. I sure couldn't ask Byrd to carry the load. There was no hope there if national interest was involved. I really did think something could be

---

* Admiral Elmo R. Zumwalt, Jr., USN, served as Chief of Naval Operations from 1 July 1970 to 29 June 1974.

done and had to be done. So I had to make my own decision and go my own way. I've never looked back on that tour as a very satisfying tour, through no fault of my own. And what I accomplished in many areas, plus the antarctic treaty, was little understood.

Q: Admiral Fechteler was the CNO during the first couple of years you were there.[*] How much discussion and so forth went back and forth between the CNO's office and OP-61?

Captain Schratz: I really have no strong recollection of what role we really filled. Arleigh Burke always overshadowed our division very, very strongly. You may recall that Count Austin was the junior division commander with Burke in his "31-knot" days during the war, and Austin doesn't show up well at all in Burke's book, perhaps unjustly so. When OP-60 needed some extra talent in connection with strategic interests of the Middle East, Admiral Burke grabbed Dick Colbert, then in OP-61, and Dick worked privately on his own with OP-60 in developing a number of Middle East papers on related problems.[†] Admiral Burke, to our knowledge, didn't go through Austin formally; he simply used Dick on a personal basis. Others were used similarly, and the impression I have is that the branch itself didn't carry an awful lot of weight simply because of a very strong personality next door and the relatively weak leadership in our group. Smedberg and Austin both, I believe, were more influential with State, more useful to State, than to OpNav.

Q: You say you were really not doing any hard thinking, pulling things together. What were you doing--mainly reacting to things as they came up?

---

[*] Admiral William M. Fechteler, USN, served as Chief of Naval Operations from 16 August 1951 to 17 August 1953.
[†] Commander Richard G. Colbert, later president of the Naval War College and eventually a four-star admiral.

Captain Schratz: Yes, which is generally what's expected. Since the U.S. claims not to have an aggressive foreign policy, we generally react rather than follow up on actions of our own creation.

Q: What kinds of things do you remember reacting to other than the Antarctic and Iceland during that period?

Captain Schratz: We had one problem of a fairly strong spreading Communist influence in Latin America at that particular time which affected my branch through ONI and State.[*] There had been some very serious uprisings, one in Bogota, lots of people killed in several countries.

During that period, I was the president and a first fiddler with the Arlington Symphony; we had the task of finding a new conductor. One applicant had some superb clippings. He was the director of music for the Pan American Union in Washington, and he wanted to become the director of the Arlington Symphony in addition. A superb talent, he had made several guest conductor appearances in Latin America and had the glossy brochures as proof. My board decided we were very fortunate to have this gentleman. There were problems over his frequent absences from the area; he couldn't be available for rehearsals many times, and we would have to be flexible. But we were all willing to accept this as the necessary price.

The next morning, by chance, I had his brochures with me and happened to notice quite by chance that places where he had conducted in Latin America, such as Bogota, Panama, and a few others, had been the scenes of serious Communist uprisings at the same time. I arranged a meeting with a contact up in another branch and dropped this folder on his desk. This was a very prominent name in his office. When I said that we had just made him the conductor of the Arlington Symphony Orchestra, he said I had two problems. I had to get him out of the conductor's appointment and do so without giving the board the reason for it.

---

[*] ONI--Office of Naval Intelligence.

I had the very awkward task of reversing the action of the board for which I had been enthusiastic 24 hours earlier. Stressing his unavailability at rehearsals, his haphazard travel schedule, and competition from other conducting duties, I drew a dire picture of the effects on our season. So I was successful in canceling our action before it got to the press. I don't know why he wanted the new job; I could only speculate that my own dual position could have been a factor. I had been working with other agencies on the common problem of Communist activities in Latin America.

Q: What was this individual's name?

Captain Schratz: The conductor? I don't recall anymore.

Q: These other agencies that you were dealing with, did they include the CIA?[*]

Captain Schratz: No, ONI. Well, CIA through the ONI, but I never worked directly with the CIA, except on the antarctic committee.

Q: On a family level, you finally had a son during that period.

Captain Schratz: Yes, I guess it did happen then. Pete was our fifth youngster.[†] We had two daughters after Pete.

Q: So did they all get involved in the community there where you were living in northern Virginia?

Captain Schratz: Oh, yes, always. We had a super community and worked together on many things. We were active with them socially too.

---

[*] CIA--Central Intelligence Agency.
[†] Paul R. Schratz, Jr., later became a naval officer himself.

Q: Did your wife take part in Navy wives' activities?

Captain Schratz: Not to a great extent. In Washington there aren't very many Navy wives' activities because everyone is so spread out. With my writing activities and being in the symphony and some other things with music and fundraising, we did a lot of entertaining for the symphony and for our neighborhood community. And we had a fair amount of OpNav social meetings.

One of the main problems when I was in OP-61 is that name of Donc Donaho.[*] I also handled new personnel; Donc was a branch head, running the foreign military aid program. Since Donc was so tough to work for, I had a serious problem in finding a bright, young submarine officer to fill a junior billet in his staff. With great difficulty, I located a very sharp officer, and the approval had no sooner been announced than an old friend in BuPers got very upset about it, claiming it would cause a serious personality conflict and ruin his career. The officer was very capable, but outspoken and would never work under Donc. Feeling obligated, I tried to kill the orders and find somebody else.

I briefed Donc's number-one assistant on the need to avoid a personality conflict and of my intention to find somebody else. After an extremely difficult search, BuPers found a replacement, an officer named Bill Racette, whom the OpNav personnel office finally approved.[†]

That night, just before quitting time, Donc came into the front office to inform me that Racette wouldn't do. "He's French. I'm Scotch-Irish. We'll have a personality conflict from the day he arrives."

I couldn't believe my ears. Nor could I explain to anybody the reason, especially after having done everything I could to find the officer and get him approved, then to turn him down because he was of a different national origin. What I didn't realize, and maybe should have, was that Donc was pulling my leg. He was known to have no sense of humor; this was the first joke he ever pulled in his life.

---

[*] Rear Admiral Glyn R. Donaho, USN.
[†] Lieutenant Commander William A. Racette, USN.

Q: Did he know what you'd been through with the other?

Captain Schratz: He had a very good idea. He thought it was really funny, and to see me squirm must have given him great delight. Well, I never expected a joke from him. This made it all the funnier. But I decided that day to have the last word. Racette was accepted, and, biding my time until the next vacancy in his office, the man I sought needed only one qualification--to be of Italian origin. And so Guy Gugliotta came to OpNav--he may never know why--because I couldn't wait to see the nameplates outside the office, marking the double personality conflict with Donc.[*]

Q: You also had some encounters during that period, didn't you, with Judge Eller?[†]

Captain Schratz: Yes.

Q: Would you like to discuss it, please?

Captain Schratz: The Judge was a very careful naval officer. He was not a strong individual as far as accepting responsibility, and at that time he was under the gun for selection to flag rank and walked a very cautious path. The staff had great difficulty in getting any paper through the Judge if it seemed in any way contrary to an opinion of a senior, however justified the action was. It was a cross we all had to bear. The Judge also was one of the few who had the God-given gift of being able to read and write. Nitpicking was driving us mad, trying to clear a paper through him phrased in the style of English which he liked.

For example, I had a memorandum of agreement with a State Department official which they wanted confirmed in writing. Paragraph one mentioned something about the

---

[*] Commander Guy F. Gugliotta, USN.
[†] Captain Ernest M. Eller, USN. The oral history of Eller, who retired as a rear admiral, is in the Naval Institute collection.

U.S. Navy still supporting the three-mile territorial limit. Paragraph two said the letter confirmed a telephone conversation between Commander Schratz and Ms. Somebody or other. The Judge nitpicked the first paragraph, rephrased it to his liking. I put it back in the typewriter, but the next draft fared no better. Before I sent up the third draft, I changed paragraph two to read, "This no longer confirms telephone conversation between Commander Schratz and . . ." Well, the Judge got quite upset. But I often wondered if he did the same to Shakespeare. When he got home to Annapolis each night, did he pull down his volume of sonnets, perhaps over an evening cocktail, and they too been nitpicked to make them express what Shakespeare really had in mind?

Q: So as this tour was winding down, I guess you were looking forward to getting back to submarines.

Captain Schratz: I was looking forward to getting anywhere. I felt I'd done as good a job I could under the circumstances, and considerably better than might have been expected. I simply was not appreciated, and I never had that experience before or since.

Q: In 1954 you reported to the submarine tender <u>Nereus</u> as executive officer.[*] Who was your skipper?

Captain Schratz: My skipper was Robert E. "Dusty" Dornin, class of '35, who had had a fantastic record during the war as a submarine skipper, one of the best in the submarine force.[†] I hadn't met him before, strangely.

The <u>Nereus</u> was a very challenging task. This was at the time when discipline, reenlistments, everything in the Navy had gone to pot. In fact, it was so bad that ComSubPac sent a letter to each skipper in the force, suggesting that his fitness report

---

[*] The USS <u>Nereus</u> (AS-17) was commissioned on 27 October 1945. She was 530 feet long, 74 feet in the beam, had a draft of 26.5 feet, and displaced 16,550 tons fully loaded. She had a top speed of 15 knots and was armed with four 5-inch guns.
[†] Captain Robert E. Dornin, USN. Dornin's oral history of his service as aide to Fleet Admiral Ernest J. King, USN, during World War II is in the Naval Institute collection.

would reflect his success in the reenlistment campaign. This might not be the best leadership technique, but it sure gets a lot of action. Nereus itself had still greater problems. When we reported aboard, there were more court-martials on that ship, more captain's mast cases, than in all the rest of the Pacific Fleet combined. The ship had simply ground to a halt to prosecute justice. Much of this was caused by some renegades from the retraining command outside San Diego, Camp Elliott. Every time a mother would write a congressman that the Navy didn't understand her Johnny, they'd parole him and send him to Nereus for a new chance.

Q: Why the Nereus?

Captain Schratz: She was in port in San Diego most of the time and needed the people. But the great majority of "parolees" from Camp Elliott were simply festering sores on the ship. Dusty and I succeeded a very sharp CO-exec team when we came aboard: Kenny Nauman, who had command of Salmon when Sterlet escorted her home after her fatal damage from depth charging, and Harry Higgs, a classmate of mine, as exec.[*] Dusty Dornin's handling of the men was totally different. The new Uniform Code of Military Justice had just come into effect, and fortunately, neither of us had read it.[†] We had a very sharp legal officer aboard who tried to keep us out of trouble, and trouble was not long in coming.

We had been aboard less than a week when a simple case at captain's mast put the Dornin stamp on discipline. One of our Camp Elliott veterans, on his first liberty on board, had gone down to Tijuana, absorbed a few too many beers, and came back about 45 minutes over leave the next morning. Normally this would be handled at the exec's level. His record was so horrible, though, I thought he should meet the captain. In Nereus, mast before Dusty's arrival was held on deck like most ships. Present for each offender were his division officer, the reporting officer, the chief master-at-arms, the legal officer, the medical

---

[*] Captain Harley K. Nauman, USN; Commander Alfred Henry Higgs, USN.
[†] The Uniform Code of Military Justice (UCMJ) was enacted into law on 5 May 1950 with the provision that it be in full force and effect by the individual services by 31 May 1951.

officer, the duty officer, the officer of the deck, witnesses. It was a rat race. With a score or more at mast, it was like morning quarters. Everybody on the ship was there.

No man was going to break down and plead his case before friends, bosses, division officers, everybody else on the ship. So Dusty didn't do it that way. Mast was held in his cabin. A man came there to be commended or to be condemned; either way, he was going to remember the day. The captain wanted nobody else present except the chief master-at-arms behind the accused and the exec behind the CO. The legal requirement about his duty to inform the accused of his rights, of an appeal if he didn't like the punishment--this was the legal officer's responsibility before the accused ever came across the threshold. Once the man was in front of the captain, Dusty sought nothing but to dispense justice.

When this young delinquent walked in for our first case, Dusty glared at him and ordered, "Put up your fists. I could kick the soot out of you."

I was stunned. Racking my brain to find what to do to separate the captain from an affray at captain's mast, I looked across at the chief master-at-arms and could see his knees shaking through his khaki trousers. I could feel spurts of perspiration running down my arms as Dusty gave the worst dressing-down I've ever heard. The culprit burst into tears and then headed for the first door he could find, out onto the deck, bouncing off the lifeline and heading aft, with Dusty in full pursuit. I couldn't believe it. I sought out the legal officer and briefed him.

I have no idea what the chief master-at-arms told the chiefs or what the crew learned in crew's quarters, but overnight we had no more mast cases. Overnight, Nereus went from the worst to the absolute best in the fleet. Nobody showed up for mast. There was no thrill to taking on the skipper. For that first culprit, I asked the department head to keep an eye on him and report to me in a couple of months. When he reported to me later, he said, "Well, that kid ain't much. He'll never be much. But one thing I can guarantee, there's nothing in this wonderful world of ours that he won't do to keep from seeing Mr. Dornin across that little table again." If this was totally in conflict with the Uniform Code, I can only say that justice was served.

At the Naval War College on my next tour, the JAG lectured on the failure of many Navy commands to accept the new UMCJ as superior to the old "Rocks and Shoals." He said, "When you follow UMCJ, you can have superb discipline. I want to use the example of the USS Nereus, who went from the worst to the best in changing over to UMCJ." Sitting in the audience, I couldn't quite agree but held my peace.

We did one fine job in training and refitting submarines too. Nereus earned a marvelous reputation. We had a good crew, and once they set to work, nothing daunted them. In ship's training, Dusty made another major contribution. We were allowed only two days a month for seagoing training of the crew, the only time the tender could be spared from the primary task of refitting submarines. Normally, San Diego tenders took the two days for intensive exercises in the local area, which we both thought extremely dull.

Instead, we went out to witness a Regulus missile firing exercise by some of our boats, made a speed run to Long Beach, and putting two monthly periods together over a holiday, made a special trip to San Francisco. Sea drills featured realism, progressive damage control exercises as lifelike as I could make them. We filmed these and other shipboard activities and showed them before the movies at night, both as a critique and commentary of life on board. We even took two women to sea from Long Beach to San Diego--in those days highly irregular.

To help the reenlistment campaign, we examined every element of shipboard life to make it more pleasant. We killed useless routines like airing bedding, pushed reveille up a half hour, arranged for locker clubs and parking at the local Coast Guard Air Station--in exchange for repainting their hangar--and went to great lengths to counter the myth of how great was the life on the outside. I got data from VA and college deans on how many servicemen failed or dropped out of GI Bill education, and arranged special classes at local schools for the men still in uniform.[*] I went out of my way to use the plan of the day as a small-town newspaper carrying gossip, sports stories, shipboard contests, seamanship questions, all designed to pull the men together in shared common interests.

We made a trip to Santa Barbara, just a weekend jaunt, where, thanks to superb advance preparation, it may stand as the perfect example of how mutually outstanding such

---

[*] VA--Veterans Administration. The GI Bill, officially the Servicemen's Readjustment Act of 1944, provided educational assistance and other benefits to all veterans honorably discharged with six or more months of active service after 16 September 1940.

a trip can be. We replaced the fresh water supply system for the local children's hospital--a holiday for the repair gang--and donated several hundred dollars to the hospital as an expression of our gratitude to the city. A restaurant was renamed for the ship. We helped redecorate the lounge with nautical trivia, including a few souvenirs from the ship's foundry and carpenter shop. It wasn't just chance that we focused on the children's hospital. I had learned earlier that both Admiral Nimitz and SecNav, Thomas Gates, had handicapped youngsters who were patients there.* Within a very short time after the Nereus visit, Captain Dornin was ordered to Washington for interviews by the Secretary concerning his next tour of duty.

Q: You've written about Captain Dornin for Shipmate without mentioning his name. Now that he's departed, are there stories that could be told on the record?

Captain Schratz: That Shipmate series attracted wide interest among readers, but even they were largely understated.† There is no way to capture the real essence of the Dornin era and the effect of that CO-XO pair on the ship, the flotilla, and the force. The whole story is unbelievable.

At the end of the year, ComSubPac decided to give the "E" to the Nereus as the outstanding submarine in SubRon Five. The tenders were not in the competition. This decision came from ComSubPac personally. I don't think anybody in the flotilla begrudged us the "E," certainly none of our submarines. They all really thought that we'd done more than they had ever expected from a tender in everything.

We made a refresher cruise to Pearl Harbor, and ComSubPac came aboard for a visit. To Dusty he said, "I want to congratulate you. I can walk anywhere on the submarine base and see your men walking two or three abreast, arm in arm, and if I don't

---

* Fleet Admiral Chester W. Nimitz, USN, had been Commander in Chief Pacific Fleet, 1941-45, and Chief of Naval Operations, 1945-47. Thomas S. Gates, Jr., served as Secretary of the Navy from 1 April 1957 to 7 June 1959.

† These articles were published in successive issues of Shipmate in 1981: March, pages 5, 7; April, page 5; May, pages 4, 6; June, pages 7-8; July-August, pages 5, 7; September, pages 5, 8.

stop to ask them about their ship, they'll stop me. They're so damn proud of their ship and their skipper." I had seen nothing like their reaction; it was quite a lesson for me in real leadership. He had a fantastic, natural esprit with the men. He was a robust, hard-living type, and I can see that he would have been one of the greatest in wartime. When he came down with cancer, I went out to his home in Leucadia. Ellie told me later that those Shipmate columns kept him alive an extra six months.

Q: I talked to a fellow who worked with him in the Sea Fox right after World War II, and he said Dornin at that time showed a great flair for the dramatic, as you told the mast story, that captured people's attention and got them headed in the right direction.[*]

Captain Schratz: He was far smarter than he looked. He didn't give the impression of scholarly brilliance, but don't ever sell him short. I was surprised to see how high he stood academically in his class.[†]

Q: Any other things about him specifically from that tour?

Captain Schratz: He was a great sports buff and wanted to take the ship to San Francisco, his home and previous duty station. We combined two or three of our two-day training periods and made the trip. We arranged for about 200 of the crew to see Navy play Stanford in Pasadena while we were in San Fran.

Shortly after our return, I ran a sports question in the plan of the day. With Christmas coming up, I offered an extra week of Christmas leave to the first correct answer to the question "When did Navy play LSU last and what was the score?" For an extra week of leave, men will lie, cheat, and slay dragons, but nobody came up with the answer, including the CO. And Dusty had all the records of Navy sports, plus practice games, probably. Sportswriters in San Diego frequently called him for information. But everybody drew a blank on this one. People checked the news archives and called the athletic

---

[*] This is in the Naval Institute oral history of Captain Alex A. Kerr, USN (Ret.).
[†] Dornin stood number 50 of the 442 graduates in the Naval Academy's class of 1935.

association here in Annapolis. When they still couldn't find the answer, Dusty was getting tense. "I think you really blew this one. We never did play those bastards."

I confided in nobody until the answer was finally published, that Navy played Leland Stanford University (LSU) just a few weeks prior, with 200 Nereus sailors enjoying the game. You can imagine the reaction. I took a week's leave to get away from the heat. The point is, the spirit was sensational. We ran the ship as a real loose outfit, and it was just great to be part of the experience.

Q: Well, loose in some ways. Obviously not loose in Navy regulations.

Captain Schratz: We did the job. The men played hard and were happy to work even harder.

Q: What makes one tender better than another tender in refitting submarines?

Captain Schratz: You can always go by the book to avoid excessive or questionable repairs or unauthorized alterations, or you can put your own neck out to accommodate in things you're not supposed to do, the cumshaw items, the extras. You can be awfully nice or you can go by the book. Either way makes a reputation very quickly. When the crew is working overtime, it's easy to refuse requests for ashtrays, plaques, bronze dolphins, and similar souvenirs from the foundry and carpenter shops. But we filled them anyway. We scrounged every dump in the area to find scrap brass. I used this as a training school for pattern makers, carpenters, foundrymen.

Q: I take it that you were more in the generous vein.

Captain Schratz: Oh, sure. Even when we couldn't give the boats everything they wanted, they liked it better. At the end of the year, the usual routine is for the skipper and the exec of the two tenders to trade ships and get the division and squadron commander assignments in the other squadron. It isn't wise to run the squadron or division while based in the tender where you had command or exec the year before. That year, however, ComSubPac decided to break up the Dornin-Schratz team. The other tender, Sperry, was skippered by Gene Fluckey, Medal of Honor winner and another top submariner in the war. Gene worked extremely hard in Sperry, but our luck was all good, his was all bad. If it didn't rain once all summer, it would storm on the day he went to sea for training. For a number of reasons, the normally flamboyant Gene was much overshadowed by Dusty. And Gene's exec was not always helpful.

By the end of the year, therefore, considerable friction had built up between the two tenders. I, therefore, took command of SubDiv 52 based in Nereus, and Dusty took Squadron Three based in Sperry. And so I suddenly found myself working for the individual who had reason to believe that I was the main thorn in many of the things where he had come off second best the previous year. Almost from the day there were problems. A SubRon 5 boat, Pomodon, had a very serious fire and explosion while in overhaul in San Francisco several weeks prior.[*]

Gene, as CO Sperry, had been ordered to San Francisco to conduct the investigation. He hadn't taken the squadron yet. He recommended that the skipper be given a letter of admonition. When his report got to ComSubPac, the big boss sent it back to CO Pomodon for comment prior to taking final action. The CO, Charles Almy, was one of the best. He put together what I thought was a very sound cause--admittedly!--which put the casualty in quite a different light.[†] The strongest testimony against him was given by three of his men in the maneuvering room, all of whom had strong motives of self-interest in their testimony.

I, who had just become Almy's immediate superior, found his statement quite persuasive, and I was particularly impressed by his outstanding handling of the casualty subsequent to the fire and explosion. This created a major problem. I had to send my endorsement through Gene Fluckey as the squadron commander. Where he had been the

---

[*] A hydrogen explosion occurred on board the submarine Pomodon (SS-486) on 20 February 1955 while she was in overhaul at San Francisco Naval Shipyard at Hunters Point. An officer and four enlisted men were killed; three others were critically injured.
[†] Lieutenant Commander Charles B. Almy, USN.

accusing officer originally, he was now the endorsing officer. I was caught in the middle. I supported the skipper, recommending that his statement be considered carefully in elaboration of the board's finding, and I also pointed out his outstanding display of leadership after the fire.

This didn't set at all well with Commodore Fluckey. Then about two weeks later, two letters, both from ComSubPac to CO Pomodon, arrived in the squadron. The first letter stated that the force commander believed the CO was derelict prior to the explosion and fire, but because of his outstanding leadership in the crisis, no letter of admonition will be issued. The second was a letter of commendation to CO, USS Pomodon, for his outstanding display of leadership subsequent to the disaster. When that hit the squadron, it was a bit frosty in the mess for several days. Gene takes those things very seriously and usually gets emotionally involved. This is not the way to start off with a new squadron commander.

Q: How did things develop after that?

Captain Schratz: I always admired Gene very much. He is a super person, personally and professionally. He and I got on extremely well. At the end of the year, it was one of my boats that got the "E."* The other two division commanders were very able, energetic officers, and I really appreciated that the "E" boat was in my division. The primary duty of the divcom is training, hence he shares the honor. Gene did his level best, and we never had a problem.

Q: Do you have any specific memories of working with him other than that case?

Captain Schratz: Yes. Again, it comes back to the idea of realistic training exercises. When I took command of the division, I discussed readiness of all units. I suggested to my six COs that in my view it was the exec's primary role to look inward, to get the men and

---

* An "E," for excellence, is generally awarded to a ship or component of a ship as a result of top performance in competition with other ships during a given time period.

material at peak readiness. I had no question that routine drills would be executed efficiently. The CO's task, on the other hand, was to look outward, to look toward the ship performing her mission in battle.

I added, "To evaluate each one of you in this task, I plan to give an operational readiness inspection like you'd never seen before. What you'll be expected to do is carry out your war mission as realistically as I can possibly make it. I will conduct these while boats are deployed to the Far East, preferably, so as to save family time while in the San Diego area." I wanted to minimize extra underway time as far as possible. I wanted to test the skipper on how he reacted to the unexpected in a war emergency. For each ORI I used my division engineer to administer the problem and used the exec of the next ship to be examined as my chief observer. The three of us actually ran the problem.

For the first--<u>Pomodon</u>, I believe--whose wartime mission involved laying a mine field in a strategic area, we chose a nearby operating area where the navigation was almost the same as for his war mission. I emphasized that when he left the side of the tender, he was on a war basis. I gave him a top secret operation order as close as possible to what his war operation order would be, and expected him to act accordingly. If he didn't start zigzagging on leaving the harbor, he didn't know it, but another submarine was out there waiting to fire a torpedo at him. He suddenly saw a wake of bubbles right underneath the conning tower just a mile outside the entrance, which surprised the be-Jesus out of him. Arriving in the area, he commenced mining operations. Again, I didn't tell him, but a destroyer had been alerted to look for him. When he saw an impulse bubble from firing a mine, he called in an ASW patrol from North Island and commenced a coordinated air-surface attack. The CO knew only that he would be involved with air and some antisubmarine surface units.

The destroyer made contact, closed to 300 yards, and dropped a pattern of live depth charges. You asked earlier what a depth charge attack is like. Well, not having heard one from way back in World War II myself, these went off in shallow water at 300 yards, and let me tell you, they really sounded close. Probably only one or two men aboard had ever heard one go off before. Simultaneously, the report came to the conning tower,

"Serious flooding in the forward torpedo room." It was actually the start of the damage control drill, but the CO didn't know it.

As I looked into my skipper's baby blue eyes at that time, I had a far better understanding of how he would react in a real crisis than any other way I know to find out. He used full evasion, within certain limits imposed by (simulated) damage from the depth charging, to break contact with the ASW forces. Meanwhile, the (simulated) flooding began an extensive damage control problem within the ship. He did well but not too well. But he learned an awful lot. And we had a good exercise, an excellent evaluation. Of course, getting permission from ComSubPac to use live ordnance without telling the skipper about it took some second thoughts by several in the chain of command. I don't think they'd give that permission to everybody.

Well, having thoroughly surprised Pomodon, how could I hope to challenge all the other five submarines equally? It took all sorts of ideas. I was able to catch everyone by surprise. One did a photo recon of San Clemente island--into the morning haze and sun. I wasn't looking for photography sharp enough for an exhibit at the Art Association; I wanted a realistic and intelligent appraisal, to pick an objective area for a short-fuse amphibious landing, develop the pictures on board, prepare a stereo collage, and make appropriate recommendations on beach landing areas.

For one of my best boats, Catfish, I went to Okinawa for her ORI. We were fortunate in getting a carrier and a destroyer squadron for services, but the weather was wretched. A mountainous typhoon had blown through the day before. The carrier got to sea, leaving half the crew on the beach. The destroyermen were sick as dogs. When I reported to the desron commander that I had authorization from ComSubPac to use live ordnance, he was petrified.[*] He agreed only if I accepted full responsibility repeatedly. The storm had churned up the sea so there were no layers, a straight isothermal to 600 feet, making ASW very good and evasion very tough for the submarine. The submariners were also sick and largely unmotivated. When that depth charge salvo went off, I felt sorry for them. But the ship did extremely well.

---

[*] Desron--destroyer squadron.

The last ORI was for Bugara, then in a "reserve status in commission" available for limited wartime duty, primarily training. I suggested a nice, easy operational readiness exercise, and come evening time, we'd anchor out off Coronado Roads and enjoy a movie on deck. Unknown to the CO, I had called the UDT people in Coronado, run by Jon Lindbergh.[*] At the appropriate time, with the Bugara crew lolling on deck, his special teams came aboard secretly, caught the captain asleep in his bunk, painted a phosphorescent figure on his forehead, and got off without being detected. It came off like a dream.

The point is that I think that's the best way to maintain proper readiness for war. It's good fun; we all enjoyed it; we accomplished a sound realization of a war mission to be gained in no other way, and I can't help but feel that the readiness improved enormously as a result. I got a nice letter of commendation from ComSubPac, informally, and enthusiastic letters from his staff. But to the best of my knowledge, they never used that technique again.

Q: Which skippers in the division did the best in preparing their boats for war?

Captain Schratz: I think all of them adapted well to my style: "It isn't how you play the game; winning is everything." Chuck Almy in Pomodon was one of the very best. Howard Bucknell in Remora was probably tops.[†] He won the "E" and later became a nuke. When Howard did things, they were done right. He had a great ability in getting the maximum out of whatever he had to do it with.

To get advanced training about that time, Chuck Triebel, then the flotilla commander, used his influence to get the carrier groups en route to and from WestPac to block out an open sea area through which they had to transit during a given period.[‡] They were required to pass with a certain distance of one or two fixed points, and it gave a good

---

[*] UDT--underwater demolition team. Ensign Jon M. Lindbergh, USNR; his father was famed aviator Charles A. Lindbergh, who made the first solo flight across the Atlantic in May 1927.
[†] Lieutenant Commander Howard Bucknell III, USN.
[‡] Captain Charles O. Triebel, USN, Commander Submarine Flotilla One.

chance for unrestricted submarining. The CVAs tried to outwit us one way or another.* A single slow submarine against a carrier task force at high speed doesn't often promise much. When I gave Howard the task, he put homemade radar reflectors and some fake periscopes at both extremes north and south of the initial point, to fake the surface units toward the center. They came right over him and gave him several excellent attack opportunities. In thinking ahead and making things happen, I thought Howard was clearly superior.

Q: Sounds like there was a premium on imagination in coming up with these things.

Captain Schratz: Yes. He also had my absentee pennant made of metal and welded onto the conning tower, to suggest I should be absent. I thought it showed a sense of humor, if not of tact.

Q: How much attention were you in the Pacific giving to the development of the first nuclear submarines at that point?[†]

Captain Schratz: We had a monthly submarine conference of active senior submariners while I was in Washington to discuss new technology, operations, anything in the submarine future. I think I was in at the meeting when it was first decided to build a nuclear submarine. While on the West Coast, the nuclear program was well along. My concern even then was the lack of a research program other than pressurized water.

One of my Naval Academy roommates, Bill Sawyer, was trying to interest the Navy in a new idea.[‡] He was probably the best educated guy in the class in the field of gas turbines. Bill was stationed in San Diego at the time and had developed a design for a nuclear plant using gas turbine propulsion with, as I recall, lithium hydroxide as the coolant. One great advantage is a much smaller, lighter engine. Another of our roommates was Jim

---

* CVAs--attack aircraft carriers.
† The USS Nautilus (SSN-571), the Navy's first nuclear-powered submarine, was commissioned 30 September 1954. Because she did not have to come to the surface to recharge batteries, the Nautilus revolutionized submarine warfare.
‡ Commander William T. Sawyer, USN.

Dunford, then Admiral Rickover's number two, and Jim tried either to get Rickover's support or his consent to run it through the Office of Naval Research.* "Rick," however, had made his fame and fortune on pressurized water and wasn't about to risk, or let anybody else develop, a new system. That was the greatest defect in the Rickover era then and today. We finally gave it up. There was no way we could get around the Rickover empire, so Bill turned in his suit not long after that and tried it on the outside.

Q: Anything else from that tour of duty that you want to mention?

Captain Schratz: I don't think so.

Q: Then you went to the opposite coast and the opposite business, hunting submarines instead of running them. How did that assignment come about?

Captain Schratz: I think the Navy was just then realizing it had not been doing right by antisubmarine warfare, split between the air, surface, shore installations, and subsurface empires. An antisubmarine command was set up within CinCLant, with a nice slice of submariners, antisubmariners, aviators, destroyermen, and technicians. I was assistant chief of staff for readiness and training and thoroughly enjoyed the tour. We were just then getting the SOSUS network in the Atlantic, getting it out from under the rug.† The head of ASWForLant then was Vice Admiral Frank Watkins, a fine submariner, former ComSubLant.‡ I had the opportunity to try ideas we had used very successfully in submarines, like control of electronic emissions. Our air and surface people didn't know how to live in a world of radar silence. Both Germany and Japan were way ahead of us at the end of World War II in use of radar receivers for tactical purposes. They had to to survive.

---

* Commander James M. Dunford, USN.
† SOSUS--sound surveillance system, a seafloor network of listening devices used by the U.S. Navy to detect noises from transiting ships.
‡ Vice Admiral Frank T. Watkins, USN, served as Commander Anti-submarine Defense Force Atlantic Fleet from July 1957 to August 1958.

Our Navy had never thought seriously of limiting radar emissions. Subs patrolling off Japan late in the war, when the fleet was off Okinawa, found that about one-quarter, maybe half the radar scope was simply blanked out by radar noise from that enormous fleet to the south. In ASWForLant, the first major exercise out of Norfolk using control of electronic emissions left much to be desired. The operating folks shut down the massive search units but kept using the fire control radars for station keeping, thereby defeating the whole purpose of the exercise. We found quite quickly that there was a serious lack of doctrine, a lack of agreed air, surface, and subsurface dialogue on ASW.

As mentioned earlier, submariners were never given free evasion, which handicapped developing their own evasion techniques. Surface and air units were misled as to their own capabilities. Recognizing the problem, it was a wise decision in OpNav to pick some bright people for the antisubmarine warfare command. Frank Watkins, a renowned submariner, was followed by Admiral Massie Hughes, an aviator, and Charlie Weakley, a very shrewd destroyer sailor.* They finally put some life into the antisubmarine warfare game.

Q: What other things do you recall about your job? The readiness certainly should have been down your alley after what you did with the division.

Captain Schratz: Very much so. First, in order to break down the barriers between the various navies--air, surface, and subsurface--I suggested to Admiral Watkins that he start a direct personal correspondence with all the rest of his co-commanders having anything to do with antisubmarine warfare. I drafted the letters except for the personal touch which he added, and suggested three or four different areas in which we should be doing more or better, and solicited their ideas in the field of advanced training. This worked extremely well. Very few flag officers failed to give frank and complete support. It was taken in good

---

* Rear Admiral Francis Massie Hughes, USN. Vice Admiral Charles E. Weakley, USN, served as Commander Antisubmarine Warfare Force Atlantic Fleet from November 1963 to October 1967.

faith and, I think, added quite a lot to better knowledge, better exchange of information, and especially better support in the various commands.

NATO, the SACLant command in Norfolk, was interested then in doing a study of survivability of Soviet missile submarines on routine missile launching missions in the Atlantic.* So they turned it over to a team of mathematicians. I needed the same information but did my own estimate, using not mathematics but pure horse sense and operational knowledge. The figures I came up with looked like less than 50% of Soviet missile subs would survive to make a launch. The total time on station was less than ten days, far lower than predicted, and only 20% would survive their patrols. These were nonnuclear submarines. When the OEG experts finished their analysis, our answers were almost identical.†

Another question was, at that time, how many submarines did the Soviets really have for us to worry about? It seemed to me that from an operational point of view, the published figures on Soviet sub strength didn't make much sense. It was the usual problem that if an intelligence service gives the Russians the capability to build 50 submarines a year, then the estimate for the next year starts off with 50 more than the previous year. The fact that a nation may not build up to its full capacity is difficult to account for. There's no real measure when they fall short, and the errors are cumulative. I thought then they were far too high.

I took a totally different approach, again the practical approach. Based on the total square miles of training area the U.S. submarines use off New London, Norfolk, Key West, San Diego, and Pearl Harbor, and the number of submarines using that total area, it gave a crude measure of square miles of ocean for routine training per submarine. Using a similar measure for the Soviet submarine force, then estimated at 550 to our 100, it suggested first the great handicap they have in finding adequate operational training areas. Inaccessibility to the sea and poor weather areas became extremely important. If we assumed they need

---

* NATO--North Atlantic Treaty Organization. SACLant--Supreme Allied Commander Atlantic, a billet held by a four-star admiral from the U.S. Navy. At the time the individual was Admiral Jerauld Wright, USN.
† OEG--Operational Evaluation Group.

the same amount of space to retain a level of training comparable with ours, then either the number of contacts of submarines in open sea areas should have been ten or 20 times higher than it was, or the number of fully operational submarines might be far less than what they were given credit for, or they were in a very low state of training. All such possibilities are serious operational readiness factors.

Just about that time, by chance, they started their nuclear submarine program, and for several years prior had already cut back on diesel construction. Studies such as mine, therefore, gave the intelligence services a good excuse to take a new look at their estimates. The reassessment cut back the Soviet force to a much lower figure of about half the estimates. My study was only operational horse sense, but it looked to be at least as persuasive as the other techniques.

Q: Do you think we lost an important capability with the demise of the antisubmarine specialized carrier?

Captain Schratz: Definitely.

Q: What value was that to you during that time?

Captain Schratz: I'm concerned. I have not observed antisubmarine operations off the big carriers for years, but when you have first and second class citizens using the same airport, the first class citizens get all the priorities of training and operations, and I don't see how the ASW teams can possibly retain as high a level of capability as they would have if they had their own ship. I realize that there are important economic reasons why we can't do both.

Q: What ship were you in during your time there? Did you go to sea in the carriers?

Captain Schratz: I went to sea frequently in carriers, aircraft, destroyers, blimps, and submarines.

Q: Did you work with any NATO navies?

Captain Schratz: Yes.

Q: Which ones were the most capable?

Captain Schratz: I was much impressed with the Canadians at sea. The British did very well in some major NATO exercises, but my experience at sea was too limited to make a more finite judgment.

Q: Are there any exercises that particularly stand out in your mind other than that one with the radar silence that wasn't silent?

Captain Schratz: Not that I recall. They were all operating at a pretty high level all the time, too many operational commitments for the forces available. As previously, I thought too many of these operations were unnecessary.

Q: Did you run nuclear submarines into the problems?

Captain Schratz: Yes, but very few were available.

Q: What were the results of that?

Captain Schratz: Superb. Again, the limitations they put on them against free maneuverability were so high that often it was not worthwhile to use a nuclear submarine. A well-handled Guppy could do well enough. The surface and air units mislead themselves as to just what they can do against a fully evasive nuclear submarine.

Q: Just because of the artificiality?

Captain Schratz: Yes. One tends to lose sight of the limitations when they become part of the normal routine.

Q: Was there any pioneering work on tactics or doctrine during that period that you were involved in?

Captain Schratz: I made a trip to Halifax to visit the Joint Maritime Warfare School. I think I set the Canadian program back a couple of years with a semi-facetious briefing. At that time we were playing around with an unshielded nuclear reactor, a nuclear tugboat, really, requiring only 15 feet of sea water around it to give enough shielding to use as a nuclear power source. I suggested its use as an unmanned deep sea tugboat to tow large plastic containers to move POL or similar materials across the oceans.* Traveling at about 600 feet, it could be programmed to surface off Gibraltar or the channel, for instance, and handle half the transatlantic resupply in that fashion.

Well, when I discussed this with the Canadians, I suggested the possibility of using the unmanned reactor as both a tugboat and power source, towing two or three of our World War II diesel submarines to give them an antisubmarine escort capability with essentially unlimited submerged endurance. I didn't emphasize clearly enough that it was purely hypothetical. When I learned later that this became part of a Canadian research program, I was too embarrassed to discuss it.

Q: What else do you recall from that tour of duty? I don't know what questions to ask.

Captain Schratz: We participated in several NATO exercises, controlled from Petrievie Castle, near Edinburgh, during a simulated war emergency. It was fascinating to see how the Brits carried out their emergency reactivation. After my Burrfish experience, it was an

---

* POL--petroleum, oil, and lubricants.

eye-opener to see the British procedure. They started at 8:00 o'clock in the morning, pried the covers off a number of antisubmarine ships, and provisions and equipment arrived by lorry. Crewmen put down their civilian pursuits, pulled on a Navy hat, and were soon doing the same thing in uniform. By the end of the day, they were chugging around the harbor, and the next morning they'd fill them full of fuel and beans, and they were off doing their antisubmarine work.

By an unfortunate coincidence at that particular time, the U.S. Navy was hit by an Asian flu epidemic, and many of our ships couldn't get under way. We took a lot of ribbing from the British who could take a reserve ship out of mothballs and carry the brunt of the naval exercise while the regular Navy of the great Americans had to stay in port. The British did extremely well--by any measure--with very modest resources. Their communication network throughout Britain, for our emergency, was amazing. Manned by local operators doing their normal day's work, they got the message through very quickly and reliably, and with a thorough knowledge of the entire command organization.

Q: Do you have any observations on active versus passive sonar from this period?

Captain Schratz: Never having been a surface sailor in an antisubmarine vessel, my bread and butter is passive sonar, passive detection by any means. I suggested earlier that in <u>Atule</u> we had invented some passive detection devices during World War II. I feel that we stress active sonar and neglect important tactical and strategic advantages gained by using passive means. And remember, the sonar gear I saw while in the antisubmarine business was far inferior to what I had in my Japanese submarine--the German Balkon gear, really superb sonar gear. I've learned since that we have surpassed that in performance. I wait to be convinced how it works in combat.

Q: How useful were the helicopters that did use sonar?

Captain Schratz: They, too, I thought, from the submarine perspective, were overrated. I had experience with a dipping sonar type, even a towed array other than from a blimp. For any aircraft, fixed wing or rotary, using sonobuoys, in my experience, I didn't think was here to stay.

Q: Why?

Captain Schratz: If he's using an active sonar, the submarine has the advantage by remaining passive. If the helo drops a circle of sonobuoys to localize a contact passively, I never felt those to be any but the most marginal capability. They depend on cavitation, and any well-handled sub never cavitates. We have indicators to alert us. This is another artificiality in forcing the sub to cavitate during exercises, which builds up a false capability. When we got the sophisticated LOFAR sonobuoys--I don't know what they have now, but the cost is awful--they were dropping expendable Cadillacs all over the ocean.[*]

Q: What did you think was the best way of detecting a submerged submarine?

Captain Schratz: Well, a torpedo wake isn't bad.

Q: You'd like to get them before that.

Captain Schratz: The surface ASW ship is the key. I am not familiar enough with a nuclear submarine as an ASW vessel. I know the active, highly sophisticated gear we have on our surface ships now gets some pretty fantastic results, at least under peacetime conditions when the submarine isn't shooting back. But when using active sonar, we tend to overlook the fact that a megawatt signal in the water telegraphs one's own position to a submarine at least twice as far away as you can hope to get an echo. If he can get an echo, the sound has travelled twice as far for the submarine to hear it passively, and you're talking maybe 100 miles. Such a signal tells him that it's a warship, that it's big enough to be worthy of a

---

[*] LOFAR--low-frequency acquisition and ranging.

torpedo or cruise missile and it solves the fire control problem of bearing and roughly of range.

It makes a simple problem for either a torpedo or homing missile. A cruise missile may certainly be ideal in those circumstances. Not having any experience in that field for a number of years, I can only wonder if we have kept up with the best of operational thinking and experience in our antisubmarine exercises. I for one don't feel that the Russian submariner is as good as we generally make him out to be, even if it's only national pride speaking. The average American is so much a mechanical genius, I just don't see the Russians as having that innate capability to compare under the demanding conditions of submarining in the North Atlantic.

Q: You went on to the Naval War College. That was the first of many war college steps for you. Had you applied for that duty?

Captain Schratz: You didn't apply for it in those days; you just hoped you'd be selected. My class, my peers, had the misfortune of not being available for any war college until we'd made four stripes. I'll never forget the day when I finally received my first notification from Newport, along with a selection of reading material to go through before I arrived in Newport. Those readings opened a brand-new world to me. I had no idea of that world and never had occasion to think about it. Even though I had always been an avid reader, I had never read those basics of my profession until that time. I couldn't help but regret the many years I had wasted in not having ever entered that field of study of strategy. I was avid to get with it when I got to Newport.

Q: Why did it work out that your class didn't get there before then?

Captain Schratz: We were all at sea during the war. Not just my class, I guess everybody from perhaps 1937 through 1940. We had forfeited our chance for command and staff level and didn't get to the senior school until late. At the end of the war, some people were sent to school right away. But for operational reasons, our first war college experience was at sea, learning the hard way.

Q: What are the topics that you found your mind open to when you got that?

Captain Schratz: Primarily in the area of strategy. I'd had a fair education in international politics, simply by virtue of traveling a lot, previous duties, and a better than average education prior. But the whole concept of strategy and broad use of force was new. My whole experience was tactical operations, at best theater operations with the fleet. For the first time, I could think about the operations of the fleets for the purposes of nations, a much higher level of understanding, and I found it fascinating. I still do.

Q: What was the level of the course work there? How challenging was it?

Captain Schratz: Most of us claimed that the process was largely self-education. It was pretty much what you made it. Unfortunately, as the recent Naval War College Centennial History points out, that period was one of the all-time lows at the war college, both in the program and the people--quality of students and quality of faculty. There weren't very many places then, or now, I suppose. You can lose a senior captain just to keep him out of harm's way and keep him earning a decent living, other than the Naval War College, unfortunately.

The intellectual challenge came from a master's program that Boston University was conducting, as George Washington and other universities did later. The Boston U. course was head and shoulders above the others in quality of the program, the instruction, and the rigor. Unfortunately, they killed the program a few years after I left, partly because Boston U. didn't want to be associated with the low-quality programs from other universities. We, as students weren't allowed to take the course. I stayed on the faculty and took it then. But I had planned even before I had left Norfolk to start that course just as soon as I could, and so I did lots of work beyond the war college course and, as a bookworm, I relished the opportunity to do research and took the course very seriously.

Q: What sorts of things were you covering in your regular classwork?

Captain Schratz: It by and large then was a shallow international relations course, freshman level. I called it later the Rio Grande theory of education--a mile wide and an inch deep. But it was a good briefing. We did have access to the senior people in the Navy who gave lectures and subjected themselves to frank and sometimes even rude questions. It was a great experience in that respect. We all learned from thinking of common problems from different perspectives.

The student then was largely self-educated. He learned much from outstanding fellow students coming from all the services, little from the military faculty. Though my fellow Navy students themselves were below average at that time, the Army, Air Force, and the Marines did not lower their standards.

Q: To what do you attribute this period of shortcoming?

Captain Schratz: Largely from too low a priority on education in the Navy. At the end of the war, both the Army and Air Force, particularly the Air Force, had high percentages of officers without college degrees. Nearly 100% of naval officers were college graduates. The impetus was far greater in the other services to set up high-priority programs of professional education. The Navy never felt such a need and could always claim that the officers were necessary in sea billets and had no time for schooling. I just saw some recent figures on that. The Navy has one-third more college grads than the other services, one-third less with an M.A. and only one-tenth the number of Ph.D.s of the other services. There are many brilliant men but few intellectuals in the Navy. The Naval War College in its first century offers a history of anti-intellectualism, as I wrote in summarizing that century of progress in the special centennial issue of the War College Review.[*] The Navy

---

[*] "The Hundred Year Growing Pain: Opposition and Opportunity," Naval War College Review, September-October 1984, pages 71-85.

has a long tradition of learning, not from books but from command of a ship at sea. That's all one knows and all one needs to know.

Q: The war college certainly had a rocky beginning on account of that theme.

Captain Schratz: Yes, and still the all-time low came in the postwar period while I was there. Very disappointing, but a stimulating experience nevertheless.

Q: Were there any individuals that you remember from there in that period that were counter to that trend, who were pushing forward, trying to expand the program?

Captain Schratz: There were some outstanding officers up there at the time. Slim Ingersoll was the president when I arrived, an outstanding officer but not an educator.* The chief of staff, Rear Admiral Charlie Lyman, was more the educator but quite limited in what he could accomplish.† Dick Colbert was just getting well started with the foreign officers' course, later to become the Naval Command College, for which he filled a memorable role. One of the most outstanding students was Mike Michaelis, who was pulled out later in the course for command of the first nuclear carrier and later earned four stars.‡ The Navy students, as a whole, however, fell far below average in flag officer selection.

Q: Did you have much contact with foreign students there?

Captain Schratz: Almost none other than personally or socially. They were in some of our seminars such as international law, but because of security problems, they were often sent off on trips during the classified fleet operations or nuclear weapons studies. Nor did we capitalize on their special talents. For instance, some of the British, French, and Italians had

---

* Vice Admiral Stuart H. Ingersoll, USN, served as president of the Naval War College from 13 August 1957 to 30 June 1960.
† Rear Admiral Charles H. Lyman III, USN.
‡ Captain Frederick H. Michaelis, USN. The oral history of Admiral Michaelis is in the Naval Institute collection.

very interesting doctrines on antisubmarine warfare based on long experience that we could have used to great benefit. Possibly because of agreements with their governments, their research papers were generally not available. I read through some of them and was quite impressed. And they must have been disappointed on occasion with some of the lectures on the same subject, because there is much more experience in the European NATO navies which goes beyond ours.

Q: Had they asked for that kind of protection or was it forced upon them?

Captain Schratz: I never learned. I suspect it was administratively desirable for a lot of reasons. But I'm sure we could have worked out a compromise if we had any desire to use them.

Q: Did you write a thesis per se while you were in the course?

Captain Schratz: Yes. Two. My first experience with the old "Estimate of the Situation" and commander's decision form. I was quite skeptical that these procedures, so effective in an era when you could match ship against ship in planning one's Trafalgar or Jutland, would fall apart under the new complexities of nuclear war. I decided to write my first thesis, using the traditional form to develop an appraisal of U.S. versus the Soviet Union in modern war. Much to my surprise, I found it to be extremely effective. The principles behind the old decision form were solid; decisions had to be made, whatever the weaponry. It was logically sound, and logically was about the only way to tackle the problem. From a heretic, I became a very strong convert. The paper itself was chosen as the outstanding one in the class and was later published in the Proceedings.[*]

Q: What was the social life like during that period in Newport?

---

[*] See "After Communism, What?" U.S. Naval Institute Proceedings, July 1960, pages 38-47.

Captain Schratz: Very active. We did a lot of things, put on plays, wrote skits, golf, sailing, other things. Newport is enjoyable for families, too. I played in the Brown University Symphony, in the Rhode Island State Opera Orchestra, and did some fiddling in Newport with the Navy Choristers. We lived in one of those old homes near the Redwood Library and thoroughly enjoyed the Newport social life, hiking around Cliff Walk, etc. At the end of three years, we were pretty solid Newporters.

Q: As a member of the faculty, did you set out to rectify some of the shortcomings you had perceived?

Captain Schratz: I sure did. I found very shortly that as a junior member of the faculty, there was an isothermal layer of deadwood between me and the president. Any bright idea that came up from below bounced off this impenetrable layer and got deflected back into the depths. I had to challenge that system. Responsible for the long-range academic planning, I sold a number of ideas on rebuilding the course and to vastly increase the number of Navy students by working out deals with the Bureau of Naval Personnel. Despite working level agreement with BuPers, we couldn't pull it off, and in fact the reverse occurred. The number of Navy students was even less than the number of Army students.

Q: Was this Admiral Austin doing the deciding?

Captain Schratz: No, Austin didn't come until just about the time I left.* I had not very much to do in his era. It was primarily Slim Ingersoll.

Q: Why do you think this inertia existed?

Captain Schratz: Because they didn't want to send students up there. It wasn't career-enhancing because of bad luck with selection boards, which soon made students reluctant to

---

* Vice Admiral Bernard L. Austin, USN, served as president of the Naval War College from 30 June 1960 to 31 July 1964.

come, whatever the need for their professional training. The trick was to get a set of orders to the Naval War College in your record, then try somehow to get diverted, so you got recognition in your record without actually having gone. If I seem a little bit heretical, the evidence bears me out.

Q: So the problem went beyond the war college itself, it sounds like. There was an institutionalized prejudice in the Navy at large against it.

Captain Schratz: No question. It never, at least until after the Turner era, regained the stature enjoyed prior to the war.[*] For one thing, the focus prior to World War II was tactical, and the relations with the fleet were very close. It was routine to game fleet exercises at Newport, and tactics we all understood to some degree. The idea of a nuclear war changed the focus to strategic, but where the military dominated tactical thinking, it made no contribution in modern strategic doctrine, all of which evolved from civilians with no operational experience whatsoever. There are a lot of reasons why the War College did not achieve its former position after World War II. I sympathize with that, but I don't accept it.

Q: That period you were there was during the most frigid part of the Cold War. Did that have any effect on what you studied at all, on what you discussed?

Captain Schratz: It was very much anti-Communist oriented. I think the over-concentration on the Soviet Union at the expense of the other 100 or so nations of the world was fairly flagrant. It not only perpetuated but fostered a similar bias in our flag officers.

Q: What did your faculty duties consist of specifically?

---

[*] Vice Admiral Stansfield Turner, USN, served as president of the Naval War College from 30 June 1972 to 9 August 1974.

Captain Schratz: The long-range master plan took much of my time. I did some lecturing, generally on my own initiative. When I had an idea I thought should get some circulation, I set up a voluntary lecture for students and staff. Of course, I wasn't held back by modesty in those things. I also had done some work then and previously on the Navy Survivor Benefit Plan and found myself deeply involved in financial counseling of the students. And I was a speech writer for Admiral Ingersoll. Even as a student, I wrote his Global Strategy address and his graduation-retirement talk. He had no idea who wrote them, and it didn't increase my admiration for the faculty to do this task while a student.

Q: There wasn't a formal schedule then?

Captain Schratz: Oh, definitely, but I was not on the academic faculty. The military were not on the lecture program except for special events. As a long-range planner, I was primarily an administrator. Financial planning was no part of anybody's formal role, but there was reason for concern that the average military officer's personal planning was being very much neglected. Students were just then at the point of having youngsters preparing for college, and in meeting heavy expenses, the average financial estate planning was wretched. I ultimately prepared a guide which both the Navy Relief and Army Relief adopted. I tried to get out from under as quickly as I could, with not an awful lot of success.

Then about the time Count Austin arrived, a serious dispute was festering, primarily with the Air Force, on roles and missions, and a closely held Air Force plan for a single service. A Navy underground operating from Washington used the war college and CinCLantFlt for support, and I don't know who else--CinCPac, I'm sure. But there were a number of position papers, suggestions, policies, organizational problems floating all around, and a fair share of those come to Newport. Admiral Austin and I worked on it secretly with, I think, one other officer at the war college. Similar units were located in CinCLant and CinCPac headquarters, all very closely held. The Air Force and a single promotion list found new adherents in the other services. Perhaps you heard of the master plan?

Q: No, I haven't.

Captain Schratz: It was about a ten-year program called Black Valiant. I was able to obtain surreptitiously a copy of this "Air Force eyes only" plan, which I turned over to Ed Hooper, running the Center for Naval Analyses within the Naval War College.[*]

Q: Did you set up any counteraction plan as a result?

Captain Schratz: I personally didn't. I don't know what the group in Washington did. I was about to leave and never heard of the follow-up.

Q: Well, whatever they had in mind hasn't come about.

Captain Schratz: Well, I think it fell of its own weight. Even in the Air Force, smarter heads prevailed.

Q: Did any of your long-range plans come to fruition?

Captain Schratz: Yes. It's interesting you asked that question. I had really worked hard on that plan. It was a fairly extensive document. I worked alone because I couldn't find help inside the rest of the faculty. My immediate boss wasn't interested, and it wasn't until just about the time of my departure that this thing came out in the open and went to Admiral Austin for the first time. The chief of staff, Admiral Charlie Lyman, was a real solid guy, had talked with me about phases of it, but only casually.

When it got to Count Austin, he took it home in his briefcase. That night one of the big snows hit Newport, and he was snowed in his quarters for two days with nothing else to read. His comments certainly weren't very flattering. I saw little hope for selling it. But

---

[*] Rear Admiral Edwin B. Hooper, USN. The oral history of Hooper, who retired as a vice admiral, is in the Naval Institute collection.

shortly after my detachment for my deep-draft command of a submarine tender in New London, I returned to Newport in <u>Fulton</u> for a refresher cruise. My old buddies at the war college immediately asked if I had seen the White Plan, Admiral Austin's new educational structure for the war college. I couldn't wait to see. Surprisingly, it looked very much like one I'd written; only the names had been changed to protect the innocent.

Q: What was the thrust of your plan?

Captain Schratz: I recall only about four or five elements. The principle around which it was built was, first, a sharp reduction in civilian visiting lecturers who came in to carry much of the academic load, and, second, to get the military faculty into teaching. It seemed deplorable that in the halls made famous by Luce and Mahan, that we should have to have a civilian who's never been to sea, never had operational responsibility, come in and give us all of our inner thoughts on maritime doctrine.* Third, there were too many things going on. I wanted to cut down the lecture program and not just have it a nice session in the big bedroom two or three times a day. By a factor of three or four there were too many. Lectures are a weak learning device and they weren't used effectively. They weren't transcribed, for lack of funds, and weren't available for study after. The retention on a lecture is so low that we were getting a minimal return for an awfully expensive program. Fourth, I wanted better organization and integration of the course into week-length units in the various elements; use outside experts for that time, in addition to the lecture, but to use them primarily in small discussion groups rather than just one great big blast on the stage. This I was later able to accomplish at the Air War College. Fifth, I tried to get a travel program. The other war colleges made trips to the U.N. The National War College made trips around the world. I wasn't that grand in my concept, but I thought we could kill a couple of birds by visiting the United Nations in New York. So I worked out a plan to set this up with the carriers and other ships from Quonset, across the bay, and make a weekend, or a week, mid-week, or something, a two- or three-day trip by sea to get some of our sea

---

* Rear Admiral Stephen B. Luce, USN, and Captain Alfred Thayer Mahan, USN, were pivotal figures at the founding of the Naval War College in the late 19th century.

experience in submarines, carriers, destroyers, and then get the U.N. experience and a New York visit at very little cost. They did that eventually, but not on my bootstring basis; it was done fairly lavishly and didn't survive because they couldn't afford it.

There were a number of unsatisfactory elements in the academic program itself. The war college didn't then have a coherent academic program. It was just rag-tag. Every new idea that came by was jammed into the schedule and nothing taken out. Incrementalism and faddism overloaded the program and I objected to it strongly.

The big politico-military war games at the end of the year had little to contribute. The course started off with thinking about international relations, then broad strategy, tactics, fleet operations, which is all put together in a war game at the end of the year. The year I was there as a student, and two years prior, they had used Tito's anticipated death in Yugoslavia as the crisis to initiate the big war game. As these games usually went, it took about 12 minutes to nuclear war, a big nuclear exchange and it's all over. This involved little planning; students learned really nothing about the world as it really exists. Would we go to nuclear war under such circumstances? Never. Even as a student, I didn't think we could learn an awful lot from that.

I have a short tolerance for stupidity when it affects the professional training of our future leaders and could visualize no practical gain from the P-M game as planned. So when the teams were picked for the war game to climax the course, fortuitously, I was chosen to be on the Soviet Council of Ministers, and my roommate, a CIA type, was chosen to be on the National Security Council. I dreamed up a wholly new plan for my Council of Ministers starting six months to a year before the planned D-Day. An airplane was sent into the DEW line just to make contact, turn around and come home.* The next day or a couple of days, two airplanes repeated it. Then maybe three or an air refueling inside the DEW line, inside radar coverage.

I devised a gradual buildup of uncorrelated Soviet submarine contacts by our ASW forces and SOSUS networks over a period of six months. No Soviet commercial air flight ever flew on schedule nor far enough off schedule to do anything but raise doubt. The idea

---

* DEW--Distant Early Warning, a network of radar sites to detect the approach of Soviet bombers coming over the North Pole.

is that every operation would raise doubt, uncorrelated with previous experience. Then, on the scheduled D-Day, I wanted to confront the West with 459 or so uncorrelated incidents the day before as being not serious enough for war, and 461 on the day war became most likely, the obvious point being to flood the decision process with doubt. It placed the Americans and NATO leaders in an impossible position, and it might well happen that way in the real world.

Well, the Council of Ministers thought this was great, so they bought that plan and commenced putting it in operation. Whereupon I leaked my plan to the West via my roommate, the CIA type on the NSC. The NSC began taking countermeasures, all this happening before the game officially started. I became a mole inside the NSC. I emphasize that this was all student activity of which the faculty had no knowledge. When D-Day arrived to launch the formal war college plan, the faculty announced the death of Tito as expected and commenced their P-M game. It fell like a leaf in deep water. The students ignored it and went back to the other problem, far more fascinating. It turned out to be a valuable exercise, but throughout the whole college, only my roomie and I had any idea what was really going on. Everybody learned a lot.

The faculty in time decided to indulge in more realistic thinking about the world, an element previously absent. But I often wonder what sort of writeup the P-M game got in the war college records. I had no intention of ruining a preplanned exercise. We all gained extensive experience in operational planning in a realistic crisis situation that would never have ensued from the highly artificial plan devised by the staff. Nor could I be so critical of staff weakness in retrospect without the knowledge that it was then at its nadir and was soon to improve so markedly following the Turner revolution.

Q: How big a part did war gaming play in your master plan?

Captain Schratz: That glamorous new war gaming facility had just been completed. It had great potential, but we didn't use it at all as students. We went through it once on a tour, but much to my surprise, we never used it as part of the course.

Q: I wonder, did you plan for greater use of that in your plan?

Captain Schratz: Definitely. It's a fantastic operation, really beautiful. There's no way I could have visualized what they do with it now.

Q: How much of the Austin White Plan ended up being implemented?

Captain Schratz: Oh, I suspect a fair amount. I know he gave it a good shake. When he "originated" it, that just about put it into operation. And you'll recognize from the above most of the elements of the Stansfield Turner academic revolution soon to follow.

Q: What do you recall about your Boston U. off-campus studies?

Captain Schratz: It was run by about three or four professors, very good, very dedicated. It was done almost entirely on the war college premises, except for one seminar on a Saturday morning and an occasional lecture in Boston. We studied in the classroom for about three hours, then adjourned to the local tavern for lunch and completed our discussions. We built a bit of social life around the B.U. programs, but it was a very tough drag. Admiral Ingersoll thought it was too competitive with the war college program, and he actually canceled it about three times, I think, during the year I was doing my studies. And remember, students were not eligible, just faculty. He fostered basket weaving and golf and other sports as being not competitive with the war college program, but somehow he thought a master's course was. A very capable Army liaison officer on the faculty appealed to Slim's ego as an educator and kept the program alive. It was a good program, really tough exams, which most of us bilged the first time and had to repeat. In addition, they arranged for us to go to Boston for a series of lectures by George Kennan, which later became his book on Lenin and Stalin.[*] And I spent a lot of time and effort on that. We all did.

Q: What sorts of subjects did you cover specifically in that course?

Captain Schratz: The usual slice of international--there were choices each term depending on desires of students and availability of professors. One on international economics was quite good, another on geopolitics which was very good, given by a prominent geopolitician, Saul Cohen. Plus the usual ones on Soviet system, Communist system. One outstanding Communist expert was an East European, Andy Gyorgy, who was on the Naval War College faculty, and head of the department, Professor Gibbs, a U.S. international relations expert. Gibbs and Gyorgy together ran a very solid course.

Q: Was the university's program in any way tailored to military students as opposed to their regular foreign affairs program?

Captain Schratz: The four or five professors involved taught their specialty. Their specialty fit in very well with the war college program except in the field of strategy. We all took more courses than we really needed just for the degree, just because it was a high quality education.

Q: Did you write a thesis in that one?

Captain Schratz: No. We used a number of small theses for individual courses but none for the degree as a whole.

---

[*] George F. Kennan, Russia and the West Under Lenin and Stalin (Boston: Little, Brown, 1961).

Q: Admiral Burke by then was CNO and set up a long-range planning group within OpNav. Was there any effect of that in Newport, that you incorporated the study of long-range planning into the curriculum or saw ways to use that for the Navy's benefit?

Captain Schratz: Not to the best of my knowledge. In fact, Ed Hooper's group, the Center for Naval Analyses, was my resident long-range thinker. Ed was considering moving out of the Naval War College either to Boston or to Washington, and asked if I would do a staff study for him on it. I saw a lot of advantages in going to Boston, the academic hub of New England, but I saw a lot more advantages in staying in the war college, where he could not only use war college students for specialist expertise, but also contribute to the war college what it lacked most, to make much broader horizons available for war college students. For this reason primarily, I recommended strongly he stay in Newport. I didn't want him to go to Washington because of the problem getting involved in day-to-day operations business, rather than the deep think. I thought he could do a better job being remote from the operations and still close enough to academics and the Navy itself, by staying in Newport. I never learned what convinced him to move to Washington, but they seem to have done pretty well there.

Q: Did you leave Newport with a satisfied feeling after your three-year tour there?

Captain Schratz: Oh, very much. For the first time I recognized my academic deficiencies. It became a matter of great concern. I guess a little bit of learning was a dangerous thing. Frankly, I found less and less confidence in the capabilities, the knowledge of modern war of most of our flag officers--not just Navy, all services. I felt that they were far too shallow in their knowledge of what was necessary, to my mind, to fight a modern war and to avoid a modern war. Along with my own need for more education to do what I could to remedy our common deficiencies in the art of war, I found far less enthusiasm for my selection to flag rank. Should the chance come my way to become a flag officer at that time, I would have turned it down. I don't think one ever knows how he feels about that until it happens.

But I lost much of my ambition or drive for flag rank at that time, the first time I really thought about it seriously.

Q: There are two ways to look at it: if that's the way flag officers are, I don't want to be one. Or, now that I have this heightened perception, I can help the Navy as a whole if I do become one.

Captain Schratz: A good point. I simply felt that my horizons were broader than the Navy seemed to be able to fill. I simply was beyond what seemed to be limiting them in their own horizons. You can call it egotism or whatever, but that's how I felt.

Q: Well, you got to sea in the <u>Fulton</u>.* That was the next natural progression for a submariner. How did that tour turn out?

Captain Schratz: That was, again, fascinating and most challenging. <u>Fulton</u> was the first nuclear support ship, the first tender equipped specially, though crudely, to support the nuclear submarines. I learned very quickly that with the great need of the Navy to train nuclear submariners, there was none left they could afford to put on submarine tenders. It was too tough getting them qualified for submarines themselves. So the only way we could get nuclear talent, nuclear-trained people to use in our nuclear repair business was to get psychological rejects from the submarines.

That task of remotivation turned out to be the toughest I ever faced. A man who fails in the nuclear program is thrown out and his pay sharply reduced, must then be motivated to do the same job he's been doing, without the pay and with no halo of a nuclear submariner over his head. It generally required a tremendous selling job to turn them around. Some few cases were situational. A bright young man who had a 17-year-old wife, pregnant, living in a cold water flat and just couldn't afford to go to sea or leave her home

---

* The USS <u>Fulton</u> (AS-11) was commissioned on 12 September 1941. She was 530 feet long, 73 feet in the beam, had a draft of 23.5 feet, and displaced 18,000 tons fully loaded. She had a top speed of 18 knots and was armed with four 5-inch guns.

alone--these men got out of submarines for personal reasons despite the heavy financial loss. By and large, the talent we could scrounge in the nuclear training business were the ones who needed some missionary work to convince. It was challenging.

For one thing, I started a series of lectures to senior petty officers. I had a tremendous leading chief petty officer who ran the leadership program. He was on the lecture circuit up and down the Atlantic, and the first chance we got to talk, he asked if I would like to start a program in talking informally with senior petty officers on their role in the Navy, or anything else I wanted to get off my chest. We set these up every ten days with a different group of 10 to 20 at a time. I probably ran every petty officer I had through at some time or another. It was great training and experience for me too. Soon I was on the lecture circuit for the enlisted submarine school graduations, and when we were in Norfolk and Charleston, I gave some lectures on roughly the same subject.

Nuclear repair was the great challenge, primarily the problem of stainless steel welding. Anybody can learn to do a traditional weld. The stainless steel weld in the nuclear primary loop was a brand-new world. Out of 100 people trained to be good, conventional welders, maybe only two or three could ever become stainless steel welders. And, of course, they needed those in nuclear submarines, too, and we had a really tough time getting enough trained to help both the submarines and our own needs. And the devotion of some of these guys was remarkable. My repair officer, Lieutenant Commander Randy Zelov, class of '48, was outstanding and really burned himself out the year I had command of the tender.[*] I found all this really fascinating.

A nuclear repair was like surgery. A sterile area had to be set up around the job, and every person, tool, and piece of equipment that went into the work area had to be checked in and checked out again for radiation contamination. We were spending half of our quarterly allotment just for special clothing, equipment, and decontamination procedures. The acceptable standards of welding by which the Nautilus and the early nukes were put together changed so radically in the early years that we would have had to grind out and replace almost every weld in the ship just to attain the new minimums. All those

---

[*] Lieutenant Commander Randolph D. Zelov, USN.

submarines left General Dynamics, Electric Boat Company, across the river and became the responsibility of the tender for subsequent repairs. My men did a fantastic job. It was very little appreciated how good they were.

Q: Why were they deficient coming out of Electric Boat?

Captain Schratz: No, no. They met existing standards, but the standards changed as we got into the business of nuclear shipbuilding. A few welds were bad, we found on X-ray examination.

Q: Were you able to get these misfits turned around?

Captain Schratz: Oh, yes. They did a remarkable job. Again I tried the old idea of bread and circuses.

Q: Well, describe bread and circuses.

Captain Schratz: You make life interesting, prove that they've got a role to do, that they're important, and give them a challenge.

Q: What gimmicks did you use in that ship?

Captain Schratz: In my first weeks aboard, I was invited to a Kiwanis luncheon. And the person at the table with me had a son in boot camp, and he was grousing about his son's life in the military, the lousy food and no liberty. After the luncheon was over, I made a proposal to the chapter president: "Many of your members are about the age to have sons in the military as a result of the draft. They all complain about the food and the military life. How would you like to have your next chapter meeting on my ship? I'll serve whatever happens to be on the menu that day in the crew's mess, and you can judge what kind of food your kids are getting in the service. Then we'll take you through a nuclear submarine after." They thought it was a fantastic idea. If nothing else, it was a free lunch.

Well, since I made the deal for one of the service clubs, I had to do it for all of them. I made only one exception, for the Navy League, charging them a buck and a half and turning over the money to the submarine scholarship fund, and for the lunch I served lobsters. <u>Fulton</u> was one of the best feeders in the Atlantic, and I was pretty confident. But when you make a blanket promise of the menu on any given day, there's always an element of risk. The first two were great. One had steak and one had something equally glamorous, but the third one came by, I think we had--what's the purple cabbage German meal-- sauerbraten. After a few moments of panic over whether I should switch the menu away from leftover cabbage, I decided to stick with my promise. To my amazement, they put away sauerbraten like it was going out of fashion. I found later that the cook had done a beautiful job. He had seasoned it in these big kettles for 24 hours, marinated in something beforehand, and it was delicious. For the Navy League I couldn't believe the number of lobsters they went through. It ran me in the hole for a year. I took $1.50 contributions and many quite a bit larger and turned those over to the scholarship fund, for which they were most grateful.

On taking these people through the ship, they were very enthusiastic. They were community leaders and began inviting our men to all sorts of activities in town and in their homes. I suspect that if one of their sons said something about food in his camp or somewhere later, why, he got no sympathy: "I've tasted it, and I know exactly how good it is." Our men loved it, to see these people eating in their own mess. One member was Otto Graham, the big professional football Hall of Famer who was then coaching at the Coast Guard Academy. We went out of our way to get town leaders to go through the ship. They were anxious also to reciprocate. A trip through a nuclear submarine is very good bait. It was a great thing for the men just to act as a host to people rather than the wardroom for a change.

As part of the better life program, I also tried to counter the lure of the neon lights and New London bars for men on liberty. We volunteered to repair damaged playground equipment for local schools and parks, to repair school equipment. My carpentry, metal, and foundry trades were underused in the nuclear repair business. Again, the men were able to meet interesting and grateful people in town, and enthusiastically pursued the program.

I was playing then with the Eastern Connecticut Symphony Orchestra and was able to arrange some free Pops concerts by the orchestra at the sub base. The ship got some publicity from that, which always helps the morale of the troops.

Q: Had you had to go through any nuclear indoctrination program before taking this job?

Captain Schratz: None. I'd read some books, but I found that as soon as I got into the job, why, I could stay pretty much on the outside. Randy Zelov, my repair officer, and many of his people were nuclear-trained and did superb jobs. One problem I had, Admiral Rickover had informers in the Electric Boat Company and on the nuclear submarines and often knew of planned repairs before I did.

Q: How much did you hear from Admiral Rickover?

Captain Schratz: He came up to visit his submarines, and always made a point of not really wanting to see the skipper or anybody else on the tender. I made sure he had a bowl of fresh fruit and a jar of Brach's hard candy in the commodore's cabin, which he never requested, always expected, and never indicated that he knew or appreciated it.

We had one major problem during that time, when my crew was working their butts off to try to stay ahead on the nuclear repair workload. The Chinese conducted an A-bomb test, and it was apparently a very "dirty" bomb. About a week or ten days later, one of my people, who was making the check of nuclear contamination in the clean-up area following a repair job, found radiation along the whole main deck of the submarine. It looked initially like a serious nuclear leak but was so extensive we soon knew it could not be. I called EB and reported we had just detected some nuclear fallout which might be from the Chinese bomb.[*] They had just found the same thing in the shipyard. We agreed that we had to keep

---

[*] EB--Electric Boat Company.

it totally quiet for political reasons and a possible panic reaction in the American people. We agreed on the necessity to put a total clamp on any publicity, but we felt an obligation to determine how widespread it was through New England at least. Some of the readings were already high enough to cause concern.

At that time, the non-violent action people were protesting all of the nuclear sub launchings and commissionings. When the nuclear submarines went to sea, the "boat people" protesters were always there. A normal headache, but nuclear fallout would really send them off the deep end. I suggested that if General Dynamics would cooperate, we could check the rooftops of the cars driven by workers and our commuters, who came from all over New England, from Boston to New York. We set up a routine of wiping samples off car tops in the parking lots every morning to check on how extensive and how concentrated. Meanwhile, we prayed for rain.

In the nuclear repair business, it's a different type of radiation from fallout than from a spillage from our own operations, but you don't know until you've analyzed it in the lab. Then to make sure a possible spillage didn't get disguised in the Chinese fallout, we had to wash down the decks of all our nuclear submarines every night, and I couldn't tell our overworked people why. Even if they thought it was only the captain's fetish for cleanliness to scrub down the decks of our submarines before quitting every night, they took it with a good grace. It was a week before we got a nice, heavy, fresh rainstorm, for which I thanked the Lord, because the problem was about to get out of hand. That ended it; we had no reoccurrence.

Q: Were these strictly attack submarines that you were dealing with?

Captain Schratz: Yes, plus the Triton.[*]

---

[*] In the spring of 1960, the USS Triton (SSN-586), commanded by Captain Edward L. Beach, USN, made the first submerged circumnavigation of the world. She was an experimental two-reactor submarine, given a role as a radar picket.

Q: She being a special case. That would have been after Captain Beach had her, wouldn't it?

Captain Schratz: Yes. I don't recall when he got back in from the world cruise, but I was on the dock when he came in. He was on the dock in Pearl when I departed in <u>Pickerel</u> to set my world's record too. But I didn't deal with Ned during that period. I don't recall his ship being in New London more than momentarily while I was there.

Q: How close have you two been over the course of your career?

Captain Schratz: Quite close. We've been good-natured rivals in many things, a nice friendly rivalry.

Q: Did you take your ship out on training cruises as Captain Dornin had with the <u>Nereus</u>?

Captain Schratz: That's a surprising thing. I did it, yes. We went down to Fisher's Island once because Connecticut law says you can't drink beer till you're 21, but New York then said 18. We made a pleasant cruise down there, not for the beer; it's a delightful port and so close to New London, nobody goes there. We also made a memorable trip to Boston. During my master's program at Boston U., one of my seminars made a survey of voter responses in a Boston mayoral campaign, using the best of modern survey techniques. We predicted the "machine" candidate would win, and we were wrong. The "good guy" won for a lot of irrelevant reasons. Then the "machine" organization hired us to do a resurvey and find out why people voted as they did. Hence I had a special interest in the Boston mayor, and always relished a visit to Boston for the seafood houses.

The mayor set up a special visit for us, but for lack of time I counted on slipping through the Cape Cod Canal. If the Fulton's not the biggest ship to get through that canal, it must be next largest. We had just barely got under way when a heavy fog rolled in, closed the canal, and forced us to go around Nantucket. So I made a full-power run on the seaward route at 18 or 19 knots. In zero visibility, everything depended on the radar, and I prayed that some little fisherman wouldn't get impaled on our bow. Arriving in the sea-lanes, those big old tankers saw us charging through and fell in astern to let us do the blocking. We had no common communication frequency, and soon, three or four of them were astern in column, all heading for Boston. If anything forced us to slow down, these monsters would drive right up my stern sheets.

The ODs, all mustangs or temporary officers, technicians not really comfortable on a bridge watch, were far more concerned than I. One in particular on the midwatch asked about three times for permission to slow down. When I demurred, he asked the quartermaster to make a log entry that the officer of the deck recommended we slow down, but the captain objected. I, of course, was on the open bridge the entire time at sea, my eye glued to a superb radar repeater. We got to Boston on time and had a great weekend with the mayor and other people in that fine old liberty town. Fulton also made a trip to Charleston, South Carolina, to take over refit duties with Squadron Six while their tender was in the yard.

And naturally, we made a trip to Newport, so I could visit the War College. At that time, by chance, Arthur Schlesinger was visiting President Kennedy at the Auchincloss estate on the bay, and when I read Schlesinger's A Thousand Days several years later, I discovered that he mentioned looking out over the gorgeous Narragansett Bay at that time and seeing "a Navy battleship come up the bay," which, naturally, was the submarine tender Fulton.[*]

One thing which did not work as successfully on Fulton as in the Nereus was discipline. I used the same technique which Dusty followed, of holding all NJP--non-

---

[*] Arthur M. Schlesinger, Jr., A Thousand Days: John F. Kennedy in the White House (Boston: Houghton Mifflin, 1965).

judicial punishment--in private in my cabin. It worked very well with the men, but in my administrative inspection, I earned an unsat because it didn't follow UMCJ exactly.

Q: Did you have an aboard squadron commander?

Captain Schratz: Yes, ComSubRon 10.

Q: Who was that?

Captain Schratz: Captain Frank D. Walker.[*]

Q: What do you recall about him?

Captain Schratz: A fine officer, good submariner, good record, easygoing.

Q: What was the overall quality of your technicians, leaving aside the special nuclear people you inherited?

Captain Schratz: Extremely high. These were all volunteers, of course, even on the tenders. We took a lot of misfits from the submarines, but they were good people. Given half a chance, they produced.

Q: How did that compare in enjoyment with command of your own submarine?

Captain Schratz: Not quite the same. Of course, the perks are very nice in the CO cabin mess when a special birthday or anniversary came along. For a captain's dinner party, or other members of the mess, a smart-looking Filipino steward stood behind each chair to make sure each steak was exactly right. Our children weren't the only ones who were

---

[*] Captain Francis D. Walker, Jr., USN, Commander Submarine Squadron 18.

impressed. Those were the days when a staff car picked you up at home every morning and drove you home every night. I lived only about a mile and a half from the ship, so it took only about five minutes. But it was very nice.

Q: Then normally the squadron job would have followed. Was that the pattern?

Captain Schratz: Not immediately. It would have been the pattern after shore duty at that time.

Q: You went instead to the arms control duty.

Captain Schratz: I went to the Joint Staff, JCS. Just before I left Fulton, Admiral Rickover had his first heart attack. My nuclear division commander in Fulton was one of those summoned to sit around his bedside in Bethesda, ostensibly to pick his successor. He told this group a story. He said, "You know, any time a flag officer has a serious heart attack or condition which might prove fatal, hospital routines at Bethesda require a statement on his preference for a cemetery."

This poor hospital corpsman at Bethesda was petrified. He phoned all around the area for information, and finally took the form in to the admiral, reporting a very nice plot nearby at Burning Tree, 1,500 bucks--and Rick cut him off in mid-sentence.

"I'll never pay that. That's ridiculous."

So in total disorder, the corpsman retreated and resumed his search, finally locating a spot in southeast Washington offering no advantage but cost. He went back in and said, "I have a new place, admiral. It's not very nice, but it's only $150.00"

"That's fine," he replied. "I'll be there for only three days anyway."

I'm sure you've heard this story. Well, it's in Norman Polmar's book on Rickover.[*] He got it from me, but didn't tell it very well.

---

[*] Norman Polmar and Thomas B. Allen, Rickover (New York: Simon and Schuster, 1982), page 460.

When my division commander came back from that meeting, he was really enthused. He said, "You know, Admiral Rickover really has a great sense of humor, and I think it's a shame that the country doesn't know more about it. I can't publish this, but you can."

I agreed with him and wrote it up for submission to True magazine, then promptly forgot the whole incident. Months later, after I was detached and hard at work with the Joint Staff--the following spring just before Easter--I was visited by some scared Navy captain who asked if I was the Captain Paul Schratz who submitted this article. He showed me a galley of the next issue of True magazine. What that idiot editor had done was to hold the Rickover story until the Easter issue and then put a scurrilous cartoon about a crucifixion on it. I took one look and couldn't believe my eyes. It just destroyed any humor there was in it, especially at Easter time. An attached note from Admiral Rickover asked, "Are you the Captain P.R.S. who submitted this? Have you received any money for it? What proof do you have that it's true?"

I admitted I was the author; I was totally convinced that it was true, and I had not received money for it. I spent the whole weekend on the telephone and telegraph to New York to try to kill that page before it came out. It was too late then. I got telephone calls from admirals all over the country, suggesting that I should buck it up to the CNO, who really had the responsibility.

Then Admiral Rickover called, asking me to send a letter of apology to the editor. I already had that under way, accepting full responsibility for submitting the story in the first place, but criticized his deplorable editorial taste in adding the cartoon, which destroyed the humor and made it sacrilegious, especially to an officer who happens to be very religious--a fact I didn't know previously. Admiral Rickover wouldn't accept my letter. He wrote one for me to sign and submit to True, but I couldn't accept it because it was libelous and left me no leg to stand on in case of a suit. He also called BuPers, who happened to be Admiral Smedberg.* What he was really seeking through all this, I soon discovered, was the name of the person who had told the tale out of school. It was to save his reputation that I had to

---

* Vice Admiral William R. Smedberg III, USN, served as Chief of the Bureau of Naval Personnel from 1960 to 1964.

protect my source at all costs. Admiral Rickover kept insisting, "How do you know it's true?" I insisted I could not tell.

Smeddy called me and ordered, "Do whatever it takes to make him happy and do it immediately." As my former boss, this really wasn't the kind of help I needed or expected. I leaned as far as I could on my statement, and though still unacceptable to Admiral Rickover, sent it off to the magazine.

Admiral Smedberg pulled my name off the major command list--without any investigation--simply on the basis of what he had heard from Admiral Rickover. Then I had my Rickover interview about the action he would take. I learned firsthand the truth in all those rumors about the venetian shades throwing sun into your eyes and the shortened front legs of the chair, just to keep one tensed up, pushing against the back of the chair. To prove I wasn't really trying to embarrass him, all I could really say was that I published my name on the story; all I had to ask was that my name be withheld.

I said, "My source and I were sincere in trying to show that you have a sense of humor, and the story I submitted was quite humorous." I accepted responsibility for the editor's idiocy as far as possible, but beyond that, I couldn't go. He asked again how I knew it was true. I replied that I simply would not divulge my source. The interview lasted close to an hour, and on departure I thought I had done very well. Despite an obvious attempt, he didn't rattle me, but I couldn't do much except repeat the same statement.

I was then about to leave for Switzerland as the JCS-DoD representative on the U.S. delegation to the Eighteen Nation Disarmament Conference. Arriving in Geneva, the first letter was from the editor of True magazine, enclosing a check for $100.00 for the anecdote, along with a totally irrelevant postscript: "Have you heard any funny stories lately?" I really could have killed that guy.

To conclude, I didn't give the name of the division commander, nor did he learn that I was in trouble over it. There was no point in dragging him in. I watched him make captain, then rear admiral, and then vice admiral. Several years later when he was near retirement, I happened to meet him here at homecoming. I asked innocently, "By the way, Shannon, do you want to hear a funny story?" That was the first he ever heard of it.

Q: Can we put this gentleman's name on the record here?

Captain Schratz: Yes--Shannon Cramer.* But the story has since been claimed by many people. Norman Polmar said he's heard it from half a dozen, claiming they were responsible. I can assure you that <u>True</u> magazine in the Easter 1963 issue will find my name on it. It was a very unhappy week for us.

Q: I'm sure you've given thought to that many times since too.

Captain Schratz: I would probably have done about the same thing.

Q: Oh, really?

Captain Schratz: I think so.

Q: Would you have still sent it in in the first place?

Captain Schratz: Probably. If the editor had handled it right, it was a cute story. I've since heard it told about the German President Konrad Adenauer. You know, it is a funny story.

Q: What happened at JCS?

Captain Schratz: I checked in with the new Kennedy-McNamara team.† It was my first tour of joint duty. It isn't generally very inspiring duty. Joint staff action officers on JCS papers are brokers, men on a treadmill trying to compromise three service views. You don't

---

* Vice Admiral Shannon D. Cramer, Jr., USN, retired in 1977.
† John F. Kennedy served as President of the United States from 20 January 1960 until he was assassinated on 22 November 1963. Robert S. McNamara served as Secretary of Defense from 21 January 1961 to 29 February 1968.

have a chance for imaginative thought. They really don't want new ideas. On any issue which comes up, find out what was said before and say it again.

I tried to cut down on useless paper and wheel spinning. The first time I had an action paper, to get agreement of the service action officers, I suggested they list their objectives as category A, B, or C. A included typos and misspellings which went straight to my secretary; B included minor language changes which I would accept or reject as I saw fit; C included substantive issues on which we argue until reaching agreement. This seemed wholly sensible and unobjectionable to me, but the Army officer insisted it was totally improper. I took it to my three-star Air Force general, who thought it was excellent, immediately taking it to the G-1 section to put it formally into JCS staffing procedures. It was still there when I left at the end of my tour. Nobody objected; it just had to go through the proper procedures. Meanwhile, nobody ever used it. Perhaps in a nutshell this is the problem of the Joint Staff. The service action officers have the whip hand and aren't about to concede anything.

The Joint Staff did a superb job in planning the logistic reorganization when France dropped out of the NATO organization and we had to withdraw all our very extensive facilities on French soil. They are the best planning agency in the world in this type of action. But short-fuse problems such as the Cuban Missile Crisis present stumbling blocks I'll refer to later.

So when the chance came for temporary duty with the delegation in Geneva, I was really delighted. I had gone there previously for one crisis or another and saw how the delegation worked. We had then three flag officers, one from each service, on the U.S. delegation. The ambassador blew his stack one day and said, "I can't even get a pencil sharpened without getting a three-service position. I want one person who will speak for both the JCS and for the Secretary of Defense, and one person only."

Well, the services couldn't agree on a flag officer they would be able to control, so they settled for a captain or colonel, and I had that delightful opportunity to relieve three flag officers and take over the duty. The ambassador was correct--the split between the political and military people in the delegation at that time was worse than between the U.S. and the Russians. The Potomac was a greater barrier than the Atlantic. Both sides were very suspicious. Internal papers were very closely held. Defense supplied two typists to the delegation pool, and they had private instructions that any time they typed a speech draft, they were to insert an extra carbon and slip it to the military. Sometimes we'd see maybe a third or a half of a draft presentation to be given at the Palais, but rarely had the opportunity to clear, discuss, or develop issues under consideration.

Just after I got there, the ambassador died quite suddenly, and Bill Foster, the head of the Arms Control and Disarmament Agency, went over personally to run the delegation.[*] He was the new Kennedy appointee as head of ACDA, and his deputy was Adrian "Butch" Fisher. Foster was a distinguished negotiator who had served as Under Secretary of Defense under Eisenhower, and knew the Defense Department quite well. He didn't feel he needed that same secretiveness within the delegation, and I walked into a much happier situation.

Thanks partly to my graduate education, he immediately gave me the responsibility for the Western Four discussions--U.S., British, Canadians, and Italians, which usually preceded the private meeting of the conference co-chairmen, the U.S. and U.S.S.R. I ran all the agendas for the weekly discussions, picked the subjects for discussion, and wrote up the reports for the delegation. For State and Defense problems, I served with Tom Pickering, largely as an informal policy planning council for the delegation.[†] Tom, then a FSO-7, was a very bright young Foreign Service officer. We worked extremely well together and soon became close personal friends. Tom is just completing a tour as ambassador to Salvador, en route to the ambassador's chair in Israel. I thought Tom was the sharpest person I had ever met in the Foreign Service. He had a meteoric career and pretty well dominated State and Defense policymaking. The rumor was if we couldn't reach agreement, it needed a hard new look. Bill Foster and I also had a very friendly relationship. And when Butch Fisher came over to chair the delegation, it was much the same.

---

[*] William C. Foster became director of the Arms Control and Disarmament Agency in 1961.
[†] From 1962 to 1964 Thomas R. Pickering served as political adviser to the U.S. delegation during the 18-nation disarmament conference in Geneva.

Q: How well prepared were the Soviets?

Captain Schratz: Quite well. Ambassador Tsarapkin and most of his staff had been in the disarmament business since William Tell and knew all the nyets.* What we lacked in similar continuity we often gained through leaks. The Rumanian delegation was very disloyal to the Soviets. They would harshly criticize the Americans formally at the Palais during a session, but frequently at embassy parties before an important meeting, they would tip the Russian hand on negotiating positions. They were quite helpful.

There were "national days" for one of those delegations about every week, and the social obligations were heavy. I can't imagine circumstances where so much of the cocktail party conversation hit the cables the following day back to the various capitals. Everybody pumped everybody. And the smaller nations in particular wanted to be on good terms with the U.S. military. A Swedish general, friendly and hospitable, invited us to his command in Gotland, and we spent a weekend visiting first the Swedish nuclear expert at his home in Stockholm, then to Gotland, a gorgeous island in the Baltic. I visited most of the European and Mideast delegations at one time or other, and found it was a unique and very useful experience.

The Limited Test Ban Treaty terms were negotiated while I was on the delegation, plus the exchange of observers, and the Washington-Moscow hot line. We worked out the details in Geneva--the limits within which governmental agreement could be reached at head of state level. Unfortunately, that's the only time any significant productive output came from the Geneva conference.

Q: That was something President Kennedy was really eager to get.

Captain Schratz: That's right. But it was fascinating duty. My day frequently started with a swim in Lake Geneva with the Russians, Swedes, and a couple of others. The chairman of the Russian delegation was always there with his key people. One man patrolled in a

---

* Ambassador Semyon K. Tsarapkin.

rowboat out beyond the swimming area. They said it was a life boat. I teased them about it being for security, what with France being on the other side of the lake.

Then late in my session there, my Soviet KGB opposite number defected. They turned the place upside down for several days before admitting it publicly. This caused a major stir in the papers. He was Yuri Nosenko, who had come to Geneva after an assignment to shadow Harvey Oswald, Kennedy's assassin, during his visit to the Soviet Union. Part of my duties involved covering the CIA responsibility. I had a radio station--on-line crypto--inside my office direct to the Pentagon or CIA via Paris. An Army officer from the U.S. Military Liaison Mission in Potsdam, East Germany, came down to Geneva on rotation to run my radio station.

If anything came up in the delegation, I could get a message off to the Pentagon and return in the time it took for the State people to write it up on a message pad and walk it two blocks to the U.S. Mission headquarters to get it encrypted. They were still a few years behind. That was one of the problems before I arrived, because it gave Defense the jump on everything State was trying to do, and many times they used the time advantage to State's disadvantage, unfortunately.

When Bill Foster arrived, he simply asked if I would let him know beforehand when I reported a delegation position in which State might have an adverse reaction. I appreciated his position and since he gave me full discretion, I was careful to use it wisely. I had no secrets from him. We had an extremely harmonious arrangement. I thought it extremely effective and the delegation did too.

We were in Geneva when the President was assassinated.[*] Those were dramatic days in our lives. When the news arrived, we were at a U.S. delegation party hosted by the DCM, Don MacDonald, at his home on Lake Geneva that evening.[†] The other delegations were all represented. It broke up the party, but their expressions of sorrow, with most of the ladies in tears, were most touching. Three American couples--the Pickerings, the Schratzes, and the MacDonalds--sat around for a while in a state of shock.

---

[*] President John F. Kennedy was killed in Dallas, Texas, on 22 November 1963.
[†] Donald S. MacDonald.

We lived in a villa south of Geneva. The next morning our next-door neighbor walked all the way into town to a florist and had a beautiful red rose to greet me when I left at 7:00. The little old lady who sold the New York Herald Tribune outside the delegation headquarters that morning refused to accept any money from the Americans. So many things happened among those generally cold and unemotional Swiss, and with the other delegations, it was really remarkable. Our young President, despite his few months in office, seemed to have a remarkable effect on other peoples in the world. It was a day to live through, a day to remember.

Q: Where did your children go to school during that period?

Captain Schratz: Our eldest daughter was a senior in college and couldn't find an adequate university in her field, sociology, so she stayed in the States and allowed the Air Force to fly her over for the summers and at Christmastime. Our number-two daughter, a sophomore, caught a junior year abroad program at the University of Freiburg, about 50 miles outside Geneva, and did her junior year, certifying in both French language and literature. Our two high school age went to the International School in Geneva on the American (English) side. For our two grade-schoolers, we were content that they would lose a year, but we believed they'd gain at least as much by going to a Swiss public school. The headmaster was a very nice young man who put Pete in his own classroom. Our second-grader went into his wife's class. Our youngest, Mary, went to a primary school in French run by a Rumanian.

When we returned, our number-three daughter, Marjorie, who was in the International School, wanted to stay in Geneva for half of her senior year. She wanted to live with a neighbor and switch from the International School to the Swiss public high school, with the neighbor's daughter. By the time she came back to the U.S., she was jabbering French like she was born and raised there. All of our children became bilingual in French, which eventually shaped their futures in very important ways.

Q: Was it a place you enjoyed living?

Captain Schratz: Very much, yes. The Swiss are very strange people, but it's a wonderful place to live. We'd go back in a minute.

Q: Was there a specific time limit put on that tour of duty? How did it come to end when it did?

Captain Schratz: Defense had never previously sent dependents with their TDY representatives.* And they certainly wouldn't in my case if they knew we had seven children. I didn't ask for it; a bright young kid in DoD thought it up.† We ended up with an augmented per diem, State Department representation funds, diplomatic privileges on gas and liquor, Army educational funds, and unlimited travel with the family. Geneva is very expensive, but we could swing it. The repeat travel helped me when I was invited to visit other delegations, particularly in the European and Middle East capitals.

Q: Would you describe the tenor of the negotiations themselves? What had induced the Soviets to make an agreement during that period that hasn't occurred since then?

Captain Schratz: I think they wanted a limited test ban agreement just as much as President Kennedy did. The hot line was extremely important to both sides, who realized its vital role in time of a nuclear crisis. There wasn't nearly as much emotional reaction at that time as there is now. Nor was there a serious ideological problem between East and West. When Gromyko opened the proceedings in March 1958, his opening address set very interesting guidelines for Soviet-American talks: "We don't trust you and you don't trust us, and any agreement reached here must be reached with this in mind."‡ Blatant, outright, and absolutely accurate. And that's exactly the way we worked.

---

* TDY--temporary duty, as opposed to a permanent duty station.
† DoD--Department of Defense.
‡ Andrei A. Gromyko was the foreign minister for the Soviet Union.

Q: What kind of substance did you get into the negotiations themselves? What did you go back and forth on?

Captain Schratz: There were two areas. We met at the Palais on Tuesdays and Thursdays. On one of those days the subject was always "general and complete disarmament." When the talks were first set up, general and complete disarmament was a necessary subject; it is part of the Communist ideological utopia and useful for propagandizing the West as aggressors. Many small nations in the world, like the Nigerians, didn't realize that the Soviets were playing games. They thought both sides were seriously trying to reach complete disarmament.

Many of the small country representatives arrived with shopping lists. They wanted truckloads of rifles, Colt .45s, ammunition, rockets, and whatnot, which they were going to buy on the cheap when the big powers disarmed. They couldn't believe it was a pure propaganda exercise. When they became convinced of Soviet cynicism, the Russians moved to enlarge the conference and bring in some more innocents. That's why it went from 10 nations to 18, to 28, to 45, or whatever it is now. These meetings played for the world press and that's all.

The other weekly plenary sessions were on collateral measures, on actual disarmament measures, and those were the sessions which produced fruit. We worked out limits of the test ban: nuclear detectability of underground tests, how one can control an underground test, national means of detection vice on-site observers, limits to be set on underground explosions, and so forth. All the major delegations had had nuclear experts. George Bunn, who is on the War College faculty now, was there.[*] The Swedes always had their best people there. Jan Prawitz, now head of Swedish nuclear research, was there then. Madame Myrdahl ran the Swedish delegation. We also worked out areas of agreement on nonnuclear weapons and capabilities, developed a number of measures in the way of crisis control and such policies, wholly apart from reduction of armaments. By and large, it was useful.

---

[*] George Bunn was serving as the general counsel for the Arms Control and Disarmament Agency.

Negotiating tactics inside the delegations I found fascinating. The Russians had secret signals to Eastern European patsies. Whenever they got caught short on something, Tsarapkin would pass a signal to the Bulgarian delegation, and the Bulgarians would make a statement in Bulgarian, which few people understand. That ambassador was also an oaf, but he would talk until the Russians got themselves together. Then they shut him off and we'd go back to work. The Bulgarians were known privately as the "fools of the eastern European delegations," and the Italians, I regret to say, shared a not dissimilar role among the western delegation. The interplay of the delegations was fascinating, and I thrived on it.

Q: What was your personal contribution other than communications back with Washington?

Captain Schratz: I did a fair amount of work on the background on all the nuclear questions, working out technical details, the limits on detectability of underground explosions, objections to a complete test ban or a limited test ban, technical details of how far we could go in concessions. Thanks to a fantastic research service back in the Pentagon, the service was useful. I also wrote a number of background studies and speech drafts, and contributed to others. A non-typical example of a speech draft was prompted by the Bulgarian ambassador in the exercise above.

The U.S. delegation had contingency drafts by the score. But we had nothing like the Bulgarians to fall back on when we really got caught short. So I wrote, facetiously, "A Contingency Plan for the Contingency for Which We Have No Contingency Plan." It contained every cliche and soft, soothing words I could find, yet said absolutely nothing. Bill Foster got quite a kick out of it, sent copies back to Washington to pull some legs there.

There was a serious internal problem which made my job tough. When ACDA was founded by Kennedy, peaceniks flocked from State and elsewhere to take it over, some of whom were far-out. It took several years to weed these people out. <u>Any</u> agreement for them was a good agreement, and Defense had to hold the line. This trying problem was aggravated by a difference in negotiating tactics between State/ACDA and Defense. JCS positions were not reached as "negotiating" positions from which agreement might be worked out at a considerably lower level.

In developing a U.S. position within the U.S. policy structure in Washington to present at Geneva, all the negotiating leverage was expended to find a common view supportable on both sides of the Potomac. When this position was presented at Geneva and earned a "nyet," it was natural over time to seek agreement on a more acceptable level. This came naturally to the diplomat but was very difficult for the military man, who had the ultimate responsibility for security in any event. Here the intractability of the Joint Staff became a serious roadblock to any new position. In my position of representing both McNamara, the SecDef, and General Maxwell Taylor, the CJCS, it often required both tact and skill.[*] The "whiz kid" influence in Defense was just as much in need of restraint as the Joint Staff in need of tractability.

Q: How much contact did you have with Paul Nitze during that period?

Captain Schratz: Nitze, as head of ISA, McNamara's little State Department, was my reporting senior in DoD, and Bud Zumwalt was his senior military aide.[†] All of my output went through a deputy assistant secretary and through Bud to Nitze. I knew Nitze only casually. I was in the Pentagon only a short time before going to Geneva and didn't stay in DoD staff long after I returned. I'm not sure when he shifted over to SecNav.

Q: November of '63.

Captain Schratz: That was not long before I moved into DoD/ISA. Zumwalt was the front man. I talked primarily with Bud. I can't recall Nitze visiting Geneva when I was there.

---

[*] General Maxwell D. Taylor, USA, served as Chairman of the Joint Chiefs of Staff from 1 October 1962 to 3 July 1964.
[†] Paul H. Nitze was Assistant Secretary of Defense for International Security Affairs, 1961-63; Secretary of the Navy, 1963-67; Deputy Secretary of Defense, 1967-69. Captain Elmo R. Zumwalt, Jr., USN, was his military aide.

The ISA deputy assistant was Art Barber.* Art came to Geneva twice during my tour. He was quite nice, rather erratic, but very brainy and a good man to work with.

Q: What are your recollections of Captain Zumwalt from that period?

Captain Schratz: Bud was always extremely helpful. Primarily, I suppose, it was the difference between working in ISA and working in the Joint Staff. I mentioned earlier the lack of room for original thought in the Joint Staff, and the deadly procedure of absolute compliance with any previous statement on the subject. If a paper sold then, it was easier to sell it again, rather than fight something new through the service staffs against the precedent. Even if a JCS recommendation was disapproved by the SecDef, it didn't automatically change the guidance to the chiefs. The previous recommendation would come back again in its original form.

In the ISA and the DoD level, the contrary happens. Especially in the early days of the Kennedy team, they had no idea at all of staffing procedures and the responsibilities of moving papers through the chain of command. They worked more or less as attorneys. A case would come in; it was given to a consultant. There was a strong rumor that the way they chose military officers for ISA was by giving each new man in uniform--here, I'm leaping ahead to my tour on the ISA staff--they would give a tired old problem to you for an answer. If you came up with the standard stale solution, they condemned you to administrative duties in ISA. If you came up with an original thought or a serious attempt to try to change the direction of something, then you earned "consultant" status.

Nobody could tell by the nameplates on the doors in ISA what problems were really handled. As a "consultant" you were tagged for any problem that came by. Anybody inherited any job for which they felt he had a talent, whatever office he called home. And so Bud was in his world and I in mine. We had a good working relationship.

---

* Arthur W. Barber, Deputy Assistant Secretary of Defense for International Security Affairs.

Q: Did he seem to have a good grasp of the details of the things you were involved with in Geneva?

Captain Schratz: Oh, yes. He was interested, also, which always helps.

Q: Where were you at the time of the Cuban Missile Crisis?*

Captain Schratz: In the Joint Staff.

Q: What are your recollections from that period?

Captain Schratz: Compared with the Bay of Pigs fiasco, I thought the Cuban Missile Crisis was a superbly managed government crisis.† And when people criticized the structure of the decision-making in Washington during the Bay of Pigs, they should remember that the identical people played in both. If the organization is at fault, how could the same people be so bad in one and so good in the other? Kennedy took an active role in the Missile Crisis. I saw him in the Joint Staff during that time about as often as I saw my own boss. It was a good time for me to be there. Many times--this is in my later period in ISA--a lot of people were searching for ideas. If they heard that you happened to have a new approach to something, the chain of command didn't stand in the way of a direct phone call. It gave a sense of importance which didn't exist earlier, certainly.

---

* In mid-October 1962, U.S. reconnaissance plane photographed a Soviet nuclear missile site in Cuba and the presence of Soviet bombers. On 22 October President John F. Kennedy went on national television to announce a naval quarantine of Cuba, to be implemented on 24 October. On 28 October Premier Nikita Khrushchev of the Soviet Union notified President Kennedy that he was ordering the withdrawal of Soviet bombers and missiles from Cuba.

† In mid-April 1961 a force of 1,400 Cuban exiles, secretly trained by U.S. personnel in Guatamala, landed in the Bay of Pigs, on the southwestern coast of Cuba, in an attempt to overthrow Fidel Castro, that nation's Communist dictator. The invasion attempt was a disaster. President Kennedy decided that U.S. naval intervention would worsen the situation, so ships and aircraft offshore were prohibited from taking part.

Q: How much of a personal contact was there with Kennedy? What instances do you recall?

Captain Schratz: None for me personally. I saw him as a fluster in the corridors, but nothing directly.

Q: Anything else to recall on that period combining the arms control and the JCS?

Captain Schratz: My JCS office was directly involved in the Missile Crisis, providing the military input to the ExCom, generally in the form of guidance for Ambassador Adlai Stevenson at the U.N. These developed into endless around-the-clock drafting sessions for a team of Joint Staff operational planners and arms controllers. As each of us became too exhausted to continue, he summoned his alternate who took over until he was ready to collapse.

Many, including McNamara, moved cots into the Pentagon for the duration. Unfortunately, it was a search for an agreed word rather than an effective plan, hence a highly inefficient process. One evening I was scheduled to play a concert in Washington. My alternate was exhausted, so I couldn't call for a relief. I slipped into a tux in a washroom, rushed to the Pentagon's river entrance, where my wife was waiting, drove quickly to Lisner Auditorium, did my fiddling, and rushed back. When I got back to my seat around the conference table, the team hadn't moved more than a line or two through the draft telegram in my absence. I'm sure you can realize how this cramped my style of operating. Stultifying is the word.

Things looked up immediately, however. I and an Army colonel were sent to New York as U.N. delegates to augment the U.S. delegation staff. This I found thoroughly interesting, particularly because of the recent experience in Geneva.

I was also involved with the Berlin Task Force. This was the time the wall was built.* Affairs were very tense between East and West. Incidents frequently arose with our Military Liaison Mission in Potsdam, either with the Soviet forces or the thugs in the East German Vopo [Volkspolitzei].

Q: How did these wonderful orders come to an end? Was there some event in the negotiations that brought you back?

Captain Schratz: I think the session ended probably in the summer of 1964, and I was due for my rotation, having finished two years in the Joint Staff--with 18 months on TDY. An Air Force general in ACDA wanted me to join his staff, but I was happy to be preempted by Paul Nitze to go on the DoD/ISA staff.

Q: So had he asked for you?

Captain Schratz: Yes. And that was really the pinnacle. Having gone from the service staff in OpNav, to the Joint Staff, to the DoD staff, all in policy-forming assignments, DoD was the ultimate, a fascinating tour. I was technically the chief of plans on the ISA policy planning staff, but there were no job descriptions. You had your hand in everything that came by. One lived and died by his contacts in the services, State, NSC, throughout the bureaucracy who could be depended on. You really had to rely on people when you got in a bind.

For instance, when the Russians announced deployment of their first missile submarine, it caused near panic in Congress. The information was widely known throughout Washington in detail, and it happened right on schedule. Yet people in Congress and somebody in the White House thought we better speed up deployment of Polaris to the Pacific. Well, there was almost no flexibility in the Polaris program, having

---

* Soviets sealed off the eastern section of the city on 13 August 1961 by erecting concrete and barbed wire barriers--a wall 26 and a half miles long. The two sectors settled into an uneasy truce. Several people were killed while trying to escape from east to west. The wall was finally opened for free passage on 9 November 1989. The following day East German troops began dismantling the wall, which was entirely demolished by the end of 1990.

had the highest priority in government for several years. Yet there was suddenly intense pressure to get the first one on station off China immediately.

Wearing the blue suit, this became my problem. Just by chance I had a schedule of deployments of our first missile-launching submarines from a Nitze speech draft. I took the date the first one was supposed to go through the Panama Canal, guesstimated the great circle distance from Panama to a point within missile range of Shanghai, and figured an arrival time at maximum speed, bypassing routine planned stops at San Diego, Pearl Harbor, and Guam. Likewise with the next three subs. My three or four new estimated times on station did great violence to all sorts of planning and logistics, but the Secretary wanted it within two hours to present to the President for a noon speech. He got it. Then you start screaming for help from the Navy people, plus source backup. All OpNav could do was much the same as I did. Except for one boat where the missiles were unavailable, their answers were about the same as mine. By early afternoon the crisis was over; the data were not used, and one could relax until the next crisis.

A much more illustrative problem emerged when General Westmoreland recommended mining of the Han River and the approaches to Hanoi to cut off North Vietnamese logistic support by sea.[*] The plan originated in Saigon and was strongly supported by Westmoreland, CinCPac, the services, the Joint Staff, and the JCS. When it got to DoD, I had the task of drafting the SecDef endorsement on the red-striped JCS paper. Unfortunately, I thought it was a bad idea from the beginning. McNamara had no reluctance in overruling a unanimous vote of the Joint Chiefs, except that when he did, he wanted some convincing evidence. This was a rare paper which had gone from the field command through the entire joint structure and to the DoD without a dissenting vote.

But I had made a war patrol in that area and knew that the Han River had to be dredged almost continuously or it silts up and becomes non-navigable. A mine is a terribly indiscriminate weapon. The first ship to be hit may be a Polish hospital ship, a key neutral, or an important non-military cargo. And there was a second problem: there were no mines available at the time. Nobody thought to check. I suggested a far simpler and more

---

[*] General William C. Westmoreland, USA, served as Commander U.S. Military Assistance Command Vietnam from 20 June 1964 to 2 July 1968.

Paul R. Schratz #2 - 245

effective alternative. A Russian-built dredge, Zembales, was working the lower channel trying to keep it navigable. I recommended, since there was no tactical emergency requiring the channel be closed instantly, that the dredge be destroyed and let nature take its course to silt up the channel in about six months, and without any acute political liability.

McNamara leaped on the idea with enthusiasm, ordering that night that the dredge be destroyed. By a strange accident of history, however, the dredge had left the morning before to go to Vladivostok for overhaul. By the time it came back many months later, somehow the whole idea was forgotten. Not until years later did President Nixon, almost on his own initiative, recommend to Admiral Moorer, then the JCS Chairman, to carry out the mining.[*] I have no idea why the much better idea didn't again come to the surface. I think it's an excellent illustration first of the lack of a corporate memory in the civilian bureaucracy; second, of the different scope of possibilities for initiative in the DoD staff, and largely of the paralysis of the joint staff today versus the DoD staff.

Q: After Mr. Nitze became Secretary of the Navy, Townsend Hoopes became the Assistant Secretary of Defense for ISA. What do you remember of him?

Captain Schratz: Yes, very well. He was not in my circuit in DoD, but he asked for the loan of my services for a special project. An analysis of Thailand's strategic significance had been done for DoD by Rear Admiral Richard Craighill.[†] But the money ran out before he completed it, and he wasn't anxious to do it on his own. Unfortunately, I disagreed strongly with the entire project. Craighill and I were in different worlds. I preferred dropping the study in the trashcan, particularly since my boss agreed to the loan of my services provided it was all outside normal working hours. I spent about a month trying to make sense out of it and put it in the mill. I made it clear that I didn't want it to be my paper, because I just didn't agree with what I could understand of it.

---

[*] Admiral Thomas H. Moorer, USN, served as Chairman of the Joint Chiefs of Staff from 3 July 1970 to 30 June 1974. His oral history is in the Naval Institute collection.
[†] Rear Admiral Richard S. Craighill, USN.

Q: Who was your boss?

Captain Schratz: Let's see. Henry Rowen was, I guess, the Deputy Assistant Secretary under John McNaughton.* Adam Yarmolinsky and Dan Ellsberg were special assistants who always had ideas, some good.† Art Barber and, I guess, Tim Hoopes, and General John Vogt, USAF, came under McNaughton too.‡ Vogt was my boss. I knew Tim Hoopes casually before ISA, actually more than I knew Paul Nitze. I got to know Nitze later when I wrote his bib for the Naval Institute history of the Secretaries of the Navy.

Q: What do you remember about McNaughton, who almost became Secretary of the Navy?

Captain Schratz: A great man and a major loss to his country.§ I don't recall any familiarity or love for the Navy. He had done some pioneer studies in nuclear strategy, which he gave in a conference at Ann Arbor just before the famed McNamara "counterforce" commencement speech at Ann Arbor. I was at the conference when McNaughton spoke. It was a good piece of work. His main problem--some of his assistants were a bit flaky: Adam Yarmolinsky, a brain but rather unmilitarized. Another, I forget his name now, was carrying a heavy cross against chemical warfare. And then there was Dan Ellsberg. Even though a Marine Corps veteran and very bright, he couldn't remember to close the big vault before going home at night, so a colonel or captain had to check the security behind him. A rather strange person.

Q: We were talking at lunch about John Vann's role. Would you discuss that, please?

---

* Henry S. Rowen, John T. McNaughton.
† Daniel Ellsberg became widely known in 1971 for his role in releasing government documents that came to be known as the "Pentagon Papers."
‡ Townsend W. Hoopes; Arthur W. Barber; Brigadier General John W. Vogt, Jr., USAF.
§ With the departure of Paul Nitze in June 1967, McNaughton was nominated to replace him. On 19 July 1967, when he had not yet taken office as Secretary of the Navy, McNaughton and others were killed in an airplane crash near Hendersonville, North Carolina.

Captain Schratz: Vann was a very controversial Army type.* He had great courage, possibly too much courage, very capable, and one of the few who thoroughly understood the Vietnam War. With the courage of his own convictions, he was sure to run afoul of his Army superiors, often going in a different direction. A lieutenant colonel on General Harkins's staff, they had a total falling out. And much the same with his successor.

Q: Westmoreland.

Captain Schratz: Yes. I first learned about him through a close friend, Vince Davis, now with the University of Kentucky and custodian of Vann's papers.† When John completed his tour in Vietnam, as a lieutenant colonel, he was scheduled to brief the Joint Chiefs on Vietnam. I did what I could to grease the skids for him to ensure that the JCS talked with him. There were rumors that he would not be allowed to see the Chiefs, and at the last minute, the briefing was canceled. Then I tried to get Vann assigned to DoD/ISA, but learned that he was unassignable to Pentagon duty. Realizing that he had no future in the Army, he decided to get out of the service.

Q: What was the thrust of what he was planning to say?

Captain Schratz: He and I both thought we were fighting the wrong war and didn't understand the problem in Vietnam. He was sincere in "winning the hearts and minds of the people" and equally convinced that U.S. policy was alienating them. He returned to Vietnam as a civilian, an AID official, and resumed his missionary work to change U.S. policy.‡ I think he was shot down 26 times in a helicopter, the last when he was killed. The Viet Cong had a price on his head at that time. He was revered by the South Vietnamese,

---

* For the definitive story on Vann see Neil Sheehan's A Bright Shining Lie: John Paul Vann and America in Vietnam (New York: Random House, 1988).
† Professor Vincent Davis has written a number of books on the subject of Navy policymaking.
‡ AID--Agency for International Development.

and is really a great person. Vince Davis hopes to get a book out on John, I don't know when. It may put a different picture on some of the war in Vietnam.

Q: How much did you personally get involved with the Southeast Asia question?

Captain Schratz: Almost not at all. It was really not in my circuit for some reason. Because of the fluid organization in DoD, my chief of plans duties rarely involved planning. More as a consultant, I handled any problem that came my way, and a good idea sometimes brought instant fame.

For example, President Johnson was deeply concerned about finding a way out of the Vietnam morass. A young Army lieutenant colonel in ISA came up with a brand-new idea one day, which he put into a casual, internal paper to his boss. To his amazement, he had a telephone call from the President within hours to come over and brief LBJ directly.[*] The President was really desperate to find anything, any ray of hope to get that millstone from around his neck.

Q: Grasping for panaceas, it sounds like.

Captain Schratz: Yes. Of course, my enthusiasm for the Johnson era was nowhere near what I felt during the Kennedy years, particularly for Mrs. Kennedy then. After the assassination, always hard-pressed for an idea for my monthly Shipmate editorial, I did one on "The Eighth Profile in Courage." I used Kennedy's technique in his book Profiles in Courage and developed an eighth profile on Kennedy himself, really an epitaph and written largely in his own words. When that was published, Mrs. Kennedy learned about it from someone and phoned me in the Pentagon to ask for an autographed copy. She also promised that it would be one of the special papers and mementos from his desk to be in the museum in Boston. She wanted to know how she could repay me; I suggested an autographed photo of the family. When it arrived in the Pentagon with the special franking

---

[*] LBJ--President Lyndon B. Johnson, who succeeded to the presidency when Kennedy was assassinated in November 1963 and served until January 1969.

privileges and the Jacqueline Kennedy return address, it was worn thin from handling before it ever got to me. I was very much impressed.

Q: What other problems do you recall dealing with?

Captain Schratz: One of the biggest problems was me getting out of there. I was then feeling a strong need for more education, and about that time, for reasons unknown, I started getting offers of full-tuition fellowships at universities for a doctoral program. I think I received 10 or 12, including Yale, Princeton, Michigan, Northwestern, American, and Ohio State. I couldn't understand it.

Q: How did they come about?

Captain Schratz: I was taking some graduate courses at American University and was fairly well known in the university circuit. I'd been writing and speaking on the conference circuit and came to know people like Harold Sprout at Princeton, a distinguished scholar. Sprout had planned to do a third book in his sea power series, a book called <u>Mahan in the Modern World</u>. When the Sprouts got diverted into the energy and conservation field, they realized they'd never get back to Mahan again, and suggested I do it. We had a meeting in Pittsburgh and later at Princeton, where he turned over all of his files on the project. It was he who offered a doctoral fellowship at Princeton which I thought looked very good. Bill Crowe was just completing his doctorate under Sprout.[*]

When I went up to work out a program, however, Sprout found, to his chagrin, that Princeton has a regulation against granting full-tuition scholarships to anybody on active duty in the military. But the word apparently got around that I was interested, and, out of the blue, I started getting offers from other universities. I applied to BuPers to be allowed

---

[*] Commander William J. Crowe, Jr., USN. As an admiral, Crowe served as Chairman of the Joint Chiefs of Staff from 1985 to 1989.

to accept a fellowship at Ohio State, run by a Sprout protege and good friend, Ed Furniss.[*] The BuPers attitude was not only no, but hell no. I could understand their problem. In the first place, I was already in a job for which they couldn't find anybody qualified to fill. And if I was already qualified to fill that job, what was I going to train myself for in a university? Above all, I was doing the unpardonable thing of giving up my major command for some education. You'll recall that Smedberg pulled me off the major command list in the Rickover incident. After he left BuPers, his relief restored my name to the list, but I had already lost my chance for a submarine squadron.

Q: What were the options at that point?

Captain Schratz: All they could offer was a service squadron, which I thought was neither challenging nor rewarding. By then I felt beyond all that. Even though it was just a ticket-punching operation, I really was too involved in too many areas. Giving up the major command wasn't all that tough, but it was unforgivable for the Chief of Naval Personnel and convinced him that I was merely preparing myself for a career after retirement. And beyond all that, the Navy simply doesn't favor graduate education anywhere near the extent of the Army and Air Force.

I appealed the BuPers action to Paul Nitze, and that went around and around for months, with no decision until the week before I was due at Ohio State. I finally gave up, took the family to Pittsburgh for the Labor Day weekend. I was telling my sad story to the folks about how I almost got to graduate school, when the phone rang. It was Under Secretary Bob Baldwin calling to tell me he had just decided in my favor and wanted to talk with me as soon as I got back to Washington.[†] I couldn't believe it. The answer to all my dreams.

That was the time when Nitze and Baldwin were feuding with BuPers over the direction of the Naval Academy curriculum. He favored a much broader course, with accreditation of college courses to allow the midshipmen far more range in their academic

---
[*] Dr. Edward S. Furniss, Jr.
[†] Robert H. B. Baldwin served as Under Secretary of the Navy from 1965 to 1967.

program. He was just starting on that road, and BuPers was against it. When I returned to Washington to talk with the Under Secretary, who handles personnel matters, he explained his great reluctance to overrule BuPers on an individual officer's assignment, but found special circumstances in my case. In exchange for his support, he wanted me to give him two pledges: first, on the completion of my doctoral studies I would go to the Naval Academy as the academic dean; second, that I would use my extra education to improve the attitude toward education in the Navy. I accepted both gladly and I was off to Ohio State.

I chose Ohio State because of Ed Furniss, an established scholar and super gentleman, who was finally getting the Mershon program at Ohio State set up as it should have been in national security studies. He was looking for pioneering students to bring out there; I was the first naval officer to get a Mershon fellowship. I don't think there has been more than a handful, maybe only two or three since. This is part of the Navy attitude toward education that I was to do something about. When I finished my program, Ed unfortunately died within the month--a terrible loss.

On graduation, BuPers gave me my choice pretty much of where I wanted to go-- Naval Academy, PG school in Monterey as the dean. I chose the National War College, because I was doing a dissertation on the McNamara era. I went to the Naval Academy for interviews on setting up a civilian dean's office. I believe Bob McNitt was doing the equivalent as secretary to the academic board.[*] What Nitze foresaw was that I would be the intermediary between SecNav and BuPers and perhaps more likely, between Admiral Rickover and BuPers.

What I learned in my interviews was that much of the enrichment program and any major changes would not have smooth sailing in Annapolis either. More and more it seemed to me that what they really needed in Annapolis was a yaller-haired tiger of about 35 who didn't mind burning himself out charging through solid masonry. Having finally received the education I sought, it didn't seem right to tie myself down to an administrative assignment. I felt I could make a contribution in writing, in carrying out my other pledge. After much thought, I regretfully asked to be released from that pledge, and so I continued

---

[*] Rear Admiral Robert W. McNitt, USN.

at the National War College while working on my dissertation. There I started a voluntary elective on the history of strategic thought, a blend of theory and operational experience. It became very popular and soon involved almost the entire student body. Dozens of future Air Force and Army generals later told me that seminar changed their entire career outlook: Brent Scowcroft, Bennie Davis (CinCSAC), Ray Furlong, commandant of the Air University, et al.*

Primarily I ran the Defense Strategy Seminar, a two-week program for carefully selected senior reserve officers including a number of prominent public officials. Previously the course was done on contract with outside scholars. If my second pledge meant anything, I thought the faculty should conduct that program without outside assistance. Here I was successful, but the opposition was heavy and resourceful. To ease the teaching load, I prepared a book-length syllabus for the course and did the same for the international relations phase of the regular academic program. Getting the military faculty involved in the teaching brought back most of the difficulties encountered earlier at Newport. One other idea I was able to set up toward this end was a faculty research seminar. I visualized different military faculty members drafting papers and thrashing them out in group sessions. This was much the same as Ed Furniss had done very successfully at Ohio State with the Mershon program. I didn't do quite as well. The civilian professors contributed some papers, but I think I wrote most of them. And to improve the quality of the discussions, I found it necessary to invite top students to participate. They were extremely helpful in my own writings. During that tour, I won two Naval Institute essay prizes.

In the beginning, the research group was slow and often discouraging. Better days soon arrived. The National War College Research Foundation is now a booming operation, producing several books in print by military officers each year.

Then, early in my third year at the National War College, I had a very unusual day. Tom Moorer, who was then CNO, called one morning to tell me that I had just been

---

* Lieutenant General Brent Scowcroft, USAF, held a number of prestigious positions, including serving in various national security capacities on the White House staff from 1972 to 1977. Lieutenant General Raymond B. Furlong, USAF, was commandant of the Air University from 1 September 1975 to 1 July 1979. General Bennie L. Davis, USAF, served as Commander in Chief of the Strategic Air Command from 1981 to 1985.

nominated by the JCS for the SALT delegation soon to gather in Helsinki.[*] I was very flattered and thought I could be of considerable help. Then, the same day, Rand Corporation called and asked if I would like to take off the uniform and join as a researcher with the Rand team in Washington, and an invitation came to return to Ohio State as deputy director of the Mershon program. Shortly before that, the University of Missouri had expressed an interest in me joining as a director to set up an Office of International Studies.

Missouri had just gone to the California multi-campus system, and they wanted a university-wide office to handle all international studies programs on the four campuses. That looked very interesting. I had made two trips to St. Louis, Columbia, and Rolla, Missouri, for interviews. By coincidence, the contract arrived from Missouri also on that same morning. And I still had the possibility of the Naval Academy academic dean post which Paul Nitze said would include the grade of commodore. Not having really thought seriously about retirement, and with no initiative on my part, I suddenly found I had four or five important job offers to consider.

The Helsinki duty looked very good. The Russians were apparently serious about negotiating on nuclear weapons. What gave me the tipoff then, based on my Geneva experience and their use of the discussions largely for propaganda purposes, the Helsinki meetings were to be secret with only the U.S.-U.S.S.R. participating. The Rand job would be pure research, and I could largely do my own thing, but I didn't really think long before turning it down. So I finally decided for Missouri; it looked like a great opportunity to set up a maritime studies center, control my own program throughout the state, and the pay was about double what others were being offered in comparable university positions.

Q: What were the reasons you decided not to come to the Naval Academy?

Captain Schratz: I guess age had to be one of the most important ones. And I wanted the chance to do some writing rather than administration. In this respect, my two pledges were contradictory. As the dean position worked out in the years since, I could probably have

---

[*] Admiral Thomas H. Moorer, USN, served as Chief of Naval Operations from 1 August 1967 to 1 July 1970. SALT--Strategic Arms Limitations Talks.

had time to do some writing. I don't know any details, but the function of the dean, as I see it, has not worked out as it would had I taken the job. It appears to be more social than academic, but I don't really know the facts, only what I hear from professors.

Even though I still had about eight months payback time for the year at Ohio State, it was clear that a decision had to be made then on my future. I didn't want to retire and didn't want to leave the National War College, but the job opportunities were not likely to recur. After much thought, I put in my retirement papers, accepted the Missouri proposal, and then discovered the Secretary wouldn't approve my retirement. Part of the reason was lack of a qualified relief; my obligated service added some weight. I joined the university and continued to carry my war college duties. This went on week after week. Only TWA was making out.[*]

When Christmas arrived, I decided it was time to break the roadblock. The SecNav's EA was an old friend.[†] I convinced him it was in the Navy's interest to let me go. He agreed on condition that my boss would accept no contact relief. Thus armed, I went to the NWC commandant, then General Andy Goodpaster, and asked if he would release me on condition that I could get SecNav approval for retirement on the first of January 1969.[‡] So convinced was he that I couldn't get it through on a short fuse in the middle of the holiday period, he consented.

I wasn't at Missouri very long when Dean Drought, the first USNA academic dead, died suddenly, and I was called back again for interviews.[§] By that time, Jim Calvert was the new Superintendent, an outstanding officer who had made great strides in the new academic program.[**] By that time, also, I was well dug in with my new empire in St. Louis; we loved the duty and the area. I was five years older, and the age factor was no less a

---

[*] TWA--Trans-World Airlines.
[†] EA--executive assistant.
[‡] Lieutenant General Andrew J. Goodpaster, USA, who in 1969 became NATO's Supreme Allied Commander Europe.
[§] Dr. A. Bernard Drought had been officially appointed as the first civilian academic dean of the Naval Academy on 1 July 1964 after serving a year in the position on a pro tem basis. He died of cancer on 18 September 1970.
[**] Rear Admiral/Vice Admiral James F. Calvert, USN, served as Superintendent of the Naval Academy from July 1968 to June 1972.

consideration. Then 54, I wasn't sure the dean should be younger than the Superintendent or safer if a bit older. I was greatly encouraged by my program at Missouri, and finally said, "Thanks but no thanks."

Q: Well, the age there wasn't really that far apart, was it?[*] You were only four classes senior to him.

Captain Schratz: But I was concerned more about the whole concept of work with the midshipmen, the professors, the average naval officer on the faculty. That was the group I wanted more empathy with. I didn't want to appear to them as a white-haired old goat. I wanted to inspire them to an academic side of their careers and increase the prestige of the military teaching faculty. I saw less chance there than there probably was.

Q: How long did you stay there?

Captain Schratz: Almost five years. The civilian professors on the National War College faculty warned me it might be a hornet's nest. I was an ex-military at the peak of the anti-military feeling over Vietnam. I was filling a top post in the university, which every subordinate would think should have been filled by fleeting up from inside the system, and I was to be a university-wide official on the new St. Louis campus--not with the "home office" in Columbia--where the other university-wide directors were and where every campus begrudges anything done for the other campuses.

Properly warned, it was rarely a serious problem. The reception was superb. I never saw anti-militarism in any form. I was awarded a Legion of Merit a few months after retirement, and the award was presented during the annual ROTC parade in Columbia. During the presentation, Vietnam protesters marched around the oval carrying a casket and chanting the names of Vietnam dead. It was peaceful, and there was no other incident. I did have some problems as the only university-wide director not residing in Columbia.

---

[*] Calvert was in the Naval Academy's class of 1943.

The Columbia people tended to look out for Columbia first. As "Mister International" for the University, the international life was in St. Louis and Kansas City, and I used great care to make sure I didn't favor the St. Louis campus overtly, or appear to in the eyes of others.[*] Nevertheless, cooperation and support was super.

Just before leaving the National War College, I had been awarded a fellowship from the British Foreign Office to a conference in Wilton Park, a magnificent manor in Sussex, England, a very special European conference center. I was the first U.S. military officer to go there. Quite by chance, both the president and vice president of the University of Missouri were Wiltonians. The president, John Weaver, was also formerly at Ohio State, where we first met, and we were at Wilton Park together and had become very friendly. He had no prominent role when I was being considered for the Missouri appointment, but it was a warm reunion. This helped cool any possible jealousy and if there was any, I never saw it.

I quickly went about building my own empire in St. Louis and flying my own flag. The chancellor's flag was gold on a black background, mine the reverse and much brighter. I generally took precedence before him. We were fortunate in falling into an estate sale of a gorgeous home on Forsythe Boulevard--nicknamed by some the "Taj Mahal West"--and it helped tremendously to do all our extensive entertaining there. Using a superb caterer, it still cost the university less than using restaurants.

The first thing I wanted to do was set up an international conference center on the St. Louis campus. When the university first approached me for the job, they had mentioned that Jim McDonnell of McDonnell Douglas was very much an internationalist, and that U.N. anniversaries were paid holidays for all McDonnell Douglas employees.[†]

Earlier he offered Washington University in St. Louis a million dollars for an international studies center, with certain conditions, which didn't work out. He still had his million, but I was assured he'd never give it to the state university. Nevertheless, he was my prime candidate to fund my international center. Toward that end, I first set up a

---

[*] Schratz had his office at the University of Missouri-St. Louis.
[†] James S. McDonnell was chairman and chief executive officer of the McDonnell Douglas Corporation, a major defense contractor.

distinguished visitors program to bring in prominent people from abroad. From Wilton Park I lured a faculty member each year from Wilton Park to the U.S. for our American-style conference somewhere in the U.S. That helped considerably. More important, I wanted a member of the Soviet Institute of USA and Canada, Georgi Arbotov's institute, then being set up in Moscow, and I really wanted to get Anatoly Gromyko, the son of the Soviet foreign minister, a member of the Institute.

Thanks to my former Defense, CIA, and State Department contacts, all of whom were extremely interested in finding out more about the Arbatov Institute, this also was successful. Little information was available, and that contradictory. I returned to Washington for some briefings by State and CIA. At that time, I was serving also on the executive board of the International Studies Association, then making arrangements for our annual meeting in San Juan. I proposed to my ISA fellow board members to put Gromyko on the speakers' list and that I would offer to pay Gromyko's expenses from New York to San Juan, to St. Louis and back to New York; he would pay for the leg from Moscow.

This was exactly the type of bait the Soviets needed, I learned later. Puerto Rico was out of bounds for all Soviet personnel, and they were really itching to get their nose in. When he accepted, his escort was the Soviet deputy ambassador to the U.N., Ambassador Viktor Issraelyan, a most charming individual. I paid Gromyko's freight by the night coach--a cattle car. The ambassador flew first class. They didn't meet on the plane and didn't meet in the airport. They didn't like each other when they did. To complicate my problem further, San Juan was in the middle of an anti-Communist uprising. San Juan University, hosting our conference, was closed down; several people were killed. Bringing these big Communists into the area was really cause for concern. I had gone to San Juan earlier to work out security arrangements with the naval district, the local chief of police, and the governor. The details of the visit were intriguing, fascinating, funny, and occasionally perilous, but are probably not needed here.

The Soviet Institute of the U.S.A. and Canada aroused special interest because a half a dozen sons and daughters of the Soviet leaders work there. Among other things, it looked like a training ground to perpetuate the Soviet elite. After spending three weeks with Gromyko in San Juan, St. Louis, and on my three other campuses in Missouri, I was sick of that arrogant, pompous ass. But it launched my conference program in great fashion. He was a participant in the discussions--and did quite well--and conference speaker. I put him on a Council of World Affairs program for a major address, extremely well publicized. He never saw his honorarium. I applied it to his expenses, then loaned him to Washington University for seminars and used these fees also for my university account.

We hosted a large dinner party at our home with all the proper people from all over the state. Most important for my plans was Jim McDonnell. McDonnell was also a conference participant. The St. Louis campus had risen almost overnight from a golf course to about a 10,000-student university. To subtly impress on him our acute need for an adequate conference room, I seated him close to the doors to the kitchen, where scullery noise impressed him as much as the discussions. For such parties, McDonnell was always the first to accept.

When the Gromyko fete was over, Jim asked me privately if I could bring Gromyko and his KGB escort to a stag dinner at his home the following evening. Present then were McDonnell, Mike Witunski, who handled his foreign affairs, Gromyko, his KGB shadow Eugene Kotovoj, and I. "Old Mac" did everything himself, including tending the fire and the bartending. With some gorgeous steaks flown in from Kansas City, Russian caviar, and some good Stolichnaya vodka, it was a night to remember. Late that evening, on our second bottle of vodka, Mac told Gromyko to get some word back to his people that if they wanted to market their new TU-141 internationally the next year, they better talk to Old Mac first. McDonnell Douglas was just then finishing the DC-10, which was displayed at the Paris Air Show about a month later.* Jim and his crew flew nonstop from St. Louis to Paris in record time with about 26,000 pounds of fuel remaining. The Soviet TU, despite a delay for engine failure in Warsaw, was already there. They were the first to give McDonnell the red carpet treatment--literally.

The following day, however, an engineer off the Soviet team defected. He turned out to be a deputy in the Soviet space program, a most important intelligence coup. So Jim was still riding high when he returned to St. Louis and very shortly called me. Commenting

---

* The DC-10 was one of the first of the wide-body transport jets. It is still in service more than a quarter century later.

on the difficult acoustics at our conference, he asked me to send over what we needed for a proper conference center and said he would pick up the tab. That was the first gift he ever made to the University of Missouri, and is probably a good example of how university politics work.

Q: What other problems interested you at Missouri?

Captain Schratz: Some early programs university-wide were designed for a collateral benefit of creating enthusiasm and support for international programs. I had to build a constituency, and I thought I could use Wilton Park for the purpose. Virtually every European legislator and senior civil servant is a Wiltonian. About the time I joined Missouri University, the American Wiltonians, largely university presidents, deans, and senior professors, were trying to set up a similar organization in this country.

First, with John Weaver's strong support, was an agreement with Wilton Park and the British Foreign Office to grant the university two fellowships annually for a Wilton Park conference, the university to pay travel and incidental expenses. This policy, still in effect, gave me considerable leverage as a plum to dangle in front of deserving faculty and staff. Second, I hosted an American Wilton Park conference on Washington University's beautiful campus in St. Louis, then later was able to get Wingspread, the Frank Lloyd Wright conference center in Racine, Wisconsin, to host several American Wilton Park conferences, and I thought we were well on our way to establish that as a fixture by the time I left the university. In fact, the Johnson Foundation at Wingspread made me a flattering offer to run all their programs, which I was able to turn down. The point is that the Wilton Park connection absorbed a fair amount of my time and energy.

Other international programs for the four campuses varied widely, depending on local interests. In Kansas City, the talent I found was in the law center, and we set up a conference on international law shortly after my arrival. I gave the banquet address on "International Law and the Pueblo Crisis," which was later published. The conference report was put out in book form and sold very well. It paid for the whole conference, in fact.

The Columbia campus was interested more in social and cultural programs of international interest. Since I thought the future of our international academic programs lay more toward the interdisciplinary, I started an interdisciplinary seminar on the Columbia campus, which I chaired and used bright, young faculty members to do most of the work in developing papers. That was quite successful and largely unappreciated. The academic climate, I thought, was much too narrow in Columbia.

The Rolla campus, the old Rolla School of Mines, was always my favorite. It was too small a campus in too small a city to ever hope to have a university-wide director resident there, even though their interests were more internationally oriented than any of the campuses except St. Louis. The Rolla students and faculty built a satellite and flew it over certain areas of Missouri and other places to verify a number of metallic traces in the terrain below. They were able to uncover some major new lead fields in Missouri. Then in passes over South America, they were able to detect similar traces in Para, Brazil, in the upper Amazon delta. On the basis of the satellite evidence, the university devised and set up a program to develop the resources of the Amazon, including training the engineers to run it, which we could then turn over to the Brazilians as a self-supporting economic program. We started off initially with five different resource area programs. Despite the economic chaos in Brazil, it was quite successful, but I haven't heard for a number of years.

On the St. Louis campus, the early stress, because of Jim McDonnell, was on the United Nations. Our U.N. conference report was also published in book form and did extremely well. It went into a second printing, which is unusual for a conference report. Another program looked toward the inner cities, primarily St. Louis and Kansas City, seeking to salvage some of the superior people in the inner city minorities--German, Poles, Italians, French, and primarily blacks--they've got lots of them. The goal was a half a dozen or so initially, who, because of their deprived backgrounds couldn't qualify to enter the state university. We guaranteed them entrance into the university, special tutoring, and a terminal master's degree in due time, seeking to train them primarily as inner city administrators. The special tutoring was required initially to bring them up to speed; if they progressed beyond that, there was no limit, they competed like any other student.

One of the myths we had to break down with those people, primarily blacks, was the idea that they had strong cultural ties to their native lands, primarily Africa, more than to their American heritage, which I thought was preposterous. The blacks are so remote from African culture, and understood so little, it was largely a psychological crutch used to pressure the university into all sorts of minority programs of questionable value. I wanted to give each of these students, after his graduation, six months in his native culture. This was a great attraction. The results would, I hoped, be far different from their expectations. I was sure they'd become far more productive Americans.

This was fitted into a master's program built around international economics or business economics, primarily from the perspective of inner city administrators. In requesting funding from HEW, they were enthusiastic but claimed we didn't have the qualifications in the faculty to teach it.[*] While trying to build our faculty, Stanford University grabbed the whole program and marched off with it, including our federal funding, and that's the last I ever heard of it. It is a very good idea, and I was sorry it didn't work out.

Q: You came back to this area, then, a couple of years later to work on a study on government reorganization, didn't you?

Captain Schratz: I first came back to the Pentagon for another task, when Bud Zumwalt was Chief of Naval Operations. He had gone to a football game at Annapolis the Saturday before. Between the halves, George Anderson, his predecessor, and Hanson Baldwin corralled him.[†] I have Bud's direct quote on this; no other source. Hanson was extremely concerned about the hundred blacks coming to the Naval Academy the following year, and

---

[*] HEW--Department of Health, Education and Welfare.
[†] Admiral George W. Anderson, Jr., USN, served as Chief of Naval Operations from 1 August 1961 to 1 August 1963. His oral history is in the Naval Institute collection. Hanson W. Baldwin was a 1924 graduate of the Naval Academy. Following several years of naval service, Baldwin began a distinguished career as a newspaperman, culminating as military editor of The New York Times. His oral history is also in the Naval Institute collection.

unless Bud could prevent it, he promised a very highly critical article about rioting and drugs in the Navy for Reader's Digest the following spring, just to prevent any possibility of Bud's selection for the Chairman's job.

Bud called me in St. Louis the following Monday to ask if I'd come up and chat with him. He reported this conversation and, to counter the effects of the promised Baldwin piece, asked if I'd like to take a refresher cruise with the Sixth Fleet in the Mediterranean, to see the Navy in operation and write some articles on Navy leadership and the real status of integration. We were both fully aware that only President Johnson could prevent integration at the Academy, which would be contrary to the times and politically impossible.[*] Paul Nitze was doing everything he could to maintain a single standard of admission for all midshipmen, to avoid the greater danger of compounding racial difficulties with two sets of academic and physical standards.[†]

I made arrangements to leave from Dover, Delaware, and, fortuitously, coincided almost to the hour with the big airlift to Israel for the October 1973 war. Arriving in the Med, I spent several days at sea in the Independence, thrilled to watch round-the-clock flight operations, discussing Navy life with everybody on the ship: small groups of men, the CO and exec, wardroom officers, and I was quite favorably impressed. They had serious drug problems. They also did extremely well when called upon for that little bit extra. So I wrote a couple of editorials for the Wall Street Journal or Christian Science Monitor and a Shipmate column on leadership in the Navy based on the experience.

Q: Whatever happened to Hanson Baldwin's article?

Captain Schratz: Reader's Digest refused to publish it, so he ran apparently a milder version in the Saturday Evening Post, which I didn't realize was still alive. I saw the article, but don't think it had any effect. By that time Bud's chances for the Chairman were remote anyhow, so it didn't matter.

---

[*] This reference is puzzling. By the time Admiral Zumwalt became CNO in 1970, Richard Nixon was President.
[†] In 1973 the Secretary of the Navy was John W. Warner, not Paul Nitze.

Shortly after, I invited Bud to Missouri to talk with the ROTC in Missouri-Columbia, which turned out to be a great day for the Navy and the University. Mobs of students met him with a big black and gold banner, maybe 50 feet across, to "Welcome Big Z" to the campus. He gave an excellent talk to a packed auditorium.

A few months later, State Department was looking for a new High Commissioner For the Trust Territories of the Pacific Islands (TTPI), and so they asked the JCS for nominations. Bud threw my name in; it was approved by the JCS, and I terminated at Missouri and returned to Washington for my White House, State, and Interior Department interviews. These were quite memorable. State was anxious to grab the job for a senior Foreign Service officer, which they then had in excess. Because of difficulties with the incumbent, the government planned to make it a non-political position. The occupant, who was a protege of Senator Fong of Hawaii, was under investigation for malfeasance.[*]

The job required administration of 2,000 islands of Micronesia, which the U.S. held under a United Nations trust: about 100,000 people and 2 million square miles of ocean. Negotiations were then under way toward independence, or associated, or federated status. The JCS were interested in order to save certain base rights for U.S. forces in strategic areas as a fallback position should our existing bases in Korea, the Philippines, Guam, or Vietnam be hazarded. State had a lesser interest, but they wanted to make sure that their candidate prevailed. I wasn't very enthusiastic.

I thought my talents could be better used elsewhere, but it's like prostitution: it's not the money, it's the honor. The headquarters were on Saipan and among the perks was a Boeing 727 for travel among the six capitals. The idea was that the job would last only a year or two until the negotiations for the status of the islands were completed, when a native governor would take over. When my interviews started, State had two candidates in competition at each level. If I succeeded at any level, two brand-new State Department competitors arrived for the next. Tom Pickering, my old friend from the delegation in Geneva, now an assistant secretary, was my mole at State to help me with the briefings.

---

[*] Senator Hiram L. Fong (Republican-Hawaii).

Surviving all the Interior and White House interviews, the last was with the Deputy Secretary of State. We had a very nice chat, following which I returned to St. Louis. Barely in the front door of our home, Tom phoned to report "a very embarrassing conversation." After my interview with the Deputy Secretary, Kenneth Rush, he called Tom to nominate him for the post. He had no idea that Tom had been helping my candidacy, and Tom respectfully declined. Rush then confided in him the importance of the position to State. Rush, by chance, had been Under Secretary of Defense just prior to that time, and had reviewed the JCS emergency plan for bases in the Pacific, which disturbed him very much. He claimed that the JCS wanted to concrete the whole of Micronesia, and he was opposed on principle to a Defense candidate getting the job. Hence the urgency to use Tom, then a blue-chip Foreign Service officer.

The stalemate was broken from an unexpected quarter. President Nixon was just then beginning his decline and eventual disgrace.[*] For some relatively unimportant issue, he twisted the arm of Senator Fong for a key vote. Fong agreed only on condition that Nixon reappoint the high commissioner in Micronesia to a new term, even though he was then under investigation by the Senate Foreign Relations Committee. So the job suddenly disappeared.

Since I was in Washington and available, I was interviewed for a new commission, the White House-Congressional Committee on the Organization of the Government for Foreign Policy (COGFP). Having done my Ph.D. dissertation on Defense organization and the McNamara era in the Pentagon, this was right up my alley. I became the senior staffer on that organization, and responsible for defense and arms control. A GS-17 Civil Service rating gave enough horsepower to handle three- of four-star military people.

Q: What are the highlights of the job?

Captain Schratz: The Murphy Commission, as it's known, was an initiative of Senator Fulbright.[†] As a leading member of Congress, he was concerned about the slipping power

---

[*] Richard Nixon resigned as President in August 1974 in the wake of the Watergate scandal.
[†] Senator J. William Fulbright (Democrat-Arkansas).

of Congress with respect to the executive branch. The commission was bipartisan. Half the commissioners were in government, half from private life; half were Republicans, half Democrats; half executive branch, half congressional. The senior member the first year was Senator Mike Mansfield, the second year Vice President Rockefeller.[*] Ambassador Bob Murphy, the old warhorse, widely known throughout the government, a truly remarkable person then in his 80s, chaired the meetings.[†]

We examined the entire structure of government, scrutinizing the roles and influence of Defense, CIA, State, the NSC, Congress, and other participants in the formation of U.S. policy. Conducting our formal meetings in the beautiful conference room of the Senate Majority Leader, we interviewed every important person in government. The staff usually prepared questions for the commissioners to ask of witnesses (including the answers). Many of the outsiders hired consultants to draft the answers to our questions, sometimes the questions for our answers. There were some very bright people involved and we worked hard and well.

Unfortunately, when the Nixon Administration really began to fall apart, the last thing either party wanted was a commission looking at the structure of government, but it made for a fascinating time to study the organization of the government. Everybody was doing it anyhow. Yet we were able to do a very fine job, particularly under Nelson Rockefeller, who impressed me enormously with his detailed knowledge of the government. We used every possible classified source, but for maximum utility, kept the report unclassified.

The final report by the commission is a miracle of production by the Government Printing Office. We finished, I think, on a Friday afternoon, and the 254-page printed report was on the desk of every member of Congress and the executive branch by Monday noon. Only a Vice President could have made that happen. Unfortunately, the content of the report could never justify the urgency behind its publication. Senator Mansfield called

---

[*] Senator Mike Mansfield (Democrat-Montana). Nelson A. Rockefeller became Vice President in 1974 after Gerald Ford moved up to take over from Richard Nixon.
[†] Ambassador Robert D. Murphy, who was born in 1894.

it, accurately, "very thin gruel in a very thick bowl." True, but we had a secret. The real value is in an unappreciated jewel.

It includes six or seven volumes of appendices on the research program, including one volume on Defense, which I edited. This, too, is unclassified, and includes some excellent, straight-shooting, frank case studies of Defense programs such as the politics behind the Trident submarine, the "smart" bomb, bureaucratic constraints on policy, and many others. How we were able to bring this about is itself a case study in government organization. Everybody had a hand in the formal report of the commission, pushing, pulling, compromising, hiding. With so many vested interests throughout the government, the staff could do little here. Therefore, to protect our real work, we waited deliberately until the commission died, the day the report was submitted, and everybody else disbanded. Then we completed the research appendices--eight volumes about a foot thick--so they didn't need to go through the commissioners for clearance. From the staff it went straight to the print and came out about six months later. Because the main volume was so mushy, however, few people persisted to look at the rest of the work. It is very good.

It's a good time to quit.

Interview Number 3 with Captain Paul R. Schratz, U.S. Navy (Retired)

Place: U.S. Naval Institute, Annapolis, Maryland

Date: Tuesday, 11 December 1984

Interviewer: Paul Stillwell

Q: Captain, in going back to some of your previous tours, I think there are some additional things you want to talk about in relationship to the Naval War College.

Captain Schratz: One of my main interests at the Naval War College, I mentioned earlier, was what a great stimulus it was to my own personal thinking, starting with the readings sent me even before I went to Newport. Then my job on the faculty as long-range academic planner stimulated me to think seriously about the overall professional training of naval officers, and the great weakness I saw before me in the military faculty at the War College. My long-range academic plan, my driving motive, was a look primarily toward a much improved progressive education of the maritime professional, starting from Naval Academy days.

The slice of our art which is not covered adequately at any level, has never been covered adequately, is the same problem Admiral Luce complained about when he wrote for the Naval Institute in 1911. Lawyers study law, doctors study medicine, but naval officers don't study the art of war, which is their profession. I believe that the seeds of our professional education in the art of war should be planted more here at the Naval Academy--which they are not--and nourished through study of military history, elements of strategy and strategic planning, elements of the planning and decision-making process.

The command and staff colleges and later the senior war colleges offer the advanced training based on early study and matured in career operational experience. Obviously professional examinations are necessary for all officers from lieutenant and above for promotion, largely to stimulate them in their habits of reading and self-education. I saw none of that in the product before me at the Naval War College, in small part because my own peer group of officers lost their staff college when we were away at war. We learned much of the art of war the hard way. But war experience is severely limited for the career or senior officer who has not prepared himself or been prepared properly. We learned some different lessons; we also failed to learn an awful lot.

Now we are repeating that circumstance in the Rickover navy through concentration--over-concentration--on the technician at the expense of the seaman, the training of the engineer and the neglect of the warrior. The routine reexamination or recertification of the nuclear-trained officers may be necessary. All well and good. But the training as engineers must not substitute for their training as warriors.

If the nuclear program siphons off the cream of the officer class year after year, then there is a double responsibility that these future leaders of the Navy not be deprived of their professional training as other than engineers. These men are being deprived of a normal war college experience where they have so much to give as well as receive. The result, in the opinion of many, is a class of Rickover clones, superb engineers but severely undernourished as strategists. Military leadership has always demanded the skills of people-oriented generalists rather than technically oriented specialists. We are technicians in an era that worships technology. Where, oh, where, have the warriors gone?

At that time the immediate focus of my key interest had to be the role of the Naval Institute in its mission and responsibility for the professional training of officers. Bill Greene was then the secretary-treasurer. He and I had extensive correspondence on what we saw as the role of the Naval Institute and the Naval War College in working together for a common goal.* I thought it a curious oversight that the president of the Naval War College, or the chief of staff, had never sat on the Naval Institute's board of control, as far as I could tell, at least not in modern years. We both believed that war college membership should be as natural as the Superintendent of the Naval Academy to sit on the Naval Institute board of control.

---

* Commander William M. A. Greene, USN, served as secretary-treasurer of the Naval Institute from 1959 to 1962.

We thought there should be a much better and closer relationship between the publishing of essays and war college theses in the Naval Institute. I later learned that the Air War College goes overboard in this respect. The Air University Review preferences for articles for publication determine the length of theses and the general subject areas. Both are physically on the same campus, but that's a bit much. I would think that the Naval War College could concentrate, say, on a 4,000-word paper by the students at some phase of their senior war college work, maybe junior war college. The Naval Institute could also concentrate on getting and grooming some future writers, scholars for the Naval Institute's own writing programs in fostering creative writing by professionals.

We also thought that there should be a closer tie between the Naval Institute Proceedings and the Naval War College Review. I was concerned about an excess of technical, practical articles on nuts and bolts in the Proceedings, which even Mahan complained about as too much "gears and grease," and which don't thrill me very much. I'm sure they are useful and appeal, maybe, to young readers. My concern is the lack of articles in the higher level of war and strategy. I've stated a few times that it's always a surprise to me that of all the 130 or so books the Naval Institute has in print, only one is on strategy, and that on Soviet strategy. Bill and I thought that the Naval War College Review should function more or less like Foreign Affairs, the prestigious, high-level organ of maritime thought, and the Naval Institute Proceedings as a more popular middle level keyed to professional ideas and discussion. But both of the publications, we thought, could work very well in tandem, informally, maybe even under a closer managerial relationship to coordinate their common goals. The organizational and financial details are for others to work out.

The more I thought, the more the need of revitalizing the Naval Institute stuck with me. When I got to the National War College a number of years later, I had a new educational background and I had a pledge to SecNav to do what I could on the Navy's backwardness in professional education. I started again on the same idea of revitalizing the Naval Institute. By then, others were becoming interested. I was working fairly closely with Chick Hayward, John Hayes, Vince Davis of the University of Kentucky, Henry Eccles of Newport, and other similarly motivated individuals on what we thought we could do or should be done to help the Naval Institute in its mission.[*]

But not till I got to St. Louis did I take a major new initiative. I had a meeting in Chicago with Vince Davis about that time, and he was distressed at the slow pace of progress. Our bright new ideas were not only not being accepted at the Naval Institute; there was even hostility in some quarters. Vince suggested that the only way ever to be able to talk to the Naval Institute and get a reaction was to talk directly to the membership. And the only way one can do that, probably, was to write an essay and get himself three minutes' time at the annual meeting. This was the day before Thanksgiving; the deadline for reception in the Institute was the first of December.

Q: I believe 1971 was the year.

Captain Schratz: You have prepared yourself well. Yes, I think that is right. I got back to St. Louis and scribbled off an essay at great speed, a cut and paste of ideas I had been kicking around, and submitted it. It was a pretty dreadful piece, but somehow it won a prize that year.[†] I'm afraid I shocked the board of control by taking my allotted three minutes to talk, not about why I had written the essay as expected, but about what I thought should be done by the Naval Institute toward a much greater stress on professional education, with a few additional gratuitous gems on improving the management. That put me in the doghouse with the Naval Institute for the next ten years, but I think it accomplished a lot too. I think we can come back to further ideas on that when we get to the Air War College.

---

[*] Vice Admiral John T. Hayward, USN (Ret.), who had served as president of the Naval War College in the 1960s. Rear Admiral John D. Hayes, USN (Ret.); a frequent contributor to the war college. Upon retirement from active duty in 1952, Rear Admiral Henry E. Eccles began a 25-year second career as head of the logistics department of the Naval War College; he was a prolific author.

[†] The article, which won the prize for first honorable mention in the 1972 contest, appeared as "The Nuclear Carrier and Modern War," U.S. Naval Institute Proceedings, pages 21-25.

Q: Specifically, what did you see as the things it did accomplish? What changes did it bring about?

Captain Schratz: I don't know what success I can claim. It was only natural that the institute was most grudging in giving me credit and in drying up any internal sources I might have had. One small but significant change was a managerial survey on the financial affairs of the institute. I was concerned. I can't read a financial report, but I didn't think USNI was in very good shape. It seemed that the reserves were dropping--and the Institute's bank account was always a major factor of strength. It seemed, or so I heard, the organization was cashing in blue chip stocks to pay current bills. Maybe not that bad, but it didn't look very wholesome to me.

I took a more practical approach. I compared the Proceedings over a 30- or 40-year period with Shipmate over that period on the cost of the magazine, the number of people producing it, the number of pages, etc. The Naval Institute staff had increased many times over, the number of pages per issue had decreased fairly sharply, whereas Shipmate kept the same size editorial staff of three people, the magazine increased in size by a factor of about six to ten times, the increase in quality and appearance was remarkable, and the cost had hardly followed the inflation line.

Q: That wasn't really the main thrust of your complaint. Did you see subsequent improvement in the professionalism and the kinds of material that you thought should be published?

Captain Schratz: Again, I must be somewhat vague. The Institute can't publish a book on strategy unless somebody writes one. They tried to do one on contract with Ted Ropp as editor and Vince Davis, Frank Uhlig and me among the contributors. We met several times in Annapolis, but the idea aborted for lack of an overall contribution. This was one more stimulus to my book on strategy, still in gestation, after a long period of self-education.

One major change began to appear, the sharply increased participation of members through letters to the editor. The editor's mailbox is always the best guide to what people are reading and how critically they're reading. And somewhere around that time, the Naval Institute really took off, and, greatly nourished by Fred Rainbow, it's the most useful element of the entire magazine.* The letters are the most valuable part of the magazine, better than the essays. This reflects mainly the lack of progress in creating thinkers in uniform. The Institute can't write its own essays.

Q: What was the reaction at the meeting itself when you made this speech?

Captain Schratz: There was a certain coolness with Bud Bowler, the secretary-treasurer.† Bill Mack, the vice president, Superintendent of the Naval Academy, gave me the feeling that he took it personally.‡ And if there was anybody I was not thinking of in this respect, it was Bill. In many ways, his reputation in the Navy as a dissenter was much similar to my own. At his retirement address at the Naval Academy two years later, many people looked at me and asked if I had written it. Bill and I had much in common and I never thought of him in any but a strongly positive role with the Institute.

Q: What contact did you have with the publisher, Commander Bowler, about trying to implement what you saw as desirable changes?

Captain Schratz: Almost none. He never fostered the type of relationship I had with Bill Greene. Bud's interest on the educational side seemed to be far less. It wasn't at all his interest. I was trying to reach the board of control, the editorial board. On the business side, Bud had squelched a rambunctious officer at the annual meeting several years in a row

---

* Fred H. Rainbow joined the staff of the <u>Proceedings</u> as departments editor in 1975 and became the editor-in-chief in 1986.
† Commander Roland T. E. "Bud" Bowler, Jr., USN, became secretary-treasurer of the Naval Institute and publisher of the <u>Proceedings</u> in 1962. He retired from active duty in 1984, then remained with the Naval Institute until 1984.
‡ Vice Admiral William P. Mack, USN, served as Superintendent of the Naval Academy from June 1972 to August 1975. The Superintendent serves, ex officio, as vice president of the Naval Institute.

who was attempting merely to find out how much the editorial board members were paid, but never did. The membership wasn't encouraged to pry into "family" matters.

Q: What is your view of the Institute now? Has it moved closer toward what you view as a desirable role?

Captain Schratz: You probably wouldn't have raised the question if you didn't know the answer. Nor would I have been as frank in criticism above if things had not improved significantly. My view is fairly obvious. Now that we have a new publisher just taking office, I have some ideas of where I think the Institute should be going in the next few years.[*] I talked some of these ideas over with Fred Hartman and John Hattendorf and others at the Naval War College when we were at a conference in Avignon, France, last summer. I have a letter in the mail right now on that.

Q: Would you expand more, please, on a discussion of yourself as a dissident? You used that term. How would you use examples of that throughout your career?

Captain Schratz: That's a little hard to pin down. I was a non-conformist throughout my career, even in high school. I just got terribly bored by doing things the traditional way to come up with a traditional answer. This made no contribution to anything but a dull routine. I had the belief throughout my career that if it isn't fun, you weren't doing it right. We had an awful lot of fun in the way we did things over the years, no matter what the assignment. Looking back now, when I didn't have fun, I probably wasn't doing it right. But we did things with a flair and panache. We did things differently. A routine exercise was never a routine exercise; those things turned me off. I did everything I could to get away from that type of thing.

---

[*] Captain James A. Barber, USN (Ret.), relieved Bowler as secretary-treasurer of the Naval Institute in 1984.

Then gradually, especially in the Pickerel operations, we were known as the ship which was never in port. We were off on some cruise we had dreamed up or talked somebody into. Soon most of the Pickerel crew were bachelors, because the wives were home alone too much. The officers' wives, I guess, fretted now and then, but it was good fun for all of us, and, as far as I ever knew, not very many would have traded the experience for the more prosaic life on another submarine.

Q: I see a difference between being a dissident and doing things with a flair. I don't think those are synonymous.

Captain Schratz: True. Procedures such as in the Joint Staff--"Find out what we said last time and say it again"--drove me up the wall. I was also a dissident with my pen. We often hear the comment, "Wait till I retire and take my suit off, and I'll really blast them." I never accepted that. I always thought that if one didn't have the moral courage to express his ideas, to joust with policy when he was active, he really doesn't have the integrity to do so when he retired. His effectiveness is gone. I often hear praise on my writings for honesty and objectivity. I value such opinions very highly. I thought it necessary that I avoid being captured by the power barons in any particular fiefdom, and felt that the most salable commodity I had was objectivity.

Perhaps I can explain by an example. Shortly after retirement, when I arrived at the University of Missouri about June of '69, I was rather discouraged over where the Navy as a whole was going on its role as the leading edge of national policy. I sent a long letter to Admiral Moorer, then Chief of Naval Operations. The points I tried to make were, first, my concern over the deep suspicion of the military in Congress, not just because of the Vietnam War, but suspicion of military in general.

I was concerned with the lack of hard analytical thinking in the military, and especially with the role of maritime power in serving national policy goals. I was concerned with the overestimates of the Soviet submarine force, based on numbers--themselves questionable--rather than on capability. I was concerned that the Navy was talking about power vacuums in the Indian Ocean or the Mediterranean, which harkened largely to a bygone era of kings and empires, now replaced by the colonels and the coups, with the guerrilla as the leading resident in the "vacuum." Few of the people around the Mediterranean or the Indian Ocean or South China Sea recognize any "power vacuum." The thing they want most is to get rid of big power control, of the kings and empires that created their problems.

Much of our thinking was irrelevant or out of date. We were not doing our homework to make past experience relevant to what the challenge was today. We had a sorry appreciation of maritime strategy, and therefore it had become more and more dominated by technology. I suggested to the CNO that, in my position of responsibility in some measure for the international programs for 40,000 students and 10,000 faculty, that I could be influential in an international or maritime study center within the university. It was a frank letter and earned a rather unusual response.

Moorer sent copies to Dick Colbert, who was then the president of the Naval War College, and Jim Calvert, the Superintendent of the Naval Academy, for whatever action they could take on it.[*] He included it in his newsletter to all flag officers, and I started receiving comments from a great many people around the world, all of whom were supportive. And he gave me a set of invitational orders to come to Washington for a week of briefings by the OpDeps and a number of others. I had a very fascinating week and thought it a useful exchange. The last of my briefings was with Vice Admiral Tom Connolly, then OP-05.[†] In a private meeting, he made a proposal to divert funds then being used to glamorize the Navy with P.R. firms to help me financially with my writing, mentioning a figure which I thought very generous, and in addition to any reimbursement I would receive from publishers.

Q: This was personally?

---

[*] Vice Admiral Richard G. Colbert, USN,, served as president of the Naval War College from 30 August 1968 to 17 August 1971.
[†] Vice Admiral Thomas F. Connolly, USN, served as Deputy Chief of Naval Operations (Air) from 1 November 1966 to 31 August 1971. Admiral Connolly's oral history is in the Naval Institute collection.

Captain Schratz: Personally, yes. He said he thought they could get far more value for a dollar by subsidizing me and get a better return all around. I said it wouldn't take me long to give my answer. I had three problems. First, I didn't need the money--foolish thing to say, but I was young then. Second, the Navy might be disappointed because they had reason to believe they were buying a service, and since I prized my objectivity, they might not feel they were getting full value. But, above all, if my peers in the academic world knew I was subsidized by the Navy, I would lose my credibility with them for much the same reason, which I thought was hardly worth the risk. George Fielding Eliot severely compromised the little credibility he had in this manner a few years prior.[*] I had no problem in turning down the offer, but I did find much sympathy and support in various halls of the Navy for a maritime center.

Yet I was never able to set up the maritime studies program visualized. The Jim McDonnell tie required first efforts toward an international studies center, and it was placed wholly under the chancellor of the St. Louis campus. A maritime center required my personal and continuing supervision and would never have survived the other competing campuses who wanted a slice of everything.

Q: Before we started the tape, you were mentioning a conversation you had with Admiral Zumwalt during his Missouri visit. Could you put that on the record, please?

Captain Schratz: Yes. At that time, Bud's internal problems with the Navy had not come to the point they reached subsequently. Yet I thought that had an officer of Bud's caliber not come into the CNO job at the time, the Navy would really have had far more serious racial problems. We had a number of flag officers within my knowledge whom I thought were extremely racist. It bothered me very much. I could only imagine the deadly effect these senior people had on their subordinates in the command.

After Bud's presentation at Columbia, I drove him back to his plane, and the two of us had a good half hour to chat. We discussed racial problems, and I suggested an area of

---

[*] Eliot was a prominent book author and military-naval correspondent for the New York Herald Tribune.

preventive surgery in getting rid of a number of vice admirals whom I didn't think were doing either him or the Navy any good. This apparently echoed his own sentiments, and a march of vice admirals toward the exits began in the succeeding months. I sympathized with his problem. The whole point is, had a CNO who was not very conscious of the need for integration in the Navy come into office at that time, we would have had far more serious problems than Bud ever did.

Q: Why don't you address the subject of racism as a whole from your time as a midshipman forward, personal experiences you had in regard to that.

Captain Schratz: Having been born and raised in Pittsburgh and gone to a public high school, I never had a problem. During my Naval Academy days, a Chicago congressman was trying hard to get a black midshipman through the course.[*] One candidate in particular seemed extremely well qualified and was, in fact, red-haired and 85% Irish. I personally had no contact with him. Despite his best efforts to be a good plebe, the conduct of some of his fellow midshipmen was quite despicable. He was given many demerits unjustly for the condition of his room. For some reason, perhaps the difficulty in questioning the grades, he failed English some time during plebe year and was discharged.

It took World War II to change American attitudes toward recognition of some kind of equality both in the public and inside the military. Perhaps today we don't realize how radically some of those attitudes had to change. Do you know what the Naval Academy mascot was before Bill the goat? A Negro boy. And apparently for 50 years it raised no question of inappropriateness either inside or outside these walls. Can you imagine the reaction today? Since it was so remote a problem while I was a mid, I was neutral. I neither objected nor carried a torch.

---

[*] James Lee Johnson, appointed by Representative A. W. Mitchell of Illinois, a black Democrat, entered the Naval Academy in June 1936. He dropped out the following February for being academically deficient. See R. L. Field, "The Black Midshipmen at the Naval Academy," U.S. Naval Institute Proceedings, April 1973, page 31.

Our children show very much the changing public attitudes. They show absolutely no consciousness of racial differences. Our eldest daughter is married to a Nisei Japanese. It's a very happy marriage; he's a fine son-in-law.

Q: Wasn't it a case that there was not a lot of overt racism because the Navy was so segregated that there were not confrontations to produce it?

Captain Schratz: I suspect. Yes. And many of those segregated, like the Filipinos, apparently preferred it that way, even when promotions within the stewards' branch became nearly impossible.

Q: Switching to another subject, I had a conversation a couple of weeks ago and told someone I was about to start interviewing you. I forget who the individual was. He said, "I'm delighted to hear that. One of our top officers. It's unfortunate he didn't make flag rank, but maybe it was because he was too broad for the Navy." I wonder if you have a reaction to that?

Captain Schratz: I think that's an accurate statement. When I left the Naval War College, my horizons had broadened far beyond what I thought the Navy had to offer. I thought at the time that I would turn down flag rank if it were offered to me. Of course, that's a rather fatuous statement. You don't know how you'll react until it is offered, and I'd seen too many people who would give a right eye to be on that chosen list. I crossed my Rubicon when I felt it was very necessary for me to give up my major command in order to get a doctorate to further my own professional education and do some writing to change some primitive attitudes on many things. I think that was a wise decision on my part. I had mentioned that the Rickover incident had caused me to be taken off the major command list. Even though my name was returned to the list later, I saw that as no real tradeoff.

It was no heart-wrenching problem for me to sacrifice the command and pursuit of a star for the chance to get my doctorate, an attitude the Navy could hardly sympathize with. I would do that again today without a second thought. I think it was in the best interest of

Paul R. Schratz #3 - 279

the nation. I'm sure I've done a more valuable service to the Navy in writings, in rebuilding three war college academic programs, in lecturing around the country than I could really have done as a flag officer. Had my drive for a star been that strong, I could have accepted the Nitze suggestion of a commodore's star to go with the Naval Academy dean's chair.

Q: Do you think that the anecdote about Rickover was the thing that really derailed you?

Captain Schratz: Oh, no. But it certainly helped.

Q: What would have happened had you been offered a submarine squadron at the appropriate time?

Captain Schratz: That's a bit different. I had really earned it; I could have done a superior job and certainly would have accepted it.

Q: Let's talk more about rebuilding these programs. You've talked about the Naval War College. Anything to add on that subject?

Captain Schratz: Well, the Naval War College--let me generalize a bit further. When I got to the Air College, it was my third tour on a senior war college faculty. You may recall that the Secretary of Defense, via the Clements Committee, had studied all the war colleges.[*] The Air War College came out at the bottom, and the committee recommended rebuilding the academic program and civilianizing the faculty to broaden the scope of instruction. The only civilians they could find acceptable were largely military retired who had continued their education after they got out of the military.

I went down there and walked into a very happy experience. I would say two-thirds of the visiting flag officers, plus the three-star head of the Air University, Ray Furlong, and the commandant of the Air War College, Dick Schoeneman, had been my former students at

---

[*] William P. Clements, Jr., served as Deputy Secretary of Defense from 1973 to 1975.

the National War College.* People like Brent Scowcroft, three members of the JCS, Bennie Davis, CinCSAC, made every week a homecoming. I had an automatic built-in reputation with these officers.

The voluntary elective in the "history of strategic thought" that I had started at the National War College probably reached 90% of the students, and many of the wives and secretaries sat in the audience. It was good fun all the way through, and I was able to get some outstanding guest speakers from all over the world. General Andre Beaufre, probably the best educated and most prominent strategist that France has produced in many years, was happy to spend an afternoon with us for a $50.00 honorarium and a glass of sherry at lunch. He paid his own expenses. It was a delightful learning experience, the highlight of the National War College year for most of the students. General Furlong was one of many who claimed that my seminar turned his whole career around. He became an ardent disciple, a conscientious student of Clausewitz, Mahan, and others. Naturally I had great rapport with these flag officers when they came through the Air War College as visiting general officers.

And here, let me digress for a moment. I gradually came to feel that whatever reputation I had earned was different in the Army and Air Force from the Navy. With the Army and Air Force, my prestige was as a scholar and student of strategy; in the Navy as an operator who is also a writer, speaker, or fellow graduate, and secondarily a scholar. It's difficult to express, but I gradually came to realize an educational difference where strategic principles were less important for study in the Navy than in the other services. Mahan had given easy and glib answers to the toughest problems of strategy. Satisfied in the soundness of his teachings, we accepted those principles as givens; our major intellectual effort went into technology. That the Mahanian gospel may no longer be relevant to modern war was not subject to challenge, and hence scholarship in this field earns few admirers. A second and strongly contributing element is the lack of a military teaching faculty at the Naval Academy in contrast to West Point and Colorado Springs. The pressure for advanced

---

* Major General Richard H. Schoeneman, USAF, became commandant of the Air War College and vice commander of the Air University in November 1977.

academic degrees to qualify as a teacher is far less; rarely does a naval officer, at the Naval Academy, the war colleges, or elsewhere, establish a reputation as a scholar.

If I have an essay to circulate for review by experts before publication, a dozen names come to mind in the other services, rarely one in the Navy. This, in essence, may be the heart of the challenge given me by Paul Nitze and his Under Secretary, Robert Baldwin, so many years ago; it is this attitude which I sought to change. It may be I could have done that best by accepting the chair of academic dean. I see that more clearly today than at the time. After all, my own ideas were only then taking shape. It was the subsequent experience with the other services which brought these ideas to fruition.

For my second year at the Air War College, we installed the new course. I became a professor of military strategy rather than of international politics. There was a new commandant who was a straight SAC bald eagle type, never noted as a thinker or strategist, pretty much the pure SAC distillate.

Q: "Bomb them into submission."

Captain Schratz: Exactly. And I anticipated that my honeymoon had ended. Not so. Dave Gray was eager to learn, an activist, and became one of the best friends I had down there.[*] It was he who was primarily responsible for getting me a contract to write a book on my "history of strategic thought," which I was again giving as an elective. And every time I saw him on return visits to the campus, his first question was, "How's _my_ book coming along?" Dave was a solid person. Also, during that time Senator Dole asked if I would prepare testimony for the Senate Foreign Relations Committee on ratification of the SALT II treaty.[†]

Meanwhile, two or three of us were given blanket authority to rebuild the curriculum. When the new program was installed, Ray Furlong and I co-directed a fairly important conference, with all the war colleges and educational commands participating, on

---

[*] Major General David L. Gray, USAF, became commandant of the Air War College and vice commander of the Air University in August 1979.
[†] Senator Robert J. Dole (Republican-Kansas).

"How to teach strategy at the war colleges." I thought it was extremely valuable. By the time I completed my two-year contract, the Air University curriculum was rated tops among all the war colleges.

Q: By whom?

Captain Schratz: By DoD, the other commandants, and informally around the "circuit." All the colleges recognized it. The new quality was verified also by preferences of students in where they want to go to war college. John Collins wrote a book on the war college education for the Congressional Research Service. At that time he found the Air War College tops. Another is in a book published by Johns Hopkins on American national security policy, now in its fourth or fifth edition.

In one of the earlier editions, a study mentioned that the National War College program reached its peak in 1968-69 when Fitzhugh Lee was commandant.[*] The Air War College reached its peak under Dave Gray, the Naval War College a few years after Stan Turner rebuilt the curriculum. It is significant that both the National and Air War colleges fell from that peak very quickly. The Naval War College has been far more successful. Whatever role I had in the National and Air colleges reaching their peaks while I was a faculty member is not particularly important. What bothers me is the fact that both of them fell away so quickly after.

I realized that the one thing I couldn't do, and which was the key to success of the Turner revolution at Newport, was that he institutionalized his changes so that they would be impervious to the meddlers who succeeded him. He took a station wagon full of prestigious civilian professors to Newport and gave them five-year or so Civil Service contracts carrying them to retirement. Hence, they were able to get that program installed with a high academic credibility and a good receptivity by the rest of the operating Navy, even after Stan's departure, and that program is in much the same shape today. It's extremely important, of course, to institutionalize those changes so succeeding regimes

---

[*] Rear Admiral Fitzhugh Lee, USN, whose oral history is in the Naval Institute collection.

don't destroy the core studies through nibbling at the fringes with new fads. But the military officers have not accepted their share in the "new think," and the civilian professors have reverted largely to their areas of specialization. A hodge-podge of history has taken over for strategy study.

Q: What advantages do you see in the Turner innovations over the way the Naval War College was before Turner?

Captain Schratz: Well, academically the program was the pits. They were using the Rio Grande technique when I was up there--a mile wide and an inch deep. And it was very easy to add any new fad that came along and nothing ever got thrown out. The core of the program was carried by outside lecturers. There were many times too many. Visiting lecturers were not used effectively; they were brought in for a lecture and sent on their way after the lecture and a question period. Admiral Turner sharply reduced the number of lectures. Because a lecture has a very low payoff in the receptivity and retentivity by students, Stan brought lecturers in for several days and made them available to students through small seminars to pick their brains and really learn something. He also increased the in-house lecturing by the faculty, including the military members. Once such a program gets well set, it tends to perpetuate itself, if properly trained military officers can be found.

Q: What do you see about the value of the curriculum at a war college itself plus somebody simultaneously studying for a master's degree? Is that too much at one time?

Captain Schratz: It should be too much, but--more frequently than not--the university programs on campus were the only intellectual challenges the students received. This was true even when the university standards were low--nobody ever failed--and second-rate teachers were used. Some of the programs for master's degrees were good and some were poor. I don't want to criticize any particular university program. Those who took them realized that they many times used second-rate professors for their off-campus programs. My experience was with Boston University at the Naval War College, and shortly after,

Boston University pulled out because they didn't want to be compared with second-rate programs. At Newport in my era students were not allowed to take outside courses; only faculty members. It was considered by Admiral Ingersoll to be an interference in the student academic load. This restriction sharply limited the program from what the other war colleges were doing.

Incidentally, another indication of the comparative merit of the Naval War College today is the accreditation given the resident course by universities offering a master's program. Normally the war college course is given about six to ten academic hours credit. I hear that the Naval War College today gets about 20. That's a measure by people in the field as to the quality of the program. I don't know when the Naval War College again resumed an outside university program on campus. I would not favor that for students even if the university were high-ranking, which this one is not.

Q: Are you pleased by the current emphasis that Admiral Watkins is placing on the value of the war college?*

Captain Schratz: I think it's outstanding, perhaps the most positive action by a CNO in many years. My concerns are three. First, will he be able to institutionalize his changes so that the program survives this watch? The increased quality of students, the stress on sending officers immediately following a successful command tour, the increasingly close ties with the fleet in the war gaming center can only help. The new policy of admitting students at different times of the year into the trimester program with students entering in December, March, and August, may be necessary to give detailing officers more flexibility, but it is not preferable. If it makes 10% more students eligible or increases the quality, it will be very worthwhile. Second, the short eight-week course for officers who can't be diverted for a full year sets a dangerous precedent.

Of the four service arms, only the Navy has failed to understand the necessity of top quality officers attending both a command and staff course and senior war college. We do

---

* Admiral James D. Watkins, USN, served as Chief of Naval Operations from 1982 to 1986.

one or the other, far too often neither. Would we send our children to high school or college but not both? Both the college and the student would suffer. If we now accept an eight-week temporary alternative until the student is available for a full year, will such top-notch students ever become available to return for the normal course? I would much favor stress on a correspondence course stopgap as a better and safer all-round alternative. My third concern is that the CNO, I believe, tends to think of the war college role as tactical or operational rather than the deep think necessary for a longer range strategically oriented experience. In short, his attitude may be toward training rather than education. This I surmise largely from his role with the Naval Institute, as I understand it.

Q: One way to help reinforce his ideas is to somehow influence selections so that those with that background prosper.

Captain Schratz: Yes, and I think he's done that too. Despite my concerns, I have hopes that in a few years his program should pay off very well.

An indication of the difficulty in getting quality students to the war colleges is that when Tom Hayward was the CNO he was very supportive of the war colleges.[*] Tom had been one of my students at the National War College and a good friend. When I was at the Air War College, there was ample cause for concern about the lack of quality of the Navy students. Never in the history of the Air War College had a naval officer made Distinguished Graduate. For years the Navy students who went to the Air War College were by and large the least qualified of all of our war college students. At least this is the strong impression held at Maxwell.[†] In general, those I saw bore it out. Many should not have gone to any war college, and clearly were merely filling a quota.

I wrote to Tom to plead for a higher quality student. I was successful for one year. The Navy student in my seminar made Distinguished Graduate, the first time ever. I thought he was a pretty good student. The year after my departure there was a shortage of

---

[*] Admiral Thomas B. Hayward, USN, served as Chief of Naval Operations from 1978 to 1982.
[†] Maxwell Air Force Base, Alabama, is the site of the Air War College.

Navy students for all the war college quotas. To fill their quota, the Navy decided to order in two TAR reserves for the purpose of going to the National War College, and the war college objected. The Navy then took the two students fingered for the Air War College and diverted them to the National, to be replaced by the two TARs.[*]

Q: It's an oversimplification, obviously, but an observation has been made that in peacetime the Navy still has the requirement to operate its ships, whereas the Army officers have the job of going to school. Is there any way to remedy that?

Captain Schratz: Perhaps we could send the Army officers to operate ships? The Army operated more ships in Vietnam than the Navy and flew more airplanes than the Air Force. That might not be a full solution. I think more important is the ingrained attitude in the Navy that the way to become a naval officer is to be on the bridge of a ship at sea, and everything else is secondary. Education never had a high priority. The essay I did for the centennial issue of the <u>Naval War College Review</u> is essentially a history of 100 years of anti-intellectualism in the Navy. I think it's very prominent in a great many of our officers. Every now and then we get an outstanding CNO like Admiral Burke, who screams that in our planning and staffing, "We are being eaten alive by the other services."[†] And for a year or two, a little node appears in the quality of the students, or maybe a few Naval War College graduates will be sent to the National War College as students the following year to help improve the Navy's image, but those things are temporary and don't do much good in the long run.

Q: One of the crying needs--and this should strike a sympathetic chord with you as a submariner--is that nuclear submariners are so scarce anyway that they're needed in those boats and can't seem to be spared for war colleges. And yet they're the most talented

---

[*] TARs are active-duty Naval Reservists who specialize in the training and administration of inactive Naval Reservists.
[†] Admiral Arleigh A. Burke, USN, served as Chief of Naval Operations from 17 August 1955 to 1 August 1961.

people getting into this tight screen and are winding up with the two-, three-, and four-star jobs in the Navy. Shouldn't there be some mechanism to get them better educated before they get to the top?

Captain Schratz: Yes. I published something on the Naval Academy of 25 years into the future--Shipmate in 1970--in which I thought it was a crime not to send high-quality nuclear-trained people to war colleges, both for what they had to learn and what they had to give the other students.* I thought a way should be found to do that. A few years ago I was being briefed in the Pentagon by a three-star nuclear officer who claimed that when he became the SecNav executive assistant, the Secretary, uneducated in the ways of the sea, knew more about the Navy than he did. His 17 years prior had been almost continually at sea. Today, perhaps, we recognize the danger of that over-concentration. I noted just recently that the rotation of nuclear-trained officers has been changed. Instead of 17 out of the first 20 years at sea, the ratio will be roughly half and half, maybe one year more at sea than ashore in their first 17 years. This was necessary to ease the rush for the exits. Even the bonuses couldn't overcome the separation and the operating hours.

Q: You touched only lightly on what you did at the National War College. Could you cover that in more detail, please?

Captain Schratz: Yes. I started a formal "history of strategic thought" seminar. A civilian professor, Jim Huston from Purdue, who had previously been on the Naval War College faculty with me, had worked somewhat informally with students at the National War College on strategic thought before my arrival; when he left, I was happy to take over.

I changed the focus of it from straight history--since I'm not a historian--to a more or less operational development of American strategic thought, concentrating on the soldier-scholar: military officers whose theorizing was based on war experience, such as Thucydides, Clausewitz, Mahan, or Douhet. It was a fine experience, and turned on many

---

* "And in Twenty-Five More Years," Shipmate, October 1970, pages 20-23.

bright students into a far deeper study of their profession. I was concerned at the National War College, once again, with the same old bugaboo about the military faculty administering the program and leaving the civilians to do all the teaching. To stimulate thinking by the military, I started a faculty research seminar, trying to encourage the military officers to write papers, even operational experience, anything, just to get them into writing and thinking about their profession. This I discussed earlier, and it's mushrooming into a major publications effort today. My main writing effort then, of course, went into the dissertation.

Also, I was "hired out" on a number of projects. A high-level study of future base requirements in the Pacific, stimulated by the White House, captured my attention to serve on the OpNav-ONI task group. General Goodpaster allowed me only a week away from regular duties, so I spent a weekend blocking out the entire study and developing certain parts of it within my immediate capability, which the others then fleshed out for the final report.

The Army Research and Analysis Corporation, RAC, also offered me a contract to analyze the rise of Soviet power in the Mediterranean. This was a straight civilian contract, and seemed to be a direct conflict of interest with my war college duties. I passed all the papers to the JAG for an opinion. Much to my surprise, he found no legal objection.*

So I taught my Middle East seminar by day, then spent six hours at home writing the same thing for RAC and added $200 a day to my income. This was published as an oversized pamphlet.

While on the National War College faculty, I also was elected a trustee of the Naval Academy Alumni Association, when Admiral Smedberg was president. Stimulated by some letters I was getting from numerous university fund drives, I developed a proposal for the Naval Academy to tap some major funding sources through prominent graduates worldwide. At that time the Alumni Association was struggling to eke out $1,500 annually from membership dues to support the Naval Academy Foreign Affairs Conference (NAFAC). My proposal was quickly adopted, and in a few years, dramatically changed the

---

* JAG--Judge Advocate General.

entire function of the association. The donor program is now a multi-million dollar operation. In addition, the association had offered to contribute $6 to $13 million to the new activities center, reducing federal funds accordingly.

Somewhat earlier, I became interested in getting Andy Goodpaster, with all the trappings of a first-rate scholar and a highly successful career in broad policy matters, to relieve Fitzhugh Lee. Fitz had done a great job, and I wanted as his successor somebody likely to continue the support I had been receiving on a rebuilt academic program. It was the Army's turn as commandant, and General Goodpaster was recovering from a heart attack suffered while director of the Joint Staff. It looked ideal, during his recovery, to spend a year or two at the National War College. I had no influence in detailing Army generals, but at my instigation, a number of friends in academic life wrote letters to McNamara in Goodpaster's behalf. McNamara sent them to the National War College to prepare a reply, and they were given to me to prepare, a task I eagerly welcomed. Out of the blue the impossible happened, and Andy became my new boss.

My elation was short-lived. Goodpaster had too little energy left for the college. He helicoptered to Gettysburg frequently to work with Eisenhower on his memoirs, never broke clear of the Joint Staff, and served a lot of other interests.[*] Involved in everything, we saw too little of him. Even when present, he was never able to get into the academic program. The day that General Andre Beaufre came from Paris to spend with my seminar, Goodpaster made no apparent attempt to meet or greet, merely presenting a note of apology to me that he was not able to participate in the seminar. The students couldn't believe it, nor could I.

Q: Could you discuss somewhat more Admiral Lee's role there?

Captain Schratz: Yes. Fitz had a broad background of experience in the Navy. He had been executive assistant to the Secretary during the unification hassle, I believe, and was

---

[*] Dwight D. Eisenhower served as President of the United States from January 1953 to January 1961, following a distinguished Army career that culminated with his service as Chief of Staff from 1945 to 1948.

well qualified in this area. A fine person to work with, congenial with subordinates, he never professed to be an expert in the academic field and was modest, too modest about his talents in other things. I found him most supportive in my programs. In his own way, he was an extremely effective commandant, far more than most. It was a refreshing change for the other services to work with him. And just as I had become involved at the Naval War College with Admiral Ingersoll's retirement, I became involved at the National when Admiral Lee retired.

Years before, General Eisenhower, concerned about attempts to politicize the U.S. military forces in Europe, pushed through an idea to set up a program for military schools on the dangers of Communism. The National War College at that time brought in a team of civilians to put the program on each summer. This program, which was in its tenth year when I arrived, became my primary responsibility. It was a two-week program, mentioned earlier, coming at the end of the academic year, called the Defense Strategy Seminar, or DSS. It is similar to the Current Strategy Forum at Newport. The program at McNair was run by a quite outstanding group of people. It bothered me, because it's the sort of a program the war colleges should put on with the regular faculty, not with civilians under contract. I first had to con Admiral Lee into killing the contract for that year.

The civilian team, then run by the silver-tongued Frank Barnett, was looking forward to a special tenth anniversary program. Fitz agreed with me, and Barnett was shocked when his contract wasn't renewed. Naturally, I became the <u>bete noire</u>. Barnett had been a graduation week fixture at both the Naval and National war colleges for years. The only way I could get around using him was to substitute Admiral Lee and his farewell address. And of all Fitz Lee's great accomplishments, public speaking was not included. The curriculum board bought the substitution of Lee for Barnett as the wrap-up speaker, assuming I had worked it out directly with him. But Fitz had not even read the changes on the last page of the curriculum in which he was to be so directly involved.

After waiting quite some time, I finally raised the question of writing his speech. He was taken totally by surprise and his reluctance grew day by day. Barnett, meanwhile, was very much in the wings. In desperation, I finally suggested a compromise to Admiral Lee. The DSS includes distinguished Americans, congressmen, judges, and others whom we lectured to death for two weeks. I suggested that maybe it would be a good idea to give them a chance to be heard. I suggested a short, pithy introduction by Admiral Lee, after which we would entertain one-minute interventions from the floor either as a question or a message. He agreed quickly, on condition that I take the other rostrum and do it together. This put an entirely new cast to the program and was extremely well received.

Frank Barnett came to town on his own and picked up the tab for a freebie informal banquet for the DSS at the Mayflower Hotel, in direct competition with our program. Fortunately, very few students attended, favoring the war college program instead. The ghost of the hired brain trust was finally laid to rest. Again, this was somewhat the gimmick approach. The whole point was, as always, to get the War College to do its own academic work as well as administering the program, to participate in more than the athletic program and the field trips.

Q: Do you have any suggestions for areas that the war colleges might profitably go into from now on?

Captain Schratz: Yes. Right now we're in the midst of a hassle over reorganizing the Joint Chiefs, to try to make the Joint Chiefs more effective. Almost nobody will deny that the Joint Chiefs organization today is ineffective. The purpose of the National War College is to train future leaders for JCS and unified command. It was set up as a joint school specifically for that purpose. If that's the goal, it should be the primary focus of the National War College course. It is not. When I was there, what a future unified commander learned that would benefit him was whatever he might have absorbed at the command and staff level many years before, but for his own responsibilities in strategic planning or making his budget for the forces needed, very little.

The most important element in military strategy is the prepared mind of the commander, achieved, regardless of the genius of his staff, through hard study by the commander, not by the staff. We have no body of joint doctrine on which to base such instruction. In its absence, the body of strategic doctrine is no more than a series of tired cliches, a new set for each administration, and I regret to say that the Navy in its blind adherence to outdated doctrines of Mahan, is the worst offender. The simple reason is that the service staff so totally dominates the Joint Staff, that unless the services are willing to give up some sovereignty to the joint organization, the JCS will never be effective. There is nobody around to teach such a course except ex-commanders who survived the hard way.

When President Eisenhower pushed the 1958 amendments to the National Security Act through Congress, it was Eisenhower's postwar experience encapsulated in the statute. That piece of legislation placed joint planning and joint doctrinal development as the prime responsibility of the Joint Chiefs of Staff, repeated three times in his message to Congress. The Chiefs, however, delegated the responsibility to the services. The JCS had neither the training, facilities, or test grounds then, for doctrinal development. But the services were concerned with service doctrine, not joint, and joint doctrine never appeared.

How wonderful it would be if the Navy and Air Force had a body of doctrine for use of tactical air comparable to the body of doctrine in the Navy and Marine Corps for amphibious operations. A formal post-mortem on the Korean War found a major defect to be the lack of a body of common tactical air doctrine for joint actions against common targets. Aircraft had no common control nor even a radio frequency through which they could communicate. The same failure was repeated--aggravated--in Vietnam, and guess what?

Observers of the Grenada operation found to their surprise that we had no joint tactical air doctrine, not even a common frequency for control of aircraft. When a junior Army officer allegedly uses a telephone credit card to call Fort Bragg in North Carolina to get word to the Navy to supply air support for his beleaguered troops, something is seriously wrong with the joint organization.

For joint doctrinal development, what the services do today is a crime. The doctrinal bibles of the three services are terrible as far as any help to a unified commander. By law the unified commanders control all the combat forces in time of war. The services have the responsibility only to "provide, train, and equip" forces for the unified commands. There is no body of joint tactical or strategic doctrine, because the Joint Chiefs never assumed their legal responsibility. This is where the National War College in particular has fallen down. I understand that a new course has been set up at the National specifically for training of senior joint commanders. This is a wonderful initiative, but it is far too late in their career. The whole educational preparation should be focused on the need.

I had a recent meeting with the head of planning and policy on the Air Staff last week. He mentioned 31 initiatives which the Army and the Air Force are working on toward interservice cooperation. The orders to the Air Staff are that those 31 initiatives will be graded as green, red, or yellow--green, we do right now; yellow, we better take a pretty hard look at; and red, those which we can't do without giving up turf or sacrificing service values. He claimed the Air Force made major concessions and is willing to make others to improve joint command. The biggest battle he fights is the "iron majors" who know how things were always done, and they refuse to break the service stranglehold over the joint structure.

I believe the joint structure is also at fault in misuse of component commanders. I thought for many years that service component commanders on each unified staff simply build in a service compromise in all unified command actions. The unified commander himself is too prone, because of the deficiencies of his own background, to accept responsibility for control of three service performance under him as a joint commander. He therefore delegates each service slice of the action to the component commander representing that service and continues to make every action a three-service action. It's probably necessary to have component commanders as long as we fail to develop a body of common doctrine, but I would look with great care at how the responsibility is shared by component commanders in joint operations. The Grenada experience is a laboratory case. I see serious defects in the whole joint structure in strategic development and in the JCS role in controlling it.

Specifically to answer your question, the service war colleges have a role in teaching and developing maritime or land or air warfare, but their main role at the senior level is the common task of developing joint strategy, strategic planning, and training of carefully selected future leaders for their role as unified commanders. All that is already provided for in the law. If we attack this problem forthrightly and energetically, no legislative action is necessary. And unless we attack it forthrightly and energetically, new legislation now pending or proposed will have little effect.

Q: Might some improvement in that area be made at the Armed Forces Staff College?

Captain Schratz: Yes. As the mid-level educational facility, the staff college is designed to indoctrinate a select body of officers in the principles of staff planning procedures and unit or small joint command. General Eisenhower, as Army Chief of Staff, visualized all higher education under joint control. He gave up the superb Army War College at Fort McNair to found the National War College. He wanted to use the Naval War College as the Armed Forces Staff College in 1947, and not to reopen it as the Naval War College. But the Navy thought it needed its own war college to teach the elements of maritime warfare, and instead turned over a piece of land in Norfolk for the Armed Forces Staff College.

Eisenhower's successor as Chief of Staff still believed the Army needed its war college, particularly since the Navy reopened Newport, and they founded the new Army War College at Carlisle Barracks. Eisenhower never forgave the Navy. When he became President, his major goal, little mentioned in the press, was to close "that goddamn Naval War College," or at least to put all the war colleges under joint control. I happened to be on the Naval War College faculty during the new attempt to put all the service war colleges, including the infant Air War College, under the JCS.

It was clear to me at that time that he wouldn't accept a simple no answer. I thought it was time to bring out the gimmick approach again. So as the staff action officer to prepare War College comments for the CNO, I suggested that the three service war colleges had much in common in the way of teaching joint doctrine, but also had a service responsibility in teaching maritime war and all its complexities, for which it was vital to have an adequate school. To help orient the three service colleges in bringing together their common responsibilities in the joint area, I suggested a semi-annual or annual meeting of the commandants of all the senior war colleges to work out common problems. The JCS grabbed at this straw and quickly adopted it. I understand the MECC still convenes twice a year and has been very helpful. Yet the stress on joint education is nowhere near adequate either at the senior colleges or at the Armed Forces Staff College. The failure is through the void in broad strategic doctrine more than in the organization.

Q: You've covered some of this in your article in a recent issue of the War College Review.

Captain Schratz: Yes.

Q: What suggestions do you have for reorganizing the Joint Chiefs organization to make it more effective?

Captain Schratz: As I implied before, the present organization will work when a Secretary of Defense or Chairman wants it to work. We discussed earlier the McNamara reforms in which he took full advantage of the 1958 amendment to gain total control of the civilian side of defense and policy control of the military. The same 1958 act creates the authority to put the military side of Defense under the same tight control. McNamara and his successors--the few who understand--won't do it; it isn't in their interest to unify the "opposition" through a unified military voice. I emphasize strongly that this does not mean a single chief of staff running a Prussian style general staff. That is specifically against the law. The authority is provided the service chiefs in their JCS role, not as a chief of service.

Insufficient understanding of the present law is a major weakness in new direction to improve the JCS. The main direction of the Davey Jones Plan--a fine name for an Air Force general--most prominent around the village now, is to increase the power of the chairman, give him his own staff, and put him on the National Security Council.* I think there is more bad than good here. The whole structure of command is keyed to civilian control of the military forces. That is why the unified commanders are under the Secretary of Defense, who, as deputy to the commander in chief, is legally a military officer. I see little point in putting one more layer of authority between him and the unified or specified commanders by inserting the JCS. The JCS are the legal advisers to the Secretary. There was never any intention in the law to have the Secretary create a duplicate staff to parallel the Joint Staff.

---

* General David C. Jones, USAF, served as Chairman of the Joint Chiefs of Staff from 21 June 1978 to 18 June 1982.

The Jones plan is flawed first in putting the Chairman of the JCS on the National Security Council. Such membership could not give him equality with the Secretary as long as he is legally only an adviser to the Secretary. It would also further overbalance the military input to the NSC in comparison with the State Department influence, for example, on the political side. The Jones idea of increasing the influence of the Chairman by legal means is also flawed. The NSC amendments of '49, '53, and '58 all sought to strengthen the Chairman and "clarify" the role of the Secretary; each clarified the role of the Chairman and strengthened the Secretary. If either the Chairman or the Secretary can't get an adequate opinion out of the JCS structure, it is time to find a new set of chiefs. The absence of an agreed body of strategic doctrine will forever kill the JCS effectiveness. We overcame it in World War II by fighting three separate wars, especially in the Pacific, and we had abundant resources to do so. We don't now and won't again have that luxury.

To amplify the first point above, contrary to many cherished beliefs about being dominated by civilians, the reverse is far more the case. The American military professional today is the best educated, trained, disciplined, and organized element of the federal government. The State Department can only lament its inferiority in producing major staffing efforts on short notice, a task wholly beyond its capability.

Military officers dominate the NSC structure, many of the assistant secretary positions in Defense, 18 in "policy" roles in State, on loan from the Pentagon. But a military officer, trained in the use of violence, tends to think of national security problems in military terms, and, as George Marshall claimed, "Thinking of political problems in military terms soon makes them military problems." Yet military advice is flawed by the lack of the body of professional knowledge in the higher direction of power and the lack of joint doctrine so heavily dependent on that knowledge. The military now dominates the civilian policy through its organization, not through its philosophy. Ergo, a militarized national policy structure.

If the military thought in political-strategic terms, i.e., on the role of force in seeking a political objective, it would tend to politicize military power toward a national objective. Lacking a proper doctrinal base, he concentrates on the tactical role of military force only, and supports policy in military terms. As stated earlier, this is the sure road to militarism and the primary reason for the present extreme in militarizing national policy objectives.

Q: The JCS, though, has some kind of amorphous role between the SecDef and the unified commanders.

Captain Schratz: Yes. The broad concept behind the Army and Air Force plans lies toward centralizing the whole JCS structure, and this, however sound in principle, needs far deeper understanding. When McNamara came to the Pentagon determined to centralize the Defense Department, he was concerned about civilian direction. He couldn't care less about centralizing the military side of the house. It was in his interest to do the opposite, to let the military fight each other. If they couldn't decide on anything, he always had a stable of eager young assistants all too happy to assume responsibility and make decisions for us.

As an indication of this attitude, McNamara went out of his way to make sure that "the admirals" wouldn't have an inside track to that blue water sailor in the White House, John Kennedy. Kennedy had promised FDR, Jr., that he would be named the Secretary of the Navy. Ably qualified and, like his father, a longtime friend of the Navy, this was an ideal appointment. But to McNamara it could only solidify the back channel from the admirals to the White House. That McNamara had to prevent at all costs. He wanted John Connally for two reasons.* Connally was a Navy veteran with a fine combat record. More important, he was the defeated rival and the biggest Kennedy-hater in government. Connally therefore seemed ideal to cut the umbilical to the White House, and McNamara insisted vehemently on that appointment despite strong objections by JFK. You may gathered that--from my research in doing the John Connally chapter for the Naval Institute's American Secretaries of the Navy-- I didn't get a very good impression of him.

The McNamara goal was to centralize the managerial side of Defense, and what has grown today is the most massive bureaucracy imaginable, wholly impervious to human control. The primary cause of the $5,000 coffee pots and the $800 screwdrivers is that one

---

* John B. Connally served as Secretary of the Navy from 25 January 1961 to 20 December 1961.

can't slice his way into the structure to prevent such abuse. The experience in corporate life today is the opposite; not centralization but decentralization. There are limits toward which centralization is no longer beneficial, and if one takes a look at our largest corporations--the big auto companies--they show an effective type of decentralization. AT&T may be the exception; time will tell.

But the military staff, if we must accept centralized management, must get its act together on a common philosophy. It's dangerous to centralize the military side, either under a single chief or by adding another layer in the middle of the command structure. The common body of doctrine gives the individual services enough scope for strategic thought unique to that service environment. Such ideas contribute to the richness and variety of the strategy without imposing three separate solutions to every crisis, and creating the fiascoes of joint planning evidenced in every joint action since Inchon. I think the Chairman of the Joint Chiefs should control the Joint Chiefs. The Joint Chiefs should, as a first order of business, remove doctrinal development from the services and put it into the Joint Chiefs, as a Joint Staff responsibility called for under the law, the same law McNamara used to his advantage on the civilian side.

If the services want to comment, to initiate, to assist, accept their thoughts with pleasure. But the responsibility must be, and is by law, in the Joint Chiefs of Staff, for both doctrinal development and for strategic planning. The unified command must do its strategic planning, develop, and recommend force levels and draft its own budgets. The Chiefs objected initially to the unified commanders developing doctrine, because it was feared they might come up with eight different sets for the eight different commands. That's what the Joint Chiefs are for. If they can't resolve doctrinal problems among the unified commanders, they are evading their statutory responsibilities.

To answer your question specifically, therefore, I see no need for the legislative change to the JCS organization that would be either fruitful or necessary.* What needs to be done is wholly within the present law. The only area where legislative change would be

---

* In fact, the law was changed. The Goldwater-Nichols Defense Reorganization Act of 1986 went into effect on 1 October of that year. For details, see "DoD Reorganization," U.S. Naval Institute Proceedings, May 1987, pages 136-145.

useful is one not yet suggested by the reformers. That is a need, which I first developed 20 years ago for my doctoral dissertation, for a professional civil service in specified under secretary level and subordinate positions, primarily in the Pentagon and State Department. This would decrease the turbulence and add significantly to stability, continuity, and corporate memory, and help ease the urge of each new administration to establish its own track record in foreign and defense policy.

Q: Do you have any philosophical thoughts on the management versus leadership controversy and its role in the military services?

Captain Schratz: I'm just now in the middle of looking at recent leadership texts used at the Air Force Academy and the Naval Academy for a study on leadership techniques, especially here at Annapolis. In my era, an officer spent most of his time at sea in leadership positions small and large. A JO was junior, but he was an officer in the firm with executive duties. He had responsibility, and the system produced excellent operational leaders. Much of one's education came naturally at sea. From earliest experience with enlisted men, he learned the hard way the elemental lessons of leadership, an opportunity far less available today. That part of the career experience now is fabricated somewhere else and pumped into young--and even not young--officers. Complex technology now dominates his best efforts.

I think we've gone through a very long period where the changing needs were either overlooked or wouldn't fit into the master plan. I believe we have some outstanding people running the leadership program at the Naval Academy. But of the two activists with whom I've worked, one is a civilian with no sea experience, the other is a junior Marine Corps officer. They have energetically sought the comments and ideas from senior officers in the Navy, but "professional development" as a non-credit course must compete with all the major programs. I'm not sure how the program influences the whole of leadership training. I have not made a study of it, I emphasize, but the head of the program should be very close to the Superintendent himself. This is the impression I get from a bit more than a casual look.

It again gets back to the idea of the need to use the Naval Academy to plant and fertilize the seed of professional education in the art of war. And that theme has got to be so dominant in the training program throughout one's career that unless started here, precious time is wasted in establishing habits of thought, interests, and trends of study, even in first trying to get people to read. I am an avid reader, yet for some reason, that phase of my professional development, other than reading about great leaders of the past, simply escaped me until I was wearing four stripes. As a JO, we had to do a book review every three months. Bright young ensigns chasing German raiders or escorting convoys in the middle of the Atlantic, we had to get our book reviews in. But those were designed to broaden us culturally and to teach creative writing, not as a professional aid. Each review had to come from different categories: religion, the arts, sciences, and various disciplines. That task fell on its face because a lot of people refused to comply and not much could be done about it.

Q: Do you think the Navy, with its emphasis on managerial techniques and weapons acquisition and that sort of thing, squeezed out the kind of individuality of a Dusty Dornin or a Paul Schratz in this flair for doing things?

Captain Schratz: I would say half and half. I think that the "squeezees" have been equally liable. I mentioned that Dusty Dornin, for instance, was not at all fazed by the strictures, as we saw them, of the Uniform Military Code of Justice. We simply bent it to suit operational, leadership needs. Discipline is a major element of leadership training, and his ideas had obvious and immediate results in the ship which would not have come had we gone with the tide and used normal procedures as envisioned and developed by civilian attorneys. In the old "rocks and shoals," justice prevailed because it was rightly based on the assumption that we had good leadership.

The UMCJ is based on the need for protection of the rights of the accused, because of its assumption that leadership was bad. Few realize the special effort needed to stay marginally within the Code and still use discipline as a major technique of leadership. I can't see myself as a commanding officer accepting the degree of interference from a remote commander, even the White House, on tactical operations. I can't see myself ever doing that, no matter what position I had in the command chain. I just would not accept it. You may feel that these sentiments emerge after years on the retired list, but I have not changed. In all honesty, I'm sure I would have done exactly the same thing then as I had done in the past.

Q: Isn't it possible, though, that the "squeezees" have decided they didn't want to retire as lieutenant commanders or commanders and so went along with the program?

Captain Schratz: Well, obviously that is likely, but I can't buy it either. My career was full and rich, and if I had it to do over again, I'd do it much the same, pretty much.

Q: It's possible, I think, that you were much more able to do it then than your counterparts today would be able to.

Captain Schratz: Well, in the submarine service, I think this is as true then as now. You could do an awful lot then because so much depended on personal reputation. It happened time and time again. For instance, when Pickerel was coming back from Hong Kong on that submerged cruise, the mere fact that when all of our antenna were wiped away and had lost all means of communication, as far as Admiral Radford was concerned, we were an overdue submarine unreported for several days. He wanted SubPac to bring us up. Admiral Brown said, "That's the best boat I've got. I have absolute faith in them. I've been with them in the shipyard; I've seen them operate here. I'll accept full responsibility." That doesn't happen very often. It may never happen now.

In submarines, I mentioned earlier the Rickover influence toward technical clones rather than seamen. The idea of checking and rechecking everybody might be necessary for technical reasons or for reasons of safety or health, but I can't see how that doesn't very quickly absorb a lot of command responsibility. This type of attitude can get pervasive. For example, a recent case involved two P-3 airplanes, one of which had a wheels-up landing with no casualties and only slight damage to the airplane; the other was a strike accident and loss of the crew through a navigational error. A very bright, young squadron commander was relieved and given a letter of admonition as being responsible. As far as command responsibility was concerned, it looked to me, from a very careful examination of the record, that he had done everything he could. Both pilots were well-qualified, trained, and experienced. Aircraft by their nature are subject to hazard in advanced training operations when fatigue or other reasons take their toll. Even if somebody in the plane just goofed off, one could still make a case for a training deficiency, but relief of the CO without even an investigation is a shafting. He's becoming a civilian next month.

Another case appeared in the press last week about the carrier <u>Ranger</u>, where a fuel valve was missing, and somebody squirted fuel over the area. The command gave the junior enlisted men court-martials; the CNO reversed that and assigned a reprimand long after the fact to the CO and XO, and he's apparently thinking about something further for two flag officers who had deferred a scheduled overhaul and sent the ship to sea on a routine deployment. Based on the information available in the press, a missing valve is not really attributable to a delayed overhaul. Ships coming out of overhaul are more likely to have valves missing than when they go in. If this sets the precedent for an admiral's responsibility, it has vast implications elsewhere on flag officers' responsibility that can only produce a wave of CYA at all levels.[*] I just don't see that.

I was happy to accept responsibility, even remotely, for the things which happened during my career, but I don't see that standard of responsibility in the Navy today. And it's interesting that both of these acts were taken by nuclear submariners whose training has been very, very much more toward the senior person being responsible for details generally far below his ken. I regard our nuclear submariners as by far the best and brightest, but the system makes them technicians rather than warriors.

Let me suggest a similar experience while I was a submarine division commander. One of my submarines was going through an advanced training exercise against a "heavy" escorted by two destroyers. Normally he would try to penetrate the screen, get into attack position on the heavy and fire his torpedoes. I modified the instructions to the extent that

---

[*] CYA--cover your ass.

he fired only water slugs on the attack, then paralleled the formation and went deep at high speed while reloading for a reattack, then fired his torpedoes for record on the reattack.

To ease his problem slightly, I instructed the surface force, on receiving the signal of his first attack, to simulate damage and slow down somewhat. The submarine CO made an excellent attack, went deep smartly and was returning to periscope depth for the reattack. Quite properly, he placed one sonar on tracking the near escort. Since he was paralleling the formation, he expected a constant bearing. The change of course and speed following the initial attack, however, placed him on a collision course with the escort. When he raised the scope just before reaching periscope depth, he almost put it into the DD engine room. The scope was bent over at a sharp 120 degree angle by the collision, but no other damages were suffered.

We surfaced immediately to assure the very tense OCE that no other damage had been suffered.[*] To his plaintive plea of, "What do we do now?" I suggested opening out to at least five miles before we try it again, suggesting that since we still had one periscope left, we could repeat it at least once. There is no way I can minimize his misgivings, but we completed the test successfully and returned to port. The tender, Nereus, my old happy home, pulled the damaged scope, replaced it, and the ship was ready for full operations by the following morning.

In his report, the CO explained the incident essentially as stated above. In my endorsement, I stated that a submarine, by the nature of close, uncoordinated, high-speed operations with surface ships, accepts the risk of collision. To nourish the aggressiveness of commanders in war, considerable realism was necessary in peace. The CO was fully experienced, the crew at a maximum state of training, and he had followed doctrine carefully. The risk involved was minimized and to preserve a proper attitude for all submarine commanders, I recommended no further action. Both the squadron and force commander supported me, and the incident was closed. Many senior people in the Navy would find this wholly unbelievable today.

---

[*] OCE--officer conducting the exercise.

Q: You haven't talked much about your civilian teaching career. Would you provide a brief summary of that, please?

Captain Schratz: I did some teaching, occasionally, in political science in St. Louis but couldn't accept regular course work for administrative reasons usually concerning frequent absences and possible favoritism to one campus. With never enough money to go around, each and every penny spent on any other campus was a penny wasted. I also wanted to get an overseas program started university-wide.

Friends in Annecy, France, where some of our children went to summer camp when we were in Geneva, had restored a magnificent ninth century chateau on the lake front--one of the most scenic spots in Europe, where they were willing to set up a summer program for the University free of charge. My idea was to use University of Geneva to teach and administer a program assisted by two or three Missouri professors. I had arrangements for housing and meals at a pair of very nice pensions nearby. This promised to be the lowest cost and the highest quality overseas program of any U.S. university. I was really high on it.

Then came the critical day when I presented it to the trustees, I was shocked to learn that any accreditation of an off-campus program was within the empire of a little pipsqueak within the university who runs the farm agencies, the extension course in every county in the state. In my ignorance of the university system, I had neglected to involve him in the program, and it was far too late to convince him then that he had thought it up. He didn't think any infringement on his sovereign turf was justified. The merit of the program didn't matter; it just simply got killed on the spot. This individual at that time was politicking to become the president of the university, a position for which I was also nominated. The capital holding his interest was not Paris or Rome, but Jefferson City. He eventually succeeded in relieving John Weaver on John's departure to become president of the 26-campus University of Wisconsin system.

Q: Was this Brice Ratchford?*

Captain Schratz: Yes. When he killed my program, Tufts University grabbed it, and a few years later my aging benefactor on Lake Annecy turned the whole building over to Tufts. They now have a super, low-cost graduate program in Annecy, France.

Also in St. Louis, I spent a considerable amount of time on radio and TV. KMOX, the all-talk radio station, kept me on their list for short notice on anything international. I made the program frequently and found it an excellent way to get ideas across to the listeners. In St. Louis everybody listens to KMOX. After a short discussion with one of the staff, they open the line for questions, and they run the gamut. I happened to be on one of those broadcasts the day George Wallace was shot, and since I was already in the studio, we stayed on the air for almost two hours.† I fielded questions on the political campaign, the assassination attempt, and related subjects. It was an eye-opening experience to see how a major network handles a big news break like that.

Then with Jim McDonnell's public relations expert, I served as panelist on a television series on NBC channel four, the Sunday morning talk program, a current news forum interviewing every distinguished visitor who came through the area. McDonnell's representative, Mike Witunski, moderated; he chose representatives from the press and one from the university, usually me if I was in town. After a while, we got some sponsors, and it was able to pay its own way. I thought it was a very good program.

As a member of the executive board of the International Studies Association, I co-hosted a number of their conferences in St. Louis and elsewhere in the state. In my spare time, I played my fiddle with the St. Louis Philharmonic. And I was always ready with encouragement for bright young Missouri graduates like Paul Stillwell to further their

---

* Dr. C. Brice Ratchford.
† On 15 May 1972 would-be assassin Arthur H. Bremer shot and seriously wounded Governor George C. Wallace of Alabama while he was campaigning in Laurel, Maryland, for that state's upcoming presidential primary election.

careers by going to the Naval Institute.* But a regular teaching role was not possible. I ran the seminar in Columbia on a regular basis, but this was about the limit.

Q: There is frequently a mutual distrust between military services and the news media in this country that you seem to have bridged. Can you address that from your viewpoints on both sides?

Captain Schratz: Well, with less intensity than most, I share the problem of the military in getting adequate press coverage without allowing the press too much liberty in coloring what they see of military operations for their own benefit, simply to satisfy vocal minorities or sections of their leadership. I'm sure the Vietnam problem over the years fundamentally changed the military attitude toward press coverage, and the role of the media in doing what they see as their job. For those willing to stay inside Saigon and absorb the canned briefings, the war they knew was far different from the one they would have seen if they went out into the field.

I read Peter Braestrup's Big Story, an excellent piece of research on the press in Vietnam.† I sympathize with General Westmoreland in his trial today.‡ I can't imagine he'll win anything but a Pyrrhic victory where only the lawyers will get rich. I think press relations are something which every commander should look at very seriously, not as an adversary but as a cooperative effort toward harmonious goals. Both, after all, share a

---

* The interviewer joined the staff of the Naval Institute in 1974 as the result of a recommendation from Captain Schratz.
† Peter Braestrup, Big Story: How the American Press and Television Reported and Interpreted the Crisis of Tet 1968 in Vietnam and Washington (Boulder, Colorado: Westview Press, 1977).
‡ In September 1982 General William C. Westmoreland, USA (Ret.), filed a $120 million libel suit against the CBS network in response to a program telecast in January of that year. Titled "The Uncounted Enemy: A Vietnam Deception," the documentary implied that General Westmoreland had participated in a conspiracy to underestimate enemy troop strength in Vietnam and thus to deceive the American public. In February 1985 General Westmoreland dropped his suit as part of an out-of-court settlement in which the network paid him no money. Afterward both sides claimed victory.

common superior--the American people. Things happen which can't be anticipated, and they can promise a black eye, particularly if somebody is looking for sensationalism.

That Pickerel big angle photo was first stimulated by a newspaper reporter in Houston, Texas, a reserve officer who went to sea with us and told me if he could write up a story on our operations at sea that day, including a picture of the big angle, which I always did at the end of reserve training cruises and the like, his fortune would be made. I covered earlier the long time in planning and carrying off that big angle picture, and it might have made a couple of media fortunes. Any time we took a newspaperman to sea, he became a convert, at least after his heart returned to normal. I could never use canned press handouts.

When Pickerel finished her world's record snorkel cruise, The New York Times wanted me to do a story on it for the Sunday magazine. Even if I shed my traditional modesty, the cruise really was no big deal, and my colleagues knew it. I suggested to The Times I might have problems doing it and asked that they try it with my assistance. The story ran under a feature writer's byline and was later sold to International News Service.

Q: Who was the writer?

Captain Schratz: I forget now. Dick something.

Q: You also spent some time at Georgetown. What were your experiences there?

Captain Schratz: When I left the Murphy Commission, I was invited first to the University of Virginia as director of the Burke White Miller Center; I think the name is correct. Miller had made a multi-million dollar grant to the university for a new program in national security studies, with certain strings attached. In order to make an immediate splash, the people setting up the program wanted total concentration on the all-volunteer force. I thought this was a mistake. Morrie Janowitz and the Inter-University Seminar on the Armed Forces in Chicago, of which I was a member, had this program locked; all University of Virginia could hope to be was a satellite in Morrie's orbit. Second, I thought the all-volunteer Army was a non-starter from the beginning, with little opportunity for making a worthwhile contribution.

I suggested emphasis on the commander in chief and the role of the military in security policy-making as influenced by the President and Congress. Ambassador Fritz Nolting was serving as temporary director. He was all set on the Al-Vol, and I said I was not interested on that basis. I learned later that the donor was also displeased, favoring a focus almost exactly as I had described, and withdrew all but the initial seed money from the program.

Meanwhile, I was invited to start a new graduate level program at Georgetown University in national security studies. My course was again an adaptation of the history of strategic thought seminar from National War College days. At this time, also, I was invited to join Brookings as a visiting scholar. Most visiting scholars there don't carry much clout or even gain free access to the regular staff unless they're big news in the trade and somebody needs an endorsement. They're happy to take your ideas, but you'll rarely get credit for them. I enjoyed it, but when the call came from Georgetown, I was ready to go. I also had a partial commitment to join the Stanford Research Group (SRI) in Washington, which I got clear of.

My students at Georgetown were largely foreign embassy staffers in Washington, deeply interested and with widely varied backgrounds. I was just entering my second year in this program when the Air Force offer came by.

Also at this time, I became more and more deeply involved in my Naval Academy class memorial for 1978, commemorating our 39th anniversary of graduation. As a member of the class executive committee, I inherited the task of finding a suitable gift, "utilitarian rather than statuary," and costing $39,000. After much thought and discussion, I recommended an atomic clock, to be located in Michelson Hall, for midshipmen and faculty research, with a suitable readout of local time accurate to nine decimals to be located in the Bancroft Hall rotunda.

This project soon took almost full time for two years. Much of it depended on new technology just then evolving--the large size of the numerals in the readout, the signal transmission from the cesium frequency unit in Michelson Hall to Bancroft, the material of the memorial--polyester bronze, specially designed to be proof against midshipmen doodling or horseplay by fire, flood, or facile fingers. The project required repeated trips to New York to work out the design with the overall architect Viggo Rambusch and sculptor Domenico Facci, inventor of the self-sealing gasoline tank for aircraft in World War II.

Not least of the problems was the first estimate of cost--$175,000--which put me in shock for a week. We finally reduced it to about $69,999, which gave us the same percentage overrun as for the first three frigates built for the Navy in the 1790s and of the more recent Air Force C-5A military transport. My deepening involvement in exceedingly complex details with a dozen corporations removed me more and more from any guidance from the class; more and more major decisions I had to make on my own. The project caught everybody's enthusiasm. Funding rolled in easily despite the overrun; three separate donors offered to cover any shortage. We ultimately asked one of these sources for about 70 cents to put us over the top. The inscriptions in Michelson and Bancroft are heavily edited Tennyson and Longfellow; I also wrote a glossy brochure as a special handout for VIP visitors. This task was completed only a few days before our big reunion at homecoming, October 1978, just a few months after I joined the Air War College.

Meanwhile, in early 1977, the Marshall Foundation in Lexington, Virginia, held a major conference on the evolution of the American military establishment since World War II, and I was asked to participate and edit the book. The participants were largely heavyweights: Paul Nitze, Andy Goodpaster, conference chairman, Arleigh Burke, Maxwell Taylor, Larry Norstadt, Ed Hooper, and most of the people who had been in the ring during the big unification battles of the '40s and '50s. I edited that book and it was very successful, undoubtedly helping my reputation on the war college circuit also just about the time when I was invited to go down to the Air War College.

My first problem there was financial. While on the Murphy Commission, I won the battle to be exempt from dual compensation limitations. In addition, the war college salary ceiling was a GS-15. Since I'd been a GS-17 on the Murphy Commission, there were problems. Fortunately, a recently enacted law, the Interdepartmental Personnel Act, or IPA, was designed to help university people get a government job without too much punishment by salary limitations. With a bit of pulling and hauling, it fitted my case. I was serving as an adjunct professor at Georgetown with no share in tenure or retirement benefits. The IPA was stretched to fit. It also allowed me to accept a job with the Air Force without forfeiting any of my military retired pay.

Based on my academic record, Georgetown equated me to a full professor of moderate seniority. To that salary level the Air Force added one-third for a full calendar year versus an academic year, and a similar slice for fringe benefits and to bring me into the Georgetown retirement system, then added per diem for the entire two years I was down there, which their comptroller decided was non-taxable. To top it off, I was given a professional development fee each year for travel and conference fees, which made a quite handsome total. I was earning more than Stan Turner as CIA director, more than the Vice President, less than Jimmy Carter, which I thought was a nice neighborhood.[*]

Q: What induced you to leave that neighborhood?

Captain Schratz: I really burned myself out two years down there. The commandant, Dave Gray, wanted me to stay a third year and use that period to write the book. He wanted to get it in print within that third year for student use. It seemed simple at first--take ten lectures and put them into ten chapters and add a cover. But I thought it necessary to get away from the hurly-burly life at Maxwell. I was the first in every morning and the last one home, took a big briefcase home to work on and really earned my salary. It was also necessary, as the senior Navy person there, to be at every party and generally the last to leave. Often as not, I wore my military full dress uniform "when appropriate," just to show these young upstarts we had some Navy heroes around too. Great public relations.

In town I was concertmaster of the Montgomery Symphony, played with a chamber group at the art association and professionally on occasion with the Birmingham Symphony, all of which was hardly the atmosphere to do some intensive writing. We looked for a place in Florida away from it all. All I asked for the book was necessary expenses plus a dollar,

---

[*] Admiral Stansfield Turner, USN, was director of the Central Intelligence Agency from 1977 to 1981; Jimmy Carter was President of the United States those same years. Walter Mondale was Vice President.

and Dave gave me a contract on that basis. When I returned for a progress report with the faculty a year later, they wanted more time to review the book than they were giving me to write it. The contract allowed me to copyright it in my name and market it elsewhere, which came as quite a surprise to them. After some discussion, I became convinced it would hardly work out, and I suggested we drop the contract. Meanwhile, the Naval War College had approved a similar support arrangement through the Center for Advanced Research, and they're still sponsoring me.

Q: What have you done since leaving the Air War College?

Captain Schratz: Primarily writing. I was invited to join the Marshall Group in Washington, primarily of retired generals. Admirals Roy Johnson and Rivets Rivero are members, as are a few press editorial writers.[*] The purpose is to prepare position papers on current foreign and defense policy issues for submission to State, Defense, or the NSC. We also plan to produce a book. I am working on two chapters on "the continental and maritime philosophies in modern war." We meet monthly and usually find a secretary or senior official to lead the discussion. I find it useful, but I'm more a user than a producer.

I've also been associated with the American Committee on East-West Accord, at the invitation of Noel Gayler, and I can't find time for that either.[†] I've been trying to get the strategy book out. The University of Kentucky is interested in sponsoring both my strategy book and a memoir, "Submarine Commander, World War II and Korea." They are anxious to get their hands on both manuscripts. I've cut out most everything else except work on our 50th USNA class memorial. I dropped the monthly Shipmate contribution after 40 years, but have promised to put the best of these columns into a book also.

---

[*] Admiral Roy L. Johnson, USN (Ret.); Admiral Horacio Rivero, Jr., USN (Ret.). The oral histories of both are in the Naval Institute collection.
[†] Admiral Noel A. M. Gayler, USN, was at the time running the committee. His oral history is in the Naval Institute collection.

Q: Admiral Gayler is one of the individuals whom I've interviewed. I'd be interested in anything you have to say about that committee he's involved with.

Captain Schratz: I can say very little, because I know very little. I was interested in his nuclear arms reduction proposal, which is so simple and sensible that it may never fly. The membership is prestigious; the annual meetings draw scientists and scholars from all over the world. Last year at the meeting, Carl Sagan and Paul Erlich first disclosed their concept of the "nuclear winter," followed by a joint press conference from Washington and Moscow.

Q: What do you see on the horizon after you shed some of these other responsibilities to concentrate on your writing?

Captain Schratz: Arlington, maybe. We do a lot of traveling, about five months away from home last year, which hurt the writing business terribly. Maintaining a Florida home takes time. We don't get down there very often. I just want to get that submarine book and the strategy book out of the way, start enjoying some life in Florida now and then. We have a beautiful home down there on the golf course waiting for us, but I doubt I ever get back to my golf game again.

Q: We've come to the present. Is there anything you'd like to talk about in addition that we haven't discussed?

Captain Schratz: Not that I can think of at the moment. I may go over some notes and see what I can find.

Q: On behalf of all the people in the future who will wind up using this, I am grateful to you for taking this time to make a contribution.

Captain Schratz: I am delighted and highly honored to be chosen.

Q: Do you have a concluding thought?

Captain Schratz: Yes. When I was on the Naval War College faculty, I was asked for an epigrammatic inscription for a bust of Admiral Luce. After some digging, I suggested, "He taught the Navy to think." I would be flattered and honored to be thought of in the same terms some day.

Index To

Reminiscences of

Captain Paul Richard Schratz

U.S. Navy (Retired)

Accidents
The submarine Pomodon (SS-486) had an explosion and fire on board in February 1955, 189-190; one of the boats in Submarine Division 52 suffered a collision with a destroyer during a training exercise in the mid-1950s, 302-303

Ahearn, Lieutenant John A., USNR
Edited the ship's newspaper as the captured Japanese submarine I-203 made a voyage to Hawaii in 1945, 113

Air Force, U.S.
Around 1960 the Naval War College supported Navy efforts to ward off an Air Force proposal for a single U.S. military service, 210-211; initiatives in the 1980s toward better interservice cooperation, 293

See also Air War College, Montgomery, Alabama

Air War College, Montgomery, Alabama
In the 1970s, while on the college staff, Schratz wrote a paper on Captain Milton Miles's role in China in World War II, 172-173; link between student papers and publication in the Air University Review, 269; Schratz's work in the late 1970s to upgrade the college's program, 279-282; as Chief of Naval Operations in the late 1970s, Admiral Thomas Hayward arranged for the Navy to send better qualified students to the Air War College than it had been, 285-286

Alcohol
Drinking was infrequent for Navy men on liberty in Iceland in 1941, 45; the crew of the submarine Burrfish (SS-312) bought liquor while on a shakedown cruise to St. Thomas in late 1948, then hid it upon returning to New London, 142-144

Almy, Lieutenant Commander Charles B., USN (USNA, 1944)
Was commanding officer of the submarine Pomodon (SS-486) when she had an explosion and fire on board in February 1955, 189-190; did a fine job as skipper, 193

Anderson, Admiral George W., Jr., USN (Ret.) (USNA, 1927)
Retired Chief of Naval Operations who was concerned in the early 1970s about the number of blacks at the Naval Academy, 261-262

Antarctica
Planning in the early 1950s for a U.S. expedition to Antarctica as part of the International Geophysical Year, 167-168; State Department position on U.S. claims in Antarctica, 168-170; in the early 1950s U.S. Rear Admiral Milton Miles tried to resolve conflicting claims to Deception Island between Argentina and Chile, 171-172; lack of high-level OpNav attention to antarctic issues in the early 1950s, 176-177

Anti-Submarine Defense Force Atlantic Fleet
Developmental work in a number of areas in the late 1950s, 195-203

Antisubmarine Warfare
Feeble antisubmarine capabilities of the heavy cruiser Wichita (CA-45) in 1941, 33; Japanese depth-charging of the U.S. submarine Sterlet (SS-392) during World War II, 66-67, 78; quality of Japanese magnetic anomaly detection gear near the end of World War II, 86; antisubmarine warfare drills out of Pearl Harbor in 1951, 158-160; a destroyer dropped depth charges on the submarine Pomodon (SS-486) during a training exercise in the mid-1950s, 191-192; practice depth charging of the submarine Catfish (SS-339) in the mid-1950s, 192; work of Anti-Submarine Defense Force Atlantic Fleet in the late 1950s, 195-203

Argentina
Visit by the heavy cruiser Wichita (CA-45) in 1940, 29; had a territorial dispute in the early 1950s with Chile over Deception Island in Antarctica, 171-172

Army, U.S
Laws regarding "tombstone" promotions of Army officers following World War I, 116-117

Army Air Forces, U.S.
A B-29 shot down Japanese planes near Kure near the end of World War II, 86; Schratz flew in a B-29 bombing raid near Nagasaki in the summer of 1945, 90-91; B-29s laid mines in the Inland Sea of Japan in 1945, 109

Army War College, U.S.
Establishment of new campus at Carlisle, Pennsylvania, in the 1940s, 294

Atomic Bombs
Japanese reaction to the bombs dropped by the United States in 1945, 100

Atule, USS (SS-403)
Successful war patrols during the latter part of World War II, 84-89, 93-94

Austin, Vice Admiral Bernard L., USN (USNA, 1924)
Personality of while running the politico-military division of OpNav in the early 1950s, 166; indecisive qualities, 173-177; as president of the Naval War College in the early 1960s, 210-212

B-29 SuperFortress
Shot down Japanese planes near Kure near the end of World War II, 86; Schratz flew in a bombing raid near Nagasaki in the summer of 1945, 90-91; laid mines in the Inland Sea of Japan in 1945, 109

Baldwin, Hanson W., (USNA, 1924)
Retired newspaperman who was concerned in the early 1970s by the number of blacks at the Naval Academy, 261-262

Baldwin, Robert H. B.
As Under Secretary of the Navy in the mid-1960s, ruled that Schratz could seek a doctorate from Ohio State, 250-251

Baseball
Schratz's wisecrack as members of the OpNav staff watched the National League pennant playoff game on television in October 1951, 172

Basketball
Ship's team in the heavy cruiser Wichita (CA-45) shortly before World War II, 43

Bass, Commander Raymond H., USN (USNA, 1931)
Used steep down angles while conning his submarine during World War II, 164

Bathythermograph
Value to U.S. submariners during World War II, 69

Beach, Captain Edward L., USN (USNA, 1939)
Came to the erroneous conclusion that the Japanese submarine I-58 used kaiten suicide torpedoes in sinking the cruiser Indianapolis (CA-35) in 1945, 101; commanded the submarine Triton (SSN-586) in the early 1960s, 223-224; friendly rivalry with Schratz, 224

Benson, Lieutenant Roy S., USN (USNA, 1929)
Taught navigation at the Naval Academy in the late 1930s, 16-17

Berkeley, Colonel James P., USMC
While stationed in Japan in 1945, provided Schratz with passes to seek Japanese war souvenirs, 102

Bethesda Naval Hospital
See National Naval Medical Center, Bethesda, Maryland

Blacks
Attempt to set up a program for minorities at the University of Missouri around 1970, 260-261; concern in the early 1970s on the part of retired Navy men about the number of black midshipmen at the Naval Academy, 261-262; a black midshipman who entered the Naval Academy in 1936 dropped out shortly thereafter, 277

Blair, Clay, Jr.
Author whom Schratz believes misrepresented the skipper of the submarine Scorpion (SS-278) in writing his book Silent Victory, 60-61; comments on command opportunities in World War II, 89

Boatwright, Midshipman Victor T., USN (USNA, 1939)
Brilliant person who finished near the top of his Naval Academy class, 8, 12

Bombing
Schratz flew in a B-29 bombing raid near Nagasaki in the summer of 1945, 90-91

Boston, Massachusetts
Visited by the crew of the submarine tender Fulton (AS-11) in the early 1960s, 224-225

Boston University
Offered a master's program for Naval War College students in the 1950s and 1960s, 204, 215-216, 283-284

Bowler, Commander Roland T. E., Jr., USN (Ret.) (USNA, 1945)
As secretary-treasurer of the Naval Institute in the 1960s and 1970s, was unresponsive to criticisms of the organization made by Schratz, 272-273

Brazil
Visit by the heavy cruiser Wichita (CA-45) in 1940 because of a political crisis, 28; around 1970 a U.S. satellite detected lead deposits in Brazil, 260

Brown, Rear Admiral John H., Jr., USN (USNA, 1914)
As Commander Submarine Force Pacific Fleet in 1949, sent out a letter telling skippers not to surface at steep angles, 131; gave Vice Admiral Charles Lockwood a photo of the Pickerel (SS-524) at a steep angle, 131-132; supported the Pickerel during a long submerged transit in 1950, 135, 301; reaction to the Pickerel's patrol report, 137

Brown, Paul
After World War II, Congressman Brown asked Schratz to handle the case of a widow's benefit for one of his constituents, 121-123

Bucknell, Lieutenant Commander Howard III, USN (USNA, 1945)
Did an outstanding job as skipper of the submarine Remora (SS-487) in the mid-1950s, 193-194

Buenos Aires, Argentina
Visit by the heavy cruiser Wichita (CA-45) in 1940, 29

Bugara, USS (SS-331)
Submarine that underwent a challenging operational readiness inspection in the mid-1950s, 193

Bureau of Naval Personnel
Administration of various types of retirements by naval officers shortly after World War II, 115-126; in the late 1940s the bureau did not do orderly career and promotion planning for various Naval Academy classes, 126; detailing of top-notch officers to the new submarine Pickerel (SS-524) in 1949, 128-129

Bureau of Ships
  Interested in a long underwater endurance run made by the submarine Pickerel (SS-524) in 1950, 134, 136-137; concerns about batteries in the Pickerel, 138

Burford, Lieutenant William P., USN (USNA, 1923)
  Put erring midshipmen on report as a duty officer at the Naval Academy in the 1930s, 6

Burke, Rear Admiral Arleigh A., USN (USNA, 1923)
  Was a workhorse as director of strategic plans for OpNav in the early 1950s, 174, 177

Burrfish, USS (SS-312)
  Reactivated in 1948 to test the readiness of the reserve fleet, 141-142, 146-148; shakedown cruise to St. Thomas in late 1948, 142-143; the crew bought liquor in St. Thomas, then hid it upon returning to New London, 142-144; operational readiness inspection around Christmas in 1948, 143-144

Byrd, Rear Admiral Richard E., USN (Ret.) (USNA, 1912)
  Questions following World War II on the status of his retired pay, 119-121; had a reluctance to get involved in meetings in the Pentagon in the 1950s, 167-168; lack of interest in pursuing U.S. claims in Antarctica, 168-169; a Boy Scout who accompanied Byrd to Antarctica in the 1920s later claimed that Byrd did not reach the South Pole, 170; lacked knowledge about his committee's accomplishments, 170-171, 176

Canadian Navy
  Schratz gave a facetious briefing about a nuclear-powered tugboat while in Halifax in the late 1950s, 200

Carpenter, USS (DDE-825)
  Involvement in antisubmarine warfare drills out of Pearl Harbor in 1951, 158-160

Catfish, USS (SS-339)
  Submarine that underwent a challenging operational readiness inspection in the mid-1950s, 192

Catlin, Lieutenant Allen B., USN (USNA, 1942)
  Served as executive officer of the captured Japanese submarine I-203 in the autumn of 1945, 111, 114

Censorship
  Of personal mail on board U.S. submarines in World War II, 95-96

Center for Naval Analyses
  Rear Admiral Edwin B. Hooper ran the CNA program within the Naval War College in the late 1950s, 211, 217

Chiang Kai-shek
Offered Chinese troops to fight when the Korean War broke out in 1950, 150-151

Chile
Had a territorial dispute in the early 1950s with Argentina over Deception Island in Antarctica, 171-172

China
In the 1970s, while on the Air War College staff, Schratz wrote a paper on Captain Milton Miles's role in China in World War II, 172-173

See also Taiwan

China, People's Republic of
Chinese Communist nuclear weapons tests in the early 1960s produced contamination problems as far away as Connecticut, 222-223; deployment of U.S. Polaris submarines off China in the mid-1960s, 244

Civil War
Military retirement laws enacted during the war were still in effect in the 1940s, 123-124

Codebreaking
U.S. submariners effectively used Ultra information in World War II operations, 70, 87

Colbert, Commander Richard G., USN (USNA, 1937)
Worked on Middle East strategic issues while serving in OpNav in the early 1950s, 177; work with foreign officers at the Naval War College in the late 1950s, 206

Collisions
One of the boats in Submarine Division 52 suffered a collision with a destroyer during a training exercise in the mid-1950s, 302-303

Communications
Ship-shore radio traffic with U.S. submarines during World War II, 94-95; during a long submerged transit in 1950 the submarine Pickerel (SS-524) lost her ability to communicate by radio, 135, 301; by the U.S. delegation to the Eighteen-Nation Disarmament Conference at Geneva, Switzerland, in the early 1960s, 234

Communism
A man named as conductor of the Arlington, Virginia, symphony in the 1950s lost his job because of suspected Communist links, 178-179; the National War College ran a program on anti-Communism in the 1950s and 1960s, 290-291

Congress, U.S.
After World War II, Congressman Paul Brown asked Schratz to handle the case of a widow's benefit for one of his constituents, 121-123; testimony on retirement laws in 1947 by Secretary of Defense James Forrestal, 123-124; set up a commission in the mid-1970s to study government organization for foreign policy, 264-266

Connally, John B.
Though John F. Kennedy promised Franklin D. Roosevelt, Jr., the job of Secretary of the Navy in 1961, Connally got it instead, 297

Connolly, Vice Admiral Thomas F., USN (USNA, 1933)
As OP-05 in 1969, suggested that the Navy divert some funds to Schratz to support his writings, 275-276

Cooley, Commander Thomas Ross, Jr., USN (USNA, 1917)
Served as executive officer of the heavy cruiser Wichita (CA-45) shortly before World War II, 38-39

Craighill, Rear Admiral Richard S., USN (USNA, 1932)
Made an analysis in the mid-1960s of Thailand's strategic significance, 245

Cramer, Vice Admiral Shannon D., Jr., USN (Ret.) (USNA, 1944)
Told Schratz a facetious story about Vice Admiral H. G. Rickover that got Schratz into trouble in 1963, 227-230

Cuba
Liberty for officers of the heavy cruiser Wichita (CA-45) ashore on the island in the late 1930s, 26127

Cuban Missile Crisis
Handling of in the autumn of 1962 by the President and Joint Staff, 241-242

Damage Control
Shortcomings in the damage control arrangement in the heavy cruiser Wichita (CA-45) in 1941, 39-40; drills conducted on board the submarine Pomodon (SS-486) during an operational readiness inspection in the mid-1950s, 191-192

Davies, Ensign Thomas D., USN (USNA, 1937)
As a junior officer in the heavy cruiser Wichita (CA-45) in the late 1930s, solved a difficult fire control problem involving the main battery range keeper, 26, 41-42; involvement with the cruiser's antiaircraft battery, 41; as a catapult officer in the Wichita, 41

Davis, Captain Henry F. D., USN (USNA, 1908)
While serving as manager of the Portsmouth Navy Yard in 1943, rented a retirement home to Schratz and his wife, 53

Davis, Professor Vincent
University of Kentucky historian interested in publishing a book on John Paul Vann and the war in Vietnam, 247-248, joined Schratz in attempts to improve the Naval Institute, 269-271

Dawson, Lieutenant (j.g.) Cosby Homer, USN
Officer whose widow Schratz helped with pension benefits following World War II, 121-123

Defense Department
Description of the method for staffing during the beginning of the Kennedy-McNamara era in the early 1960s, 240; work of the International Security Affairs section in the mid-1960s, 243-250

Denebrink, Commander Francis C., USN (USNA, 1917)
Popular as an instructor at the Naval Academy in the late 1930s, 17-18

Depth Charges
Effect of depth-charging on the crew of the submarine Sterlet (SS-392) during World War II, 66-67, 78; used in training of the crew of the submarine Pomodon (SS-486) in the mid-1950s, 191-192

Diesel Engines
In March-April 1950, the submarine Pickerel (SS-524) made a long submerged run from Hong Kong to Pearl Harbor, using her engines and snorkel, 133-140; the Pickerel damaged her engines during a high-speed run to Japan in 1950, 150

Disarmament Talks
U.S. Joint Staff contribution in 1963-64 to the Eighteen-Nation Disarmament Conference at Geneva Switzerland, 231-240

Discipline
Infractions by Naval Academy midshipmen in the mid-1930s, 5-7; the submarine tender Nereus (AS-17) had a great many disciplinary problems in the mid-1950s, 183-185, 300; procedures on board the submarine tender Fulton (AS-11) in the early 1960s, 225-226; discipline was assigned to the commanding officer and executive officer of the aircraft carrier Ranger (CV-61) for an incident in the mid-1980s when a fuel valve was missing, 302

Donaho, Rear Admiral Glynn R., USN (USNA, 1927)
Was a demanding training supervisor as the submarine Sterlet (SS-392) prepared to go into combat in 1944, 77-78; tough to work for while serving in OpNav in the early 1950s, 180; not noted for having a sense of humor, 180-181

Dornin, Captain Robert E., USN (USNA, 1935)
Demonstrated his strong personality as commanding officer of the submarine tender Nereus (AS-17) in the mid-1950s, 182-184, 186-188, 300

Dunford, Commander James M., USN (USNA, 1939)
Finished third in his class at the Naval Academy, 5, 8; served as a deputy to Rear Admiral Hyman Rickover in the nuclear power program in the 1950s, 195

Education
In Pittsburgh, Pennsylvania, in the 1920s and 1930s, 1-5; at the Naval Academy in the late 1930s, 8-14; the Navy has traditionally provided less education in international affairs and the art of war than the other U.S. services, 165; program of study at the Naval War College in the late 1950s and early 1960s, 203-218; in the late 1950s the Naval War College provided students much more knowledge than they'd had previously about strategy, 204; Boston University offered a master's program for war college students in the 1950s and 1960s, 204, 215-216, 283-284; of Schratz's children while he was in Switzerland in the early 1960s, 235-236; Schratz earned a doctorate from Ohio State University in 1966, 250-251; Schratz ran the international studies program at the University of Missouri, 1968-73, 253-261, 276, 304-306; Schratz's proposals for improved progressive education of maritime professionals, 267-273; anti-intellectual tendencies in the Navy, 286; as Army Chief of Staff in the late 1940s, General Dwight Eisenhower saw the need for joint higher education, 294

Eisenhower, General of the Army Dwight D., USA (USMA, 1915)
Work on memoirs in the 1960s, 289; initiation in the 1950s of a course in anti-Communism at the National War College, 290; push for amendments to the National Security Act in 1958, 292; as Army Chief of Staff in the late 1940s, saw the need for joint higher education, 294

Electric Boat Company, Groton, Connecticut
Construction of nuclear submarines in the early 1960s, 219-220; monitoring of radiation fallout from Chinese nuclear weapons testing in the early 1960s, 222-223

Eller, Captain Ernest M., USN (USNA, 1925)
Cautious officer who nitpicked papers sent to him for approval while serving in OpNav in the mid-1950s, 181-182

Ellsberg, Daniel
As a Defense Department official in the mid-1960s, he was sometimes careless about security matters, 246

Emission Control
The Anti-Submarine Defense Force Atlantic Fleet did developmental work in the late 1950s on the importance of controlling electronic emissions, 195-196

Engineering Plants
Difficulty running the former Japanese submarine I-203 after Americans captured her in 1945, 103-104, 112; in March-April 1950, the submarine Pickerel (SS-524) made a long submerged run from Hong Kong to Pearl Harbor, 133-140; the Pickerel damaged her engines during a highspeed run to Japan in 1950, 150; in the 1950s

Commander William Sawyer developed a nuclear plant using gas turbine propulsion, 194-195; discipline was assigned to the commanding officer and executive officer of the aircraft carrier Ranger (CV-61) for an incident in the mid-1980s when a fuel valve was missing, 302

Euryale, USS (AS-22)
Went to western Japan in 1945 to support the U.S. disposal of captured Japanese submarines, 97, 106-108; trip to Hawaii in company with the former I-203, 111-112

Fenno, Captain Frank W., Jr., USN (USNA, 1925)
World War II submarine skipper who was chagrined to lose out on a house lease while at Portsmouth Navy Yard in 1943, 52-53

Fife, Rear Admiral James, Jr., USN (USNA, 1918)
As Commander Submarine Force Atlantic Fleet in late 1948, gave Schratz directions on taking the submarine Burrfish (SS-312) on a shakedown cruise to St. Thomas, 142-143; demanding as type commander, 146, 148-149

Fire
The submarine Pomodon (SS-486) had an explosion and fire on board in February 1955, 189-190

Fire Control
In the heavy cruiser Wichita (CA-45) in the late 1930s, Ensign Tom Davies solved a problem involving main battery range keepers, 26, 41-42; visual range finder in the Wichita, 35; antiaircraft range keeper in the Wichita, 41; role of the torpedo data computer during World War II attacks by the submarine Scorpion (SS-278), 70-72

Fluckey, Captain Eugene B., USN (USNA, 1935)
Wrote excellent patrol reports while commanding the submarine Barb late in World War II, 86-87; as commanding officer of the submarine tender Sperry (AS-12) in the mid-1950s, 189; as commander of Submarine Squadron Five in the mid-1950s, 189-190

Fog
See Weather

Food
Supplies were meager for the crew's mess in the heavy cruiser Wichita (CA-45) when she was operating out of Iceland in 1941, 34; problems storing food on board the captured Japanese submarine I-203 during a voyage in 1945, 112; for several reasons, the submarine Pickerel (SS-524) was not a good feeder during the early part of the Korean War, 156-157; quality of the mess on board the submarine tender Fulton (AS-11) in the early 1960s, 220-221; quality of the captain's mess in the Fulton, 226

Formosa
See Taiwan

Forrestal, James V.
　Testimony on retirement laws in 1947, in his capacity as Secretary of Defense, 123-124

Foster, William C.
　Civilian official who ran the U.S. delegation to the Eighteen-Nation Disarmament Conference at Geneva, Switzerland, in the early 1960s, 232, 234, 238

Fulton, USS (AS-11)
　Tender stationed at Guam in 1944 to provide repair services to submarines, 82-84; in the late 1950s became the first tender specifically equipped to service nuclear submarines, 218; difficulty in the early 1960s in motivating crewmen who were rejects from the nuclear program, 218-219; challenges involved in nuclear repairs, particularly welding, 219-220; outreach to the local community in New London, Connecticut, 220-222; quality of food on board, 220-221; monitoring off radiation fallout from Chinese nuclear tests, 222-223; training cruises, 224; disciplinary procedures, 225-226; perks for the commanding officer, 226-227

Gallaher, Lieutenant Commander Antone R., USN (USNA, 1933)
　Taught an informal submarine attack seminar during World War II, 55, 68

Gayler, Admiral Noel A. M., USN (Ret.) (USNA, 1935)
　Work during the 1980s for the American Committee on East-West Accord, 311-312

Geneva, Switzerland
　Site of Eighteen-Nation Disarmament Conference in the early 1960s, 231-240; reaction in Geneva to President John F. Kennedy's assassination in November 1963, 234-235

German Navy
　Operations in the Atlantic Ocean in 1941 included attacks against U.S. ships, 31-33; suffered heavy losses in U-boats World War II, 51

Giffen, Rear Admiral Robert C., USN (USNA, 1907)
　While serving as Commander Cruiser Division Seven in the autumn of 1941, had little opportunity to retaliate when German U-boats attacked U.S. ships, 31

Giles, Commander Donald T., USN (USNA, 1921)
　Became a prisoner of war when Guam fell in December 1941, lost considerable weight in prison camp, 97-98

Goodpaster, Lieutenant General Andrew J., USA (USMA, 1939)
　As president of the National War College briefly in the late 1960s, 254, 288-289

Grady, Commander James B., USN (USNA, 1933)
While serving as skipper of the destroyer Carpenter (DDE-825) in 1951, was involved in ASW exercises out of Pearl Harbor, 158-159

Gray, Major General David L., USAF
Approach to the study of strategy while serving as commandant of the Air War College in the late 1970s and early 1980s, 281-282; got Schratz to write a book on the evolution of the American military, 310-311

Great Britain
Anti-British feelings in the U.S. Navy during the early years of the 20th century, 15

Greene, Commander William M. A., USN
As secretary-treasurer of the Naval Institute, 1959-62, corresponded with Schratz on the organization's mission and possible ties with the Naval Institute, 268-269, 272

Grenadier, USS (SS-210)
When this submarine was scuttled in April 1943, her crew became prisoners of war, 97

Gromyko, Anatoly
Soviet foreign minister's son who took part in international conferences at the University of Missouri around 1970, 257-258

Groundings
The submarine Scorpion (SS-278) ran aground off Midway Island in 1943, 64

Guam
Launching point for B-29 bombing raids against Japan in the summer of 1945, 90-91

Gunnery-Naval
April 1943 gun duel between the submarine Scorpion (SS-278) and a Japanese patrol vessel, 61-62

Hashimoto, Captain Mochitsura, IJN
After sinking the cruiser Indianapolis (CA-35) in 1945, this Japanese submarine skipper went to Washington to testify against the captain of the cruiser, 98-99; did not use kaiten suicide torpedoes against the Indianapolis, 101

Hawkins, Lieutenant (j.g.) David D., USN (USNA, 1930)
Taught English at the Naval Academy in the late 1930s and invited midshipmen to his home, 13-14

Hayward, Admiral Thomas B., USN (USNA, 1948)
As Chief of Naval Operations in the late 1970s, arranged for the Navy to send better qualified students to the Air War College than it had been, 285-286

Hensel, Commander Karl G., USN (USNA, 1923)
Was a tough taskmaster while serving as officer in charge of submarine school in 1942, 47, 50-51

Hong Kong
In 1950, the submarine Pickerel (SS-524) made a long submerged run from Hong Kong to Pearl Harbor, 133-140, 301

Hooper, Rear Admiral Edwin B., USN (USNA, 1931)
Ran the Center for Naval Analyses program within the Naval War College in the late 1950s, 211, 217

I-58 (Japanese Submarine)
Torpedoed and sank the U.S. heavy cruiser Indianapolis (CA-35) in 1945, 98-99

I-203 (Japanese Submarine)
Operated by U.S. Navy personnel after being captured from Japan in 1945, 98, 102-104, 106-107, 111-114

Iceland
U.S. military forces occupied the island in the summer of 1941, 30; torpedoed destroyer Kearny (DD-432) was saluted on her arrival at Hvalfjordur in October 1941, 31; difficult conditions for U.S. Navy ships there in 1941, 34; liberty was not too appealing for U.S. Navy men there in 1941, 45-46

Indianapolis, USS (CA-35)
Post-World War II discussions with the Japanese submarine skipper who sank this heavy cruiser in 1945, 98-99, 101

Ingersoll, Vice Admiral Stuart H., USN (USNA, 1921)
Served as president of the Naval War College in the late 1950s, 206, 208, 210, 215, 284

Ingling, Ensign Alan L., USN (USNA, 1934)
Had difficulties on board the heavy cruiser Wichita (CA-45) in the late 1930s, after having failed previously to be promoted, 24-25

Inspections
The submarine Burrfish (SS-312) had an operational readiness inspection right around Christmas in 1948, 143-144; operational readiness inspection of boats in Submarine Division 52 in the mid-1950s, 191-193

Intelligence
U.S. submariners effectively used Ultra information in World War II operations, 70, 87; the submarine Atule (SS-403) captured a Japanese antisubmarine warfare officer near the end of World War II, 86; the submarine Pickerel (SS-524) patrolled off

Vladivostok, Soviet Union, in 1950, 152-154; photo reconnaissance mission off Wonsan, Korea, in September 1950, 153-154

International Affairs
The Navy has traditionally provided less education in international affairs and the art of war than the other U.S. services, 165; planning in the early 1950s for a U.S. expedition to Antarctica as part of the International Geophysical Year, 167-168; State Department position on U.S. claims in Antarctica, 168-170; in the early 1950s U.S. Rear Admiral Milton Miles tried to resolve conflicting claims to Deception Island between Argentina and Chile, 171-172; Geneva was the site of an Eighteen-Nation Disarmament Conference in the early 1960s, 231-240; Congress set up a commission in the mid-1970s to study government organization for foreign policy, 264-266

International Geophysical Year
Planning in the early 1950s for a U.S. expedition to Antarctica as part of the International Geophysical Year, to be held in 1957-58, 167-168

J. Fred Talbott, USS (DD-156)
Made a midshipman training cruise on the East Coast in the summer of 1937, 19

Jackson, Lieutenant Ralph F., USN (USNA, 1944)
Served as the engineer officer in 1949-50 in the submarine Pickerel (SS-524), 129, 138

Japan
The submarine Scorpion (SS-278) laid a minefield near Tokyo Bay in 1943, 61; a B-29 shot down Japanese planes near Kure near the end of World War II, 86; Schratz flew in a bombing raid near Nagasaki in the summer of 1945, 90-91; surrender in the summer of 1945 after being hit by atomic bombs, 91-92; U.S. occupation of the country in 1945 included the takeover of Japanese submarine facilities and demilitarization of submarines, 96-100, 107-109; reaction to the bombs dropped on Japan by the United States in 1945, 100; condition of the country in the fall of 1945, 103-104, 106-107, 110; Americans on liberty in Japan in 1945, 104-106

Japanese Army
Intense rivalry with the Japanese Navy during World War II, 99-100

Japanese Navy
April 1943 gun duel between the submarine Scorpion (SS-278) and a Japanese patrol vessel, 61-62; depth-charging of the U.S. submarine Sterlet (SS-392) during World War II, 66-67, 78; quality of Japanese magnetic anomaly detection gear for ASW near the end of World War II, 86; U.S. occupation of Japan in 1945 included the takeover of submarine facilities and demilitarization of individual submarines, 96-100, 107-109; the Japanese submarine I-58 sank the cruiser Indianapolis (CA-35) in 1945, 98-99, 101; U.S. Navy personnel operated the Japanese submarine I-203 after capturing her in 1945, 98, 102-104, 106-107, 111-114; discussion of submarine tactics following the conclusion of World War II, 99; intense rivalry with the Japanese Army during

World War II, 99-100; Japanese rationale for using kaiten suicide torpedoes late in the war, 101-102

Jarvis, Midshipman Benjamin C., USN (USNA, 1939)
Served as Schratz's large dancing partner at the Naval Academy in the late 1930s, 12; finished at the top of his submarine school class in 1942, 49

Johnson, President Lyndon B.
Desperate search in the mid-1960s for a solution to the Vietnam War, 248

Joint Chiefs of Staff
Nominated Schratz in the early 1970s for a job as high commissioner in Micronesia, 263-264; reorganization of in the 1980s, 291-292, 295-299; need for development of joint doctrine and education among the services, 292-294, 298

Joint Staff
Schratz found little opportunity for creative thought while serving on the Joint Staff in the early 1960s, 230-231; Joint Staff contribution in 1963-64 to the Eighteen-Nation Disarmament Conference at Geneva Switzerland, 231-240; handling of the Cuban Missile Crisis in the autumn of 1962, 241-242; response to a proposal in the mid-1960s to mine the Han River in North Vietnam, 244-245

Jones, General David C., USAF (Ret.)
Expression of views in the mid-1980s on reorganization of the Joint Chiefs of Staff organization, 295-296

Joy, Vice Admiral C. Turner, USN (1916)
Actions as Commander U.S. Naval Forces Far East during the early part of the Korean War, in 1950, 153-154, 158

Judge Advocate General, U.S. Navy
Involvement in the administration of various types of retirement by naval officers in the years shortly after World War II, 115-121, 124-125

Kaitens
The Japanese submarine I-58 did not use kaiten suicide torpedoes in sinking the cruiser Indianapolis (CA-35) in 1945, 101; Japanese rationale for using kaitens late in World War II, 101-102

Kearny, USS (DD-432)
After being torpedoed by a German U-boat in October 1941, she received a warm welcome from other U.S. warships when she arrived in Iceland, 31

Kennedy, Mrs. Jacqueline
Asked for a column Schratz wrote about her husband after his death in 1963, 248-249

Kennedy, President John F.
   In 1963 desired a nuclear test-ban treaty, 233, 236; reaction in Geneva, Switzerland, to the President's assassination in November 1963, 234-235; role in the Cuban Missile Crisis in the autumn of 1962, 241-242; was not able to keep his promise to name Franklin D. Roosevelt, Jr., Secretary of the Navy in 1961, 297

King George V, HMS
   British battleship that operated out of Iceland in 1941, 31, 33, 39-40

Koiso, General Kuniaki
   Former Japanese premier who in 1945 discussed his nation's defeat in World War II, 100

Korean War
   The Pickerel (SS-524) was the first submarine sent to Korea after war broke out there in 1950, 149-150; U.S. submarine operations off Wonsan, Korea, in September 1950, 153-154

Kure, Japan
   Demilitarization of captured Japanese submarines in the autumn of 1945, 107-109

Laning, Lieutenant Commander Richard B., USN (USNA, 1940)
   Was executive officer of the badly damaged submarine Salmon (SS-182) when she was escorted to Saipan following the Battle of Leyte Gulf in October 1944, 82-83

Leave and Liberty
   For officers of the heavy cruiser Wichita (CA-45) ashore in Cuba and South America in 1939-40, 26-29; liberty was not too appealing for U.S. Navy men in Iceland in 1941, 45-46; rest periods between patrols of the submarine Scorpion (SS-278) in World War II, 72-73; U.S. naval officers ashore in Japan in the autumn of 1945, 104-106

Lee, Vice Admiral Fitzhugh, USN (USNA, 1926)
   Served as president of the National War College in the mid-1960s, 289-291

LeMay, Major General Curtis E., USA
   In the summer of 1945 authorized Schratz to fly in a B-29, 90

Loran
   Used on board the submarine Pickerel (SS-524) during a long submerged transit in 1950, 139

Lyman, Rear Admiral Charles H. III, USN (USNA, 1926)
   As chief of staff at the Naval War College in the late 1950s, 206, 211

Mack, Vice Admiral William P., USN (USNA, 1937)
As vice president of the Naval Institute in the early 1970s, seemed to take personally Schratz's criticisms of the organization, 272

Mackerel, USS (SS-204)
Fired on a German U-boat while on a war patrol in the Atlantic in mid-1942, 50; crew members were given only limited access to torpedo magnetic exploiters in 1942, 53-54; training of prospective submarine skippers in 1942, 55-56

Mail
Excellent service to deployed U.S. submarines during World War II, 95; censorship of, 95-96

Marine Corps, U.S.
Selection of graduating Naval Academy midshipmen in the late 1930s to become marine officers, 19-20

Maurer, Commander John H., USN (USNA, 1935)
Did a fine job as commanding officer of the submarine Atule (SS-403) in the closing stages of World War II, 83-85

Maynard, Lieutenant Commander Harry C., USN (USNA, 1933)
Became executive officer of the submarine Scorpion (SS-278) in 1943 after his predecessor was killed in action, 63-64, 74; though he had a hand in the grounding of the Scorpion at Midway in 1943, he was given a command of his own, 64-65

McDonnell, James S.
St. Louis defense contractor who enthusiastically supported the University of Missouri's international studies program in the 1960s and 1970s, 256, 258-260, 276, 305

McKee, Captain Andrew I., USN (USNA, 1917)
Did a superb job while building submarines at the Portsmouth Navy Yard in World War II, 57-58; role in the salvage of the flooded submarine Squalus (SS-192) in 1939, 58-59

McLean, Rear Admiral Heber H. McLean, USN (USNA, 1921)
As naval base commander in Japan in 1950, treated visiting submariners well, 151

McNamara, Robert S.
As Secretary of Defense during the Cuban Missile Crisis in the autumn of 1962, 242; reaction to proposals in the mid-1960s to shut down the Han River in North Vietnam, 244-245; use of his power as Secretary of Defense, 295, 297-298; prevented Franklin D. Roosevelt, Jr., from becoming Secretary of the Navy in 1961, 297

McNaughton, John T.
>Defense Department official who was killed in an airplane crash in July 1967 after having been designated as the prospective Secretary of the Navy, 246

Medical Problems
>In the early 1960s Vice Admiral H. G. Rickover was treated at Bethesda naval hospital after suffering a heart attack, 227-230

Michaelis, Captain Frederick H., USN (1940)
>Was an outstanding student at the Naval War College in the late 1950s, 206

Micronesia
>The State Department talked to Schratz in the mid-1960s about a possible job in Micronesia, 263-264

Midway Island
>Served as a U.S. submarine base in World War II, 64; grounding near Midway in 1943 by the submarine Scorpion (SS-278), 64

Miles, Rear Admiral Milton E., USN (USNA, 1922)
>As head of Pan American affairs in OpNav in the early 1950s, tried to resolve friction between Argentina and Chile over Antarctica, 171-172; in the 1970s, while on the Air War College staff, Schratz wrote a paper on Miles's role in China in World War II, 172-173

Mines
>The submarine Scorpion (SS-278) laid a minefield near Tokyo Bay, Japan, in 1943, 61; the submarine Atule (SS-403) blew up a number of Japanese mines in the closing stages of World War II, 85; laid in the Inland Sea of Japan by B-29s in 1945, 109; while serving as U.S. commander in Vietnam in the mid-1960s, General William Westmoreland recommended mining the Han River near Hanoi, 244-245

Missiles
>Exercises in the mid-1950s simulated defense against submarine-launched missiles, 175-176; the staff of the NATO Supreme Allied Commander Atlantic did studies in the 1950s on the survivability of Soviet missile-launching submarines, 197

Missouri, University of, St. Louis, Missouri
>Schratz ran the international studies program for the university from 1968 to 1973, 253-261, 276, 304-306; participation of Soviet diplomats in conferences, 257

Moorer, Admiral Thomas H., USN (USNA, 1933)
>Response to a 1969 letter from Schratz about the Navy's strategic interests, 274-275

Moseley, Captain Stanley P., USN (USNA, 1925)
>Was in charge of operations in western Japan in the autumn of 1945 as U.S. Navy personnel disarmed captured Japanese submarines, 108-109

Mothball Fleet
    See Reserve Fleet

Moyer, Commander John G., USN (USNA, 1914)
    Capable ship handler while serving as exec of the heavy cruiser Wichita (CA-45) in the late 1930s, 26, 39; eager for sports and liberty, 26-27

Music
    Schratz's experiences in the high school symphony in Pittsburgh in the early 1930s, 1-3; Norfolk Symphony Orchestra in the 1950s had a demanding conductor, 6-7; a man named as conductor of the Arlington, Virginia, symphony in the 1950s lost his job because of suspected Communist links, 178-179; Schratz's symphony experience in Rhode Island in the late 1950s, 208; in Northern Virginia in 1962, 242; in Alabama in the late 1970s, 310

National Naval Medical Center, Bethesda, Maryland
    Treated Vice Admiral H. G. Rickover after he suffered a heart attack in the early 1960s, 227-230

National War College, Washington, D.C.
    In the mid-1960s Schratz initiated a seminar on the history of strategic thought, 251-252, 287-288; Lieutenant General Andrew Goodpaster as president in the late 1960s, 289; Vice Admiral Fitzhugh Lee as president in the mid-1960s, 290-291; program on anti-Communism in the 1950s and 1960s, 290-291

Naval Academy, U.S., Annapolis, Maryland
    Top-ranking midshipmen in the class of 1939, 5, 8, 11; plebe summer in 1935, 5-6; disciplinary infractions, 5-7; academic work in the late 1930s, 8-14; social life for midshipmen, 12-13; summer training cruises in the late 1930s, 16-19; submarine command opportunities for members of the class of 1939 late in World War II, 89-90; in the mid-1960s, Secretary of the Navy Paul H. Nitze sought a broader course of study at the Naval Academy, 250-251; concern in the early 1970s on the part of retired Navy men about the number of black midshipmen at the academy, 261-262; Schratz's belief in the need for the Naval Academy to do a better job of planting the seeds of professional education, 267-268; a black midshipman who entered the Naval Academy in 1936 dropped out shortly thereafter, 277; leadership training over the years, 299; the class of 1939 donated an atomic clock to the academy in 1978, 308-309

Naval Institute, U.S.
    Around 1960 Schratz had extensive correspondence with the secretary-treasurer of the Naval Institute about its mission for the professional training of officers and possible ties with the Naval War College, 268-269; Schratz's attempts in the 1960s and 1970s to revitalize the organization, 269-273

Naval Reserve, U.S
Reservists on board the heavy cruiser Wichita (CA-45) for training shortly before World War II, 43-44; the reserve officers in the submarine Scorpion (SS-278) during World War II were high-quality individuals, 68

Naval Torpedo Station, Newport, Rhode Island
Provided briefings on torpedo exploders during World War II, 53-54; seemed unwilling to correct mistakes, 54-55

Naval War College, Newport, Rhode Island
Because of the duty requirements of World War II, many members of the Naval Academy classes in the late 1930s did not get to the war college until they were fairly senior, 203-204; provided education in strategy, 204; Boston University offered a master's program for war college students in the 1950s and 1960s, 204, 215-216, 283-284; shortcomings in the educational program in the late 1950s, 204-209, 267-268, 283-284; relatively poor quality of Navy students around 1960, 205-206, 208-209; foreign officers at the college, 206-207; teaching of the "estimate of the situation," 207; social life in Newport for students and their families, 208; Schratz provided financial planning guidance to students, 210; supported Navy efforts around 1960 to ward off an Air Force proposal for a single U.S. military service, 210-211; Schratz's plan, completed in the early 1960s, to improve the war college, 210-214; Rear Admiral Edwin B. Hooper ran the Center for Naval Analyses program within the war college in the late 1950s, 211, 217; war games, 213-215; around 1960 Schratz had extensive correspondence with the secretary-treasurer of the Naval Institute about its mission for the professional training of officers and possible ties with the Naval War College, 268-269; as president of the war college in the early 1970s, Vice Admiral Stansfield Turner institutionalized valuable improvements in the curriculum, 282-283; the Navy does not make it necessary for top-notch officers to attend the war college, 284-285; not many top-notch nuclear submariners study at the college, 286-287

Navigation
Training in celestial navigation by the Naval Academy in the late 1930s, 16-17; on board the submarine Pickerel (SS-524) during a long submerged transit in 1950, 139

Nereus, USS (AS-17)
Submarine tender with a great many disciplinary problems in the mid-1950s, 182-185; did a fine job in the 1950s of training and refitting submarines, 185, 188; crew training, 185; civic contributions by the crew, 185-186; morale of the crew, 186-187; repaired a periscope damaged when a submarine collided with a destroyer during a training exercise in the mid-1950s

New London, Connecticut
Community outreach program by the captain and crew of the submarine tender Fulton (AS-11) in the early 1960s, 220-222

See also Electric Boat Company, Groton, Connecticut; Submarine School, New London, Connecticut

News Media
Schratz's views on the fairness of news media coverage of the military services, 306-307

Night Vision
Experiments in interior lighting in the submarine Scorpion (SS-278) in 1942 to improve night vision topside, 56

Nitze, Paul E.
As Secretary of the Navy in the mid-1960s, he sought a broader course of study at the Naval Academy, 250-251, 253

Nixon, President Richard M
His difficulties over Watergate in the mid-1970s limited his effectiveness as President, 264-265

North Atlantic Treaty Organization
The staff of the NATO Supreme Allied Commander Atlantic did studies in the 1950s on the survivability of Soviet missile-launching submarines, 197; NATO at-sea exercises in the late 1950s, 199-201

Nuclear Power
In the 1950s Commander William Sawyer developed a nuclear plant using gas turbine propulsion, 194-195; Schratz gave a facetious briefing about a nuclear-powered tugboat while in Halifax, Canada, in the late 1950s, 200; Schratz believed the nuclear power program over-emphasized the technical aspects of an officer's career, 268, 302

Nuclear Weapons
Chinese Communist nuclear weapons tests in the early 1960s produced contamination problems as far away as Connecticut, 222-223; a limited test-ban treaty was achieved at the Eighteen-Nation Disarmament Conference at Geneva, Switzerland, in the early 1960s, 233, 236-238

Ohio State University, Columbus, Ohio
National security studies program in the mid-1960s, 250-251

Okinawa
The submarine Sterlet (SS-392) picked up downed naval aviators off Okinawa late in World War II, 80-82

Operations Analysis
The staff of the NATO Supreme Allied Commander Atlantic did studies in the 1950s on the survivability of Soviet missile-launching submarines, 197

OpNav
Dealt with a variety of international affairs issues in the early 1950s, 167-174, 177; shortcomings in crisis-response procedures in the early 1950s, 175

Oyhus, Lieutenant (j.g.) Frederick A., USNR
Brilliant electronics officer who served in the submarine Atule (SS-403) during World War II, 93-94

Parks, Captain Lewis S., USN (USNA, 1925)
Innovative skipper who took over a submarine squadron in 1943, 52-53; was involved in the takeover of submarine facilities when U.S. forces occupied Japan in 1945, 96

Patterson, Lieutenant Commander George W., Jr., USN (USNA, 1924)
Made a useful contribution as an instructor at submarine school in 1942, 50-51

Patrol Reports
Those written by U.S. submarine skippers in World War II were quite effective in spreading the word throughout the submarine force, 68-69; varied in quality, depending on who wrote them, 84-86

Pay and Allowances
Difficulties for naval officers with previous enlisted service when they tried to collect retirement pay after World War II, 117-119; efforts by polar explorer Richard Byrd to help his retirement situation, 119-121; efforts by presidential aide James Vardaman to improve his retired pay in the mid-1940s, 119-120; case of a widow's benefit for a deceased officer, 121-123; work of lawyers whose clients tried to outwit the system on retirements, 124-125; Schratz moved up the commissioning of the submarine Burrfish (SS-312) in November 1948 to get more submarine pay for his crew, 147-148

Pearl Harbor, Hawaii
In 1950, the submarine Pickerel (SS-524) made a long submerged run from Hong Kong to Pearl Harbor, 133-140, 301; antisubmarine warfare drills out of Pearl Harbor in 1951, 158-160

Perch, USS (SS-313)
Carried a landing force during a mission on the east coast of Korea in 1950, 153-154

Photography
The submarine Pickerel (SS-524) was photographed surfacing at an unusually steep angle soon after her 1949 commissioning, 130-133, 307; the Pickerel conducted a photo reconnaissance mission off Wonsan, Korea, in September 1950, 153-154; photo reconnaissance training for a submarine in the mid-1950s, 192

Pickens, Rear Admiral Andrew C., USN (USNA, 1904)
Congenial cruiser division commander embarked in the heavy cruiser Wichita (CA-45) in 1940, 35-36

Pickerel, USS (SS-524)
Schratz's method of getting quality officers assigned to the boat when she went into commission in 1949, 128-129; establishment of the ship's organization, 129-130; was photographed while surfacing at an unusually steep angle soon after commissioning, 130-133, 307; in March-April 1950, the boat made a long submerged run from Hong Kong to Pearl Harbor, 133-140, 301; was the first submarine sent to Korea after war broke out there in 1950, 149-150; damaged engines in high-speed transit to Japan, 150; patrol off Taiwan and mainland China in 1950, 150-151; patrol off the Soviet Union in 1950, 152-154; photo reconnaissance operation off Wonsan, Korea, in 1950, 153-154; problems with supplies for the mess during the Korean War, 156-157; crew training, 157-160; trials conducted off Portsmouth when the boat was new, 160-161; went through some wild maneuvers while in a VIP cruise out of Pearl Harbor, 163-164; was frequently under way during Schratz's command, 274

Pickering, Thomas R.
Foreign service officer who served as the political adviser to the U.S. delegation during the Eighteen-Nation Disarmament Conference at Geneva, Switzerland, in the early 1960s, 232, 234; talked with Schratz in the early 1970s about a possible job in Micronesia, 263-264

Planning
Planning in the early 1950s for the International Geophysical Year, to be held in 1957-58, 167-168

Polaris Submarines
Deployment off China in the mid-1960s, 244-245

Pomodon, USS (SS-486)
Submarine that had an explosion and fire on board in February 1955, 189-190; underwent a challenging operational readiness inspection in the mid-1950s, 191-192

Portsmouth Navy Yard, Kittery, Maine
Construction of thin-skinned submarines early in World War II, 52; Captain H. F. D. Davis, the shipyard manager, rented a house to Schratz in 1943, 53; fitting out of the submarine Scorpion (SS-278) in 1942, 56-58; fitting out of the submarine Sterlet (SS-392) in 1944, 75-76; Schratz's handling of the submarine Pickerel (SS-524) during trials out of Portsmouth Harbor in 1949, 160-161; the Pickerel went through some wild maneuvers while in a VIP cruise out of Pearl Harbor, 163-164 in the early 1950s, 163-164

Prisoners of War
Release of captured U.S. submariners when Japan was occupied in 1945, 96-98

Promotion of Officers
Application of laws concerning "tombstone promotions" in the years shortly after World War II, 116-119; in the late 1940s the Bureau of Personnel did not do orderly

career and promotion planning for various Naval Academy classes, 126; promotion examinations for U.S. naval officers were restored in the late 1940s after being suspended during World War II, 161-163

Proteus, USS (AS-19)
Went to Tokyo Bay in 1945 to support the U.S. takeover of captured Japanese submarine facilities, 96

Racette, Lieutenant Commander William A., USN (USNA, 1943)
Capable submarine officer who served on the OpNav staff in the early 1950s, 180-181

Racism
As Chief of Naval Operations in the early 1970s, Admiral Elmo Zumwalt kept racial problems from being worse than they might have been otherwise, 276-277; a black midshipman who entered the Naval Academy in 1936 dropped out shortly thereafter, 277

Radar
Various types installed in the submarine Scorpion (SS-278) during construction in 1942, 57; use of air-search radar by the submarine Atule (SS-403) in World War II, 93-94; tests of the importance of controlling electronic emissions from submarines in the late 1950s, 195-196

Radford, Admiral Arthur W., USN (USNA, 1916)
As Commander in Chief Pacific in 1950 was concerned when the submarine Pickerel (SS-524) lost radio communications during along submerged transit, 135, 301; reaction to the Pickerel's patrol report, 137; dispatched the Pickerel to Korea when war started there in 1950, 149-150

Radio
Ship-shore communication with U.S. submarines during World War II, 94-95; during a long submerged transit in 1950 the submarine Pickerel (SS-524) lost her ability to communicate by radio, 135, 301; Schratz was a commentator on radio station KMOX in St. Louis in the early 1970s, 305

Ranger, USS (CV-61)
Discipline was assigned to the commanding officer and executive officer for an incident in the mid-1980s when a fuel valve was missing, 302

Raymond, Lieutenant Commander Reginald M., USN (USNA, 1933)
Brilliant individual who served as the first executive officer when the submarine Scorpion (SS-278) went into service in 1942, 60; made submarine patrols with the British early in the war, 61; death in April 1943 during his submarine's gun duel with a Japanese patrol vessel, 61-63, 65; Schratz named a daughter in honor of Raymond, 62

Regulus Missile
Launched from surface ships and surfaced submarines in the mid-1950s, 175, 185

Religion
   An enlisted lay leader conducted divine services on board the submarine Sterlet (SS-392) during World War II, 155-156

Remora, USS (SS-487)
   Lieutenant Commander Howard Bucknell III did an outstanding job as skipper in the mid-1950s, 193-194

Rescue at Sea
   The submarine Sterlet (SS-392) picked up downed naval aviators off Okinawa late in World War II, 80-82

Reserve Fleet
   Reactivation of the submarine Burrfish (SS-312) in 1948 to test the reserve fleet, 141-142, 146-148; British drill to reactivate mothballed ASW ships in the late 1950s, 200-201

Retirement
   In the years shortly after World War II, the Bureau of Naval Personnel administered various types of retirements by naval officers, 115-126; testimony in 1947 by Secretary of Defense James Forrestal, 123-124; various benefits for retirees, 125-126

Rickover, Rear Admiral Hyman G., USN (USNA, 1922)
   While running the Navy's nuclear power program in the 1950s, was not interested in examining new systems, 195; visits to the submarine tender Fulton (AS-11) in the early 1960s, 222; Schratz believed he lost his opportunity for major command because he published a facetious story in 1963 about Rickover's burial plans, 227-230; Schratz believed the nuclear power program over-emphasized the technical aspects of an officer's career, 268

Rio de Janeiro, Brazil
   Visit by the heavy cruiser Wichita (CA-45) in 1940 because of a political crisis, 28

Robbins, Commander Orme C., USN (USNA, 1934)
   Served as first commanding officer of the submarine Sterlet (SS-392) when she was commissioned in 1944, 75-76; reluctant to stand up for his submarine's officers, 77; lacked aggressiveness in combat while commanding the Sterlet, 78-82; got rid of Schratz as the Sterlet's executive officer in the autumn of 1944, 83-84

Roddis, Midshipman Louis H., USN (USNA, 1939)
   Finished at the top of his Naval Academy class, 8, 12, 16-17

Ronhovde, Andreas G.
   State Department representative to a committee that met in the early 1950s to deal with a planned expedition to Antarctica, 167-168

Roosevelt, President Franklin D.
As President in 1941, he authorized various naval operations against Germans in the Atlantic Ocean, 30-31; attempt to provoke the Japanese, 32

Roosevelt, Franklin D., Jr.
Though John F. Kennedy promised him the job of Secretary of the Navy in 1961, John B. Connally got it instead, 297

Royal Navy
Submarine patrols in the Mediterranean Sea during World War II, 61; drill to reactivate mothballed ASW ships in the late 1950s, 200-201

St. Thomas, Virgin Islands
The submarine Burrfish (SS-312) made a shakedown cruise to St. Thomas in late 1948, 142-143

Saipan, Marianas Islands
The tender Fulton (AS-11) was in Tanapag Harbor to provide repair services to submarines, 82-84

Salmon, USS (SS-182)
Was escorted to Saipan in the autumn of 1944 after being badly damaged by the Japanese, 82-83

Sawyer, Commander William T., USN (USNA, 1939)
Finished high in his class at the Naval Academy, 8; in the 1950s developed a nuclear plant using gas turbine propulsion, 194-195

Schratz, Henrietta Frank
Connection with her husband's musical career, 7, 242; dated Midshipman Schratz in the late 1930s, 13; work before her marriage as a home economist in New Jersey, 20-21, 37; marriage of in June 1941, 30, 37; first pregnancy ended in miscarriage, 37, 47; life-endangering second pregnancy, 74; sent word of birth of second daughter, 94; mail to her husband during World War II, 95

Schratz, Captain Paul R., USN (Ret.) (USNA, 1939)
Boyhood in Pittsburgh, Pennsylvania, in the 1920s and 1930s, 1-5; parents of, 1-4, 15, 20; education of, 1-5, 8-14; musical career, 1-3, 6-7, 178-180, 208, 222, 242, 310; as a midshipman from 1935 to 1939 at the Naval Academy, 5-20; wife of, 7, 13, 20-21, 30, 37, 47, 74, 94, 96, 114, 180, 242; service from 1939 to 1941 in the heavy cruiser Wichita (CA-45), 20-47; marriage of in June 1941, 30, 37; children of, 47, 94, 179, 235-236; as a student in submarine school in early 1942, 47-48, 52; service in the submarine Mackerel (SS-204) in 1942, 50, 53-56; service in the submarine Scorpion (SS-278) in 1942-43, 51-52, 56-64; service in the submarine Sterlet (SS-392) in 1944, 70, 75-83; service in the submarine Atule (SS-403) in 1944-45, 84-90; work in disarming and operating captured Japanese submarines shortly after the

end of World War II, 98-114; duty from 1946 to 1948 in the Bureau of Naval Personnel, 114-128; command of the submarine Pickerel (SS-524), 1949-51, 128-165, 274; stint as temporary skipper of the submarine Burrfish (SS-312) when she was reactivated in 1948, 141-149; duty in the political-military policy division of OpNav, 1951-54, 165-182; served as executive officer of the submarine tender Nereus (AS-17) in 1954-55, 182-189; as Commander Submarine Division 52, 1955-56, 189-195, 302-303; duty from 1956 to 1958 on the staff of Commander Anti-Submarine Defense Force Atlantic Fleet, 195-203; as a student and staff member at the Naval War College, 1958-61, 203-218, 267-268; commanded the submarine tender Fulton (AS-11) in 1961-62, 218-227; believed he lost his opportunity for major command because he published a facetious story in 1963 about Vice Admiral H. G. Rickover's burial plans, 227-230; duty from 1962 to 1964 on the Joint Staff, including service as a delegate to the 18-nation disarmament conference in Geneva, Switzerland, 230-243; duty in the Department of Defense in 1964-65, 243-250; earned a doctorate from Ohio State University in 1965-66, 250-251; service on the faculty of the National War College, 1966-68, 251-252, 287-291; ran an international studies program at the University of Missouri, 1968-73, 253-261, 276, 304-306; retirement from active duty in January 1969, 254; held a variety of short-term jobs in the mid-1970s, 261-266; attempts in the 1960s and 1970s to improve the Naval Institute, 267-273; on the faculty of the Air War College in the late 1970s, 279-282, 309-310; taught at Georgetown University in the mid-1970s, 308, 310; post-retirement book writing, 309-312

Scorpion, USS (SS-278)

Commissioned in 1942 with Lieutenant Commander William Wylie in command, 48, 51, 60; was designed with too thin an outer skin, 52; experiments in 1942 in improving night vision, 56; installation of various radars, 57; Lieutenant Commander Reginald Raymond as first executive officer, 60; laid minefield near Tokyo Bay in 1943, 61; gun duel with a Japanese patrol vessel in April 1943 proved fatal to the Scorpion's executive officer, 61-63, 74; second patrol, in the summer of 1943, was a successful one, 63-64; lost in early 1944, 63, 74-75; grounded at Midway Island in 1943, 64-65; high-quality Naval Reserve officers in the crew, 68; role of the torpedo data computer during attacks, 70-72; rest periods between patrols, 72

Security

As a Defense Department official in the mid-1960s, Daniel Ellsberg was sometimes careless about security matters, 246

Ship Design

Poorly designed arrangement of firerooms in the heavy cruiser Wichita (CA-45), 51; excellent design of World War II fleet submarines, based in part on prewar depth-charge testing, 51; the submarine Scorpion (SS-278), commissioned in 1942, had too thin an outer skin, 52

Ship Handling

When the heavy cruiser Wichita (CA-45) went into commission in 1939, the skipper's wife was a better ship handler than he was, 21-23; formation steaming in the Wichita,

23-24; Schratz's handling of the submarine, Pickerel (SS-524) during trials out of Portsmouth Harbor in 1949, 160-161

Sims, Lieutenant Commander William E., USN (USNA, 1942)
Did a superb job as executive officer of the new submarine Pickerel (SS-524) when she went into service in 1949-50, 129, 133-134, 139, 161

Siple, Paul A.
Boy Scout who accompanied Richard Byrd to Antarctica in the 1920s, later claimed that Byrd had never been to the South Pole, 167, 170

Smedberg, Vice Admiral William R. III, USN (USNA, 1926)
As head of politico-military policy in OpNav in the early 1950s, was not interested in work on issues pertaining to Antarctica, 168-169, 171, 176; working habits, 176-177; as Chief of Naval Personnel in 1963 took Schratz off the major command list for publishing a facetious story about Vice Admiral H. G. Rickover's burial plans, 227-230, 250

Smith, Lieutenant General Holland M., USMC
Presented a fictitious award to Schratz when they were stationed in Japan on New Year's Eve of 1945, 102

Snorkels
In March-April 1950, the submarine Pickerel (SS-524) made a long submerged run from Hong Kong to Pearl Harbor, 133-140, 301

Sonar
Use of in antisubmarine warfare exercises in the late 1950s, 201-203

South Pole
A Boy Scout who accompanied Richard Byrd to Antarctica in the 1920s later claimed that Byrd did not reach the South Pole, 170

Soviet Navy
The submarine Pickerel (SS-524) observed Soviet submarines as they made a transit between fleets in 1950, 152-154; the staff of the NATO Supreme Allied Commander Atlantic did studies in the 1950s on the survivability of Soviet missile-launching submarines, 197; U.S. study in the number of Soviet submarines that posed a threat, 197-198; deployment of missile submarines in the mid-1960s, 243-244

Soviet Union
The submarine Pickerel (SS-524) patrolled off Vladivostok in 1950, 152-154; participation in Eighteen-Nation Disarmament Conference at Geneva, Switzerland, in the early 1960s, 233-234, 236-238; conclusion of nuclear test-ban treaty in 1963, 233, 236-238; participation of Soviet diplomats in conferences sponsored by the University of Missouri in the 1960s and 1970s, 257; display of aircraft at the Paris Air Show, 258

Spain
>The USS Wyoming (AG-17) helped evacuate Americans in July 1936, during the Spanish Civil War, 16

Sperry, USS (AS-12)
>Did a fine job repairing the submarine Scorpion (SS-278) at Midway in the summer of 1943, 64

Sprout, Harold
>Princeton scholar who sought out Schratz in the mid-1960s to do work on Alfred Thayer Mahan, 249-250

Spruance, Commander Edward D., USN (USNA, 1937)
>Made liberty in Japan in the autumn of 1945 while commanding a captured Japanese submarine, 104-106

Squalus, USS (SS-192)
>Role of Commander Andrew I. McKee in the salvage of the submarine after her sinking in 1939, 58-59

State Department
>Position in the early 1950s about U.S. claims in Antarctica, 168-170; involvement in the Eighteen-Nation Disarmament Conference at Geneva, Switzerland, in the early 1960s, 232-240; its communications were not as effective as those of the Defense Department delegation at the Geneva conference, 234; talked to Schratz in the mid-1960s about a possible job in Micronesia, 263-264

Sterlet, USS (SS-392)
>Reaction to depth-charge attacks during World War II, 66-67, 78; fitting out at the Portsmouth Navy Yard in 1944, 75-76; initial sea trials, 76-77; crew training, 77; war patrols in 1944 with a skipper who was not aggressive, 78-82; rescue of downed aviators off Okinawa, 80-82; escorted the badly damaged submarine Salmon (SS-182) to Saipan in the autumn of 1944, 82-83; divine services conducted by an enlisted lay leader, 155-156

Strategy
>In the early 1950s Schratz articulated a number of strategic goals the Navy should be achieving, 175-176; in the late 1950s the Naval War College provided students much more knowledge than they'd had previously about strategy, 204; DoD analysis in the mid-1960s of Thailand's strategic significance, 245; Schratz's concern in the late 1960s that the Navy was trying to fill power vacuums in the Mediterranean Sea and Indian Ocean, 274-275; the others services put greater emphasis on the study of strategy than does the Navy, 280-282

Submarine Force, U.S. Pacific Fleet
Patrol reports written by submarine skippers in World War II were quite effective in spreading the word throughout the submarine force, 68-69, 84-86; distribution of operation orders to individual submarines, 69-70; administrative hierarchy within the command, 73; role of relief crews in repairing submarines between patrols in World War II, 92-93

See also individual submarines: Atule (SS-403), Salmon (SS-182), Scorpion (SS-278), Sterlet (SS-392)

Submarine School, New London, Connecticut
Adopted a shortened course in early 1942, 47; training of prospective submarine skippers in 1942, 47-48, 50, 55-56, 68; curriculum and practical training for prospective submariners, 48-50; few combat veterans among the staff in 1942, 52; psychological screening of potential submariners, 67; the submarine Burrfish (SS-312) provided training services for the school in 1949, 145-146

Supreme Allied Commander Atlantic (NATO)
Did studies in the 1950s on the survivability of Soviet missile-launching submarines, 197

Switzerland
Geneva was the site of an Eighteen-Nation Disarmament Conference in the early 1960s, 231-240; reaction in Geneva to President John F. Kennedy's assassination in November 1963, 234-235

Tactics
Following World War II Japanese submarine officers discussed the tactics they had used in wartime, 99

Taiwan
The submarine Pickerel (SS-524) was directed to patrol the Taiwan Strait in 1950 to report if the various Chinese factions attacked each other, 150-151

Thailand
Department of Defense analysis in the mid-1960s of Thailand's strategic significance, 245

Thomas, Dr. C. R. Walther
Naval Academy professor in the late 1930s who was later interned as a Nazi sympathizer, 14

Thomson, Captain Thaddeus A., Jr., USN (USNA, 1907)
Reputation as a martinet while at the Naval Academy in the 1930s, 11-12; difficult as first commanding officer of the heavy cruiser Wichita (CA-45) in 1939-40, 11-12, 21-22; Thomson's wife was a better ship handler than he, 21-23; had a solid

understanding of the role of a professional naval officer, 25; social relationship with junior officers, 27-28; had a meek son, 27, 38-39

Torpedo Data Computer
Role during World War II attacks by the submarine Scorpion (SS-278), 70-72

Torpedoes
Problems with the magnetic exploder in U.S. submarine torpedoes in World War II, 53-55; Japanese rationale for using kaiten suicide torpedoes late in World War II, 101-102; Japanese torpedoes captured at war's end, 109-110

Toulon, Lieutenant Alfred J., Jr., USN (USNA, 1939)
Considerably debilitated while a prisoner of war in Japan, 1943-45, 97

Training
Summer cruises from the Naval Academy in the late 1930s, 16-19; Naval Reservists on board the heavy cruiser Wichita (CA-45) for training shortly before World War II, 43-44; submarine school course in early 1942 at New London, 47-50; training of prospective submarine skippers in 1942, 47-48, 50, 55-56, 68; Commander Glynn Donaho was a demanding training supervisor as the submarine Sterlet (SS-392) prepared to go into combat in 1944, 77-78; the submarine Burrfish (SS-312) provided training services for the submarine school in 1949, 145-146; crew training for the submarine Pickerel (SS-524) during the Korean War, 157-158; antisubmarine warfare drills out of Pearl Harbor in 1951, 158-160; training of the crew of the submarine tender Nereus (AS-17) in the mid-1950s, 185; of the boats in Submarine Division 52 in the mid-1950s, 190-191, 302-303; as Commander Submarine Flotilla One in the mid-1950s, Captain Charles O. Triebel set up training opportunities for aircraft carriers and submarines in the Pacific, 193-194; leadership training at the Naval Academy over the years, 299

Triebel, Captain Charles O., USN (USNA, 1929)
As Commander Submarine Flotilla One in the mid-1950s, set up training opportunities for aircraft carriers and submarines in the Pacific, 193-194

Turner, Vice Admiral Stansfield, USN (USNA, 1947)
As president of the Naval War College in the early 1970s, he institutionalized valuable improvements in the curriculum, 282-283

Ultra
Results of codebreaking used by U.S. submariners in World War II, 70, 87

Uniform Code of Military Justice
Captain Robert Dornin, the skipper of the submarine tender Nereus (AS-17) generally ignored the UCMJ when dispensing discipline in the mid-1950s, 183-185, 300

Uniforms-Naval
White works worn by Naval Academy midshipmen in the mid-1930s, 5-6

University of Missouri
See Missouri, University of, St. Louis, Missouri

Vann, Lieutenant Colonel John Paul, USA
Role in mid-1960s during the Vietnam War, 246-248

Vardaman, Commodore James K., Jr., USNR
After serving as President Harry Truman's naval aide in 1945-46, tried to enhance his retirement status, 119-120

Vietnam War
While serving as U.S. commander in Vietnam in the mid-1960s, General William Westmoreland recommended mining the Han River near Hanoi, 244-245; John Paul Vann's ideas for conducting the war, 246-248; President Lyndon Johnson's desperate search for a solution, 248; fairness of news media coverage, 306

Walsh, Lieutenant Commander William C., USN (USNA, 1941)
Served briefly as executive officer when the submarine Burrfish (SS-312) was reactivated from the reserve fleet in 1948, 142

War Games
As part of the Naval War College program in the late 1950s and early 1960s, 213-215

Watkins, Vice Admiral Frank T., USN (USNA, 1922)
Fine submariner who commanded the Anti-Submarine Defense Force Atlantic Fleet in 1957-58, 195-197

Watkins, Admiral James D., USN (USNA, 1949)
As Chief of Naval Operations in the mid-1980s put an emphasis on the importance of the Naval War College but tended to favor tactical studies, 284-285

Weather
The heavy cruiser Wichita (CA-45) had difficulties with a temperamental whistle while steaming in fog around 1940, 24-25; cold conditions for U.S. Navy ships operating out of Iceland in 1941, 34; the Wichita faced some terrible weather in Iceland in early 1942, 47; reaction of the crew of the submarine Atule (SS-403) to heavy seas late in World War II, 88-89; the submarine tender Fulton (AS-11) had to steam through heavy fog while going to Boston in the early 1960s, 225

Welding
The advent of nuclear submarines in the U.S. Navy in the 1950s demanded much higher standards for welding than in effect previously, 219-220

Westmoreland, General William C., USA (USMA, 1936)
While serving as U.S. commander in Vietnam in the mid-1960s, recommended mining the Han River near Hanoi, 244-245

Whaling
   19th century whaling voyages had an effect on U.S. claims in the 20th century concerning Antarctica, 169

Wichita, USS (CA-45)
   Traits of Captain Thaddeus Thomson, the first skipper, in 1939-40, 11-12, 21-25, 27-28; anti-British sentiment during wardroom discussions prior to U.S.involvement in World War II, 15; fitting out in 1939, 20-22; balky steam whistles during early cruises, 22, 24-25; formation steaming, 23-24; full-power runs and gunnery tests, 25-26; officers' liberty in Cuba, 26-27; social calls by junior officers, 27; cruise to South America in 1940, 28-29; operations in the Atlantic in 1941, 30-35, 45-46; feeble ASW capability in 1941, 33; poor air-conditioning and ventilation in belowdecks spaces during battle conditions, 39-40; antiaircraft gunnery, 41-43; operation of the ship's catapults to launch aircraft, 41; ship's basketball team, 43; Naval Reservists on board for training, 43-44; operation of shipboard aircraft, 44-45; faced terrible weather in Iceland in early 1942, 47; design defects in terms of fireroom arrangement, 51; the ship's junior officers were required to write a book review each quarter, 300

Wilton Park
   An English manor that served as the site of a special European conference center in the 1960s and 1970s, 256-257, 259

Wylie, Lieutenant Commander William N., USN (USNA, 1930)
   Took command of the new submarine Scorpion (SS-278) in 1942 after training at New London, 48, 51, 60; as a combat leader in the Scorpion, 60-66; grounding of the Scorpion in 1943, 64-65; wrote that the detachment of Schratz from the Scorpion led to her loss in 1944, 65, 73-74

Wyoming, USS (AG-17)
   Took midshipmen on training cruises to Europe in the late 1930s, 16-18; helped evacuate Americans from Spain in 1936, during the Spanish Civil War, 16

Zelov, Lieutenant Commander Randolph D., USN (USNA, 1948)
   Did an outstanding job as repair officer of the submarine tender Fulton (AS-11) in 1963, 219, 222

Zumwalt, Admiral Elmo R., Jr., USN (USNA, 1943)
   Served in the mid-1960s as executive assistant to Defense Department official Paul Nitze, 239-241; as Chief of Naval Operations in 1973 sought to counter a threatened article that would be critical of the Navy, 261-262; was excellent in his dealings with racial problems, 276-277

www.ingramcontent.com/pod-product-compliance
Lightning Source LLC
Chambersburg PA
CBHW080619170426
43209CB00007B/1467